Praise for *ZOKOLOGY*

"In the mid-'80s on the PGA Tour, there was a giant influx of foreign golfers who had gravitated towards playing in the United States. Names like Seve Ballesteros, Nick Price, Greg Norman, and Nick Faldo made their names among the golf elite. Golf was becoming more and more global, with many lesser-known players working their way up the rankings. One of them was Canada's Richard Zokol. I had heard of Dick as a player for BYU and became friendly with him in 1984, my rookie year. We played many practice rounds together, often talking about the game between the ears. In *Zokology*, you will learn how you can improve your game and your score without just making your swing better. Dick has an incredible way of giving you examples of how to use your mind to overcome the inevitable obstacles this game throws at you. The only thing he forgot to write in his book is that it will guarantee you shooting better scores!"

—BRAD FAXON, eight-time PGA Tour winner and NBC golf analyst

"Richard Zokol is one of the finest golfers to come out of Canada. As a young man, seeing a Canadian win at the highest levels of the game was an inspiration and helped with our vision for ourselves. Having known Zoke for over 20 years, to think of him only as a golfer would be a disservice to this curious, educated, and very wise man. He said process and execution before it became a popular thing to say. He was okay with being different, knowing that the game of golf would recognize the importance of what he was teaching us."

—SEAN FOLEY, renowned golf instructor

"I was fortunate to have Zoke's guidance when I was a young pro when perspective mattered as much as performance! This book is for anyone wanting to learn how success really happens . . . it's never in a straight line, navigating obstacles on the path with enduring perseverance that continually gets tested. A great read!"

—MIKE WEIR, 2003 Masters champion and eight-time PGA Tour winner

"Richard Zokol has lived a high-performance life. He has spent years understanding how people perform their best under the gun on the golf course when it matters most. His simple and effective system worked for him on the PGA Tour and will help you to play your best golf as well. Read and apply to play better AND enjoy the game more."

—DEREK INGRAM, PGA Tour, Golf Canada pro/amateur, and Team Canada Olympic coach

"MindTRAK Golf absolutely helped my performance. It got me back to the way I think when I played my best. I don't get attached to my bad shots anymore."

—TAYLOR PENDRITH, PGA Tour winner and member of the 2022 Presidents Cup International Team

"Playing on the PGA Tour is the ultimate pressure situation in golf. Not having a plan and a reliable pre-shot routine means you won't be there long. This is one man's journey of how he overcame that crushing pressure. I really enjoyed sharing so many great moments on tour with Zoke and watching him climb to the heights he did in our wonderful sport of golf."

—JIM NELFORD, former PGA Tour player and Canadian Golf Hall of Fame 2013 inductee

"The story of Dick's golf journey, its challenges, ups and downs, and his quest to develop an effective approach to the sport makes for an interesting read."

—DR. SAUL MILLER, sports psychologist and author of *Winning Golf: The Mental Game*

Zokology

CHANGE YOUR PERSPECTIVE NOT YOUR SWING

HOW I COMPETED AND WON ON THE PGA TOUR BY CHANGING THE WAY I THOUGHT

Richard "Disco Dick" Zokol

FOREWORD BY LORNE RUBENSTEIN

Published by ECW Press
665 Gerrard Street East
Toronto, Ontario, Canada M4M 1Y2
416-694-3348 / info@ecwpress.com

Editor for the Press: Michael Holmes
Cover design: Jess Albert
Cover photo: PGA TOUR Archive / Contributor

Unless otherwise specified, all photos are from the author's personal collection. Every effort has been made to credit copyright holders. The publishers would be glad to amend in future editions any errors or omissions brought to their attention.

To the best of his abilities, the author has related experiences, places, people, and organizations from his memories of them. In order to protect the privacy of others, he has, in some instances, changed the names of certain people and details of events and places.

LIBRARY AND ARCHIVES CANADA CATALOGUING IN PUBLICATION

Title: Zokology : change your perspective not your swing : how I competed and won on the PGA Tour by changing the way I thought / Richard "Disco Dick" Zokol ; foreword by Lorne Rubenstein.

Names: Zokol, Richard, author. | Rubenstein, Lorne, writer of foreword

Identifiers: Canadiana (print) 20260121673 | Canadiana (ebook) 20260121681

ISBN 978-1-77041-873-8 (softcover)
ISBN 978-1-77852-573-5 (ePub)
ISBN 978-1-77852-574-2 (PDF)

Subjects: LCSH: Zokol, Richard. | LCSH: Golfers—Canada—Biography. | LCSH: PGA Tour (Association) | LCSH: Success—Psychological aspects. | LCGFT: Autobiographies.

Classification: LCC GV964.Z65 A3 2026 | DDC 796.352092—dc23

This book is funded in part by the Government of Canada. *Ce livre est financé en partie par le gouvernement du Canada.* We acknowledge the support of the Canada Council for the Arts. *Nous remercions le Conseil des arts du Canada de son soutien.* We would like to acknowledge the funding support of the Ontario Arts Council (OAC) and the Government of Ontario for their support. We also acknowledge the support of the Government of Ontario through the Ontario Book Publishing Tax Credit, and through Ontario Creates.

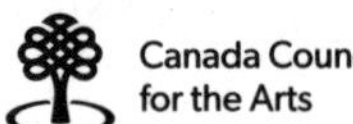

PRINTED AND BOUND IN CANADA

PRINTING: MARQUIS 5 4 3 2 1

CONTENTS

FOREWORD

It was in the early 1980s when I first became aware of how unusual and interesting a golfer Richard Zokol was. We were starting *SCORE*, now *SCOREGolf Magazine*, Canada's national golf publication. Zoke, as I came to call him, had won the 1981 Canadian Amateur in Calgary in August. He had distinguished himself as the captain of the Brigham Young University golf team and had led the squad to a win in the 1981 NCAA Championship. Having turned professional after that summer, he entered the grueling PGA Tour qualifying tournament at the Waterwood National Golf Club in Huntsville, Texas. He qualified on the number to play on the 1982 PGA Tour.

Zoke and I had spoken a few times by then. It occurred to me that, thoughtful young pro that he was, he might have a lot to contribute to the magazine I was editing. I asked if he would be interested in keeping a journal of his experiences. He agreed and regularly sent me his unfiltered accounts of his experiences, handwritten on yellow foolscap sheets.

It quickly became apparent that he was open to trying new things to get the most out of himself on the PGA Tour. Zoke had long ago recognized what he referred to as his "hyperactive" nature. He had inserted cotton batting into his ears while competing as an amateur, in an attempt to quell the thoughts that raced through his mind. He had difficulty staying in the present, as his mind zipped ahead to holes he had yet to play, how he wanted to play them, and what would happen if he ran into problems. Possible bogies or worse became bogies in his mind.

Zoke had been in Toronto in the late fall of 1981 to accept the SCORE Award as the top Canadian male amateur of the year. He ran into the great Canadian professional George Knudson in an elevator in the hotel where the ceremony was taking place. Knudson, then 44, had won eight times on the PGA Tour. He had tied for second in the 1969 Masters. Knudson, like Zokol, had a vivid, often frenzied mind that could be both good and bad for his golf—good in the sense it could help him play imaginative golf, bad in the sense he couldn't focus on the moment. He sought a quiet mind on the course. Knudson walked slowly. He drove to the course slowly. He played what I came to think of as "introverted, silent golf."

Knudson congratulated Zoke on qualifying for the PGA Tour and asked how he felt about getting there.

"I'm very excited about playing the PGA Tour," he told Knudson. The veteran golfer had been there, felt that. "Don't be excited," he advised Zoke. "It can only hurt you."

Zoke took that advice to heart. He's always referred to himself as a "journeyman" on the PGA Tour. What did he need to do to progress? What was the most effective approach to train his mind? Did the answer lie in his mindset rather than his swing? He concluded the correct path for him was to change his mental approach and game. So it was that, as a newly minted PGA Tour player, he began his quest to play what he called "cold-blooded golf," where a well-played shot, hole, round, or tournament wouldn't excite him for more than a moment. He recognized that he needed to learn to "stay in the present," as he would often say. *Zokology* is based on that desire. It would never be easy, as he details in these pages.

It was challenging enough in his first year as a tour professional that he wore headphones during the 1982 Greater Milwaukee Open. This was a golfer, human all too human, who would try what seemed like extreme measures to quiet his fevered brain. Zoke had a Walkman with him as he started the opening round at the Tuckaway Country Club in Milwaukee and put headphones on while walking down the fairway. Ronnie Black and Larry Rinker were in the threesome with Zoke. They quickly dubbed him Disco Dick. He shot 7 under par, 65 in the first round to take the lead, followed by 69 and 70 while continuing to listen to music between shots. He was still tied for the lead with four holes to play, but went bogey, double bogey, bogey from the 15th through the 17th holes. He finished fifth. Listening to music had obviously helped. But he understood he needed to rely more on himself than on listening to music.

"Golf can lead the industry in the mental health area," Zoke once told me, speaking of what athletes in all sports could learn from studies of golf and golfers. We were chatting via Zoom. I spotted a bottle of wine he was given during the 2000 US Open at Pebble Beach. He shot 30 on the front 9 in the final round but came back in 39 to finish T-32. Tiger Woods won by 15 shots—yes, 15. There was a photo of Zoke's dad, Joe, who introduced him to golf at the Marine Drive Golf Club in Vancouver, and another of Ben Hogan at his finish position—what a swing. A photo of the third hole at the Sagebrush Golf Club in Quilchena, BC, that Zoke founded—he's no longer involved but plays there every Sunday during the summer—was on his office wall.

Our call led me to reminisce about the times Zoke and I have enjoyed together during our 45-year friendship. I remembered going to a Toronto Raptors game that Zoke had invited me to during the week of the Canadian Open. He had been provided tickets on the floor. We found ourselves sitting beside actor Burt Reynolds. That remains the only time I've watched a basketball game from the floor. I remember a party my wife and I had for Zoke and some fellow Canadian pros, including Dave Barr, at a friend's home during the Honda Classic, now called the Cognizant Classic in The Palm Beaches.

I've often thought as well, and repeatedly, of that 1982 Greater Milwaukee Open where Zoke had listened to music while walking the fairways. That action says so much about his journey. Ten years later, he would win the 1992 Greater Milwaukee Open—there was something so appropriate about his winning in Milwaukee. Prior to the tournament, Zoke and his wife, Joanie, had been informed they would have to move out of the home they were renting in Vancouver. He was furious and upset, given that they had three young children. He channeled his anger and vowed to win in Milwaukee.

I watched the last round in Toronto's downtown Kensington neighborhood, at the home of my beloved Auntie Goldie. A Holocaust survivor, she was the kindest person one could hope to meet. She and my mom talked in the kitchen while I watched Zoke in the final round in Milwaukee. Every so often, they would inquire as to how he was doing. I can still see him walking up the final fairway, about to win. The $180,000 first prize enabled him and Joanie to buy their first home.

Zokol has been working since those long-ago days on the issues that a hyperactive, tetchy mind can cause a golfer. They're the foundation of MindTRAK, an app he created to help golfers with their own mental issues on the course, while providing a means of assessing their progress. Over the years, I have heard Zoke develop a golf vocabulary all his own, a fascinating and insightful vocabulary: key performance markers; SWOT (strength, weakness, opportunities, threats); logical thought; spatial thought; right-brain golf; left-brain golf; lost-shot events, and more. They're the foundation of *Zokology* and his hard-won awareness that the road to improvement is changing one's perspective at least as much as, or in most cases, more than changing one's swing.

One more memory. I was working on my book *Moe & Me: Encounters with Moe Norman, Golf's Mysterious Genius.* That was during Sagebrush's early days. Zoke invited me to spend a few days at the club. He stocked the comfortable yurt near the 13th green with scotch and snacks, and I completed the manuscript. That was 13 years ago, and here we are, still talking golf and enjoying each other's company after all these years. I'm honored that he invited me to write this foreword to *Zokology*.

Zoke's approach to improving one's golf is unique. He's the only golfer I know who has read books such as Jill Bolte Taylor's *My Stroke of Insight*, Tae Yun Kim's *The Silent Master*, and *The Four Agreements* by Don Miguel Ruiz. My friend is a searcher and a student. You, the reader, are sure to benefit from his explorations and adventures in the game.

Lorne Rubenstein

CHAPTER 1

Family Background—Caddying—Marine Drive Golf Club—Getting Into and Out of Drugs

My very first recollection of golf was alongside my father. We lived in Kitimat, British Columbia, where I was born, and my dad took me with him to the golf course. I must have been four or five years old at the time. Right after my dad struck his first shot down the fairway, I took off running as fast as I could to go get the golf ball. I proudly picked it up and ran as fast as I could back to him so he could do it again. I didn't know that wasn't what you were supposed to do.

In 1964, I was six years old when our family moved from Kitimat to our grandmother's home in Vancouver on King Edward Avenue near Main Street. Three years later, when I was nine, my cousin Neil and I, along with a couple of friends, came across some golf clubs and balls in my grandmother's basement. We took them to the wide-open space of Hillcrest Park to hit them without fear of breaking windows. That was the first time I felt the delight of hitting a good golf shot. This happened on a couple of occasions, but soon we gravitated to Queen Elizabeth Park's Pitch & Putt.

On Friday, December 13, 1968, when I was ten, the family moved to Vancouver's Kerrisdale neighborhood. Our new home was three houses in from 57th Avenue, right across the street from the Marine Drive Golf Club (MDGC). Both my parents were already members at Marine Drive, but at the time, I had no idea how large a role MDGC was going to play in shaping my life.

Both my parents came from immigrant families. My mother, Elsie, was born in 1921 to Slovenian immigrants in a small company-owned mining town in Northern British Columbia called Anyox. It has since become a ghost town following the closure of the mine in 1935. My father, Joseph, was born in Cerklje, Slovenia, and immigrated to Canada with his parents as a seven-year-old boy. They arrived at the Port of Quebec on June 16, 1929, aboard the *Empress of Scotland.*

I was the youngest of my parents' four children. My brother, Ron, is nine years older than I am, my sister Janet is seven years older, and my sister Deb is a year older. We grew up in a loving, proud, and ambitious family.

Both my parents grew up in the immigrant neighborhood on Vancouver's East End called Strathcona. Strathcona was a hardscrabble ethnic community that bordered on Vancouver's Chinatown. In 1942, prior to volunteering for the Canadian Army for World War II (4 Company, Royal Canadian Dental Corps), my father began to play golf. I came across and have saved an invoice dated April 11, 1942, the date he purchased his first golf clubs—a set of ten clubs, a golf bag, and head covers from the Pro-Made Golf Company for a total of $93.55, a tidy sum at the time. My father's golf was shelved when he set off to Basic Training in Vernon, BC, and the Canadian Army's Basic Infantry Training Centre and support camp for Coldstream Ranch Battle Drill School before shipping overseas to England. My father came into France right behind the Normandy Invasion at Juno Beach on D-Day Plus 6 (June 12, 1944) in *Operation Overlord.*

PRO-MADE GOLF COMPANY
Owned and Operated by
B. C. LEATHER CO. LTD.
VANCOUVER, B.C.

MAKERS OF
PRO-MADE
Reg. Trade Mark
GOLF CLUBS
"The Finest Golf Clubs in the World"

M Mr. Joe Zokol,
45 West 10th Ave.,
Vancouver, B.C.

Vancouver, B.C. April 11th 1942

No 8758

Order No. Shipped Via Terms:

Quantity	DESCRIPTION	Price	Total
	CONDITIONAL SALE ACCOUNT		
2	model #129 woods		15.90
7	model #165 irons		34.65
1	model #55 putter		7.50
1	golf bag		32.50
2	head covers		2.00
			92.55
	carrying charges		1.00
			93.55

My father's first golf club purchase before going to WWII.

In 1946, after the war ended, the troops repatriated to Canada, and my father went back to school to complete his high school equivalency, an undergrad at the University of British Columbia, and then advanced to the University of Oregon's Dental School. My brother, Ron, and sister Deb followed our father's path and became dentists too, but my sister Jan and I had other ideas.

Joseph Zokol, 1944.

Elsie Zokol, 2007.

Both my parents evolved into passionate golfers and MDGC members. Our family was very involved with the club. My Uncle Bob was a past president of the club as well. My father played a regular weekend game with his buddies, playing to a six handicap in his prime. I can still remember the excitement I felt when my dad asked me to caddie for him on Saturday and Sunday morning games. I jumped at the opportunity. When I watched my father play golf, I thought my dad was the best golfer in the world. For a Father's Day gift in grade two, I addressed his Father's Day card to the King of Golfers.

When my parents told me that when I turned 12, I could become a junior member at Marine Drive, I was so excited. Nothing sounded better to me than that. My dad saw I was eager to play golf and made arrangements with the pro shop staff to cut down a driver, a 5-iron, and a putter for me. My eyes lit up when he gave them to me. Mondays were a day off for golf club staff in those days, so after dinner on Mondays, my dad would take me down to the club and sneak me onto the course to play either 6 or 9 holes. My three cut-down clubs were tucked out of sight in his golf bag. A few prying eyes exposed our secret breach of club rules, but once we got to the second hole and out of sight of the clubhouse, Dad would throw a ball on the ground for me to play with my cut-down clubs. Every Monday meant playing a few holes on a grown-up golf course, and it was the best thing in the whole world. I so looked forward to those Monday nights with my dad every week.

Looking to Pick a Fight

Chris Rivers and I became best friends in grade four, right after we had a schoolyard fight that started during a lunchtime soccer game at Dr. R.E. McKechnie Elementary School. I was the new kid in class who came in halfway through the fourth grade year, and I guess you could say I came in with a chip on my shoulder, needing to prove something. I had spent a couple of years playing soccer at Vancouver's Riley Park–Little Mountain neighborhood and attending General Wolfe Elementary School, which bordered on a rough area of town with housing projects, and in the schoolyard there, you either learned to fend for yourself or you got bullied. I had to repeat the third grade at General Wolfe, which resulted in me getting teased in the schoolyard, so I'd had my share of fights, and these fortified my fighting skills. My father knew what I had to face in the schoolyard and told me, "I will teach you to box, but if I ever catch you starting a fight, you're going to get it from me. But if someone starts a fight with you, I want you to be able to finish it." My father, in his younger years, was an amateur boxer and grew up in the rough side of Vancouver's immigrant neighborhood; he knew how to fight. After dinner, we would go into our living room, my father would get down on his knees, and we would put on the boxing gloves, him showing me the fundamentals of boxing. He always said, "If you let your guard down, I am going to hit you, and so you will learn. All you need to do is hit the guy as hard as you can right on the nose, and I will teach you to do just that."

As the new kid in school, I instinctively started trying to figure out where I stood in the schoolyard pecking order. From my perspective, sports and the odd fight fleshed things out pretty fast.

As we were playing soccer in the schoolyard, this kid named Chris Rivers was on the other team. Rivers was the fastest kid on the soccer field. Nobody could catch him in a race. In this soccer game, he beat me to a loose ball, and I didn't like it. The next time we both went for the ball he beat me again and, out of frustration, I tripped him. Chris went down on the gravel and got up and got right in my face for my foul play. We got into a pushing match. Then the challenge was made, I said, "Let's fight after school under the willow tree in the far field." My challenge was accepted.

Throughout that afternoon, word of the pending fight went through the school like wildfire. Kids in the class were telling me, "Rivers is going to kill you. He knows Judo." My anxiety about the fight grew as the three o'clock buzzer loomed. When the buzzer finally sounded and I went outside, I could see the gathering of kids excited about this fight walking to the far field under the large willow tree. All the kids were on Chris Rivers's side.

As we squared off, the large group of kids encircled us and started to chant, "Fight-Fight-Fight," and it was on. I went straight into my boxing position, and Rivers ran straight at me, and we wrestled on the ground for a bit. We both got on our feet and squared off a second time. Once again, Rivers was so fast and came at me and got me on the ground, but I got loose from him again and stood up. He wanted to grapple on the ground, and I wanted to box. We squared off one more time. I got back into my boxing position and punched him in the face with a left jab. I hit him in the face again with another left jab. Then I hit him with a hard right with everything I could right on the nose. A cut formed under his nose, and his nose started to bleed—the fight was over.

Immediately after the fight, Chris and I became best friends, inseparable from that point forward. In the sixth grade, Chris and I started to hang out with some older kids who introduced us to smoking pot. We both thought getting high was a pretty cool thing to do and we started smoking regularly. In fact, still in the sixth grade, another buddy of mine got me some LSD called Purple Barrel Microdot. I was curious and tried it. Hallucinating was a fascinating experience—watching the walls breathe was a little freaky—and it was the first and last time I took LSD.

When Chris and I got to grade seven, we were smoking hashish on a daily basis with our buddies after school. We'd walk to Ian Phelps's house and smoke a gram of Blond Lebanese, our favorite hash. A couple of our buddies were doing a little dealing so we had easy access to whatever we wanted.

In 1970, when I turned 12, I became a junior member of the MDGC. For Christmas that year, my parents gave me a junior set of golf clubs consisting of a driver, a 3-wood, a 3-, 5-, 7-, and 9-iron, and a putter. My father got one of the club's assistant pros, Bill Carrington, to get me started with weekly golf lessons.

Marine Drive Golf Club 50 Year Member bag tag (joined 1970).

My first junior golf tournament was also in 1970, called the Little Masters at the Tsawwassen Golf Club. (Today, Tsawwassen Springs is a wonderful golf course development owned by the Toigo family, who assembled an ownership team of Bruce Allen, Michael Buble, and my late friend Pat Quinn.) It was there that I won my first golf trophy: Low Net Score for the group of boys aged 12 and under. That trophy sat on my bedroom dresser, and I looked at it every day.

As I settled into the junior program at Marine Drive, I quickly developed friendships with other junior members. Russ Jordan, who was a few years older than me, became my best friend. Our regular junior group at Marine Drive included Russ, Kelly Murray, Kevin Hayward, and Peter

Radiuk. Alvie Thompson was the head pro at the time and became a mentor to me when I turned professional. Alvie's 1962 CPGA Championship victory earned him an invitation to the 1963 Masters. Alvie's influence on the juniors was immeasurable. Our group played and practiced as much as we could, and we admired the many great players that came out of MDGC, including Alvie Thompson, Stan Leonard, Johnny Johnston, Wayne Vollmer, Doug Roxburgh, Steve Berry, Harry White, Marilyn Palmer, Val White, Mike Buckley, and Paula Phillips, among others.

Competition Golf

Our group of junior players became very competitive. In 1973, Russ and I were asked if we wanted to play in a Marine Drive junior interclub match against the junior team at Capilano Golf Club. We eagerly accepted and played as a two-man match for Marine Drive. Russ was a much better player than I was, but I played well and Russ played great, and we dominated the junior players from Capilano. We loved every minute of it and felt proud to return to MDGC with a victory over Capilano Golf & CC.

Caddying at Marine Drive for Leopold (Poldi) Bentley

At the age of 14, I started to caddie on Saturdays and Sundays at Marine Drive for Leopold Lionel Garrick Bentley (née Bloch-Bauer). In 1938, the Bloch-Bauers changed their surname to Bentley when they landed in Canada as refugees after escaping Nazi-occupied Vienna. Mr. Bentley's family and friends referred to him simply as "Poldi." Poldi and his brother-in-law, John Prentice started a new business called 'Pacific Veneer' which lead to the start of Canadian Forest Products, now Canfor. Mr. Bentley had a regular threesome each weekend that included himself and fellow Marine Drive members John Robertson and Fred Cope.

Leopold Bloch-Bauer and his wife, Antoinette Ruth Bloch-Bauer, had one son, Peter John Gerald Bloch-Bauer, born in Vienna, Austria, in 1930. The Bloch-Bauers and their extended family, the Picks and the Prentices, were prominent and wealthy Viennese Jewish families who together owned and operated a sugar refinery business controlling approximately 20% of the European sugar market at the turn of the twentieth century. They were also collectors of fine art. In fact, in 1907, Ferdinand Bloch-Bauer, Leopold's uncle, commissioned Gustav Klimt to paint the *Portrait of Adele Bloch-Bauer I*, (*The Woman in Gold*), the subject of which was Ferdinand's wife.

The Bloch-Bauer story was brought to film in the movie *Women in Gold* starring Helen Mirren and Ryan Reynolds, which told the story of Maria Altmann, Poldi's sister. Maria Altmann who inevitably landed in Los Angeles, CA, and fought the government of Austria for a decade to reclaim the *Portrait of Adele Bloch-Bauer I,* which had been stolen by the Nazis during WWII after Ferdinand Bloch-Bauer had gifted the painting to Maria Altmann, the niece of Adele Bloch-Bauer in 1937. The case ended up in the US Supreme Court, *Republic of Austria v. Altmann* (2004), which ruled in favor of Maria Altmann. She later sold it, and the painting is on display today at the Neue Galerie in New York City. In November 2006, four Klimt paintings were sold at Christie's auction house: *Portrait of Adele Bloch-Bauer II* (a second portrait he painted of her) sold for $87.9 million to Oprah Winfrey (then Oprah resold the painting in 2016 for $150 million), *Apfelbaum* sold for $33 million, *Buchenwald* for $40.3 million, and *Häuser in Unterach am Attersee* for $31 million, all went to private collections.

I enjoyed caddying for Mr. Bentley, but during these years I was not 100% focused on golf. I also played soccer and baseball in the Kerrisdale Little League program at Elm Park on 41st and Elm St. in Vancouver, and I pitched and played shortstop for the Kerrisdale Lions. The more I played other sports the more I found myself being attracted to the individuality of golf. As I got a little older, the notion of being solely responsible for your own performance was appealing.

In 1972, I made the Kerrisdale Little League all-star baseball team and was picked to open the playoffs as the starting pitcher against the Little Mountain all-star team. I was faced with a dilemma when Stan Leonard asked me to caddie for him in the British Columbia Open being played at the Vancouver Golf Club on the same dates as the Little League playoffs. I had to choose whether to pitch or to caddie. Stan Leonard was a former head professional at MDGC prior to joining the PGA Tour and was one of the greatest professional players to ever come out of Canada. Leonard won three PGA Tour events in his day, the Greater Greensboro Open, the

Western Open, and the Tournament of Champions. Leonard played well in the Masters finishing T8th in 1955, T4th in both 1958 and 1959, and T9th in 1960. How could I pass up the opportunity to caddie for one of the best players in the history of our country? I told my baseball coach, Mr. White, that I'd decided not to play in the all-star games, and I never played another baseball game after that.

Playing in Competition—1973 BC Junior Championship

My first BC Junior Championship was in 1973, played at the Quilchena Golf Club in Richmond, BC. The BC Junior was a big deal for all the Marine Drive juniors who played competition golf. My close friend Russ Jordan played well, getting himself into contention and making the BC Junior B Team. The A Team was made up of the top four players from the BC Junior Championship plus an additional two rounds in the BC Junior Invitational tournament. The next four players qualified for BC's B Team, which represented BC in an inter-provincial competition against Alberta's junior team. Making a team to represent your province was a big deal, and I admired how well Russ played in those matches. Jim Nelford won the 1973 BC Junior Championship and, without any doubt, was the best junior player in the province. I didn't know him at that time, but he was four years older than me, and we all admired him as a player.

My First Traumatic Experience in Competition

I will never forget my first round of the 1973 BC Junior Championship. When our group got to the fourth hole at Quilchena Golf Club, there was a three-group wait. The fourth hole was a long par 4 with the property boundary, out of bounds, running down the whole right side, just off the fairway. While waiting for the groups in front of ours to play, I watched closely and saw a couple of players hit their tee shots out of bounds. I could feel the embarrassment on their faces and in their body language as they rifled through their golf bag for a provisional ball. I could feel rising tension and wanted to avoid a similar, painfully embarrassing experience.

Finally, it was our group's turn to play. When it was my turn, I walked to the tee and stuck my tee into the ground to tee up my ball. The only thought going through my mind was *DON'T HIT IT OUT OF BOUNDS!* I then proceeded to hit three balls in succession out of bounds. After hitting my fourth provisional tee shot way left, I walked off the tee toward my golf bag and fought like crazy inside to not look as embarrassed as I felt in front of all those players watching. It was embarrassing and traumatizing when I shot 94 in the first round. In the second round, I shot 86 and missed the cut. It was my first real experience with the pain, frustration, discomfort, and failure in front of others that can come with playing this game.

The 1976 BC Junior Championship—Fred Couples

The first time I saw Fred Couples hit a golf shot was during the practice round for the 1976 BC Junior Championship. Our group was walking up to the 18th tee in the practice round, and the group in front of us was still on the tee waiting for the group in front of them to clear the 18th fairway. We weren't able to recognize any of the players in the group waiting on the tee, which was a bit unusual. We could tell they weren't from here.

As we approached the 18th tee, one of the guys in our group engaged with this unfamiliar group and asked the first question: "Where are you guys from?" The smallest of the three players said, "We're from Seattle." "What's your name?" The same guy said, "My name is Scott Williams, and this guy here is going to win this tournament." "Oh yeah, what's his name?" "His name is Fred Couples."

We looked over at this guy named Fred Couples, and he didn't say a word. Instead, he nonchalantly swung his driver with a shy "awe-shucks" expression. Williams was doing all the chirping and bragging on his buddy Fred's account.

When the 18th fairway finally cleared, Scott Williams stood up on the tee and with a short, fast golf swing, struck his tee shot. Then Fred teed it up and with his long, smooth, powerful swing—which has never changed to this very day—he absolutely crushed it. My eyes almost popped out of my head when I watched the ball come off his driver's clubface and heard the sound of impact that he made. *Holy shit.* I had never seen any person other than a powerful pro hit a tee shot like that.

The legend of Fred Couples began. I never got paired with Couples in that BC Junior, but word got out that on the 13th hole, Couples had hit the par 5 in two with two 1-irons. Other than Fred Couples, no other junior player in the field was capable of hitting the green in two, let alone with two 1-irons. Couples did not end up winning the tournament. And I played well, finishing T2nd with a young 16-year-old kid named Jim Rutledge. Fred Couples finished fourth.

THE 1976 BC JUNIOR CHAMPIONSHIP RESULTS

Place	Name	Club
1st	Joe Limoli	Vancouver Golf Club, Coquitlam, BC
T2nd	Dick Zokol	Marine Drive Golf Club, Vancouver, BC
T2nd	Jim Rutledge	Cedar Hill Golf Club, Victoria, BC
4th	Fred Couples	Jefferson Park Golf Course, Seattle, WA

Getting Off Track

Looking back to 1973, Chris Rivers and I entered the eighth grade at Magee Secondary School, and apparently, we had quite the reputation—as druggies. The amount of weed we were smoking and classes we were skipping started to accelerate. By the end of eighth grade, I recall regularly smoking pot on the way to school in the morning and on the way home after school, then getting really wrecked after dinner.

Ninth grade was the breaking point. I had purchased a quarter ounce of hash, and my mother found my stash. She didn't know what to do, so she turned to my older brother, Ron, who was in dental school at the time. My brother read me the riot act, said that I needed to get my shit straight, and said that I needed to break the news of my behavior to Dad when he got home from work.

Later that day, I confessed my sins to my father. Not surprisingly, he was pretty upset and came down hard on me, grounding me and saying, "You cannot see those trouble-making friends of yours that you've been hanging around with ever again. You must get home immediately after school, and there is no going out after dinner. The only place you can go to is that golf course across the street. And if you don't comply, you may have to find a new home."

My father's threats to expel me from my loving family blew my mind. It scared the shit right out of me. It scared me straight, and by letting me continue at the club, it gave me an alternate path.

The thing that impacted me most was how I disappointed my parents and family. My father's body language toward me changed when I stepped into the room, his frown clearly showing his disapproval. After dinner was finished each day, we typically sat around the table to talk as a family, but now I was uncomfortable sitting there and excused myself early, feeling I needed to leave the room. I hated it.

Not feeling my father's love was killing me, so I avoided him as much as I could, instead spending as much time at the golf club as possible. Russ Jordan and I would play and practice all day long, then, with my dad's permission, I started going to the golf course after dinner. Russ and I started to follow what fellow Marine Drive member Doug Roxburgh did—we would hit our shag bag of balls on the range until dark, then putt on the practice green with the lights of the clubhouse helping us see in the dark. This new routine went on throughout that summer of 1974 and into the next summer of 1975, and our golf games improved.

In grade ten at Magee, I had stopped doing all drugs just as most kids were starting to dabble in pot. Instead, I started to get serious about my golf game and to pull back from the high school social activities.

Chris Rivers and I are still like brothers to this day. We both came though our periods of adolescent confusion better from having experienced it, which is not always the case. Chris built a wonderful career as a successful realtor in Vancouver over the last 40 years. We often look back at our youth and laugh.

During this period, I started to really appreciate the great golf history of MDGC. It pulled me in. Marine Drive is truly the club of champions, and I wanted to pursue fitting into and being part of it.

In 2018, our family spread both of our parents' ashes on the MDGC property, right beside the practice area close to the 4th green near the Fraser River.

My father, Joseph Zokol, and me.

CHAPTER 2

1977–1981—My Cinderella Story—BYU & Amateur Golf—Walking On the BYU Golf Team

In January 1977, I was in the twelfth grade at Magee Secondary School in Vancouver. During my daily walks to school, I started to pick up on daily movement patterns in my environment. Because I left the house at the exact same time every day, I noticed people and patterns of cars pulling out of their driveway at the same time and the city bus would stop at that bus stop at the same time. This pattern made me think I was already stuck. Thoughts like *what the hell am I going to do for the rest of my life* were on a constant replay loop in my mind.

At that time, my older brother, Ron, had followed our father's path and had recently graduated from dental school (my older sister, Deb, decided to enter dental school at the age of 29). I felt the pressure to be successful. What was I going to do with my life? All I knew for certain was that I didn't want to work for anyone. I wanted to be independent and wanted to be my own boss. I was pretty good at golf, and I started to think about being a professional golfer. It was definitely appealing, so I began to question the best path. It occurred to me that the best way to the PGA Tour was to progress through the NCAA program in the United States.

Over the previous four years, my buddy Russ Jordan and I kept a keen watch on Jim Nelford, who transformed his game as part of Brigham Young University's Golf Team. It was proof enough for me. By Nelford's senior year at BYU, he elevated his playing ability and rose above the pack of Canadian players, becoming the best amateur player in Canada. Nelford won the 1975 and 1976 Canadian Amateur Championships and the prestigious Western Amateur Championship in 1977. Nelford's ascent from junior golf, followed by his four years at BYU, gave him the best possible chance to make the PGA Tour, and my plan was to follow Jim Nelford's path. I was naïve and had no real basis for this confidence, but I felt inspired by the possibility.

I decided to write Karl Tucker, the head men's golf coach at BYU, a letter highlighting my junior playing record. I didn't know how to write a formal letter, so I reached out to Harry White and Fred Welsby, who ran Vancouver's Junior Golf Tour program and were very supportive of junior golfers, to help me construct the letter.

I did not have a very robust junior golf resume, other than my second place finish in the 1976 BC Junior Championship. That didn't bother me, but I wasn't sure if it would impress the head coach of one of the best NCAA golf programs in the United States.

A few weeks later, I received a letter back from Karl Tucker basically saying, "Thanks but no thanks." This is where my naivety worked in my favor. This news didn't deter me. Because I was so determined to follow Nelford's path of success, I didn't even try to reach out to any other NCAA program and figured I'd get in the next year. From my perspective, I was going to BYU. That was some audacity on my part—I didn't have the slightest idea of what it takes to get into a top-tier NCAA Division 1 golf program, plus I'm not even a Mormon.

I planned to take a gap year to work, and following that, I would reapply to Coach Tucker for the following year. In the meantime, my golf game began to rapidly improve, and in the spring of 1977, I won the Green Acres Amateur in Richmond, BC, which had a strong amateur field, and a few weeks later, I won the 1977 Vancouver City Men's Amateur Championship right after graduating from Magee Secondary School.

My next scheduled tournament was in July: the 1977 BC Amateur Championship being held at the Kamloops Golf Club. By sheer happenstance, I got paired with Jim Nelford in the first two rounds of the tournament. Nelford had just finished his senior year at BYU and was going after his third consecutive Canadian Amateur Championship the following month before turning pro and entering the 1977 PGA Tour's Q-School.

Nelford was not only the best Amateur player in Canada; he was one of the best players coming out of the whole NCAA collegiate system in

1977. He looked like a pro, he acted like a pro, and, most importantly, he played like a pro. Jim Nelford was the quintessential by-product of a successful NCAA program. This was exactly what I wanted to pursue.

After the first two rounds of the BC Amateur, I was not only beating Nelford, I was leading the tournament.

After the second round was over, Nelford said to me, "I understand you wrote Coach Tucker a letter earlier this year and want to go to BYU?" Obviously, Coach Tucker asked Nelford about me. Aside from the two rounds we had just played together, Nelford knew absolutely nothing about my ability, being four years ahead of me. He said to me, "I will be speaking to Coach Tucker next week and I'll put in a good word for you."

Things could not have turned out better. I played well in the final two rounds but felt like I gave the tournament away with mistakes in the final round. Doug Roxburgh went on to win the event (one of his 13 BC Amateur Championship victories), but my connection with Nelford changed my world. This was one of the most significant inflection points in my life.

The following week, I received a call from Coach Tucker. He said, "Jim Nelford spoke highly about your ability. I am glad to see your advancement since you wrote me in January. Are you still interested in our program?" I replied, "Yes, absolutely." Tucker explained, "It's too late for me to come up to Canada on a recruiting trip, but are you able to come down to Provo, Utah? I'd like to have a look at you, and you can get a look at the campus and our program." I knew nothing about the Mormon religion at the time, but that was all I needed to hear.

After telling my parents that Coach Tucker wanted to have a look at me and suggested I come down to Provo on a recruiting trip, my father said, "Take my car and get your ass down there."

So I made arrangements to meet Coach Tucker and planned my drive from Vancouver, BC, to Provo, Utah. A couple of days before I set out on the thousand-mile drive to Provo, I pulled into the old White Spot Drive-In on 64th and Granville in Vancouver for a Triple-O burger and parked beside a high school buddy, Steve Cottrell. After a bit of small talk, I mentioned to Steve that I was driving to Utah in a couple of days and that, if he didn't have anything better to do, he could join me on this road trip. Steve agreed, and the two of us jumped into my dad's 1972 Ford Thunderbird and took off for Provo, Utah.

I will never forget, as Steve and I were south of Salt Lake City in Draper, UT, southbound on Interstate 15 to Provo, when I looked to the right and saw Utah State Prison for my first time and said to Steve, "Holy shit, that's where that Gary Gilmore guy was executed by firing squad a few months ago." Gilmore demanded the implementation of his death sentence.

Steve and I arrived in Provo on schedule the day before my meeting with Coach Tucker. The next morning, I made my way to Brigham Young University's Smith Fieldhouse to meet Coach Tucker. As I waited in the foyer, I was immediately impressed with the faces, plaques, and trophies of all the previous BYU players, such as Johnny Miller, Mike Taylor, Ray Leach, Mike Reid, Michael Brannan, John Fought, Stan Souza, Joey Dills, Lance Suzuki, Pat McGowan, Jimmy Blair, and Jim Nelford.

After a conversation, Coach Tucker grabbed a shag bag of golf balls, told me to grab my clubs, and we walked across the parking lot from the Fieldhouse to the Football & Golf practice field. Tucker said, "Let's see how you hit the ball." After warming up, I went through my bag, starting with my short irons, and Tucker started to ask me to hit different types of shots. From my perspective, I couldn't have hit the ball any better. After about 30 minutes of hitting shots for Coach Tucker, he said, "I'd like you to play a round of golf today at Riverside Country Club with one of our team players, Jamie Edmond." Jamie had just finished his junior year and was a solid player on the BYU Golf Team.

Jamie Edmond picked me up and took me to Riverside CC, and we played 18 holes. I played well and shot a couple under par on a course I had never seen. I was pleased and found Jamie to be a wonderful player and person. After the round, Jamie said, "Coach Tucker wants you in his office at 9:00 am tomorrow morning."

The next day, I went back to the Smith Fieldhouse and Coach Tucker's office, and he sat me down, saying, "Look, I can't give you any grant-in-aid as we are all out, but I will let you walk on the golf team. You can join us in weekly team meetings and play in all our qualifiers to see who makes the traveling squad. If you play well enough you can play your way on the team. I can get you enrolled in school on short notice. Can you afford your own tuition and room and board in the athlete dorm?" I said, "That sounds great, but I will need to talk with my parents." Coach Tucker went on to say, "I can put you in the athletic dorm; you can room with Bobby Clampett."

I didn't know who Bobby Clampett was and I said to myself, "You could put me in with Jed or Eli May Clampett for all I care." I didn't know it at the time, but Bobby Clampett was the number one recruited collegiate player in the entire NCAA. He had full ride offers to any Division I NCAA School in the country—he chose BYU.

My Freshman Year: 1977-78

School started in September, and I moved into our dorm room in Hinckley Hall and met my roommate, Bobby Clampett. The four new golf team freshmen were Clampett, from Carmel, CA; Dave DeSantis, from Tucson, AZ; Kim Carpenter, from Los Angeles, CA; and me. Clampett and I roomed together, and DeSantis and Carpenter roomed together on the same floor.

The sophomore players on our team were Tod Hensarling from Lafayette, LA; Jerry Rose from Sacramento, CA; and Chip Larson from Scottsdale, AZ. The junor players were Erich Gott and Jamie Edmond and senior players on the team were Stan Souza and Mike Brannan.

Other Great BYU Freshmen

The year 1977 was an interesting one for BYU Athletics, to say the least. Danny Ainge was a freshman and a highly recruited athlete from Eugene, OR. Ainge committed to play college basketball for BYU. Of note, Danny was also drafted in Major League Baseball's 1977 amateur draft by the Toronto Blue Jays, straight out of high school.

Danny was a three-sport high school All-American in football, baseball, and basketball. In Ainge's senior year (1981), he was named the national basketball college player of the year and won the John R. Woodmen Award for the most outstanding male college basketball player. Ainge went on to play for the Boston Celtics for eight seasons (1981–1989) and a few years with the Sacramento Kings, Portland Trail Blazers, and the Phoenix Suns.

Another freshman in Hinckley Hall in 1977 was Jim McMahon. McMahon played quarterback for the BYU football team. He was selected fifth overall by the Chicago Bears in the 1982 NFL Draft. McMahon achieved his greatest professional success with the 1985 Chicago Bears that won the franchise's first Super Bowl title in Super Bowl XX.

Bobby Clampett

Bobby Clampett was a golf phenomenon as a junior and NCAA collegiate player. He was highly motivated, and his ability to perform was off-the-charts remarkable: his golf swing was outstanding—he hit it long and straight and made every putt he looked at.

As soon as school started, Coach Tucker had all of us competing in two- or three-round qualifying events. The fall schedule was set for tournaments hosted by Weber State, Utah State, UNLV, and the W.H. Tucker Intercollegiate, hosted by the University of New Mexico in Albuquerque, NM. Most collegiate tournaments were six-man teams, so Coach would draw up the next qualifying event, which might be three rounds with all ten players on the team playing for four spots. The two senior players, Mike Brannan and Stan Souza, were exempt. If you played well in tournaments, Coach could choose to exempt you into the next tournament, but if you didn't, he threw you back into qualifying.

In our first qualifying event, Clampett absolutely smoked everyone. He was carding 62s, 63s, and 64s seemingly every round, while the senior players on the team, like Mike and Stan, were all shooting scores in the high sixties. Bobby was blowing away everyone and I was shooting scores like 74, 73, and 72, if I was lucky. Coach Tucker knew these qualifying events would hone our edge, but I was just trying to keep up and survive.

Bobby Clampett was unbelievably good. As the low qualifier, he earned one of the four spots for the six-man team in the team's first event of the fall season. Clampett then proceeded to blow the field away in his first NCAA collegiate event. In fact, Bobby won his first three collegiate events that he played in as a freshman. I remember him being the only player in the field to shoot such low scores at the University of New Mexico course in the W.H. Tucker Intercollegiate in Albuquerque, which was a long and difficult track. Clampett went on to win the All-American Intercollegiate as a freshman against all the best players in the nation, and he was named First Team All-American that same year.

In my opinion, Clampett should have won the 1978 Fred Haskins Award to honor the most outstanding collegiate golfer in the NCAA, but it went instead to Lindy Miller from Oklahoma State, but he went on to win the Fred Haskins Award in his sophomore year (1979) and his junior year (1980). Clampett's amateur titles included the Porter Cup, the Sunnehanna Amateur, and the Western Amateur. He also won the 1978 World Amateur medal in team competition for the Eisenhower Cup Trophy and the 1978 and 1980 California State Amateur Championship. He was the low amateur at the 1978 US Open and 1979 Masters.

Clampett would leave BYU before our senior year to turn pro. He joined the PGA Tour in short order and finished nineteenth on the Official PGA Tour Money List in 1981, his rookie year.

Bobby based his early golf training on the book *The Golfing Machine* by Homer Kelly. Bobby worked closely with his golf instructor Ben Doyle, the first authorized instructor of *The Golfing Machine*. Ben was like a father to Bobby.

As my freshman year ended, I managed to play in one tournament, and my roommate was the best amateur player in the world. I felt proud to be a player on the BYU Golf Team, but I was just trying to keep up with the other players, and I had no idea how much I was improving being in this kind of environment. When I got back to Vancouver after my freshman year, my perspective changed; my buddy Russ Jordan told me he saw a significant improvement in how I played.

At the end of my freshman year, in 1978, the NCAA Championship was played at Eugene Country Club in Eugene, OR. The five players on our team were Mike Brannan, Stan Souza, Jamie Edman, Erich Gott, and Bobby Clampett. BYU tied for fourth.

1978 NCAA CHAMPIONSHIP

Place	School	Score
1st	Oklahoma State	1140
2nd	Georgia	1157
3rd	Arizona State	1160
T4th	**Brigham Young**	**1174**
T4th	North Carolina	1174

Playing in My First PGA Tour Event

In the late spring of 1978, after final exams were written, when I got back to Vancouver, I went to the BC Golf Association's office to put in my entry forms for all the tournaments I could play in. On the wall, I noticed a poster for the Canadian Open Western Canada Qualifying at Peace Portal Golf Club in White Rock, BC. It was a 36-hole, one-day event. The winner of that spot would get into the 1978 Canadian Open, being played on Jack Nicklaus's new Glen Abbey Golf Course in Oakville, ON. So I took a form and mailed in my entry.

There was really no way of knowing what to expect with this qualifying. The one thing I did know was I had spent the last year playing in many qualifying events at BYU against some of the best players in the NCAA, so I had a healthy mindset going in. When I arrived at Peace Portal Golf Course, I saw Jim Gibson of the BCGA at the Registration. After I registered, Jim told me he would be refereeing the twosome I was in for 36-hole qualifying.

I said, "That's great, how many players in the field?" Jim said, "There are two players in the field. The two of you will be playing for one spot in the Canadian Open, you and an assistant pro at the Earl Grey Golf Club in Calgary."

This was an amazing opportunity. I was ready to play.

In the first 18 holes, I shot 69, and my opponent shot 75. In the second 18 holes, I think I followed up with something like 67 to his 77. I cannot remember the actual scores, but I played well and qualified in the 1978 Canadian Open. How fucking cool is that?

When I got home, and as our family sat around the dinner table, my parents asked me, "How'd it go today?" I said, "I played great, there were only two players in the field, and I won the spot to play in the Canadian Open. Can you please pass the potatoes?"

I called Coach Tucker to tell him I qualified for the Canadian Open, and he then called Billy Casper to see if he could arrange for me to play a practice round. Playing in a PGA Tour event was so exciting, hitting brand new Titleists on the range next to Arnold Palmer and passing Jack Nicklaus in the locker room was incredible for a 19-year-old kid.

At the time, Glen Abbey was one of the hardest courses on the PGA Tour. I was blown away by how difficult it was to play. The last hole in my first round, the ninth hole, still stands out to me to this very day. It was a long par 4, and your second shot needed to carry the water in front of the green. I blocked my tee shot into the fairway bunker on the right. I remember having a 2-iron in hand standing in that fairway bunker and saying to myself, "Okay, let's just hit a solid shot here, get it on the green and 2-putt for an 84." I did just that.

In the second round, I don't think I broke 80, but the experience was gold. Being able to play in a PGA Tour event and being able to say I stood next to Jack Nicklaus at the urinal relieving myself in the men's locker room in the Canadian Open was a rewarding (but intimidating) moment.

My Sophomore Year: 1978-79

A new year meant the departure of senior players, which meant I had an opportunity to fill the gap and break into the traveling squad. I was a better player in my second year at BYU, and now there were four fewer excellent players. I was excited to get back at it.

Bobby's mother had bought a three-bedroom town house off campus, and Dave DeSantis and I moved into Clampett's place in the second semester of our sophomore year. Danny Ainge lived right behind us. It was good to get away off campus and from all the pressure of being a non-Mormon at BYU. Coach Tucker was great to us non-Mormons. He said if the missionaries keep knocking on our doors, "Just let me know and I will take care of it." He did just that.

The thing was, while you didn't have to be Mormon to attend BYU, you do have to abide by their rules, which I thought was fair enough. Coach Tucker was great, but he did give us a warning that "if you are stupid enough to get caught drinking beer or any alcohol, you will be dealt with firmly and likely shown the door out of BYU."

There were five new players on the team. Barry Willardson from Houston, TX, who had just come back from his two-year Mormon Mission in San Diego. Keith Clearwater and Kent Kluba both came from Walnut Creek, CA. John Bodenhamer came in from Seattle. Another player that came back to our team was Tom Costello. Tom, or "Cozy," was my roommate in my first semester of sophomore year.

Sophomore year was a great opportunity to advance up the ladder on the golf team. A few spots opened up, and we knew exactly how to prepare to qualify and make the traveling squad, solidifying our place on the team. This was now what we lived for.

At the end of my sophomore year, the NCAA Championship was hosted by Wake Forest and played at Bermuda Run. The five players on the team were Tod Hensarling, Tom Costello, Bobby Clampett, Dave DeSantis, and me.

1979 NCAA CHAMPIONSHIP, WINSTON-SALEM, NC, BERMUDA RUN		
1st	Ohio State	1189
2nd	Oklahoma State	1191
3rd	Wake Forest	1196
4th	**Brigham Young**	**1198**
5th	New Mexico	1202

IMG's Huges Norton—In Pursuit of Bobby Clampett

Bobby Clampett made such a significant impact on the golf world; we were living in his world at BYU and we loved every minute of it.

One Sunday morning the phone rang. I picked up the phone and the person calling asked, "Is Bobby Clampett there?" I said, "No, he's not. Can I tell him who's calling, and can I take a message?" The caller said, "Yes, my name is Hughes Norton, I am calling from Cleveland, Ohio. Could you have Bobby give me a call when he returns?" This Hughes fellow gave me his number, and the conversation ended.

The following Sunday morning, the phone rang again. "It's Hughes Norton calling from Cleveland. Is Bobby in?" I said, "No, he's not, he's practicing, can I take a message?" Hughes said, "What's your name?" "My name's Dick Zokol." "Are you on the BYU Golf Team?" "Yes, I am." Hughes then said, "Let Bobby know that I called." I said, "I sure will."

The next Sunday at the same time, the phone rang again. I picked up the phone, and it was Hughes Norton again. By this time, Hughes recognized my voice and asked, "Is this Dick?" and I said, "Hi Hughes, yes, it is, and Bobby's not here, he's practicing." Hughes said to me, "Why aren't you practicing with Clampett?" I said something to the effect of I didn't have a car, and Bobby gets up too early.

Hughes Norton was a senior vice president in charge of golf operations at Cleveland-based International Management Group (IMG), the world's oldest and largest sports marketing organization, founded by Mark McCormack. Hughes Norton had his sights on signing Bobby Clampett to IMG. Hughes's efforts were rewarded three years later when Clampett turned pro and signed with IMG.

Hughes Norton's biggest claim to fame was signing Tiger Woods when Tiger turned pro and launched his career in the 1996 Greater Milwaukee Open with the Hello World campaign. Hughes put together significant endorsement deals for Woods in their two-year business relationship with Nike, Titleist, TAG Heuer, American Express, All-Star Cafe, Wheaties, and Warner Books.

IMG made the brilliant move to hire Earl Woods as a scout. In his book *Rainmaker*, Hughes explains how he introduced himself to Earl, Kultida, and Tiger and sat in their home in Cypress, California, when Tiger was still a junior player, establishing a relationship and trust that led to him becoming an IMG client. This was a brilliant move by Norton. Earl Woods wrote reports on the junior players competing against Tiger, and the unsaid obligation was to sign only one player down the road, his son when it was his time to turn professional.

The word in the locker room was that IMG didn't want to jeopardize Tiger's amateur status by signing a financial deal with Tiger's father. All they needed to do was hire Earl Woods as an IMG scout and recruiter and pay him accordingly.

I remember the 1992 Los Angeles Open at Riviera, Tiger's first PGA Tour event as an amateur. Tiger was 16 years old. At the time, I was also an IMG client, and Hughes Norton called me over to introduce me to Earl Woods. We exchanged greetings, and I immediately thought about how relentless Hughes was in his recruiting pursuits. Hughes Norton was the A-1 predator at the top of the sports agency food chain. He went after Clampett in his sophomore year in college and Tiger Woods when he was still a junior. Sports agency is a tough business with no guarantees, but

Hughes found out that things can change at a moment's notice. He explains his stories in his excellent book *Rainmaker*.

Junior Year 1979-80

In my junior year, a few other Canadians started to follow the path down to BYU: Keith Westover, or "Westy" as we called him, came to BYU as the 1980 Canadian Junior Champion, and Rick Gibson, or "Gibber," from Victoria, BC, came onto the team in my junior year. Gibber had a hilarious experience in his Bishop interview. As I mentioned, if you want to go to BYU, you don't have to be a Mormon, but you have to abide by Mormon rules, and they vet all non-Mormons in an interview with a Mormon Bishop. Gibber told the following story of his one-on-one Bishop interview:

> Bishop: Do you drink tea or coffee?
> Gibson: Yes, I do drink coffee.
> Bishop: In our Words of Wisdom, the Lord commands us (Mormons) to abstain from harmful substances. We are taught not to drink "hot drinks," meaning coffee or any tea.
> Gibson: That won't be a problem.
> Bishop: Do you smoke or do any tobacco products?
> Gibson: No, sir.
> Bishop: That's good. Do you drink alcohol?
> Gibson: Yes, I have a few beers now and then.
> Bishop: If you go to BYU, you cannot drink alcohol at all.
> Gibson: That won't be a problem.
> Bishop: Do you have a girlfriend?
> Gibson: Not at the moment.
> Bishop: Have you ever had a girlfriend?
> Gibson: Yes.
> Bishop: Have you had premarital sex?
> Gibson: Yes.
> Bishop: If you go to BYU, you must abstain from having premarital sex.

Gibson: Okay.
Bishop: Do you masturbate?
Gibson: It sounds like I am going to have to start.

Rick was smart enough to not say that last sentence out loud to the Bishop or he would not have passed the interview. But that is what went though his mind. Rick Gibson, like many of us who played for Karl Tucker at BYU, considered Coach a father figure. In fact, Rick's firstborn son was named Karl, after Coach Tucker.

The First Metalwood Used in the NCAA

In the spring of 1980, we were playing at a collegiate event in Southern California and a Los Angeles-based photographer named Chuck Brenkus, who took some famous photos of Hogan at the 1966 US Open at Olympic Club, approached Bobby Clampett and gave him this new metal-headed club with the name <Metalwood> on the top of the club. Chuck Brenkus said he'd heard about this new company, TaylorMade, and how they were producing these new "metal-headed" drivers at a foundry in Los Angeles called Alphacast.

It turned out, Clampett couldn't quite wrap his head around this metalwood thing, but I thought it was great. It was very simple to hit. I asked Clampett if he was going to use it after he hit a few shots with it. Clampett said, "Nope." I asked if I could have it, and Clampett said, "It's yours." I immediately put it into play and was the first collegiate player in NCAA golf to use a Metalwood in the 1980 Western Athletic Conference (WAC) at Torrey Pines South Course in La Jolla, CA, where we won the WAC Championship by 20 shots.

In the spring of 1980, the Royal Canadian Golf Association (now Golf Canada) asked me and Graham Cooke to represent Canada in a two-man team in an international event in Rabat, Morocco. The RCGA picked the team based on the 1979 Canadian Amateur Championship, which was played at Brantford Golf Club, won by Rafael Alarcón. My good friend Graham Cooke finished second and I finished third.

Graham Cooke and I were picked to make up Team Canada, and our non-playing captain was W. Len Goldson, so the three of us took off to Morocco to play at the Royal Golf Dar Es Salam golf course in Rabat. We got to know both Ronan Rafferty (Northern Ireland) and Gordon Brand Jr., who played for Great Britain. I played well and won the individual competition.

It was rumored that the Prince of Morocco was going to attend the reception the evening after the final round, and Rafferty and Brand noticed I was nervous, thinking I had to say a few words as the champion. It was custom to give a Moroccan dagger called a Koummya to the champion, and they asked me if I knew how to engage Morocco's royal family, which freaked me out even more. Rafferty said to me, "Whatever you do, do not ever turn your back to them. It's an insult if you do." That's when I really started to get nervous, but the Prince of Morocco wasn't able to be there in any event.

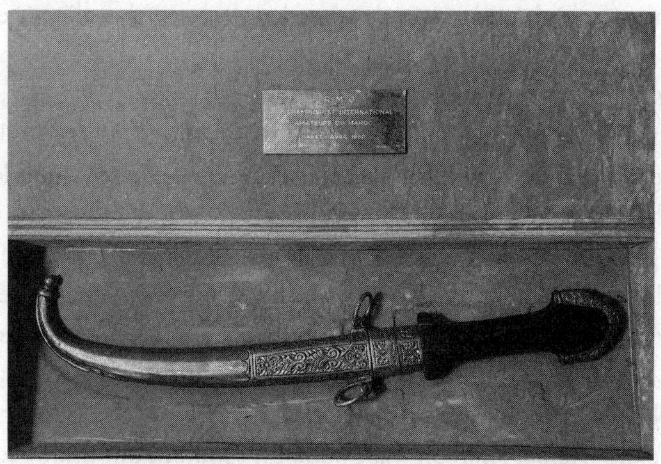

"Koummya" Moroccan Dagger. F.R.M.G. 16th Championnat International Amateurs Du Maroc Rabat – Avril 1980.

Our junior year on the BYU Golf Team ascended to the next level. Each player on our team was maturing, and of course, we had our big weapon, Bobby Clampett. We were neck and neck with the best golf teams in the nation: Mike Holder's Oklahoma State, Dave Williams's University of Houston, and Bill Brogden's Oral Roberts. We were focused hard, aiming to win the NCAA Championship being played at Ohio State's Scarlet Course.

The day before the first round of the NCAA Championship, the NCAA held a Long Drive Competition where each team would enter their longest hitter. Each player was given three balls to hit and in order to count each shot needed to finish in the fairway. The weather was cold, wet, and rainy. There were many players in the long drive contest who were considered big hitters, but Fred Couples separated himself from all the others as far as distance off the tee was concerned.

I will never forget Fred's phenomenal power with those three shots. Fred, with his wood-headed driver and Balata ball, launched his first shot, which plugged on impact in the fairway at 299 yards. Fred's second shot also plugged in the fairway at 301 yards. The crowd around the tee box was simply amazed by Fred's power and accuracy. Couples's third ball also plugged on impact in the fairway, and the person doing the measurement barked into the Walkie-Talkie, "Third ball—300." Hitting a Balata golf ball that spins too much with a wooden-headed driver at that distance in cold weather requires a clubhead speed of something like 130 miles per hour. Fred was a beast off the tee.

Our five-man playing squad was Bobby Clampett, Barry Willardson, Dave DeSantis, Tom Costello, and me, and we wanted nothing less than to win the NCAA Championship. With Clampett in full flight, we were expecting it. We played well, but Oklahoma State had a great team that included Rafael Alarcón, Bob Tway, Willie Wood, and Jeff Walser, and it was Alarcón who crushed our hopes and chances. Alarcón was second to none in his ability to scramble, truly one of the best escape artists in the whole NCAA. I remember Coach Tucker saying in the last nine holes, "That fucking Rafael Alarcón was goddamn Houdini out there the way he escaped trouble." Every time Alarcón got into trouble, he escaped miraculously, allowing Oklahoma State to win the 1980 NCAA Championship. The loss was a difficult pill for us to swallow.

1980 NCAA CHAMPIONSHIP RESULTS

Place	School	Score
1st	Oklahoma State	1173
2nd	**Brigham Young**	**1177**
3rd	Oral Roberts	1178
T4th	Ohio States	1184
T4th	Texas Christian	1184

The NCAA Individual title went to Utah State's Jay Don Blake, who beat Centenary's Hal Sutton in a sudden-death playoff.

I qualified to play in the 1980 Canadian Open at Royal Montreal as an amateur after finishing in 3rd place in the Canadian Amateur in 1979 at Brantford Golf CC. The RCGA gave spots to the top three players that year: Rafael Alarcón, who won, Graham Cooke, who finished second, and me, who finished third.

This was my second Canadian Open as an amateur. I was thrilled to play a practice round with Jim Nelford, Pat McGowan, and Bob Gilder. That practice round, I watched Bob Gilder. He was obviously a good Tour player who had a veteran's perspective, but what stood out to me was that his capability didn't seem to be too far out of reach. And when Bob Gilder won that week, I realized that the gap between top collegiate golf and PGA Tour golf wasn't insurmountable. In fact, I felt I was closing that gap.

1980 World Amateur Team Championship—Eisenhower Trophy

In the fall of 1980, the biennial World Amateur Team Championship was played at Pinehurst No. 2. Team Canada's four-man team was made up of Stu Hamilton, Graham Cooke, Greg Olson, and me. Geordie Hilton was our non-playing captain.

It's a proud moment when you can play for your country. A special bond happens and stays with you forever.

Left to right: Stu Hamilton, Richard Zokol, Graham Cooke, Greg Olson, and non-playing Captain Geordie Hilton—Team Canada at the 1980 World Amateur Team Championship—Eisenhower Trophy.

Pinehurst No. 2 is such a great golf course. What really stood out was Hal Sutton's dominant performance. Hal really separated himself from other amateur players at this time; he was ready to turn professional.

1980 WORLD AMATEUR TEAM CHAMPIONSHIP

Place	Team/Player	Scores
1st	**USA**	**Score: 848**
	Jim Holtgrieve	72-71-72-70
	Jay Sigel	71-71-75-77
	Hal Sutton	68-69-71-68
	Bob Tway	72-71-74-71
2nd	**South Africa**	**Score: 875**
	E. Groenwold	74-75-73-76
	D. Lindsay-Smith	73-71-74-80
	Wayne Player	72-73-77-76
	D. Suddards	79-72-71-70

3rd	**Republic of China**	**Score: 884**
	Dong-Liang Chong	81-74-78-78
	T.C. Chen	69-70-71-72
	Chun-Lung Wu	76-86-79-81
	Ching-Chi Yen	74-77-72-73
4th	**Japan**	**Score: 887**
	Tetsuo Sakata	73-70-76-72
	Tatsuhiko Asakawa	77-77-76-72
	Masayuki Naito	73-72-73-74
	Fuminori Sono	79-77-76-78
T5th	**Canada**	**Score: 890**
	Graham Cooke	74-77-77-78
	Stu Hamilton	76-79-74-75
	Greg Olson	71-70-74-75
	Richard Zokol	71-74-80-76
T5th	**Australia**	**Score: 890**
	A.Y. Gresham	77-77-71-72
	J.A. Kelly	80-80-73-72
	J.L. Senior	79-74-80-77
	P.J. Sweeny	75-74-69-73
T5th	**Great Britain & Ireland**	**Score: 890**
	Gordon Brand	80-74-79-76
	Ian Hutcheon	77-73-79-74
	Peter McEvoy	82-73-79-73
	Ronan Rafferty	72-70-71-73

My Senior Year: 1980–81

After the first semester of our senior year was over, we all started to come to terms with the fact that Bobby Clampett wasn't there to lead us. Clampett decided to turn pro, so we were now on our own, and Coach Tucker kept drilling us to take charge on the golf course. But our depth was strong even without Clampett, and at the beginning of 1981, we were ranked as the number one NCAA golf team in the nation. Our team consisted of John Bodenhamer, Keith Clearwater, Dave DeSantis, Rick Fehr, Neil Finch, Rick Gibson, Robert Meyer, Barry Willardson, Kent Kluba, and me. We never lost the number one ranking throughout the season, and we won the 1981 NCAA Championship at Stanford.

Some golf publications called us Snow White and the Seven Dwarfs. When we won the NCAA they said, "BYU's dwarfs rise to the occasion—a balanced effort earns us the NCAA crown." *Golf World* said, "Brigham Young has had a long line of great individual players but not until this year did it win the NCAA title, and nary a superstar around."[1]

"I've had teams with more talented players, maybe," said BYU Coach Karl Tucker—who had coached the likes of Johnny Miller, Pat McGowan, Mike Reid, Mike Brannan, John Fought, and Jim Nelford, in addition to Clampett—"but I've never, never had a better team." The NCAA victory capped a year of personal trials for Coach Tucker. In addition to losing Clampett, John Bodenhamer was forced to leave school after being diagnosed with Hodgkin's disease. Coach's wife, Joanne, also had a kidney transplant that involved a couple of tense battles with rejection.

One of the most fascinating things about our senior year was that not any one player on our team was a standout, but that all the other teams had a weak fourth, fifth, or sixth player and we did not. Coach Tucker picked the Championship team, Dave DeSantis, Keith Clearwater, Barry Willardson, freshman Rick Fehr, and me, and our strength as a team came to fruition in the second round. The format of the 1981 NCAA Championship was a five-man team with the low four rounds counting each day. In the second round, we threw out our high score of 74 and as a team, we shot 280, 4 under par: I shot 66, Rick Fehr shot 69, Keith Clearwater shot 70, and Dave DeSantis shot 73. That's when we took the lead. We struggled a bit in the third round but stabilized and played well with the lead in the final round.

In the final round and playing in the final group, after hitting my tee shot on the 18th hole, I felt we had the lead but wasn't sure by how much. Coach Tucker came up to me as I walked off the tee and I asked him, "What kind of lead do we have?" Coach said, "We got this unless

1 Jim Moriarty, *Golf World*, June 5, 1981.

you break your leg before you hole out. We've got a 3-shot lead on Oral Roberts." As I got to my tee shot that ended up on the right side of the fairway, the strategy was to not make more than a bogey 5. The pin was in the middle right portion of the 18th green, and I hit a 4-iron making sure I stayed left and away from trouble right of the green. My 4-iron shot found the bunker left of the green, and I was left with a lot of green to work my bunker shot.

This was the final group, and there were a lot of people surrounding the 18th green. Johnny Miller came down from Napa to watch us play, and ESPN was broadcasting the event. The bunker shot was not difficult if you were a good bunker player, and I felt I was. I went into the bunker shot with a smile on my face and executed the bunker shot perfectly. My ball came to rest about 10 feet below the hole—perfect for the situation. My putt for par lipped out, and I tapped my ball in for a bogey, and Coach Tucker and the team ran onto the green in celebration. We—Brigham Young—had finally won the NCAA Championship.

Above:
1981 NCAA Championship ring.

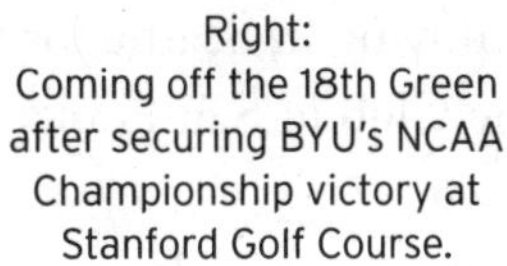

Right:
Coming off the 18th Green after securing BYU's NCAA Championship victory at Stanford Golf Course.

1981 NCAA CHAMPIONSHIP

Place	Team	Score
1st	**Brigham Young**	**1161**
2nd	Oral Roberts	1163
3rd	Houston	1170
4th	Oklahoma State	1171
5th	Arizona State	1172

The 1981 Canadian Amateur Championship

Coach Karl Tucker was like a father to us and BYU was like a second home. Being part of the Brigham Young University team that won BYU's first NCAA Championship was something very special indeed. It was the perfect end to my Cinderella story.

In July, I was off to Kelowna to play in the 1981 Ogopogo Open, which I had won in 1979 and 1980. The event always attracted some of the best amateur players in BC. That week I got paired with and met Gordy Karch from Calgary. My good play continued, and I won the 1981 Ogopogo Open for the third consecutive year. After the tournament was over, I was having a few beers with Gordy Karch and a few others, and Gordy asked me if I was playing in the Canadian Amateur Championship next month at the Calgary Golf & Country Club. I said I was.

Gordy said, "I am a member and I live close to the club and have an extra room. If you want to save a few bucks, you can stay at my place. I even have an extra car you can use."

I said to Gordy, "Thank you, that sounds like a great idea. Your offer is much appreciated."

It was early August, and I made it through qualifying in Seattle for the 1981 US Amateur Championship at the Olympic Club in San Francisco. Then I was off to Calgary for the Canadian Amateur.

Gordy could not have been a better host, and we got to know each other well. I opened up with a 64 to grab the first-round lead. I then expanded my lead in the second round with a 68. In the third round, I got paired with the Canadian legend Gary Cowan, who was known to be a tough customer, having won two US Amateur Championships and eight Canadian Amateur Championships. I recall shanking a shot on the 10th hole and Cowan got a glimmer of hope in his eye, but I salvaged a 71 in the third round and took a four-shot lead into the final round.

Heading into the final round with the lead, I felt completely in control. But as we got through the front 9 my four-shot lead started to diminish. As it happened, Blaine McCallister from Fort Stockton, TX, who was on the University of Houston golf team, was making a big charge. We, BYU, battled it out with Houston and came out victorious at the NCAA at Stanford. Blaine started the day four strokes behind me and proceeded to shoot 64 in his final round. I stood on the 18th tee needing to make par and shoot a final round 68 to get into a sudden-death playoff with McCallister.

I took care of business on the final hole, and very much remember the composure I had to make that 4-foot putt for par on the 18th hole. As good as Blaine played in the final round to close the gap, I went into the

My tee shot on the first hole at the Calgary Golf & CC in the sudden-death playoff against Blaine McCallister for the 1981 Canadian Amateur Championship. With RCGA official Jim Bruce officiating the playoff, Stephen Ross standing behind Jim and Bill Farlinger OC, Past President of the RCGA (1983) and former Chairman of Ernst & Young in Toronto.

sudden-death playoff thinking that this was Canada, it was my home turf, and I was not going to be denied. The first hole at Calgary Golf & CC is a short uphill par 5. Blaine got into a bit of trouble with his tee shot, and it looked like it was going to be difficult for him to make birdie. I played an excellent tee shot, then hit the green in two with a 3-iron. Blaine made par, so all I had to do was 2-putt for a birdie 4 to win—and I did.

Shooting rounds of 64-68-71-68 and winning the 1981 Canadian Amateur avenged my collapse in the final round of the 1980 Canadian Amateur at New Ashburn Golf Club in Halifax, NS. During the final round of the 1980 Canadian Amateur Championship, I held the lead on the back nine and lost to my good friend Greg Olson. On the par 3, the 11th hole, which had a severe slope, I 4-putted and couldn't recover. Greg Olson went on the win.

That evening after winning the '81 Canadian Amateur, I went out to celebrate with Gordy Karch, his buddy Jeff Kohn, and a few others. It was

Holding up the Canadian Amateur Championship's Earl Grey Cup at Calgary Golf & CC.

a marvelous evening, and one that I will never forget. That evening, I asked Gordy if he wanted to caddie for me the following week in the US Amateur at the Olympic Club in San Francisco. He said, "Hell yes," and we took off for San Francisco.

The US Amateur didn't go so well, and I didn't make it through the qualifying for match play. The very next day I declared myself a professional golfer. I didn't tell anyone, but in my own mind I felt very proud of what I accomplished—I was ready to take the next step.

In December 1981, *SCOREGolf Magazine* came out with the inaugural SCORE Awards, which identified Canada's top male and female professional and amateur players. Dan Halldorson was the 1981 Outstanding Canadian Male Professional player, and I was named the 1981 Outstanding Canadian Male Amateur player.

Looking back at the night of the SCORE Awards, I recall coming down the elevator in the Toronto hotel in my rented tuxedo with George Knudson. Knudson knew I had just qualified to get my PGA Tour card a couple weeks prior. Knudson extoled, "Congratulations on getting your Tour card, how do you feel about playing the PGA Tour next year?"

I replied, "Thank you, I am really anxious about playing."

Knudson said, "You never want to be anxious playing this game."

In that moment, I didn't understand what Knudson was implying. Looking back after some 30 years, I did come to understand what George Knudson meant.

CHAPTER 3

1981—Turning Pro—Arranging Sponsorship—PGA Tour Q-School

Securing financial support helps enable young aspiring players to compete without worrying about paying the bills while trying to get your legs stable as a professional player. It is one of the more important off-course obstacles. Without financial security in place, it is difficult to focus entirely on the personal and physical development that is required to succeed in professional golf. Eliminating this burden doesn't guarantee success by any means, but it reduces the obstacles. Being able to handle this challenge makes a significant difference in attrition rate. Another critical and key obstacle, of course, is how the aspiring player begins to develop their mind. You need to develop a resilient *belief system* and learn from your mistakes. The final key element is—you must get traction and perform.

The vast majority of young aspiring players who come out of the NCAA system have the physical skills, or golf swing, to make it at the highest level in professional golf. But what's going to determine whether they make it or not will be the thoughts that run through their minds when they play, in the endless number of difficult situations they will be confronted with, and the thoughts that consume their mind when they are off the golf course as well. The world is littered with thousands upon thousands of impressive swinging young players that have not developed a proper mindset—they get stuck in Golf Insanity and wash out.

After finishing four years at BYU, being part of the victorious NCAA Championship team, and then winning the 1981 Canadian Amateur Championship, I approached my father figure friend from Marine Drive,

Mr. Bentley, and told him I was planning to turn professional by entering the 1981 Fall PGA Tour Qualifying School. He asked me if I had arranged for financial assistance. I told Mr. Bentley I had four members of Shaughnessy Golf Club who had expressed interest in sponsoring me. He responded, "In an effort to help you, if you need money, I will lend you what you need." I thanked him for his generosity and let him know that I wanted to meet with the Shaughnessy group first to see what form their offer would take.

My Sponsor Agreement

My brother, Ron, mentioned he had a patient, a member of Shaughnessy, who was inquiring if I had made a sponsorship arrangement for when I turned pro. This fellow's name was Howard Cadinha. Howard was an executive of Kaiser Resources Ltd. and he invited Ron and me to have dinner at his home. We had a lovely dinner with Howard, his wife, Arlene, and their two daughters.

After dinner, the ladies excused themselves, and Howard started talking about a possible sponsorship agreement. He mentioned he had already approached three other close friends, other Shaughnessy members, about forming a four-person consortium to sponsor me. Howard also asked if there were any Marine Drive Golf Club members who were interested in sponsoring me. I told Howard I had been speaking to Poldi Bentley, but nothing had been agreed to. I instinctively thought to myself that, if there were another interested party, it could put me in a better bargaining position. Howard asked me, "How much money do you need to cover your expenses per year?" I had absolutely no idea, and I should have said, "I don't know." But instead I said, "Around US$50,000."

Howard said, "Let me give it some thought, and I'd like to run it by my friends and inquire if they are truly interested in getting involved in this deal."

I asked Howard who the other possible participants in his group were. He responded, "My good friends, Ed McGeachan, Ed is the president and COO of the Bank of British Columbia (in 1986 HSBC purchased the Bank of British Columbia's 41 branches), my friend Edgar Saba, who owns Saba Brothers Furs, and Alan Hackett, a Vancouver stockbroker. I would like to introduce them to you."

I said, "Yes, that would be nice."

Howard finished with, "This could be a lot of fun and help you at the same time."

In September 1981, I was invited by Howard to have lunch at Shaughnessy to meet with Ed McGeachan, Edgar Saba, and Alan Hackett. I found them all to be very warm and friendly. Over lunch, Howard outlined the basic terms of this proposed agreement. The agreement would be between Howard and me only. Howard's three friends participated financially with Howard, but they would not be part of the formal agreement.

The basic terms of the draft sponsorship agreement:

- A term of three years.
- Cadinha would provide US$50,000 to Zokol at the start of each of the three years, the principal investment.
- In year one, Cadinha would keep 95% of gross revenue that Zokol made as a professional golfer (prize money, golf equipment endorsements, all other endorsement earnings, performance bonuses, etc.). Zokol would retain the remaining 5%.
- In years two and three, Cadinha would keep 90% of gross revenue that Zokol made as a professional player (prize money, golf equipment endorsements, all other endorsement earnings, performance bonuses, etc.). Zokol would retain the remaining 10% for both year two and three.
- Once Zokol had repaid the principal investment back to Cadinha, the gross revenue percentage split would adjust to 75% Cadinha and 25% to Zokol.
- Once Cadinha had received 100% of his initial principle investment back AND then made an additional 100% return on money invested, the percentage split would reset to 90% to Zokol and 10% to Cadinha.

After our lunch, there was one significant condition in this agreement that wasn't discussed prior to or even at the lunch. It hit me like a ton of bricks when I discovered the deal was conditional on me holding a PGA Tour membership. My reaction? "Oh, shit, I didn't talk about that!"

After having my good friend and legal representative Lyall Knott look through the draft agreement, I had a much better sense of the strengths and shortcomings of this agreement. Among other things, it didn't cover my $1,500 entry fees into the PGA Tour Qualifying Tournament nor travel expenses to Sectional Qualifying. It really helped me learn the meaning of the saying *the devil is in the details*.

After reviewing the draft, I went back to Howard and asked him, "What will happen if I am not successful in earning my PGA Tour card?" Howard's abrupt reply, "We'd have no deal. We are only interested in investing in you if you are on the PGA Tour."

My reaction was, "Ouch, that hurt."

I was left feeling a little empty at Howard's cold comment, but I embraced the brutal reality it represented. From an investment perspective, the ROI on a PGA Tour rookie was risky enough. Trying to generate ROI on a young aspiring player who isn't on the PGA Tour carried a significantly greater risk. The more time I spent around Howard getting a sense of his character, the more it became clear to me that the desire to invest in me came from Howard's ego. He wanted to show off his prized PGA Tour player, like a thoroughbred, which was a harbinger of things to come.

The proposed agreement presented me with a dilemma. Should I go back to Poldi Bentley to ask formally for financial help? Bentley was offering a more-than-generous gift simply because he wanted to help me succeed. But I couldn't help but wonder if my long-term interest was better served with the structured business agreement that Howard Cadinha offered.

I contemplated my options and talked at length with my parents about which path to choose. In the end, I decided to go with Howard and his small group. I called Mr. Bentley and thanked him for his generous offer to help me, but I told him, "I think it's best for my independence and development that I work within a more formal business relationship." He responded, "Deek, you know I will help you anyway I can."

I called Howard Cadinha and told him the terms of the agreement were acceptable. We drew up the agreement, and I signed it. My professional golf journey had begun.

Entering The PGA Tour Qualifying Tournament—Q-School

My parents had always been there to help me every step of the way. Whether it was covering costs for university or travel expenses to play in amateur tournaments, they always supported me. I asked them to help me with the cost of entering and traveling to the two PGA Tour Q-School qualifying sites, and of course they said, "Yes."

The PGA Tour office accepted my Q-School entry, and I was assigned to play in Denton, TX, at the Trophy Club for the Regional Qualifying site. I spent a week prior to the qualifier back in Provo, Utah, practicing and preparing. I slept on my buddy Tom Costello's (aka "Cozy") couch before we both flew to Dallas to pick up a rental car and drive north to Denton, TX.

Getting Through Sectional Qualifying

I don't recall much about the qualifier other than making a 50-foot putt on my 16th hole in the final round, followed by two pars on my final two holes, which got me into a sudden-death playoff with seven other players fighting for the last six spots to advance. One person was going to go home unhappy, and I was determined it would not be me. After making a par on the first sudden-death hole, I was one of five who made par on the first hole; two poor fellows made bogey. The five of us earned the right to advance to the finals. The other two poor bastards went to the second hole to fight it out for the last spot. My buddy Cozy didn't make it through. He flew back to Salt Lake City, and I flew back to Vancouver.

The 1981 Fall PGA Tour Q-School Finals

The 1981 PGA Tour Q-School finals consisted of four rounds at Waterwood National, a par 71 Pete Dye beast in Huntsville, Texas. The course opened in 1974 and had a notorious reputation as a real ballbuster of a track as soon as it opened. This would soon become Pete Dye's new design characteristics—a sadistic 180-degree turn from what he and Jack Nicklaus designed at Harbour Town in 1969. And if the golf course wasn't difficult enough, the entire property was crawling with water moccasins, these fucking snakes scared the shit out of me. There is nothing creepier than seeing those things swimming in the water. Even worse, they could get aggressive and they were in the trees, in the bushes, and in the long pampas grass. All players walked carefully. There were crazy stories being told about how this Pete Dye course would bite you in different ways. Of course that made it the perfect Q-School venue from my perspective. If you showed up without a healthy mindset, you would effectively cull yourself before the event even started, from a psychological perspective.

I was part of a starting field of 120 players. The 120 players were whittled down from 513 players that had teed it up across the six regional qualifying sites. After 36 holes, the field was then cut to the low 70 and ties. The top 25 and ties after 72 holes would receive PGA Tour cards.

I flew into Houston, where I picked up a rental car, tuned to a local country radio station, and headed north on Interstate 45 to Huntsville to find a motel. It seemed like every time I got in the car that entire week the radio was playing country singer John Conlee's hit song "Miss Emily's Picture." The lyrics "pour three fingers bourbon in my coffee cup" were ringing through my mind. The next morning, as I made my way to the golf course to register and prepare for the week, that song was running a perpetual loop inside my head. I arrived at Waterwood National to get a lay of the land. After registering, hitting a few balls, and striking a few warm-up putts I was anxious to get on the course to see if the place matched its diabolical reputation.

Golf carts were allowed at Tour School. I picked one up from the cart staging area, headed to the first tee, and pulled up behind a parked cart already there with what appeared to be another contestant and a lady sitting in the passenger seat. You don't often see gals on the course during practice rounds. I got out of the cart, pulled out my driver, and strode toward the first tee. The player in the cart in front of me got out, walked up to the tee at the same time. He said to me, "Would you like to join me?" I responded, "Absolutely." As we got closer, he extended his hand to greet me and said, "My name is Larry, and please meet my wife, Bonnie." I reached out and shook Larry's hand and replied, "My name is Richard, nice to meet you, Larry, and it's my pleasure to meet you too Bonnie." I asked, "Where you two from?" Larry responded, "We're from Augusta, Georgia." And he asked me,

"Where you from, Richard?" I responded, "I am from Vancouver, Canada." From that day forward, Larry and Bonnie Mize became good friends.

My practice rounds revealed a golf course that came as advertised. It was brutally tough. Embedded in my belief system that I learned from Coach Tucker was the tougher the golf course or situation the better it was for me because of the mental perspective we learned under Tucker. I did my best to embrace not only the difficulty of the golf course but also the emotional strain of the PGA Tour Q-School environment itself. After 36 holes the field was cut to 73 players who had shot 150 (+8) or better. I shot 76-74 and made the cut right on the number.

In the third round, I shot 73 and made up ground. But I was still outside the number looking in with 18 holes to play. I played the final round with Rocky Thompson. Rocky was an older and exuberant player who had played the PGA Tour for many years. Both of us found ourselves on the bubble with a few holes to play. Pressure does not get any higher than when you are in a situation where you cannot afford to make a mistake with a few holes to play on a tough golf course and your job is on the line. But, playing defensively in those situations and simply trying to avoid mistakes rarely works out for the player. I was happy to par my last three holes and walk off the 18th green having shot 73 in the final round, finishing at 12-over-par 296. Then the tough part began. Sweating out the next two hours waiting for the rest of the field to finish and see what the cutoff score was going to be. After all the players were finished, the number was finally announced. Those who finished 12-over-par 296, finished T25th. I made it—I earned my PGA Tour card right on the fucking number. I was so glad they were kind enough not to have ties fight it out in playoffs that would have been too cruel.

1981 PGA TOUR FALL QUALIFYING SCHOOL

Spots available: top 25 players plus ties.

All four rounds were played at Waterwood National Country Club, par 71, 6,872 yards. A total of 513 applications were accepted, and six regional trials were held to reduce the starting field to 120. After 36 holes, the field was cut to 73 players who scored 150 (+8) or better.

Place	**Name**	**Score**
T1	Robert Thompson	75-68-69-72–284
T1	Tim Graham	71-69-75-69–284
T3	Jay Cudd	74-73-69-70–286
T3	Perry Arther	80-63-72-71–286
T5	Steve Liebler	74-68-73-72–287
T5	Ronnie Black	71-70-72-74–287
T7	Steve Jones	75-71-73-69–288
T8	Ron Commans	74-70-74-72–290
T8	Rick Pearson	72-75-71-72–290
T8	Al Morton	72-70-71-77–290
T11	Doug Black	77-72-72-79–291
T11	Bill Buttner	74-74-75-68–291
T11	Kenny Knox	73-69-78-70–291
T14	Johnny Elam	75-71-76-70–292
T14	Ray Barr Jr.	71-74-73-74–292
16	Mike Nicolette	74-75-69-75–293
T17	Michael Burke Jr.	78-70-76-70–294
T17	Hal Sutton	76-70-73-75–294
T19	Paul Azinger	74-72-76-73–295
T19	Scott Steger	77-73-70-75–295
T19	Larry Mize	77-71-72-75–295
T19	Scott Watkins	77-72-72-74–295
T19	Blaine McCallister	70-78-74-79–295
T19	Ken Green	74-68-74-79–295
T25	Bob Burton	76-74-71-75–296
T25	Clyde Rego	71-75-76-74–296
T25	Rocky Thompson	72-73-77-74–296
T25	Lance Ten Broeck	77-73-72-74–296
T25	Tommy Armour, III	72-72-77-75–296
T25	**Richard Zokol**	**76-74-73-73–296**
T25	Mike Booker	71-71-78-76–296
T25	Buzz Fly	72-77-77-70–296
T25	Steve Hart	75-69-75-77–296
T25	Skip Dunaway	72-72-75-77–296

Holy Shit—I Have a PGA Tour Card

The PGA Tour Q-School was over. I had earned a PGA Tour card in my first attempt by the skin of my teeth. But I found it surreal to grasp. I started the week without any expectations whatsoever, but at the same time, I was not surprised.

There was this awkwardness with those players who shot 296 or better, who got their PGA Tour cards, and those players who shot 297 or higher and missed. At the same time and in the same spot, you witnessed the happiest people in the world and the most devastated people in the world simultaneously.

PGA Tour officials began handing out packages to each player who qualified. Players who had previously held PGA Tour memberships could head home. The rest of us, the "rookies," had to stick around for two more days to go through PGA Tour orientation, which started at 9:00 AM the next morning.

I couldn't drive back to my motel fast enough (of course, with "Miss Emily's Picture" playing on the radio) to make a collect call to my parents and share the good news with them. They were excited for me. My mind was racing both during and after our call. I had a difficult time sleeping that night as it slowly started to sink in that I was indeed embarking on my chosen path—on the PGA Tour.

PGA Tour orientation the next morning was interesting. Not surprisingly, many of the guys showed up nursing hangovers after celebrating their success the previous evening. There was a lot of kibitzing and horsing around throughout the day. Mostly, there was a shared sense of relief at surviving. Tour officials handed out thick binders that covered everything from what to expect as a PGA Tour member and what your obligations were. It made it clear that it was mandatory to sign your TV and media rights over to the PGA Tour.

Tour officials also delivered presentations covering how to deal with caddies, gambling restrictions and penalties, the rules of golf, the commitment procedures to play in a tournament, and even what the consequences are if you were to cash a bad check. We were also required to sign, or have our financial backers sign, documentation confirming that we had the financial resources to cover the cost of playing the PGA Tour for the entire season. They also brought in veteran Tour players to speak to the group of rookies. Unfortunately, I cannot recall which Tour player spoke to the group.

Then finally came the moment when Tour officials gave out the PGA Tour cards and PGA Tour money clips that you clipped on your belt at Tour events that identified you as a player. This was what we'd all been waiting for. What we'd all worked so hard to achieve. When they called out my name, I walked up to the podium and got presented with my PGA Tour membership card with my name on it. It was a very proud moment. The horsing around had not subsided by this point, so when your name was called, the rest of the players would jeer you as you walked up to accept your membership cards. When it was my turn to head up, the group tried to sing "O Canada" but they didn't know the words past "O Canada," so that didn't last too long. One of the players who made it on the number was a former college player and all-around great guy from Ole Miss named Buzz Fly. When Buzz walked to the podium to accept his card, everyone in the room made a buzzing sound. It sounded like a raging beehive.

With orientation over, I headed south back to Houston. I drove past the Huntsville State Penitentiary, wondering if there were any scheduled executions on death row that day. For whatever reason, I recalled learning that the Huntsville State Prison had the most active execution chamber in Texas. "Miss Emily's Picture" came on the radio again. I couldn't get home to Vancouver fast enough.

One week later, I received my very first PGA Tour check as a professional golfer. It was for $33 for my T25th finish at the PGA Tour Q-School. I never cashed it. I framed it, and it hangs on my home office wall to this day.

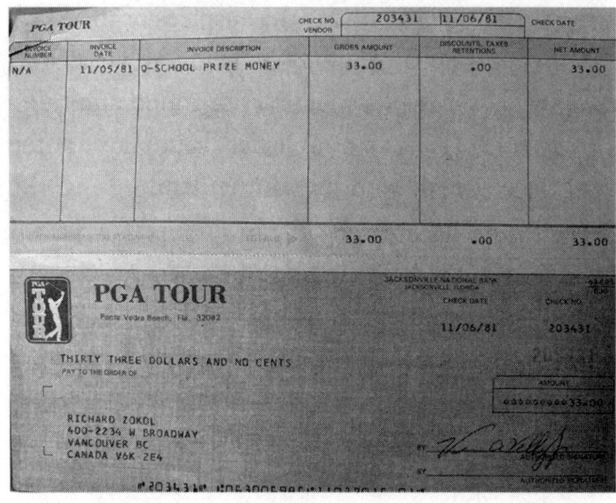

PGA TOUR

CHECK NO. 203431 11/06/81 CHECK DATE

INVOICE NUMBER	INVOICE DATE	INVOICE DESCRIPTION	GROSS AMOUNT	DISCOUNTS, TAXES RETENTIONS	NET AMOUNT
N/A	11/05/81	Q-SCHOOL PRIZE MONEY	33.00	.00	33.00
			33.00	.00	33.00

PGA TOUR
Ponte Vedra Beach, Fla. 32082

JACKSONVILLE NATIONAL BANK
JACKSONVILLE, FLORIDA

CHECK DATE 11/06/81
CHECK NO. 203431

THIRTY THREE DOLLARS AND NO CENTS

PAY TO THE ORDER OF

AMOUNT ********33.00

RICHARD ZOKOL
400-2234 W BROADWAY
VANCOUVER BC
CANADA V6K 2E4

AUTHORIZED SIGNATURE

First money earned on the PGA Tour as a professional player.

My First Tournament as a Professional

As soon as I got back to Vancouver, I gave Coach Tucker a call to let him know I had earned my PGA Tour card. He was delighted to hear the great news. The feeling of pride following a long line of BYU alumni players on the PGA Tour and coming in right after Bobby Clampett made it on the PGA Tour the year before was a proud moment.

Because of my newfound status as a PGA Tour member, Coach asked me, "Do you want to play next week in the Southern California Open in Anaheim, CA? I may be able to pull a few strings and get you in." I said, "I'd love to play, Coach." He replied, "Let me make some calls and see what I can do." Coach Tucker got back to me the next day and said, "Heber, (the term *heber* is a slang name for a country boy from Heber, Utah, that Coach Tucker used for all his players on the golf team) I got you in the tournament. They will give you an exemption into the event because you have a PGA Tour card." I was delighted and thanked Coach Tucker. Our bond was always so strong. I will never forget what he meant to me and will be forever grateful for what he did for us at BYU. Sadly, Coach Tucker passed away in January 2010. Karl Tucker was truly celebrated by Brigham Young University, the whole BYU Athletic community, Utah senator Orrin Hatch, and a long list of former BYU Golf Team players. Glen Tuckett, BYU's former athletic director, spoke eloquently about his close friend Karl Tucker at Coach's Celebration of Life. I felt so proud to be part of the BYU family, even as a non-Mormon.

The Southern California Open was run under the auspices of the PGA of Southern California. It always drew a tremendous field. About a third of the players were PGA Tour players. I played a practice round and hung out with Jim Nelford that week. Ed Fiori, an established Tour player at the time (and years later, a very close friend) won the tournament.

Slammin' Sam Snead

A memorable aspect of this event was that it was Sam Snead's last tournament before moving over to the newly formed Senior PGA Tour. Because the Southern California Open was not a PGA Tour event, there was no restriction on players asking for or receiving an honorarium (aka "appearance money") to play. The speculation in the locker room was that Sam was the only player receiving any money—rumored to be $10,000 cash plus a "woman of ill repute" sharing an adjoining hotel room with a connecting door. Snead wasn't shy and often spoke openly in PGA Tour locker rooms about his off-course promiscuity. In fact, he spoke of it as though it were a badge of honor.

In Sam's later years, Snead was in the 18th tower with Roger Maltbie and Dan Hicks in an NBC Telecast. Maltbie told the story in a *Golf Digest* article: "We decided to do an interview with Sam. He was what, 87 or something? We were advised that Sam had good days and bad days, so we decided to do the interview on tape. The last thing you want to do is embarrass anybody. Then in a moment, he snapped in, and he was lucid. So then Dan asked him what the secret was to his longevity. Sam said, 'Well, I never drank too much. Always took pretty good care of myself. Got to bed early, got lots of sleep.' Then with an old Sam Snead grin, looked directly at Hicks and said, 'Course, I did shake those bedsprings every now and then.'"[2]

I made the 36-hole cut in the tournament and got paired in the final round with Frank Beard. Frank Beard was the PGA Tour's leading money winner in 1969 and later went on to a successful broadcasting career. Meeting and playing with him was a tremendous treat for me. Frank was one of those legendary Tour players recognized as a great ball-striker. I felt fortunate to so quickly be able to step into my newly elevated status as a professional golfer and start to learn in my new environment. I made my second check as a professional at that 1981 Southern California Open. I finished in the back end of the field and won approximately $700. I went out and purchased a tweed blazer—if I was going to be a professional golfer, I needed to look and act the part.

By the end of 1981, I had made a tremendous ascent. We won the NCAA Championship, I won the Ogopogo Invitational in Kelowna, BC, for the third year in a row, won the Canadian Amateur Championship at Calgary Golf & CC, and then to top it off, I got my PGA Tour card.

It was a great year indeed.

---

2 Craig Bestrom, "Life of the Party," *Golf Digest*, June 4, 2008.

CHAPTER 4

1982—My Rookie Year—Last Year of PGA Tour Monday Q— "Disco Dick" Leads GMO—First Professional Win— Back to Q-School

Interview by Richard Saxton for Vancouver's CKVU-TV's Sports Page in 1982.

My Diary Being a "Monday Morning Rabbit" in My First Year on the PGA Tour

The 1982 PGA Tour was in its 67th season. And it was of course my first as a member. The schedule consisted of 44 events with purses up for grabs totaling just over $14 million. (In 2025, players on the PGA Tour will play for over $400 million in prize money in the regular season and three playoff events. The PGA Tour's top line gross revenue reported in 2022 was over $1.9 billion.) The Tour started in January in Arizona, then made stops in California and Hawaii before moving to Florida in February and March. And from there it meandered across the US with international stops at the Canadian and British Opens before ending the season in late October back in Florida at Disney World.

As a non-exempt PGA Tour member, my schedule would be determined by how well I played in the Monday Qualifiers and, once in an event, how many cuts I could make to avoid falling back to Monday Qualifying. As 1982 started, I was wide-eyed and excited; I was living the dream. I knew I had a lot to learn. I would soon learn that my PGA Tour career would get off to a rough start, which became a mental and emotional barrier. I struggled in the early qualifiers and was not getting into tournaments. I quickly grew to hate Mondays and began to find it difficult to sleep on Sunday nights. Here is that story of my first year on the Tour, and some anecdotes, drawn from my 1982 Tour diary and my journal entries for each event.

Monday Q—Joe Garagiola-Tucson Open—January 7-10, 1982
Purse: $300,000

Randolph Park North Course, Tucson, AZ. Monday Qualifying at Randolph Park GC on January 4th. Us non-exempt PGA Tour members (Monday Rabbits) were playing for 22 spots. I shot 76 and missed qualifying by six shots.

Monday Q—Bob Hope Desert Classic—January 14-17, 1982
Purse: $304,000

Indian Wells (Host Club), Bermuda Dunes, El Dorado, and La Quinta CC. The Bob Hope Desert Classic was an invitational event. There was no Monday Qualifying. All non-exempt players had a forced week off.

Monday Q–The Phoenix Open–January 22-25, 1982
Purse: $300,000

Phoenix Country Club, Phoenix, AZ. Monday Qualifying was at Phoenix CC on January 18th. We were playing 20 spots, I shot 72 and missed qualifying by two shots.

Monday Q–Wicks-Andy Williams San Diego Open–January 28-31, 1982
Purse: $300,000

Torrey Pines Golf Course, La Jolla, CA. Monday Qualifying at Torrey Pines (North Course) on January 25th. We were playing for 28 spots. I shot 70, got into a playoff and ended up as fifth alternate. Unfortunately, I did not get into the tournament.

Monday Q–Bing Crosby National Pro-Am–February 4-7, 1982
Purse: $300,000

Pebble Beach GL, Cypress Point Golf Club, and Spyglass Hill. Monday Qualifying was on February 1st at Spyglass Hill. Twenty-five spots were up for grabs. I shot 77 and missed qualifying by four shots.

My First Lesson as a PGA Tour Pro

After the first five events into the 1982 Tour schedule, I didn't yet have a tournament start. I was frustrated and needed answers. I had not had a formal golf lesson since I was 18 years old. At BYU, Coach Tucker knew just enough about golf swing fundamentals, but he was not a golf swing instructor. Was it now time to see someone to help me with my swing? Just a few miles from Pebble Beach was Quail Lodge in Carmel, CA, where Bobby Clampett's longtime instructor and "swing guru" Ben Doyle taught. At BYU, Clampett had spoken openly about Doyle and his teaching methods. Since I had yet another week off, I decided to give Doyle a call. We made arrangements to meet to see if he could help me with my game.

In 1982, Ben Doyle was widely considered to be one of the top golf instructors in the country. Ben was famous for being the first certified instructor of Homer Kelly's landmark instruction book *The Golfing Machine.* Doyle taught Clampett by applying the principles from Kelly's book to his work. And Clampett was taking the PGA Tour by storm and being looked at then as the next Jack Nicklaus. Like many others, I was interested in what Doyle had to offer. My hope was that it would be an immediate ticket to getting my game righted.

Homer Kelly's book *The Golfing Machine* was self-published in 1969 and was gaining recognition because of Clampett's play. Kelly had been a brilliant engineer working for Boeing Aircraft Company during WWII. In authoring *The Golfing Machine*, he used his technical acumen to break down the golf swing into its essential technical and geometric fundamentals using principles of motion, physics, and engineering. Kelly argued the golf swing had 24 separate components, 4 power accumulators, and that there were multiple variations for each component. Based on all the possible variations, he calculated there were 450 quadrillion possible swings—all I needed was one of them that I could quickly apply to my 1982 PGA Tour season.

On our appointed day, I arrived at the practice range at Quail Lodge in Carmel, CA, and set up on the practice line, ready to meet Ben Doyle. Doyle arrived in a golf cart filled with mops, clubs, shovels, and all kinds of contraptions. His golf cart looked like a garage sale on wheels. Ben himself was a wonderful person with a soft-spoken, gentle manner. He was also very serious about the principles and theories of *The Golfing Machine.* I began to hit some balls under his watchful eye. When Doyle began speaking, I immediately struggled to understand the concepts and what he was saying. It was like listening to someone speaking a foreign language. It got worse as the session went on. I didn't comprehend half of what I was being told. When the lesson was over, I could not have been more confused. I thought to myself, *How in the hell can I play golf for a living with these mechanical thoughts running through my mind?* Even if I had been able to understand what Doyle had been saying, I concluded that if this is what and how golf instructors teach, I didn't want any part of it.

My introduction to *The Golfing Machine* was over. There would not be a second session. At the conclusion of my golf lesson, for the time being at least, my interest in working with a swing instructor became a scary proposition. My intuition told me to avoid instructors who teach the "golf swing" who had never actually played in the trenches on the front line of battle at all costs.

Hawaiian Open—February 11–14, 1982

Purse: $325,000

Waialae Country Club, Honolulu, HI

Place: 68th

Score: 74-71-75-73

Made: $662.00

Monday Qualifying was played on Sunday, February 7, at Old Del Monte Golf GC in Monterey, CA. We were playing 38 spots. I shot 72, got into a playoff, and earned the third alternate spot.

Being the third alternate meant I suddenly had a dilemma. Should I incur the cost of flying to Honolulu to be ready if I got into my first PGA Tour event while running the risk of not getting into the tournament at all? Or should I save the money, remain in California, and get ready for next week's Monday Q for the LA Open at Riviera? I agonized over what to do. I finally called my sponsor, Howard Cadinha, to ask his advice. Howard was direct, "Get on a flight to Honolulu and prepare to play." That's all I needed to hear. I booked my flight for Monday morning and got ready to hope for the best once there.

My good friend and former BYU teammate Stan Souza had grown up in Honolulu, so to keep my expenses to a minimum, I arranged to stay with his uncle Howard Guerrero and aunt Grayse. When I arrived on Monday, they made me feel at home immediately.

Early Tuesday morning, I made my way out to Waialae Country Club to get an update on the field and to get in a practice round. I introduced myself to the lovely ladies at the tournament's registration desk as the third alternate. The lady replied, "It looks like it is your lucky day, as we've had two WDs, so you are now the first alternate." She continued, "Check with us at the end of the day for further updates."

That was indeed good news, and my hopes were high as I started to prepare mentally to play in my first PGA Tour event as a member.

I finished my practice round and was eager to get back to the registration desk and get an update. I asked the most important question, "How many players have not yet registered?" to the same lady. She responded, "Everyone has registered but three players. We've heard from two of them who had to change their flights into Honolulu and who are now arriving on Wednesday. The only player we have not heard from is Grier Jones." Jones was an established Tour player whose three PGA Tour titles included the 1972 Hawaiian Open.

My chance to get into the tournament had narrowed down to what Grier Jones was going to do. It was usual for players who hadn't registered by Wednesday to at least inform tournament officials about their expected arrival. I connected with PGA Tour rules official Glenn Tait (Tait was a no-nonsense retired US Marine Corps Major) to let him know that come Thursday, I'd be hanging around the range or putting green in case there were any last-minute WDs. Glenn responded, "Has everyone registered?" I replied, "All are registered except for Grier Jones." Glenn turned his head toward me and smiled and said, "Well, that could mean you're in luck." I asked, "Why's that?" Glenn shared, "Because Grier Jones is known as the first alternate's best friend. He lives in Florida, and we are a long way from Florida. Chances are that he's not coming." My spirits were buoyed.

I took note of Jones's Thursday tee time. He was paired with Andy North and Mark Hayes in the afternoon wave. Thursday morning arrived, and there was still no word from Jones. So I prepared and stood ready to play in his spot. Glenn Tait eventually drove up to the putting green where I was eagerly waiting and said, "Richard, you've got Grier's spot. He just called from Florida to WD." I was excited. I was in the Hawaiian Open, my first tournament as a member of the PGA Tour! I shot 74-71 to make my first PGA Tour cut and followed up with 75-73 on Saturday and Sunday to earn my first PGA Tour official check—$662.00! More importantly, however, because I made the cut in Hawaii, I was exempt into the following week's Los Angeles Open at Riviera. I was making progress!

The Canadian contingent at the 1982 Hawaiian Open. My first PGA Tour event played as a PGA Tour member. From left to right: Zokol, Dave Barr, Dan Halldorson, and Jim Nelford.

Glen Campbell Los Angeles Open—February 18-21, 1982

Purse: $300,000

Riviera Country Club, Los Angeles, CA. I was exempt from Monday Qualifying after having made the cut at the Hawaiian Open. I shot 74-76 and missed the cut.

Monday Q—Doral-Eastern Open—February 25-28, 1982

Purse: $300,000

Doral Resort & Country Club, Miami, FL

PGA Tour Monday Qualifying on February 22nd on Doral's Blue Monster, we were playing for 38 spots. I shot 78 and missed qualifying by two shots.

After missing the cut in Los Angeles, I headed to Miami, Florida, to prepare for the first Monday Qualifying of the PGA Tour's Florida Swing. Being a West Coast guy, it was the first time that I had ever been to Florida, and things were very different there. It was crazy humid and dead flat. But the biggest challenge was trying to figure out how to deal with the different types of grasses on Florida golf courses.

Doral was my first Florida Monday Qualifying event. It was also my first experience on Florida's grainy Bermuda grass, which was a major hurdle to figure out. I could not yet read or understand the significance that Bermuda grass grain had on a rolling golf ball. Bermuda grass thrives in the hot, humid weather of the southern US, whereas golfers in the west and particularly in the Pacific Northwest learn to play on Bent or *Poa annua* grass, which is devoid of grain.

I went into Doral's Monday Qualifying knowing 38 spots were up for grabs—Monday Qualifying doesn't get any easier than this—and I blew it. Figuring out how to read the grain in Bermuda greens was going to take more time than I had imagined. I also needed to figure out how the ball flew coming out of Bermuda rough. On top of all that, the wind in Florida seemed to blow at least 20 mph every bloody day.

My poor performance had been in full flight for a couple of months at this point; I was not settling in very well. I was getting discouraged. To make matters worse, when you missed Monday Qualifying, PGA Tour rules officials discouraged you from taking up the limited space available on the practice facilities. But I didn't feel comfortable practicing on site if I wasn't in the field. My problem was compounding. Increasingly depressed and discouraged, I neglected my practice and simply stayed in my motel room. I was starting to second-guess myself, wondering if I really belonged on the PGA Tour.

The next day, I put the past behind me and headed north up the Florida Turnpike to Orlando to prepare for Monday Qualifying for the Bay Hill Classic.

Monday Q–Bay Hill Classic–March 4-7, 1982
Purse: $300,000
Bay Hill Club & Lodge, Orlando, FL

Monday Qualifying for Bay Hill was on March 1st at Grenelefe Golf Course. Bay Hill was hosted by Arnold Palmer and was considered an invitation with a limited 120-man field. Upon arriving at Grenelefe that Monday, we heard 120 exempt players committed to play Bay Hill, which technically meant there were no spots available for us Monday Morning Rabbits to play for.

Deane Beman, the commissioner of the PGA Tour stepped in with an executive order and added six spots to the field for the 1982 Bay Hill Classic. Our large contingent of Monday Morning Rabbits played for those six spots. I was now into my fourth month as a PGA Tour rookie, and I'd only played in two PGA Tour events, having made only one cut. I was doing my best to keep my head straight and prepare for Monday, but my anxious mind made it difficult to sleep Sunday night. Then I went out and shot 79, missing qualifying for the Bay Hill Classic by 11 shots. I felt alone, and The Wall was getting bigger. With each passing week, I felt I was losing more ground, going backward.

My Encounter with the Notorious Jim King

After missing Monday Qualifying at Bay Hill I spent another lonely week in a shitty motel. The following Saturday I headed south from Orlando to Lauderhill to get in a practice round on Sunday for Monday Qualifying for the Honda Inverrary Classic. Sunday afternoon, I pulled into Inverrary CC and checked in with the pro shop and was given a green light to tee off on the back nine. My caddie and I headed to the 10th tee.

As I was finishing up putting on the 10th green, my caddie noticed a single player coming up behind us on the fairway and said, "Oh shit, that's Jim King coming up behind us." I asked, "Who's Jim King?" My caddie said, "You don't want to have anything to do with this guy." I hadn't yet heard of the notorious Jim King, who was quite the character in Florida's golf folklore. Word throughout the Florida PGA and the mini Tour circuit described King as a South Florida "collector," slang for a debt collector in the gangster world (also known as a *leg-breaker*).

Most Tour players feared Jim King. He had a series of run-ins with PGA Tour rules officials and fellow Tour players over the years. One story was that King stuffed PGA Tour player John Lister, from New Zealand, into a locker for some reason. Another tale included an altercation at a Tour event on the 16th hole at Pleasant Valley in the second round of the 1973 USI Classic in Worcester, MA. King allegedly grabbed PGA Tour rules official Pete Sesso "by the throat in a threatening manner," according to a report in the *New York Times*. King allegedly grabbed Sesso by the throat and picked him off the ground after Sesso penalized King for slow play. King denied there was an altercation, but he was suspended from the tournament nonetheless.[3]

King could be a mean son of a bitch, and he liked to push his weight around. In his early days, he had been a competitive boxer, played linebacker on the Western Illinois college football team, had been a paratrooper in the 82nd Airborne, and fought in the Korean War. He eventually had a solid golf career playing in a combined 255 events on the PGA Tour and PGA Tour Champions, ultimately notching 12 top 10 finishes over his career.

One of King's good friends, a former Tour player, Jeff Lewis, described him in a *Golfweek* profile as "one of the toughest, baddest men on this planet." On the other hand, Lewis continued, "He was also the most courageous, intense, fearless, regimented individual I ever met in my life. He always had to have a plan. From the time he woke up in the morning until he went to bed, he had a plan."

Seeing Jim King coming up behind me, I quickened my pace, walking off the 10th green to the 11th tee. I didn't want to have anything to do with him. The 12th hole at Inverrary was a short par 5, reachable in two, the last 100 yards of the hole doglegged left around a large hill. There was a pond to the right of the green. Both the pond and the green were blind to the 12th hole's second shot. As I was putting on the 12th green, I heard a ball splash into the pond, followed in quick succession by a second splash. I was playing fast, but it appeared King was playing faster.

As I walked briskly off the 12th green, I heard King's gruff voice from a distance bark, "Hey, kid." I pretended not to hear him, keeping my head down and increasing my pace. In a much louder voice, King shouted again, "Hey, kid." I stopped and looked back. King beckoned me with a hand gesture, "Hey, kid, come here." Nervously, I walked back onto the 12th green just as King was walking onto the front. King had this hard, grizzled look about him. He was big and intimidating. In contrast, I weighed in at a scrawny 130 pounds. As we approached each other he said to me, "Where are my balls?" I replied, "They are in the pond." King looked me squarely in the eye and said, "You threw my balls in the pond?" I couldn't believe what was happening! I immediately went into fight, flight, or freeze response.

---

3 Tod Leonard, "Golf tough guy Jim King dies," *Golf Digest*, August 14, 2021.

I said to him, "No, you hit them in the pond. I heard them splash while I was putting." This tough guy was threatening me, and I had no idea whether he was going to drop me in my tracks. King, looking square in the eyes, said, "Give me my balls!" And I mustered up the courage to say, "I don't have your fucking golf balls—you hit them in the pond." To my surprise, he backed off and with a smirk on his face said, "You're okay, kid, forget about it." It was as if he just wanted to see how I'd react to his intimidation.

I was absolutely shaken after my first Jim King encounter. He knew I didn't have his golf balls. He just wanted the pleasure of seeing a rookie squirm under pressure, as if to see if I'd stand up for myself in a confrontation. And I guess in his eyes, I did. Whenever I encountered King in the years that followed, he was very friendly every time our paths crossed. Perhaps I had indeed passed some kind of perverse test, or maybe it was his way of establishing his physical dominance. Most players on Tour absolutely feared King. But there was one player on Tour that wasn't intimidated by Jim King, and that was Lee Buck Trevino.

Lee Trevino & Jim King

I had the wonderful opportunity of being paired with Lee Trevino in a couple of Canadian Opens in the late 1980s. Trevino was my idol. I absolutely loved how he played against Jack Nicklaus in the '70s. Trevino is one smart dude.

When I got the opportunity to play with Trevino on the PGA Tour, it was a real treat. During one of those rounds we played at Glen Abbey at the Canadian Open, the subject of Jim King came up. I told Trevino about my encounter with King. Trevino then told me about some of his encounters.

More recently, I reached out to Trevino to get my story straight, and he told me, "In 1967, I finished 45th on the PGA Tour Money List, which qualified me as an exempt PGA Tour player for the 1968 PGA Tour season. Back in those days, it was legal to travel with a handgun and I traveled with my .38 revolver. I always kept it close, had it with me at all times. It was in my golf bag on the golf course and when I got into my hotel room I kept it on my nightstand beside the telephone next to the bed." Trevino went on,

"In 1968 when I got to Doral in Miami, I get this knock at my hotel room door. I open the door and it's Jim King. I am looking up at this big son of a bitch and he's got this big block head, and he said to me, 'I hear you're a pretty good player!' Sensing no threat at all I said, 'Come on in.' And King takes a seat on the edge of the bed, and we start talking. King is looking around and notices my .38 on the nightstand. King said to me, pointing at my pistol, 'Is that yours?' I said, 'Yes, it's mine.' King then asks me, 'What do you need it for?' I said, 'If I get in a jam with a guy your size, I stand a better chance with it.'" Trevino then told me, "I got along great with Jim King. He became my bodyguard."

Lee Trevino, Frank Conners, and Zokol at the Canadian Open.
Getty Images: Ken Faught

Cesar Sanudo & Jim King

Another story Trevino shared with me about Jim King involved Trevino's good pal Cesar Sanudo. Trevino shared, "Sanudo and King were paired together in a Monday Qualifying, it may have been at Pleasant Valley.

On one particular hole King's tee shot looked to be out of bounds by a foot or so." In those close situations, to determine whether the ball is in bounds or not, you draw a straight line between the two OB stakes on either side of the ball. "At first glance Sanudo said to King that the ball appeared to be out of bounds. King then got behind one of the OB stakes, got down on his knees to get a better look, and he said, 'Sanudo, come down here and take a look from this angle, from this side it looks like the ball is maybe touching the line.'" If King's ball was touching the line, the ball would be considered in bounds, and he could play it. If King's ball was out of bounds, he'd incur a two-shot penalty. Trevino went on, "So Sanudo comes over and gets down on one knee right beside King for a better look. The ball is clearly out of bounds, but before Sanudo could give his opinion King hits Sanudo with a hard elbow into his ribs. Sanudo goes rolling over sideways on the ground in severe pain. After Sanudo got his breath back he looks up at King and said, 'I think the ball is touching the line too.'"

After my run-in with Jim King, I was trying to get my head around the next day's Monday Qualifying. Once again, I couldn't sleep Sunday night.

Monday Q—Honda Inverrary Classic—March 11-14, 1982

Purse: $400,000

Inverrary Country Club, Lauderhill, FL

Monday Qualifying at Inverrary CC on March 8th playing for 17 spots, I shot 75 in the Monday Qualifying and missed qualifying by three shots.

Yet another missed Monday Qualifying. It meant another week alone in a shitty motel. I'm in a world of hurt. Mentally, I was in a bad place, a place where I could get lost in thought and easily spiral down the wrong mental path, alone with unrestrained thoughts that I may not be cut out for this life. Our minds can cultivate a disadvantageous mindset. In my first four months on the PGA Tour, Monday Qualifying meant pain, anxiety, and having a difficult time sleeping Sunday nights. It was a barrier that I needed to overcome. The mindset is the place where all aspiring professional players need to break through, or they get culled out. It wasn't looking good for me.

The Tournament Players Championship—March 18-21, 1982

Purse: $500,000

TPC Sawgrass, Ponte Vedra, FL

Not eligible to play. No Monday Qualifying.

Sea Pines Heritage Classic—March 21-28, 1982

Purse: $300,000

Harbor Town Golf Links, Hilton Head Island, SC

Not eligible to play. No Monday Qualifying as the tournament was an invitational event.

Monday Q—Greater Greensboro Open—April 2-5, 1982

Purse: $300,000

Forest Oaks Country Club, Greensboro, NC

Monday Qualifying March 29th we were playing for 20 spots. I shot 76 and missed qualifying by two shots.

At this point, I had two weeks off because I was ineligible to play in the Players Championship and the Sea Pines Heritage Classic, so I flew back to Vancouver for a much-needed break from the road and to be with family and friends. Then I headed back to the East Coast for the Monday Qualifier for the Greater Greensboro Open, but my poor play continued.

My buddy Jim Nelford had his van out on Tour and had planned to take a couple of weeks off after the GGO and head back to Utah for some R&R of his own. Jim asked me if I would take his van for a couple of weeks and meet him in Tallahassee, FL, when he returned to the Tour. My plans were to play the Magnolia Classic in Hattiesburg, MS, a satellite event opposite the Masters. The plan was perfect for me. Off I set in Jim's van, headed for Mississippi.

During the drive, I noticed a book in the back of Nelford's van titled *Your Erroneous Zones* by Dr. Wayne W. Dyer. I started to browse through it. Dyer spoke about the barriers that hold people back from success. It was the first self-help book I had ever read, and it made a lot of sense to me.

It opened my eyes to the value of exploring self-help books to search for insights and inspiration.

Magnolia Classic—April 8-11, 1982

Purse: $75,000

Hattiesburg Country Club, Hattiesburg, MS

No Monday Qualifying. All PGA Tour members gained access to the Magnolia Classic. Even though the tournament was a PGA Tour event, it did not count as an official win, with the privileges that winning brought, but money earned did count for the PGA Tour Official Money List. I shot 71-69-70-74, tied for 42nd, and won $345. It was my second cut made in the season.

Monday Q—Tallahassee Open—April 15-18, 1982

Purse: $100,000

Killearn Golf & Country Club, Tallahassee, FL

I was exempt having made the cut at the previous Tour event (Magnolia Classic). I shot 71-71 and missed the cut by one shot. I had the pleasure of playing with Burt Yancey who was a great Tour player, who won seven PGA Tour events before being diagnosed and institutionalized for bipolar disorder. I recall walking into the scoring tent with Burt after the second round. Burt wasn't happy with the way he played and said out loud to himself, "Goddammit Burt, your focus is so bad out there that your can hear birds farting on the golf course."

Monday Q—USF&G Classic—April 22-25, 1982

Purse: $400,000 (reduced to $300,000 since only 54 holes played)

Lakewood Country Club, New Orleans, LA

Monday Qualifying, March 19th at Lakewood CC, we were playing for 25 spots. I shot 69 and qualified, but then shot 77-72 and missed the cut by two shots.

Monday Q—Byron Nelson Golf Classic—April 29-May 2, 1982

Purse: $350,000

Preston Trails Golf Club, Dallas, TX

Monday Qualifying was April 26th at Preston Trails. We were playing for 32 spots. I shot 69 and qualified, but then shot 74-73 and again missed the cut by two shots.

Monday Q—Michelob-Houston Open—May 6-9, 1982

Purse: $350,000

Woodlands Country Club, Woodlands, TX

Monday Qualifying was on May 3rd at Woodlands. We were playing for 30 spots. I shot 72 and missed qualifying by one shot.

Most players that week stayed at the Woodlands Inn. Nelford and I were rooming together and during the evening hung out a bit in the resort's recreation area, which had a few pool tables.

Jim Nelford and I started to room together more often, and this helped stop my mind from spiraling from being alone with depressed thoughts. Nelford put me under his wing. We were in the trenches together and had someone to go out to dinner with, practice with, discuss life with, and hit a few bars when the time was right.

Monday Q—Georgia-Pacific Atlanta Classic—May 20-23, 1982

Purse: $300,000

Atlanta Country Club, Marietta, GA

Monday Qualifying was on May 17th at Atlanta CC. We were playing for 30 spots. I shot 71 and qualified. I played my best golf of the year to date, shooting 73-69-72-70 to tie for 32nd for my best finish as Tour member. I won $1,736.

Monday Q—Kemper Open—June 3-6, 1982

Purse: $400,000

Congressional Country Club, Bethesda, MD

Having made the cut in the previous event (Georgia-Pacific Atlanta Classic) I was exempt from qualifying. Unfortunately, I had a horrible first round, shot 79, and followed that with a 74 to miss the cut by four shots.

Monday Q–Danny Thomas Memphis Classic–June 10-13, 1982

Purse: $400,000

Colonial Country Club, Cordova, TN

Monday Qualifying on June 7th at Colonial CC. We were playing for 25 spots. I shot 71 and qualified. Unfortunately, I shot 78-74 and missed the cut by four shots.

Monday Q–Manufacturers Hanover Westchester Classic–June 24-27, 1982

Purse: $400,000

Westchester Country Club, Harrison, NY

Monday Qualifying was on June 21st at Westchester CC. We played for 20 spots. I shot 75 and missed qualifying by three shots.

Quebec Open (Canadian Tour Event)–June 25-27, 1982

Victoriaville Golf Club, Victoriaville, QC

After I missed the Monday Qualifying for the Westchester, Nelford called the tournament director for the Quebec Open to see if they had room to extend a sponsor exemption for me. They did, and I flew to Montreal, then drove to Victoriaville, Quebec. I played well the first two rounds but faded the last round (the tournament was only 54 holes) to shoot 70-70-75 and won $1,300 (Canadian dollars).

That was a bizarre week to say the least. The whole week was one big party. I still have this vivid memory of me, Nelford, and Dale Tallon, who had just retired as an NHL player, heading back to Gilles Marotte's home for an after-party. Marotte was also known as "Captain Crunch" for his days in the NHL playing for the Bruins, Blackhawks, LA Kings, Rangers, and St Louis. Tallon and Marotte were buddies, and the term *mon chum* (my friend) was being thrown around the more we drank that night. Back in the day, Dale Tallon had played the Canadian Tour in the summer. He was a great player and won the 1969 Canadian Junior Championship at the Kelowna Golf & CC. Then he became the second overall pick in the 1970 NHL Draft by the Vancouver Canucks and played 642 games with the Canucks, the Blackhawks, and the Penguins.

Trying to Figure Out My Problem

During this stretch, six months into the PGA Tour, I was really fighting hard to get out of the mental funk. I felt I was playing well enough, but my scores did not reflect my play. I was putting too much pressure on myself. I knew instinctively that most of my problems stemmed from being anxious. My hyperactive mind was a barrier to my success and a problem I needed to solve. During play, I was anxious over the ball. I wanted the result and the score so bad, which only added to the stress I was putting on myself. My self-talk was, "I *must* do this or I *must* do that—I *must* shoot better scores." I knew at that moment my mind was working against me, and I wondered how I could overcome my own hyperactive mind. My mind, thoughts, and emotions were killing me on the golf course.

Finally, when I asked myself for the umpteenth time the question *how can I overcome my hyperactive mind?* my inner dialogue suddenly provided an answer. It was like another personality said, *When you listen to music on your Sony Walkman, it calms you down. Why don't you listen to music between shots during play to calm you down?*

That seemed to make sense, and I started to give the idea serious thought. Nobody else on Tour did such a thing at the time. Was it even within the rules? The more I thought about it, the more I thought this might be the answer. My intuition loved the idea, and my gut said, *Do it.* I decided to put the idea to the test the following week during Monday Qualifying for the Western Open in Chicago. I said to myself, "Okay, I am going to do this." That is until Sunday night came around and my mind started acting up again. The Sunday night before the Monday Qualifying, I began to consider the consequences of not playing well while wearing a Sony Walkman in PGA Tour competition. What if I shoot 80? Would that mean even more embarrassment? My fears won out. I chickened out and decided that it wasn't a good idea.

Monday Q—Western Open—July 1-4, 1982

Purse: $350,000

Butler National Golf Club, Chicago, IL

Monday Qualifying on June 28th at Butler National, and we were playing for 25 spots. Butler National was an infamously difficult golf course. As I teed off, my inner voice was telling me the typical garbage dialogue—*Bear down, think positively, play well*—all that bullshit. I proceeded to shoot 82 and missed qualifying by six shots. I was really pissed off at myself—not for playing terribly and failing, but for surrendering to my fears and chickening out of using the Sony Walkman. I never had a problem with failing. But I had always had a problem with being weak and afraid. I vowed to use my Sony Walkman next week in the Greater Milwaukee Open.

Monday Q—Greater Milwaukee Open—July 8-11, 1982

Purse: $250,000

Tuckaway Country Club, Franklin, WI

Monday Qualifying was also at Tuckaway CC. We were playing for 61 spots. I shot 73 and qualified. Because there was 61 spots, I figured I'd save the Walkman for the first round of the tournament.

Disco Dick—My First Time Leading a PGA Tour Event

First and foremost, and for the record, I never listened to disco music. I was a classic rock guy. I loved Bob Seger. Bruce Springsteen, not so much. My favorite music came from the great rock bands, like Led Zeppelin, The Eagles, the Rolling Stones, Pink Floyd, Yes, Emerson Lake & Palmer, Santana, and Lynyrd Skynyrd. "Rock'n Richard" would have been a more appropriate handle than "Disco Dick."

Little did I know how much my life was about to change over the next four days.

As Thursday's opening round approached, I realized I still had to deal with my mental demons. The issue once again started to build in my mind. In my hotel room on Wednesday night, I wrestled with this internal dilemma.

I could feel myself starting to talk myself out of doing it once again, posing the same internal questions. *What if I embarrass myself and play horribly? What will other players think of me for doing this? Will spectators laugh at me?* All sorts of fears and insecurities were bubbling inside me, pushing me to talk myself out of the idea, again. My ego, which was clearly being threatened by this, was trying to protect me from this risk. But my gut (my intuition) reassured me that I loved the idea. I truly believed that listening to music between shots would help me. I was still waffling the night before the first round of the 1982 GMO, so I decided to make it a game-time decision at my 7:30 AM tee time the next morning. I stuffed the Sony Walkman into my golf bag and went to bed.

In the first two rounds of the 1982 GMO, I was paired with Ronnie Black and Larry Rinker. There weren't many people around that early Thursday morning tee time as we got ready to go. We started on the back nine. After we all hit our tee shots, our threesome walked down the hill from the 10th tee to the fairway. I let Ronnie and Larry walk ahead of me. When our group got about 100 yards down the fairway and Ronnie and Larry were far enough ahead, I said, "Fuck it," and took my Sony Walkman out of my bag and pulled the headphones over my ears. I stuck in the Eagles cassette and cranked up the volume. *Hotel California* was on and I thought to myself "this could be heaven or this could be hell." I thought, *How ironic is this?* But it instantly felt comfortable. I climbed into my own little world, playing great music, feeling right in my mind.

As we arrived at our tee shots in the fairway, Larry turned and looked at me, and when he realized what I had on my head, he chuckled and turned to Ronnie Black, pointing at me and said, "Look at Disco Dick." Ironically, I would later learn from a mutual friend, Greg Olson, that while at the University of Florida, Larry had been a competitive disco dancer and had been nicknamed "Shoes" by his teammates on the Gator Golf Team. "Disco Larry" had been born on the dance floor long before "Disco Dick" appeared on the golf course.

The feelings of ease and being at peace were instant once the music started in my headphones. As the round began, I started playing well. There was calmness in my mind, a harmony with my surroundings and situation. I had never felt so agile in competition. It was such an unusual feeling of freedom—I had no discomfort. I had no anxiety.

Music Allowed Me to Become Comfortably Numb

I started making birdies as we got into the round. I went 1 under, 2 under, 3 under—then 4, 5 under, then I got to 6 under par, totally blissful in my own world. I had the solitude and peace of mind that I had long craved. Walking off the ninth tee, I was 7 under par, in the lead of the Greater Milwaukee Open. I changed the cassette tape to Pink Floyd's *The Wall*. The song, "Comfortably Numb" came on, and I instantly related to the lyrics, being comfortably numb to the anxiety of the moment. In that situation, it felt great—a surreal feeling in competition golf on the PGA Tour. As I approached the green on my last hole, a photographer snapped the photo. The photo on the cover of this book, I must say—I looked comfortably numb. I was in my own world, safe inside the ropes, fully engaged in either the golf shot at hand or lost in the music. I was calm and more comfortable than I had ever been in competition golf. As we were finishing out our final hole, a slew of photographers with those huge telephoto lenses snapped photos of me wearing a Sony Walkman.

It felt great being able to shut the rest of the world out this way. Nothing else mattered—nobody else mattered. My mind was in this moment, and I was at peace. Where I stood in the tournament and what I shot simply didn't matter. Each shot I played that day was a transformational moment in my mind.

Immediately after the round, as our group proceeded to the scoring tent, the golf media was gathering and waiting to speak to this rookie player who had the audacity to wear a Sony Walkman in a PGA Tour event. But before I could sign my scorecard for my opening round 65, Jack Tuthill, the PGA Tour's tournament director, and Wade Cagle, the PGA Tour's tournament supervisor, were waiting for me inside the scoring tent. Wade Cagle said, "Richard, before you sign your scorecard, we need to speak with you." In that moment, I didn't know what to think. All I knew was that I shot the easiest 65 of my life, and I was in the lead of this PGA Tour event.

I came out of the scoring tent and engaged with a few PGA Tour rules officials that had gathered, and the questions came, "What are you listening to on your Walkman?" All hell broke loose in my mind. I felt threatened. Immediately, I thought, *Holy shit, am I going to get disqualified for this?* I responded, "I was listening to music." One of the officials said, "We've never encountered something like this, and we have a call into P.J. Boatwright at the USGA to see if listening to music is a rules infraction." They asked me, "Were you listening to any tapes relating golf instruction?" I said, "No, just music." After a tense few minutes, word came back from Boatwright that listening to music did not breach the rules of golf. I was good to go. I signed my scorecard, then I had to face the golf media's questions.

My first round score of 65 stood up through the day. I was tied for the lead with Jay Cudd, Terry Diehl, David Edwards, and Scott Simpson. The next morning, headlining sports pages across the county weren't just about who was leading. More of them referred to my radical use of the Walkman on the PGA Tour and hailed, "Disco Dick Leads GMO."

Being tied for the lead in a PGA Tour event was a brand new feeling for me. Things got a little hectic in my mind, to say the least. I remember thinking, *What the fuck just happened here?* I went from six straight months of poor performances—not being able to make the Monday Qualifying or make cuts—to suddenly leading a PGA Tour event with comfort. The only difference was listening to music between each golf shot. The music had a calming effect on me, which changed my perspective from threat to comfort. Listening to music kept me present. I didn't get ahead of myself; I just played one shot at a time and then got lost in the music between each shot. It was simple. When I got to my ball, I took my headphones off, assessed my shot, made a couple of easy decisions, committed to my decisions, then executed the shot to the best of my ability. Before my ball landed, I'd have those headphones back on before my competitors could say, "Good shot."

I thought to myself, damn this game is psychological—I had just proved to myself that I could contend if I changed the way I thought.

As I was preparing for my second round, I began to feel my expectations change. I had played well in the first round. Now there was a lot of curiosity about whether this radical rookie with the headphones was going to hold up. To be honest, I had no idea myself.

On Friday's second round, we teed off in the afternoon wave on the front nine. The first thing I did after hitting my opening tee shot was immediately pull out my Walkman from my golf bag and slap on the headphones before Larry Rinker and Ronnie Black hit their tee shots. The music once again had an instant calming effect. In that moment, the only thing that occupied my mind was the extended version of Led Zeppelin's "Stairway to Heaven," which put me right back in the present moment.

In the second round Terry Diehl and I shot 69s. We jointly held the 36-hole lead. It was a huge deal for me that the strategy of listening to music held up and kept me calm again during the second round. I climbed right back into the bubble when I put on the Walkman. *Okay, this weekend is going to be fun*, I thought.

In the third round I was paired with Terry Diehl, playing in the final group. Being paired in the final group was another environment that I needed to learn how to feel comfortable playing in. Performing well in a final group is an important milestone in all Tour players' development. It seemed that I was fast-tracking my learning curve with the Walkman. Considering this new environment I found myself in, I played well and shot 70, which kept me tied for the lead after 54 holes with Wayne Levi at 12 under par. Calvin Peete and Victor Regalado were one shot back.

As it turned out, my use of the Walkman pissed a few guys off. I had heard that when I made a good shot, which was often that week, they'd say a courteous "Nice shot," but because I'd already have my headphones back on, I wouldn't hear my competitors' kind words. As such, I missed the "thank you" reply, which is common courtesy. But I wasn't about to let that bother me; I needed to look out for myself first and foremost.

In the final round, I was paired with Victor Regalado, and things got very interesting. I continued to stay in my own bubble with the Walkman, and I played well, for the most part. But my perception changed standing on the 15th tee. I was still tied for the lead. In that moment, I thought, *I can win this thing*, and I started to project thoughts forward about winning and what it would mean to me. I did not realize at the time how quickly those thoughts would backfire on me. I hadn't learned that lesson yet. Projecting forward to results or outcomes, including winning, took me right out of being in the present moment, so these thoughts on the 15th hole were counterproductive to the calm my mind had found in the music that was causing me to do so well over the previous 68 holes.

Standing on the 15th tee with these dysfunctional thoughts of what it would mean to me if I won burst the bubble. This instant change of thought—I call this *thought shear* (just like *wind shear*, a condition change that suddenly impacts an aircraft, making it lose wind speed and drop like a rock)—put me back into anxiety mode. I finished the final four holes in my round—bogey, par, double bogey, bogey—to shoot 75 and finish T5th. When I thought sheared on the 15th tee, I lost five shots in the last four holes because of a change in my perspective; Calvin Peete went on to win.

Regardless of my finish, it was an amazing week. I had learned how important it was to control my mind and thoughts to play well. And I found a way to do it! I felt validated in my use of the Sony Walkman, and the insights it suddenly afforded me were a godsend. In one tournament, I went from feeling like I didn't belong on the PGA Tour to believing that I could win on the PGA Tour. That's an example of how powerful our minds are.

Monday Q—Miller High Life Quad Cities Open—July 15-18, 1982
Purse: $200,000
Oakwood Country Club, Coal Valley, IL

I was exempt after having made the cut in the previous event (Milwaukee). I shot 70-72 and missed the cut by two shots.

Monday Q—Anheuser-Busch Golf Classic—July 22-25, 1982
Purse: $350,000
Kingsmill Golf Club, Williamsburg, VA

Monday Qualifying was July 19th at Kingsmill GC. We were playing for 20 spots. I shot 71 and qualified. I shot 69-72-75. The event was shortened to 54 holes, and I made $770.

Monday Q—Canadian Open—July 29-August 1, 1982
Purse: CAD$425,000
Glen Abbey Golf Club, Oakville, ON

I was exempt, having made the cut in the previous event (Anheuser-Busch), but I shot 78-70 to miss the cut by six shots.

Monday Q—Sammy Davis Jr. Greater Hartford Open—August 12-15, 1982
Purse: $300,000
Wethersfield Country Club, Hartford, CT

Monday Qualifying was on August 9th also at Wethersfield CC. We were playing for 63 spots. I shot 72 and qualified. I played well and shot 67-67-68-71 to tie for 39th. I made $1,230.

Monday Q—Buick Open—August 19-22, 1982
Purse: $350,000
Warwick Hills Country Club, Grand Blanc, MI

I was exempt, having made the cut in the previous event in Hartford but shot 74-76 and missed the cut by six shots.

British Columbia Open (Canadian Tour Event)—August 27-29, 1982
Purse: CAD$20,000
Point Grey Golf & Country Club, Vancouver, BC

As had been the case at the Quebec Open earlier in the summer, I was given a non-member sponsor exemption to play in my hometown on the Canadian Tour's BC Open. Also like the Quebec Open, it was a 54-hole event. The timing was perfect for me since I was not eligible to play in the World Series of Golf in Akron. I was excited to play at home in front of family and friends and stay at home with my parents.

Donning my Sony Walkman, I shot an opening round of 68 and lead by one shot over Cec Ferguson and Jim Rutledge. Rutledge shot a second round 67 to take the lead after 36 holes. I found myself three shots back after my second round 71.

In the morning of the final round, I got distracted a bit and wasn't able to get to the golf course on time for a full warm up. I arrived at the course with just 20 minutes to my tee time. I decided to spend 10 minutes on my putting and 10 minutes stretching, warming up my body by swinging. I teed off in the final group with Rutledge and Ferguson, and I opened with five birdies in the first six holes to grab the lead. I shot an 8 under par round of 64 to win by five shots over Jim Rutledge. I had my first professional win and earned $3,000 (Canadian) in my hometown. It was a special win. Could I take my momentum and confidence back onto the PGA Tour?

MY FIRST PROFESSIONAL WIN—1982 BRITISH COLUMBIA OPEN RESULTS

Name	Winnings	Scores
Dick Zokol	$3,000	68-71-64–203
Jim Rutledge	$1,500	69-67-72–208
Cec Ferguson	$1,200	69-67-75–211
Dave Barr	$1,000	73-70-69–212
Norm Jarvis	$800	76-67-71–214
Doug Lequyer	$800	71-69-74–214
Steve Chapman	$500	72-70-73–215
Ray Stewart	$400	73-74-69–216
Rick Gibson	$400	74-71-71–216

Monday Q—Bank of Boston Classic—September 9-12, 1982

Purse: $300,000

Pleasant Valley Country Club, Sutton, MA

Monday Qualifying on September 6th at Pleasant Valley saw us all playing for 50 spots. I shot 75 and missed qualifying by an agonizing one shot.

Monday Q—Hall Of Fame Tournament—September 16-19, 1982

Purse: $250,000

Pinehurst No. 2, Pinehurst, NC

Monday Qualifying at the tournament site saw us playing for 50 spots. I shot 71 and qualified.

I was familiar with famed Pinehurst No. 2, having been named to the Canadian Eisenhower Cup/World Amateur Team with my pal Greg Olson two years earlier. It's hard not to love Pinehurst, especially Pinehurst No. 2. I played decently the first two rounds, shooting 71-72 and making the cut. In the third round, I got paired with my good friend Jeff Sanders as well as George Archer. Archer had been on the Tour for decades, having won the 1969 Masters as well as 12 other PGA Tour events. He had long been considered one of the best putters on the PGA Tour—famous for the classic Bullseye putter he'd long used.

Like many other old-timer Tour players, George called all young guys "Rookie" to their faces. It was usually expressed in a condescending or authoritarian manner. Well, I was a rookie and Sanders was a second year member of the PGA Tour, and it wasn't hard to tell Archer was unimpressed with the two of us—particularly with me wearing this contraption on my head, listening to rock 'n' roll.

We were playing the sixth hole, a 221-yard par 3 with the pin cut in the back left corner of the green. The sixth green, like most greens on Pinehurst No. 2, is turtle-backed from the center of the green, meaning the entire green slopes away from the center toward all edges of the green.

Sanders stepped onto the tee and proceeded to hit a beautiful 3-iron at the center of the green with his patent draw to the pin and dunked his shot in the hole—for a one! Sanders and I went wild, celebrating with high fives and hooting and hollering like a couple of stupid high school kids. After things settled down, it was Archer's shot, and he hit a weak shot to the front right of the green. I hit my tee shot to pin high right up the center of the green. At the green, Archer was faced with an extraordinarily long putt, one that would force him to carefully navigate the tricky turtleback green. His first putt came up way short and didn't get halfway to the hole, leaving him a very slippery and long downhill second putt to the back left portion of the green. I lagged my first putt close to the hole and tapped in for my par and walked over to where Jeff was standing to eagerly watch a Tour putting legend navigate this difficult second putt. Archer's second putt went racing by the hole and ran slightly off the green, leaving him a 20-footer for his third putt (and a bogey), which he missed. George Archer 4-putted, making a double bogey on the hole. As Sanders and I walked to the seventh tee Sanders turned and said to me, "The only thing better than my hole-in-one is watching George fucking Archer 4-putt in front of a couple of rookies." We laughed hysterically all the way to the seventh tee. It only made Archer more pissed off with us.

Monday Q–Southern Open–September 23-26, 1982

Purse: $250,000

Green Island Country Club, Columbus, GA

I was exempt, having made the cut in the previous event at Pinehurst. Unfortunately, I shot 73-75 and missed the cut by five shots.

Monday Q–Texas Open–September 30-October 3, 1982

Purse: $250,000

Oak Hills Country Club, San Antonio, TX

Monday Qualifying on September 27th was also at Oak Hills. We were playing for 15 spots. I shot 74 and missed qualifying by three shots.

Monday Q–LaJet Classic–October 7-10, 1982

Purse: $350,000

Fairway Oaks Country Club, Abilene, TX

Monday Qualifying was at Fairway Oaks on October 4th. We were playing for 18 spots. I shot 72 and qualified. I shot 73-71-76-81 to tie for 80th, good for last place money. I won $634. The last round hurt me hard. The season was winding down, and I needed to earn money to at least maintain my PGA Tour status. I needed to finish in the top 150 on the PGA Tour Money List to be exempt to the finals of the Tour Qualifying School. The clock was ticking on my 1982 PGA Tour season.

Monday Q–Pensacola Open–October 21-24, 1982

Purse: $200,000

Perdido Bay Country Club, Pensacola, FL

I was exempt, having made the cut the previous week in Abilene. Unfortunately, I played poorly, shot 76-77 and missed the cut by nine shots. I had one remaining event to desperately try and improve my status and make the PGA Tour's top 150 to at least keep my membership for 1983.

Monday Q—Walt Disney World Golf Classic—October 28-31, 1982

Purse: $400,000

Walt Disney World, Lake Buena Vista, FL

Magnolia, Palm, and Lake Buena Vista Courses. Monday Qualifying was on the Magnolia course. We were playing for 35 spots in the last official event of the 1982 PGA Tour. I shot 76 and missed qualifying by two shots.

That Monday Q I played with Jack Frenez. Jack had a reputation for smoking a lot of pot. Our group was on the 18th tee on the Magnolia Course, and we were waiting for the group in front to clear. Jack stepped off the tee box and headed toward the bushes a few yards off the tee to relieve himself. Jack was facing away from us and proceeded to relieve himself. I glanced over at Jack and I could see he hadn't figured out the Kentucky windage as he's pissing straight into a strong wind. I couldn't believe what I was seeing; the wind was blowing his urine stream right back on his shoes and he wasn't aware of it. I guess you could say Jack was comfortably numb too. When Jack looked down and saw what was happening, he quickly jumped to the side. Jack finished his business and walked back to the tee box and looked at us with his wet shoes and bell-bottom slacks and in his haze said to us, "I forgot how to piss."

My rookie season on the PGA Tour had come to an end. I finished outside the top 150 on the PGA Tour Official Money List: I finished 156th, which meant I lost my PGA Tour membership and had to go back and get through Sectional Qualifying, then get through the final stage of Q-School, and do it all over again if I wanted to be a PGA Tour player. I looked back to the last four holes in the final round at Milwaukee, and those five shots cost me a spot in the top 150.

Back to PGA Tour Qualifying School

At the start of 1982, the PGA Tour started to dramatically change how players would achieve exempt status moving forward. The Tour moved to the All-Exempt format at the start of the 1983 PGA Tour season. No longer would just the top 60 money winners from the previous year be exempt. And, no longer would there be Monday Qualifying for non-exempt PGA Tour players. Instead, at the conclusion of the 1982 PGA Tour season, under the new format, players finishing 125th or better on the Official Money List would become exempt for the entire 1983 PGA Tour season.

Those PGA Tour players finishing 126th to 150th kept their PGA Tour membership, but their category priority would fall behind the top 125 and the newly added 50 players joining from the final 1982 PGA Tour Q-School. In other words, players finishing 126th to 150th would now be in the 176th to 200th positions. Finishing outside the top 150 meant no status whatsoever (unless you fell into the Past Champions or Veteran Player categories), and a return to the Q-School was the only ticket back to the PGA Tour. It was truly a significant change for the Tour, tournament sponsors, golf fans, and perhaps most of all, for the players.

By the end of my 1982 rookie season, I had been through a mental meat grinder and finished the PGA Tour with a grand total of $15,110.00, finishing 156th on the Official PGA Tour Money List—I had effectively lost my job and was no longer a member of the PGA Tour. After my fall, I had to climb the ladder all over again. But my perspective and belief was strong. I had done it last year without the experience I had gained in my rookie year in 1982. I knew I could do it again. Anyway, I had no choice. Like all the other players who finished outside the top 150, my back was against the wall.

Sectional Qualifying

My Sectional Qualifying was November 2nd to 5th at Wellington National GC in West Palm Beach, FL. Prior to setting out on the drive south to West Palm Beach from Orlando, I reached out to my old pal Bobby Clampett, who owned a town house at TPC Sawgrass and I asked him for a favor. If I made it through Sectional Qualifying and got to the Q-School finals at TPC Sawgrass, could I stay at his place? Clampett said, "Absolutely, be my guest." That was perfect. Now, I just had to get through to the finals. With that in my back pocket I headed down the Florida Turnpike from Orlando to the Wellington area in search of a cheap motel for the week.

My focus quickly transitioned to doing everything I could to play well. I had time for precious little else and I went into shutdown mode. At the time, Vancouver's prominent golf media included Arv Olson (*Vancouver Sun*), Don Harrison (*The Province*), and Kent Gilchrest (*The Province*), and they wanted to talk with me about my rookie season on the PGA Tour. I had great relationships with each of them. But my mind was focused on prepping for Sectional Qualifying, and they wanted to ask questions about my rookie season on the Tour and the fact that I'd lost my PGA Tour card. This was all at a time before cell phones, texting, or instant communication, of course, so these media requests were being routed through my parents' home phone number. I refused them all. I did not want any distractions, and I didn't want to have to explain anything until both qualifying events were behind me. My focus was on what I needed to do right now and get through the next two pressure-cooker qualifying events. I didn't want any distractions and certainly didn't want to explain myself yet. I went into lockdown mode and went into my bubble.

My rookie year had been long, and as Q-School approached I was running low on cash. I had cashed my last check as a member of the PGA Tour for $500.00 at Disney. All the money I had to my name was in my wallet—ten $50 bills and a credit card. I told my caddie Tommy Williams ("T-Bird") to meet me at Wellington National for a practice round on Monday. T-Bird worked for me in Disney and asked to work for me in the next two Q-School events, if I made it through the Sectional Qualifying, of course. T-Bird was a free-spirited Rhode Islander who was the prototypical New England kid, spending the summer on Block Island partying and chasing girls without a bloody care in the world.

That Monday we played a practice round late in the day. As T-Bird and I walked onto the 17th tee, there was another single player who we caught up to. He said, "Please join me for the last two holes," in a foreign accent. He extended his hand to shake mine, "My name is Nick." That is when I became friends with Nick Price. Price had finished second to Tom Watson in the Open Championship at Royal Troon earlier that summer. I responded, "I know who you are . . . It's a pleasure to meet you, Nick. My name is Dick."

In the first round of Sectional Qualifying, I played steady and shot 71, a decent start. As I was changing shoes in the parking lot, I turned to T-Bird and said, "T-Bird, get my wallet out of the bag, let's head down the street to get some lunch and then we'll come back to practice." We jumped into the car and drove out of the parking lot, heading down Binks Forest Drive in search of a decent place for lunch. We found a restaurant in a strip mall that looked fine, parked, and got out of the car. I again said to T-Bird, "Got my wallet?" T-Bird looked at me with his eyes wide open, "Oh no, Zoke—didn't you get it?" I responded, "You never gave it to me." T-Bird replied, "I put it on the bumper of the car right beside you when you were changing shoes." I gasped. "I didn't see it." We immediately jumped back in the car and raced back to the parking lot. There was a group of caddies standing near the spot where my car had been parked. My heart sunk, and I said to myself, "Oh fuck, this doesn't look good." T-Bird and I approached the guys and I called out, "Anyone see a wallet?" One of the caddies replied, "We ain't seen no wallet." In that moment I accepted my wallet and its contents were gone.

So now I've got no money, no credit cards, and no identification. I was in a bit of shock. What the hell was I going to do? There was nothing to do immediately except head back to the restaurant and eat (T-Bird was buying) and figure things out while we ate. Off we went to retrace our drive back to the restaurant. Suddenly, as we turned left back onto Binks Forest Drive, T-Bird yells, "Zoke, I see a wallet on the road pull over." I jump the car onto the grass median that separates the boulevard. T-Bird jumps out, grabs the wallet, hurriedly looks inside and yells, "Zoke, this is your wallet, the credit card and ID are still here. Did you have any cash?" I replied, "Yes, I had 10 fucking $50.00 bills in there." He responded, "There's no cash in the wallet." My heart sank again.

The way I figured it, someone got a hold of it, took the cash and pitched the wallet out the window driving out of the parking lot. At least I had my credit card and identification. It was a big blow. We got back in the car and back onto the road. Before we'd even driven 30 feet, T-Bird shouted, "Is that money on the street?" I pulled the car back up on the median, and we jumped out again. We watched $50 bills spread out, blowing down the road. We ran around picking up bills all over the place and then huddled. We got every single one of those 10 $50 bills back. We were laughing like crazy as if we were kids collecting Easter eggs. I thought to myself, *Boy was I lucky, perhaps things are starting to change.*

The rest of the week could not have gone better. There were 114 players in the Sectional Qualifying playing 72 holes with the low 31 players advancing to the Q-School finals in two weeks at TPC Sawgrass and Sawgrass CC. I followed my opening 71 with rounds of 67-70-66 at Wellington and was a medalist. I finished one stroke ahead of former University of Florida player (and SEC Individual Champion) Rick Pearson of Bradenton, FL, and Jim Albus of East Norwich, NY. Happily, I also won $3,600 for being a medalist. My new friend Nick Price also got through to the finals. One down, one to go. It was time to head north on I-95 from West Palm Beach to Ponte Vedra and settle into Clampett's town house to prepare to go face-to-face with Pete Dye's monster—TPC Sawgrass Stadium Course.

The 1982 PGA Tour Q-School finals was six rounds: two rounds at Sawgrass Country Club and four rounds at the PGA Tour's new and notorious TPC Sawgrass Stadium Course.

TPC Sawgrass was the brainchild of then-PGA Tour commissioner Deane Beman. Deane assigned the most controversial (and sadistic) course designer of the time—Pete Dye—to design a freakishly difficult golf course that would become the home of the Players Championship. And true to form Beman delivered a monster of a golf course and coupled it with the best field of the year in professional golf. Beman's long-term vision was to position the PGA Tour's flagship event and elbow its way into becoming professional golf's fifth major championship.

After playing Pete Dye's final product in a practice round, PGA Tour veteran J.C. Snead famously gave his opinion on his first impression of the golf course: "They messed up a perfectly good swamp," said Snead. Ben Crenshaw piled on, "It's Star Wars golf, designed by Darth Vader." Jack Nicklaus stated, "I've never been very good at stopping a 5-iron on the hood of a car." And my good friend Mark McCumber stated, "He [Pete Dye] and Deane weren't afraid to do things that were out of the norm. We'd landed on Mars and we'd never been there. I'd never seen anything like it, and that's nothing against Mars. It was like we were on a different planet."

The great sport Vin Scully, who broadcast the Players Championship, said, "The slopes repelled even the slightest miss. The new greens also were firm, exacerbating any bounce and sending balls scurrying toward the severely undulated areas around the greens." Scully then referred to the mounding right of the 18th green as "an elephant burial ground."

Earlier in March 1982, TPC Sawgrass Stadium Course exposed itself on its maiden voyage as the new home of the Players Championship. It was a brutally difficult course that crossed the line from a playability perspective in many players' views. Players balked at Dye's penchance for creating over-the-top, artificially difficult golf courses. Dye, on the other hand, reveled in the ridicule Tour players took in his design. Pete took pleasure in pissing Tour players off. He was quoted, "Life is not fair, so why should I make a course that is fair?" Pete Dye's words embodied his design ideology. It also gave a peek into his soul. Nonetheless, following the initial backlash, the PGA Tour Policy Board decided to move in and make changes to Pete's work, to "soften the severity and improve its playability" at the end of its first year. But that also meant the 1982 PGA Tour School was going to be played on the Frankenstein version of the golf course—*before* the pending changes. The severity of the TPC Sawgrass held your attention. When you played it, you were always just one shot away from disaster all the time.

PGA Tour Q-School Is a Mental Examination—and There's No Place to Hide

Through all the controversy on Pete Dye's freakish design of TPC Sawgrass, the intimidation factor of this golf course only made matters more difficult in the minds of Q-School contestants. I knew if I was able to "keep my shit wired tight" during each round and each shot, which was another way of saying, keep my composure and not get ahead of myself—I'd do just fine. The PGA Tour Q-School is a mental test of survival. And given what I went through mentally in my rookie year on the PGA Tour, I felt my greatest asset was not so much my physical ability to swing a golf club, but it was my mental perspective. I felt I had strengthened my mettle and ability to handle extreme levels of discomfort, PGA Tour Q-School discomfort, better than the other guy I was competing against. I knew this Q-School was going to be a severe mental and emotional examination; it did not matter how good your golf swing was, what mattered was your mental skill and ability to handle stress, risk, and uncertainty on an extremely difficult golf course. I had my trusty Walkman with me to help me and I had plenty of batteries.

My plan was to climb back into my own little music bubble on the golf course and face every shot one at a time as they presented themselves.

Moe Norman Shows Up to Watch

As my first round began on Sawgrass CC, I was heading down my first fairway when I recognized Canadian golf legend and savant Moe Norman. At the time I had never met Moe but everyone in golf knew who he was. I said to myself, *Cool, Moe's coming out to watch the event.* Moe spent winters a couple hours' drive south of Ponte Vedra in Titusville, FL, at the Canadian PGA-owned Royal Oak Golf Club. After playing a few holes, I noticed Moe was still hanging around our group. He wasn't there to watch the event. He was there to check out this radical Canadian rookie who played the past year on the PGA Tour while listening to music.

After completing my first round Moe was still hanging around and I approached him and introduced myself. I cannot recall the conversation but felt privileged that he took an interest in me. Moe spent a few days watching, and the fact I was playing well helped me establish a rapport and relationship with Moe.

One of the difficulties of Q-School qualifying was trying to sleep well. After each round, whether a practice round or a tournament round, I came back to the room, or in this case, Clampett's townhome, completely exhausted. Early each evening after dinner, I found it hard not to fall asleep. But I knew if I fell asleep too early, before say 9:00 PM, I'd likely wake up in the middle of the night thinking it's time to get up, and my mind would start to get active, and then I wouldn't be able to get back to sleep. I'd lie awake through the night and feel exhausted when it was time to get up and go to battle.

1982 PGA Tour Qualifying School—November 16-21, 1982

Ponte Vedra Beach, FL

Four rounds played at TPC Sawgrass (6,857 yards); two rounds played at Sawgrass CC (7,000 yards). A total of 696 applications were accepted and eight Sectional trials were held to reduce the final Q-School starting field to 200. After 72 holes (two rounds each at Sawgrass CC and TPC Sawgrass), the field was cut to 130 players who scored 340 (+16) or better. The top 35 players and ties received spots on the 1983 PGA Tour, while the next 52 earned exemption onto the Tournament Players Series (the Tournament Players Series was the PGA Tour's initial developmental series, what is now called the Korn Ferry Tour).

1982 PGA TOUR QUALIFYING SCHOOL RESULTS

Place	Name	Scores
1	Donnie Hammond	66-68-71-65-74-74–419
2	David Peoples	72-72-70-74-73-72–433
3	Nick Price	77-70-69-69-74-74–435
T4.	**Richard Zokol**	**70-73-73-70-75-75–436**
T4.	Mac O'Grady	79-76-71-66-71-73–436
T4.	TC Chen	69-76-69-75-73-74–436
T4.	Buddy Gardner	67-72-71-74-78-74–436
T8.	Dan Forsman	75-73-73-71-76-69–437
T8.	Gary McCord	73-74-72-70-74-74–437
T8.	John McComish	72-70-75-71-75-74–437
12	Mike Peck	74-71-75-72-76-70–438
T13.	Ken Green	71-76-68-72-79-73–439
T13.	Jeff Sanders	71-73-71-77-71-76–439
T13.	Bill Sander	72-73-70-74-74-76–439
T16.	Lindy Miller	75-72-72-70-76-75–440
T16.	Steve Hart	78-73-72-71-70-76–440
T16.	Mike Brannan	76-71-70-72-72-79–440
T19.	Curt Byrum	76-69-73-73-74-76–441
T19.	Larry Rinker	76-68-72-79-69-77–441
T21.	David Ogrin	81-70-69-73-75-74–442
T21.	Russ Cochran	68-71-73-74-75-79–442
T23.	Loren Roberts	76-69-70-75-78-75–443
T23.	Tony Sills	74-77-70-74-72-76–443
T23.	Darrell Kestner	76-74-69-74-73-77–443
T23.	Wally Armstrong	69-73-72-77-74-78–443
T27.	Mike Gove	75-71-73-74-80-71–444

Place	Name	Scores
T27.	Ray Stewart	72-75-71-73-81-72–444
T27.	Ronnie Black	74-78-69-79-69-75–444
T27.	Blaine McAllister	76-69-74-73-75-77–444
T27.	Tom Lehman	71-71-71-75-78-78–444
T27.	Rafael Alarcón	77-74-67-71-76-79–444
33	Lars Meyerson	73-73-73-80-75-71–445
T34.	Rick Pearson	72-80-69-75-76-74–446
T34.	Rick Dalpos	75-72-73-75-75-76–446
T34.	Sammy Rachels	73-81-71-74-70-77–446
T34.	Jeff Sluman	67-73-73-76-78-79–446

With the final six rounds of the 1982 PGA Tour Q-School completed, I exhaled. I felt emotionally exhausted, but most importantly, I felt proud of myself for surviving. I played well under difficult circumstances and got my PGA Tour card back with my T4th finish.

I persevered through the lows of my rookie year, turned it around and emerged able to perform well around the lead of a PGA Tour event, then lost my PGA Tour card, then won the Sectional Qualifying in Florida, and finally, finished T4th in the PGA Tour Q-School Finals. All of this gave me the feeling that I'd be able to stand in and survive the trenches. I had passed the baptism by fire. Now I felt comfortable, like I belonged on the PGA Tour.

In my mind, I knew I could do this. It wasn't going to be easy, but I knew I could do this.

CHAPTER 5

1983—Year Two on the PGA Tour—Needing to Stabilize My Play

Being able to start my second year back on the PGA Tour in a much stronger priority position than my rookie year in 1982 was huge for me to advance and build a stronger belief system. Too often, aspiring players wash out after their rookie year. Obviously, the key to survival on the PGA Tour is being able to perform. Not surprisingly, the attrition rate for rookies is high. If a young player can survive to play a second season on the PGA Tour, the attrition rate significantly declines. Learning to survive strengthens you. Once you've endured the rookie battles every week on the PGA Tour, you get an idea of how this program works and what you need to do to survive. You've become significantly more familiar with the golf courses that you didn't know in your rookie year. What was initially a big mystery is now something familiar. Simply, you are in a better position at the start of year two on the PGA Tour than you were a year earlier starting blind.

As I was preparing for my second season, I went back to Poldi Bentley and asked him for some assistance. I was hoping to take a vehicle with me on Tour for the entire season. At the time the Bentley family owned the BMW distributorship for Western Canada. Having a vehicle with me would give me more freedom and flexibility. Back in those days, PGA Tour events didn't provide tournament courtesy vehicles to players—or if they did, they only went to the top players. The rest of the field relied on using player transportation to and from the airport, to the hotel, and back and forth to the golf course each day. I found this quite stifling, and having my own vehicle would help, particularly during the West Coast Swing part of the season. So I reached back to Poldi and was hopeful he would agree to help.

Mr. Bentley said, "Yes, I can help you. What I will do is give you a brand new 1983 BMW 320i to use for the year on the PGA Tour. At the end of the year, you can purchase it as a used vehicle at book value with all those miles on it." I thanked him for his generous offer. I picked up the brand new 320i at his distributorship in Vancouver, loaded it up, and drove down to Palm Springs, CA, to prepare for my second year on the PGA Tour.

In early 1983, I started to hang around Palm Springs and got to know the PGA of America professional Blair Kline, who was the head pro at Desert Horizons CC in Indian Wells, CA. Blair was a Seattle guy who was a good friend of Fred Couples (Fred was also from Seattle). Desert Horizons was a real estate development funded by the Alaska Teamsters' Pension Fund. Blair's boss, overseeing the development, was a fellow by the name of Joe Pinzone from New York. Blair and Joe both took a liking to me and asked me if I'd represent and wear the Desert Horizon logo on the PGA Tour. We signed a simple agreement, which paid me a few dollars and gave me Desert Horizon logoed clothes.

I felt like I was starting the 1983 Tour fresh with keenness. My guns were loaded, and I was full of piss and vinegar, ready to go. For me, it was such a relief knowing that Monday Qualifying was a thing of the past. I was still using my Walkman, and now, I just needed to figure out how to stabilize my play and perform well enough to make the top 125 at the end of the season and get my exempt status for 1984. I was ready to get going—with my Walkman!

The 1983 PGA Tour Season—Trying to Get Stable Footing

The 1983 PGA Tour season had 45 Regular PGA Tour Events and Official Prize Money of $17.5 million—an all-time high. I played in 31 events total and made nine cuts and missed the cut in 21 other Tour events. Here is the story of my 1983 season, the tournaments played, the nine cuts made, and a few anecdotes along the way.

Note, that if I haven't identified and outlined a PGA Tour event, I either missed the cut or did not play in the event. The PGA Tour stats did not track those that missed cuts until the early 2000s.

Joe Garagiola–Tucson Open–January 6-9, 1983
Purse: $300.000
Randolph Park GC, Tucson, AZ
Place: T26th
Score: 69-73-66-69
Made: $2,041.67

The Phoenix Open–January 27-30, 1983
Purse: $350,000
Phoenix CC, Phoenix, AZ
Missed Cut

The Birds Nest at the Phoenix Open

The Phoenix Open is run and operated by the Phoenix Thunderbirds, a civic not-for-profit volunteer organization whose purpose is to raise charitable dollars for multiple causes in the Phoenix community. The Thunderbirds did (and still do) wonderful work in the community through revenue generated at the Phoenix Open. The Phoenix Open also earned a reputation as the best party on Tour. (A reputation that has accelerated to this day!) The Birds Nest originated at the Phoenix Open at Phoenix Country Club in 1972. At that time, the Birds Nest was located beside the clubhouse, sectioned off under a large tent. By 1983, the Birds Nest had established itself as the best party spot in all of Phoenix during the golf tournament. Friday and Saturday nights were especially raucous. The band Duck Soup played the Birds Nest annually and over time came to be known as the Unofficial Band of the PGA Tour. As the Birds Nest's reputation grew, the party got bigger and often spilled out onto the golf course itself as it continued well into the night. The talk in the locker room on weekends would frequently include how many condoms and panties were found on the golf course by those players teeing off early Saturday and Sunday mornings.

My buddy Jim Nelford suggested we go to the Birds Nest Friday evening. Why not? I'd just missed the cut. Nelford and I met up with Gary McCord, and upon arrival immediately realized that there were a slew of PGA Tour players already in the tent. McCord remarked, "They just finished blacktopping the whole area under the tent a few days ago." I asked, "Why did they blacktop it?" McCord replied, "It's easier to keep clean at the end of the night when they hose down the vomit after closing."

To be honest, I was often Nelford's wingman. Nelford held legendary status on the PGA Tour as a ladies' man. He was an absolute chick magnet. Sure enough, shortly after arriving, a middle-aged cougar on the prowl locked in on Nelford and began her stalk. When she finally approached Jim, we were standing at a high-top table. Her flirtatious eyes locking onto Nelford, she said, "Can I get your autograph?" wearing her most seductive expression. Nelford picked up on her vibe, staring straight into her eyes and responded, "Where would you like it?" She handed him a Sharpie and said, "Right here," exposing a significant amount of her left breast, also uncovering part of another autograph that read, "Fuzzy." We assumed the rest of the autograph—"Zoeller"—extended across the other side of her left nipple. Nelford happily autographed her left breast as McCord and I gaped.

Fast-forward 40+ years, and the Phoenix Open party has evolved from a tent on blacktop to a massive revenue-generating party now known as the WM Phoenix Open's Coors Light Birds Nest Concert Series. It has definitely come a long way. It started with Duck Soup and grew to attract high-profile performers over the years that included Jerry Jeff Walker, Dennis Quaid and the Sharks, Huey Lewis and the News, Cheap Trick, and Glenn Frey of the Eagles. Today, top performers play Wednesday evening through Saturday evening. And of course, the tournament itself has become famous as the best attended tournament on the PGA Tour, highlighted by the stadium set up on the par 3 16th—legendary for its rowdy environment and well-lubricated spectators that can spill onto the 16th hole without any clothing.

The Bing Crosby National Pro-Am—February 3-6, 1983

Purse: $325,000

Pebble Beach GL, Cypress Point GC, and Spyglass Hill GC, Monterey, CA

Missed Cut

1983 Bing Crosby National Pro-Am, Player Decanter, the 42nd Crosby.

Isuzu–Andy Williams San Diego Open–February 17-20, 1983

Purse: $300,000

Torrey Pines GC, South Course and North Course, La Jolla, CA

Place: T66th

Score: 71-71-73-73

Made: $621.00

Playing With the King–Arnold Palmer

My first appearance at the Andy Williams San Diego Open was memorable and became a lifetime highlight when I got paired with Arnold Palmer in the third round. Coming into San Diego, I was playing poorly, having missed five consecutive cuts. My spirits were buoyed, and I felt a small reprieve making the cut at Torrey Pines—even more so when I called in on

Friday night to confirm my Saturday tee time (in those days, that's what you had to do) and was told I'd be playing with Arnold Palmer. *Holy Fuck—I am playing with the King,* I thought. I was super excited.

Arnold Palmer and I were scheduled to tee off the third round on the 10th tee on Torrey Pines' South Course. As I approached the 10th tee for my tee time, I had to fight through storms of fans massing to see Arnie. The crowd he commanded was overwhelming. I walked into the tent on the tee to pick up a pin sheet for the day and introduce myself to our group's scorer and standard-bearer. I was of course still using my Walkman at the time. Arnie hadn't arrived yet, so I said to myself, "All right, let's break the ice right now." I pulled out my Walkman, slapped on the headphones, and cranked up the volume to Led Zeppelin's "Black Dog."

Then I suddenly noticed a wave of people in the gallery starting to part, like Moses parting the Red Sea. Arnold Palmer broke through, walked up onto the tee, and strode toward the starters tent where I was standing—with a look on his face that seemed to be saying, "Who the hell is this kid and what the fuck does he have on his head?"

As Palmer approached, I took the headphones off out of respect, stepped toward him, looked straight into his eyes, and extended my hand. "Richard Zokol, it's a pleasure to meet and play with you today." Arnie responded, "Well, it's nice to meet you too, Richard." He then pointed at my Walkman and said, "What have you got going on here?" I responded, "I listen to music when I play. Would you like to try it?" The gallery was listening to our interaction with bemusement and curiosity. I handed the headphones to Arnie. Led Zeppelin was still playing. Not a good choice of music for Mr. Palmer. As he put the headphones on his head, camera shutters from the assembled press went off in a chain reaction. I could tell immediately Arnie was not impressed with my choice of music. He took off the headphones and with a baffled look on his face handed them back to me. I am not sure, but he must have wondered what the hell this young generation of golfers is coming to, listening to rock 'n' roll while playing golf.

Through the West Coast Swing, I only made two cuts and did not get off to the start I was hoping for and was still very much unstable. I had been using the Sony Walkman consistently during the start of my second season, but I wasn't playing well, missing five cuts out of the seven events on the West Coast. I did feel I learned to smell the roses between the golf shots. In other words, I was getting comfortable, and my hyperactive mind was calming. At this stage, I felt like I was ready to proceed without the Walkman. Quite frankly, I wanted to move on from being reliant on music to keep my mind in check and be able to do it myself. I felt I was ready to take off the mental training wheels the Sony Walkman represented.

I was back in Florida, where I struggled so much the previous year, but this year I was in almost all events. I couldn't get off the run of poor play and missed the next six cuts—Doral, Honda, Bay Hill, New Orleans, the Players Championship, and Greensboro. My confidence was in trouble, again. I was not eligible to play in the next three events—the Masters, Sea Pines Heritage, and the Tournament of Champions—so I flew back to Vancouver for a three-week break from my Golf Insanity. Thank goodness, I needed a break.

After three weeks off, I flew to Dallas for the Byron Nelson Golf Classic. Nelford and I were sharing a room in the Four Seasons Las Colinas right on the golf course. The week prior, Nelford had a great week and finished second to Fuzzy Zoeller at the Heritage Classic in Hilton Head. Jim was playing some great golf and seemed to be on the verge of winning. After Friday's second round, Nelford made the cut, and I missed yet another one. I can still recall the helpless look on Jim's face when I came back to the room. He was playing so well, and I was struggling so much. It was agonizing. I had now played 13 PGA Tour events and made only two cuts. I was in deep trouble again.

Prior to departing for the next event in Houston, Nelford said, "Lorne Rubenstein introduced me to this psychologist from the University of Guelph named Dr. Richard Lonetto. He helped me develop my shot routine using a biofeedback mechanism. It really helped me, and I think he can help you too. Would you like me to give him a call?" I said, "Absolutely, I need to find something."

I had noticed Nelford's newly established shot routine, which appeared to make him more contained, calm, consistent, and noticeably more rhythmic with each shot he took. Most importantly, it significantly improved Nelford's ability to perform. It seemed to me every time Nelford found himself around the cutline, he'd always manage to calm down and contain his thoughts and this helped him hold the current PGA Tour cut streak at 33 consecutive cuts. Making a cut in a PGA Tour event is no easy task.

Tiger Woods made an incredible 142 in a row between 1998 and 2005. That record will never be broken.

Nelford gave Richard Lonetto a call, and he agreed to help me out. I called Dr. Richard Lonetto and we made arrangements to meet the following week after the Houston Coca-Cola Open during the week of the Colonial National Invitational in Fort Worth, which I was not eligible to play. Instead I entered the New Hampshire Classic, one of the new Tournament Players Series (TPS) events that the PGA Tour started.

First thing Monday morning, I met Dr. Lonetto in the hotel in Concord, New Hampshire, and we had breakfast to discuss the process. I asked him if he had worked with any other athletes. Lonetto said, "Yes, even though my area of expertise is death anxiety, I've worked with a few athletes, including some NHL goalies." Lonetto described how he put a pulse rate monitor on goalies and then observed how they responded to numerous slap shots being fired at them simultaneously. Then he'd blindfolded them and resumed the slap-shot barrage to see how they'd respond. He'd look at their performance before and after being blindfolded. His students all showed improvement after the blindfolds were removed compared to their performance prior to being blindfolded. Lonetto also shared he had worked with George Knudson. He said, "Knudson was masterful with his shot routine with full swing shots, but his pulse rate went through the roof the moment he stepped foot on the putting green. It was difficult for him to get the Drop into the Still Point with his putting." I had no idea what Lonetto meant by *Drop* or *Still Point*.

After breakfast, we went to the tournament course and set up on the far end of the practice range at the Concord Country Club. Lonetto said, "Hit some balls and warm up." As I started hitting a few balls, I watched Lonetto pull this devise out of a backpack. He said, "Strap this around your chest under your golf shirt, and make sure the sensor is in contact with your xiphoid process with this contact jelly." The xiphoid process is the small, triangular concave part of your sternum. A long wire came out of the sensor under my shirt, connected to a measurement device that Lonetto monitored.

As I strapped in and looked at this contraption, I asked, "What's going to happen here?" Lonetto explained, "This device is going to monitor your pulse rate at different points, starting with your decision through the execution of your shot routine. It's very sensitive and will measure your blood volume rate (even in dilation) as you go through your shot routine for each shot. It will give us an idea of where your mind is at. We are looking to identify a rhythmic flow that you can feel in your shot routine. If this flow breaks rhythm or something disrupts your shot routine, your shot will be blown. If you feel the rhythm break and cannot feel the Drop and the calm, you abort and start your shot routine over."

Lonetto further explained, "Before you start your shot routine, you will need to assess the shot, which will lead you to making decision(s) on the shot—which club to use and/or what type of shot you choose to hit. The key here, and what really matters most, is that you believe in and commit fully to the decision(s) you make. If you have any doubt or even hesitate about your decision(s), it will show up on the monitor, and you'll be unable to get the Drop, which is vital to get into the Still Point and rhythmic flow for the shot."

At that moment, I had no idea what he meant by the *Drop*, the *Still Point*, or *rhythmic flow*. I had heard of this thing called *The Zone* but didn't really understand it.

Lonetto went on, "When you make your first step to initiate your shot routine from behind the ball, you need to put your full awareness on the rhythmic flow of your shot routine. We will figure out your shot routine with this monitor. You can shape your shot routine, shorter or longer, whatever you want. Whatever you choose, you will come to rely on it. Let's start with your 9-iron and hit shots in sets of three shots. Go through your full shot routine with each shot as best you can—as though you were in a tournament. After each shot, I want you to tell me how well the rhythm flow went with each shot."

On the first shot, I picked out a target and chose a specific shot to hit with my 9-iron. I stood behind the ball, aligning my ball and ball flight in my mind to my target with the shot I decided to hit. When I felt ready, I took my first steps forward in my shot routine. At the time, my shot routine had a couple of practice swing motions, including a couple of looks at my target. I then executed the shot. I told Lonetto, "That shot was perfect." Lonetto entered some data points on his yellow pad. Then Lonetto directed me to pick a new target and go through the same process. We repeated this process. With each shot I'd reply to Lonetto, "That shot was perfect . . . that shot was good . . . that shot was horrible," etc. We went through the process with most of the clubs in my golf bag each time in sets of three.

Rhythm of Your Shot Routine is Key

In short order, I started to feel a rhythmic flow and its pattern with each good shot, and I found it easy to repeat. I also started to feel the difference with shots when my rhythm was disrupted, and I couldn't feel the Drop when my shot routine got distracted. Those shots invariably ended up in various patterns as bad shots. After hitting about 50 balls, most of the shots I reported back to Lonetto were good or perfect. From my perspective, I hit the ball great throughout this session. The pattern Lonetto was looking for started to surface. Lonetto suddenly said, "Okay, I've got it!" What he had discovered looking at his monitor was a recognizable rhythmic pattern for each successful shot that was clearly distinguishable from that of the inconsistent patterns that appeared with my less-than-good shots.

The Drop—Crossing into the Still Point—and Explosion at Impact

After Lonetto had identified the pattern and rhythm of my good shots, he explained to me what was happening. "Being in a tournament atmosphere causes a higher-than-normal level of excitement. When you face a shot and make your decision(s) and commit to that specific shot, your excitement level starts to increase in a smooth, rhythmic manner. If there is doubt or lack of commitment in your decisions, your excitement level will spike. This can happen because of doubt, or if you have lost focus or something has distracted you, and it will break the rhythm of your shot routine. You will feel it. You need to develop awareness so you can abort when your focus breaks the rhythm and you need to start over. If you don't, you will blow the shot."

Lonetto explained, "You should make your shot routine as short and tight as possible. I'd suggest incorporating breathing into your shot routine to trigger the Drop. If you incorporate a 'breath in and a breath out' into your routine, it will help you initiate the Drop. The Drop is key, if you don't get it you won't be able to access the Still Point, and you won't deliver the

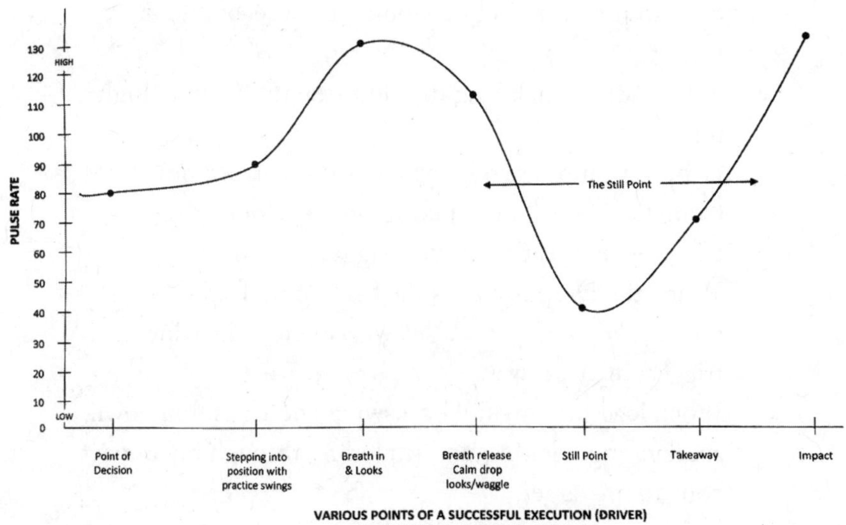

shot you want." I didn't entirely understand what Lonetto was saying, but I could feel both the Drop and the Still Point during my shot routine now. And I felt the calm prior to the takeaway and the transition of excitement with the acceleration and explosion at impact. I found it fascinating. My pulse rate at the Still Point was 40, then at takeaway it was 65, then a second later at impact, my pulse rate when using my driver went to 130, and breathing accelerated. I was shocked at how high my pulse rate was immediately after the shot was gone.

Lonetto went on, "Conditioning your shot routine is key to performing in stressful situations, and it will allow you to optimize your performance. You can change your routine from time to time, but you must train yourself to rely on the shot routine you design."

I immediately started to work on a structured new shot routine. It went like this:

- Assess the shot—make a decision(s) for the shot.
- Commit to the decision(s) of the shot.
- Initiate my shot routine with my first step from behind the ball as I move into position for my first practice swing motion (more of a half swing motion) and a look at my target with a visualized flight of my ball.

- Second practice swing motion with a second look at my target.
- Take a breath in, lifting my club straight up quite high off the ground.
- Drop my club down in sync with my breath out (sometimes out loud), taking one last look at my target—my breath out will trigger the Drop.
- When the Drop becomes the Still Point, I say to myself, *Target-Target-Target*, with a breath in, which triggers my takeaway.
- I then load into my full backswing and transition down, accelerating, rotating, and exploding through my impact zone to my target.

My shot routine took 15 seconds from start to finish. It became a reliable conditioned response in training. Keep in mind, you can change your shot routine as much as you desire. But once you have one, trust it, and take it to the golf course; it will get you through difficult situations.

When Your Shot Routine Breaks

During that initial session following one of the shots where I reported to Lonetto "that shot was bad," he responded with, "Could you feel your rhythm spike or collapse or not calm during your routine?" I said, "Absolutely, I could." Lonetto then said, "When that happens, and it will, you need to be aware that your shot routine has been compromised and you need to abort the shot and start your shot routine over. If you don't start over, you will freak out over the shot and won't be able to recover."

Developing a Healthy Conditioned Response

The purpose of developing a shot routine is to establish a structured and healthy conditioned response to help you execute golf shots under the most stressful situations. The great Bobby Jones once said, "There is golf—and there is tournament golf. And they are not at all alike." Playing a casual round of golf is very different from playing a tournament round in the mind of the player. Tournament golf has an endless number of different situations that require mental skill development to succeed. Developing a specific conditioned thought sequence (shot routine) to handle a never-ending list of possible situations to execute golf shots is critical. If a player wants to succeed in playing golf, he or she must have a shot routine that helps them succeed under the stress that comes with playing golf.

Learning my new shot routine was easy. It all started to come together, and relying on my shot routine in competition was not difficult. I was able to take it straight to the golf course, and I played well in Atlanta. Making $6,000 was a remarkable turn of events for me.

Georgia-Pacific Atlanta Classic—May 19-22, 1983

Purse: $400,000

Atlanta Golf CC, Marietta, GA

Place: T16th

Score: 71-73-69 (tournament shortened to 54 holes due to rain)

Made: $6,000.00

The week after Atlanta was Jack's Memorial Tournament, and I was not eligible to play. I did not qualify for the upcoming US Open at Oakmont and was forced to take a few weeks off. But my good play in Atlanta gave me confidence, buoyed my spirits, and gave me hope. I loved that feeling.

After three weeks off, I was eager to get back on Tour and pick up where I left off. The Western Open was played at the difficult Butler National GC in Chicago. Butler National was a men's only private golf club. There was one lady who worked at the golf club and I remember seeing a washroom on the main floor with the sign "Woman" on the door, not "Women." At least they had a sense of humor. I proceeded to miss the cut in Chicago. My focus quickly moved on to Milwaukee, where I played so well my rookie year.

When I got back to Tuckaway CC for the 1983 Greater Milwaukee Open, I felt very comfortable. It was like putting on a pair of slippers. Tuckaway CC just "suited my eye," as they say or "horses-for-courses." It was a track I loved and played well—this time without my Sony Walkman and with newfound confidence with my new shot routine.

I picked up exactly where I wanted to with my shot routine and shot 70-72-66-69 and finished sixth. This was the shift in performance I was looking for, but I was forced to take another few weeks off because I wasn't in the British Open and needed to pace myself on the road.

Greater Milwaukee Open—July 7-10, 1983
Purse: $250,000
Tuckaway CC, Franklin, WI
Place: T6th
Score: 70-72-66-69
Made: $8,375.00

The Canadian Open—July 28-31, 1983
Purse: CAD $425,000
Glen Abbey GC, Oakville, ON
Place: T24th
Score: 74-70-70-72
Made: $2,770.00

Canadians Playing The Canadian Open

To a Canadian player, there is nothing more inspiring than playing in the Canadian Open. As mentioned in an earlier chapter, my first Canadian Open was as an amateur in 1978 at Glen Abbey. I also played in two more Canadian Opens as an amateur—the 1980 Canadian Open at Royal Montreal and the 1981 Canadian Open at Glen Abbey. In 1980, I qualified by placing third in the 1979 Canadian Amateur. In 1981, I qualified by placing fourth in the 1980 Canadian Amateur, won by my good friend Greg Olson. The 1983 Canadian Open was the first time I made the cut.

BC Open—September 1-4, 1983
Purse: $300,000
En Joey GC, Endicott, NY
Place: T40th

Score: 71-71-72-69

Made: $1,024.20

Bank of Boston Classic—September 8-11, 1983

Purse: $350,000

Pleasant Valley CC, Sutton, MA

Place: T69th

Score: 70-74-70-73

Made: $700.00

Panasonic Las Vegas Pro Celebrity Classic—September 14-18, 1983

Purse: $1,052,000

Las Vegas CC, Desert Inn CC, Dunes CC, and Showboat CC, Las Vegas, NV

Place: T12th

Score: 68-68-73-68-72

Made: $15,187.50

The 1983 Panasonic Las Vegas Invitational was the first PGA Tour event with a $1 million purse. (As of this writing, the largest purse on the PGA Tour was the 2025 Players Championship at $25 million.) After making the cut and playing well, I made $15,187.50, which vaulted me into the top 125. A $1 million purse felt like an unbelievable amount to be playing for. First place money was $162,000.00, an enormous amount to win at the time.

Making that $15,187.50 was a highlight moment. It was really my first good performance on the PGA Tour that propelled me into something meaningful. It was a delightful feeling that set me up to keep my job and graduate to the next level—being an exempt player on the PGA Tour.

Pensacola Open—October 27-31, 1983

Purse: $250,000

Perdido Bay & Inn, Pensacola, FL

Place: T31st

Score: 70-73-68-70

Made: $1,387.50

My 1983 PGA Tour Season Summary

At the conclusion of the 1983 PGA Tour calendar, the Official Money Leader was Hal Sutton, who won $426,668 and two tournaments—the Players Championship and, his first major, the PGA Championship. I finished the year with official winnings of $38,106—good enough for 117th on the Money List. I had made the critical top 125 in my second year on Tour and gained exempt status for 1984. The 125th spot was nabbed by Jim Booros, who won $34,980. My T12th finish in the big money event in Las Vegas in mid-September had given me the final push into the top 125 that I needed. I was relieved to have made the exempt status for 1984 after my second year on Tour, but at the same time had to admit to myself the year had not gone the way I had hoped. While enjoying some good weeks and small successes, I spent most of the season struggling and playing poorly. I needed to play more consistently at a high level in 1984.

1983 FINAL TOUR STATS	
Tournaments Entered	31
Cuts Made	9
Cuts Missed	22
Top 10 Finishes	1 (Greater Milwaukee Open)
Stroke Average	72.62
Greens in Regulation	27th
Driving Accuracy	T35th
Official Money	$38,106.37
Official Money List Position	117th

But the most important highlights of my 1983 season were, 1) I achieved my primary objective to make the top 125 on the PGA Tour Money List, gaining exempt status, and 2) despite missing 22 cuts during the year, my play from tee to green (based on my Tour stats) placed me in the top 25% of ball-strikers on the PGA Tour. Given my ball-striking performance, it was clear that the area of my game I needed to improve the most was my putting and short game skills.

Following the last event of the season in Pensacola, Jim Nelford in his BMW 535i and I, in my BMW 320i, drove back in formation to Orlando and hung out for a couple of weeks. I eventually decided I should hit the road and drive home to Vancouver from Orlando, FL. I'd never made a drive that long but was actually looking forward to it. I took off westbound on Interstate 10 heading for California. I spent a couple days in Palm Springs and then headed north on Interstate 5 to Vancouver. It took me six days of actual driving time behind the wheel averaging 10 hours a day. I enjoyed the drive and the sights, but I was happy to be home and off the road once I got there.

Back in Vancouver, I reached out to Poldi Bentley, and we made arrangements with the Neumann family (operators of the BMW distributorship and owners of the BMW dealership on Burrard St. in Vancouver) to finalize my purchase of the BMW. My parents had sold their home by that time. So, for my entire visit, I stayed with them in their new penthouse suite atop a commercial building on West Broadway. While there, I parked my newly purchased BMW in front of the building on West Broadway. A week later, a drunk driver piledrived into the car and totaled it. The insurance company wrote me a check for the full value.

My 1983 PGA Tour official earnings were $38,107. I doubled that amount with off-golf-course revenue. The off-course revenue was generated mostly from my equipment contracts, including TaylorMade (clubs), Titleist (ball and FootJoy gloves), and various outings and Pro-Am events on Mondays and Tuesdays that paid for player participation.

I was now two years into my three-year sponsorship agreement with Howard Cadinah. By the end of my second year on Tour, I knew the agreement that provided me $50K at the start of the year was not enough to cover my actual expenses. After all, I had just picked that number out of the air when we'd had our original discussions. Now I knew better and decided to try and renegotiate the final year of the deal.

My expenses and the agreement payouts for 1982 and 1983 in US dollars:

- In Year 1, my Tour expenses were $55,000—I had to reach into my pocket for $5,000 to cover the difference.
- In Year 1, Howard Cadinha spent $50,000 and, per the

agreement, earned $30,000 as a % of my income (Cadinha lost $20,000).

- In Year 2, my Tour expenses were $65,000—I again had to cover the difference of $15,000.
- In Year 2, Howard Cadinha spent $50,000 and based on the agreement, earned $80,000 (Cadinha netted $30,000).

Net, net, over the first two years of the three-year agreement, Howard Cadinha was $10,000 ahead of his total cost of $100,000. I met with Howard and proposed to amend our sponsorship agreement for the third and final year. I explained to Howard that $50,000 per year had not been enough to cover my costs in year one, the shortfall had grown in year two, and would clearly fall further short as costs continued to rise for the final year of the agreement. Howard asked, "What are you suggesting?" I responded, "I am asking for $10,000 more than the $50,000 in our agreement. I estimate I am going to incur $70,000 in expenses in 1984, a shortfall of $20,000. And now that I am exempt on Tour, I expect to make more money. How about we split the difference and increase the guarantee from $50,000 to $60,000?" Howard replied, "Our agreement says $50,000, and that was your number." I said, "Yes, that was my number, but I had no idea what the reality was two years ago before I got on Tour." Howard responded sternly, "No, I won't agree to amend our agreement for an additional $10,000." I countered, "How about $5,000 then?" Howard stood firm, saying, "No, nothing more!"

I looked at him sitting behind his desk and calmly responded, "If we can't come to an agreement to provide additional funding for our final year, then I want to end our agreement right now. You won't have to pay the final $50,000, and we can go our separate ways." He responded with a disparaging comment about my character. I replied with something to the effect of, "I have never appreciated you parading me around as if I were your show horse, and now you're not willing to be flexible in our third year, on a number that I pulled out of thin air in good faith two years ago. If you are not open to a compromise, I am ending our agreement, and you won't need to pay the $50,000 for year three." I got up, turned my back to him, and walked out of his office. I never heard from or saw Howard Cadinha again.

CHAPTER 6

1984—Moe Norman—Clay Edwards—the Canadian Open

The 1984 PGA Tour season was another significant inflection point in my career and in my life. Once again, I met the start of a new season on the PGA Tour with a sense of opportunity and enthusiasm.

Having ended my sponsorship agreement with Howard Cadinha, I was on my own and ready to take on the risk of becoming financially independent in my third year on the Tour. I wanted to keep 100% of my earnings, which meant I needed to be able to cover 100% of my costs. I was ready and wanted to take this step.

Prior to heading down to Palm Springs after the Christmas holidays, I approached my parents and asked them for a loan of $15,000. My father wrote me the check for the full amount, and I took off for the California desert.

The first PGA Tour event of 1984 was the Seiko-Tucson Match Play Championship. I played well and won $15,000.00. I was off to a great start.

Seiko-Tucson Match Play Championship—January 2-8, 1984

Purse: $708,000.00

Randolph Park Municipal GC, Tucson, AZ

Made: $15,000

First Round Match	Zokol def. Mike Reid 3 & 2
Second Round Match	Zokol def. Curtis Strange, 19th hole
Third Round Match	Zokol def. Allen Miller 4 & 2
Fourth Round Match	Ben Crenshaw def. Richard Zokol, 20th hole

I've always loved match play competition. Match play divides all 18 holes of the golf course into 18 individual hole competitions and gives the underdog an "I've got nothing to lose" perspective, which emboldens them. Each hole represents a new individual competition unto itself. Match play rules automatically change a golfer's perspective. It's easier to access the present moment. Once the hole is over, regardless of the outcome, you reboot to a new hole competition on the next tee.

I won my first match against my good friend Mike Reid in the first round, which was a big deal for me. Mike Reid was a well-established player on the PGA Tour and a fellow BYU Golf Team player who had been a few years ahead of me at BYU. My good play continued into the second round, when I took out Curtis Strange in the morning round and then Allen Miller in the afternoon third round match. My fourth round match ended on the 20th hole in a sudden-death playoff against Ben Crenshaw. Despite losing to Ben, one of the "big names" on Tour, the week represented a big step for me, one that boosted my confidence, an important aspect of my professional development.

In 1984, Jim Nelford was going through a difficult divorce, and we decided to rent a two-bedroom property and base ourselves out of Palm Desert, CA. In spite of his personal challenges, Nelford was continuing his great play.

Bing Crosby National Pro-Am, February 2-5, 1984

Purse: $400,000

Pebble Beach GL, Cypress Point GC, and Spyglass Hill GC, Pebble Beach, CA

Place: T33rd

Score: 74-73-70-72

Made: $2,025.00

After I missed the cuts in the previous three events (Bob Hope Classic, Phoenix Open, and Andy Williams San Diego Open), Nelford and I headed up to Pebble Beach for the Crosby, once again rooming together. Every year at the Crosby, Nelford and I went to Cypress Point to play a practice round early Monday morning.

Hale Irwin's Bounce

Nelford had been playing so well that many Tour players, including me, thought Jim was on the verge of winning his first PGA Tour event. It just seemed a matter of time. I had made the cut at the Crosby and finished T33rd, shooting 74-73-70-75. Nelford, on the other hand, was surging and got himself into contention heading into the final round on Sunday. My Sunday tee time was pretty early so upon finishing, I went straight back to our hotel room to watch the final round on network TV, thinking Nelford was going to win this thing.

I sat on the edge of the hotel room bed watching the last few holes be played on the CBS telecast. Nelford's first three rounds were 67-73-70, which got him into contention. In the final round Nelford shot 68 and got in the house with a one-shot lead. There was only one player left on the golf course who had any chance to catch Nelford, Hale Irwin, who was standing on the 18th tee at Pebble Beach. Nelford was watching from behind the 18th green, anxiously waiting for Irwin to play his final hole on one of the most iconic finishing holes in golf.

Irwin pull-hooked his tee shot on the 18th, and I could see his disgust at his own shot in his body language. Luckily for Irwin, the ocean's tide was out, and his ball hit a rock and rather than splashing into Stillwater Cove, Irwin's tee shot ricocheted 90 degrees back onto the fairway. This miraculous turn of events for Irwin was catastrophic for Nelford. Walking off the 18th tee, Hale held his hands together over his head in a praying, as if to say, "Thank you, Lord." Irwin proceeded to hit the pin with his 8-iron third shot and went on to make birdie on the final hole to force a sudden-death playoff with Nelford.

The second hole of sudden death was on Pebble Beach's 16th hole. The 16th hole at Pebble is typically played with a 3-wood off the tee, which would leave you with a short iron for your second shot. Nelford drove it perfectly off the tee, which left him with a short iron to the green. Hale then proceeds to hit his 3-wood off the tee fat, which popped the ball straight up and didn't carry the fairway bunker 150 yards off the tee. Once again, things seem to be in Nelford's favor with another poor tee shot from Irwin. Hale stood in a fairway bunker with a 2-iron in his hand and made a miraculous shot from the bunker, which looked like it had a chance to go in the hole for a two. Irwin's second shot came to rest 8 feet from the hole, and with Irwin's steel focus, he made his birdie putt to win and prevent Nelford from winning his first PGA Tour event.

Unfortunately for Nelford this turned out to be one of his last opportunities to win a PGA Tour event—a genuine heartbreaker for Jim Nelford.

My cycle of good and poor play continued, and I once again found myself in a gutter, missing the next four cuts in a row (Hawaiian Open, Los Angeles Open, Honda Classic, and Doral-Eastern Open). Once again, I was getting dejected about my game. I felt like I was in trouble and didn't know what to do. With more questions than answers, I prepared for the Bay Hill Classic.

Bay Hill Classic—March 15-18, 1984

Purse: $400,000

Bay Hill Club & Lodge, Orlando, FL

Place: T55th

Score: 78-67-74-71

Made: $916.00

Moe Norman Introduces Me to Clay Edwards

My poor play continued when I opened with a first-round 78 at Bay Hill. I was now at my wits' end and had no clue what to do. After that first round, I headed back to the practice range to attempt to figure things out. I recall hitting 3-irons on the range without any purpose. As I glanced back behind the ropes, in the gallery, I saw Moe Norman watching.

Immediately, I thought, *Moe can help me*. So, I headed straight over and engaged with him. I noticed but didn't know the fellow standing at Moe's side. I said, "Moe, I need your help. I am hitting it like shit. I'm in serious trouble." Moe said, "This guy can help you," pointing to the guy standing beside him. I looked at "this guy," didn't know who he was, and I wasn't at all interested when he said to me, "I'll take care of you." In that moment, I thought, *I don't want another golf swing lesson*, but I didn't want to be rude, so I went back to Moe with, "Moe, I need your help?" Moe once again said, "Clay will take care of you." Moe clearly wanted his friend Clay to help me.

With Moe's last comment, this Clay fellow was under the ropes in a flash, saying, "Let's go—I'll take care of you." I said, "Okay, let's try it out." As we walked back to my spot on the range, I was not able to say "no" to this guy, so I asked him, "Where you from?" He said, "Clay Edwards" with a deep Texas drawl. "I am the head pro at Victoria CC in Victoria, Texas, and also a member of Bay Hill." So I thought to myself, *Well, Moe doesn't just let anyone into his world, so this Clay Edwards fellow must be good.*

As I settled into my spot, I grabbed my 3-iron again and started hitting shots under the eye of Clay Edwards. After hitting three or four shots, I said, "What do you think?" I went right back to that golf lesson experience I had with Ben Doyle, and I was not looking forward to a repeat. This Clay Edwards fellow seemed to be around my age, so I thought, *What can he know that can help me?*

The words that came out of Clay's mouth were, "On your next shot, through impact, I want you to stress the shaft—compress the ball—down your target line—as long as you can."

With Clay's directives, and my mind locked in, I found it easy to visualize "stressing the shaft—compressing the ball—down my target line—as long as I could." I immediately flushed the most perfect 3-iron shot I ever hit. The ball flew straight, higher in flight, and landed softer than any 3-iron I had ever hit before. In that moment, I connected with a perfect shot. Those few words resonated immediately. Shot after shot, I dug into stressing the shaft—compressing the ball—down my target line—as long as I could. I instantly felt control of my path, my clubface, and low point on my line of compression. It felt so simple, like throwing a ball or shooting a rifle. My ball flight pattern, on the range, instantly changed and tightened up with Clay's few words.

Needless to say, I was seriously impressed with Clay Edwards's words on the driving range that afternoon and how it immediately impacted my performance. Clay followed me during the second round, where I shot 67 before he had to catch a flight back to Houston. Prior to leaving Bay Hill Clay said, "If you really want to get your game to the next level, you should consider spending a week with me at my home in Victoria, Texas, and we can get all parts of your game sharp."

Since Clay Edwards had such a positive and immediate impact on my performance, I definitely wanted to dig in deeper with him. After

Clay Edwards watching the flight of Zokol's tee shot on tour.
Getty Images: Dick Loek

Bay Hill, I played the next three weeks at the USF&G Classic in New Orleans, then the Players Championship, and the Greater Greensboro Open. Once those three events were over and since I would not be in the field for either the Masters or the Sea Pines Heritage Classic, I decided to head back to Palm Springs the week of the Masters for a week off. I would take up Clay's offer and head to Victoria, TX, to work with him the week of Sea Pines Heritage Classic before getting back on Tour with the Houston Coca-Cola Open.

My Week in Victoria, TX

When I landed at Houston's Intercontinental Airport, Clay was there to meet me at the arrival gate. We grabbed my luggage and took off southbound on US Route 59 for the two-hour drive to Victoria, TX.

We arrived in Victoria and settled into Clay's home. It was early in the evening, and Clay said, "I am off to bed and will get you up in the morning and we can head over to the golf course." I said, "Excellent."

I awoke with Clay opening the door to my room saying, "Get up, don't shower, we're heading straight to the course." I looked at the clock and it was 4:30 AM and I thought to myself, *Geez, this guy is different.* I got dressed and walked outside, and it was pitch black as we got into Clay's car and headed to Victoria CC.

Not knowing what was going on at zero-dark-thirty I asked, "Is there a place to grab a coffee?" Clay said to me, "We'll get coffee after you putt." I curiously asked, "Why's that?" and Clay said, "I want you to wake up with your senses and attention on your putting." We arrived at Victoria CC in the dark. Clay said, "Take your putter and one ball and start putting on that green over there. I will be in the pro shop." I headed to the putting green and started putting with only one golf ball. Clay said, "I don't want you practicing with more than one ball. You never get a second chance on the golf course, so why use more than one ball when practicing? You start practicing the wrong things with more than one ball. You need to practice the way you play." Okay, I liked that.

I headed over to the putting green as light started to show on the eastern horizon. The green had some significant undulations, and the grass was Common Bermuda, which means it has significant grain. The humidity was high and dew formed on the grass. Putts that are downhill and down grain are extremely fast, and putts that are uphill and against the grain are extremely slow. To putt well, you need to identify the grain and get a sense for how the grain will affect the roll of the golf ball. This grain thing on Bermuda grass was an enigma to me.

At this point, daylight was starting to happen, making it easier to see, and I desperately needed a coffee. Clay walked back to the putting green and asked, "How's it going?" I said, "Well, I can barely see, it's dark, I can't pick up on the grain on these Bermuda greens, and I need a coffee." Clay then said, "Let me see how you putt." He went on, "I want you to putt each putt like you are in a tournament, starting with reading the putt and executing your shot routine." So, I went through each individual putt, reading the putt, lining it up from behind, looking on the other side of the putt if need be, then I went through my shot routine and executed the putt. It was blatantly clear that I was not picking up on the speed or the break on these Common Bermuda greens.

Clay watched me putt for about five minutes. Then Clay said to me, "All great putters start with reading the greens effectively. You cannot be a great putter without being able to read the greens. You are lining your putts up, but you are not feeling the putt. With each putt, you need to *assemble the feel* of this putt. It starts with building on what your senses pick up on, walking around the putt, looking at and feeling the slope with your feet, looking at the grain, and assembling the feel, gathering information from your other senses."

I asked Clay, "How do you read the grain of the green?" Clay said, "You can tell which way the grain is going by looking at the cup. When they punch in a new hole, you should be able to notice a sharp-edge cut on one side of the hole and a rough-edge cut on the opposite side. The grain goes in the direction of the sharp edge to the rough edge of the hole."

Clay continued, "Can you feel the firmness of the ground through your feet as you walk around the putt? Can you pick up on the friction of the ball as it rolls? Notice how the grain will affect the ball struck at different speeds. Put all your attention on assembling the feel of this putt right now. Practice your putting to spots on the green rather than holes to feel the pace you need to strike this putt at. It's not a logical thing—it's a feel thing. When you've got this sense of feel you assembled, go into your shot routine and *pull the trigger on the sense of feel you assembled.*"

We putted for over an hour as the morning sun came up and the morning fog in my mind started to clear. Clay then said, "Let's go get some coffee." As we sat in his office in the back of his shop with coffee in hand, Clay said, "Every morning, the first thing I want you to do is wake up, put a putter in your hand, and assemble the feel of a putt. You can putt on a rug or on a linoleum floor . . . it doesn't matter as long as you start with assembling the feel and pulling the trigger on the feel of each putt."

I had never heard a golf instructor talk like this, or think like this. Later, I came to realize Clay was studying the track of the ball and my footprints in the morning dew during this dance around the hole. After our coffee, I went back to the putting green and started practicing to assemble the feel and pulling the trigger with each putt using one golf ball. I spent that whole day on the putting green and immediately started to get the hang of it.

The next morning, Clay again woke me up at 4:30 AM, and we repeated the same schedule. The only difference was I now knew what was going on, and I was now all in on this way to improve my putting—it made complete sense to me.

The next day, after repeating this putting ritual, Clay took me to his favorite mom-and-pop TexMex restaurant for lunch. After lunch we started to hit shag balls. Under the watchful eye of Clay Edwards, we worked on incorporating "the sense of feel" into my shot routine for all shots. This fit perfectly with my biofeedback work with Dr. Richard Lonetto. We spent the rest of the week reinforcing my new perception to assembling the feel and pulling the trigger in all my shots. Clay also wanted me to use his custom-made T.P. Mills putter. I did and started to putt great. I didn't know it at the time, but Clay Edwards and I would become like brothers. His family was like family; Clay also caddied for me on many occasions. Clay has caddied for me in Tour events, US Opens, and PGA Tour Q-Schools. As a caddie, he was also able to give me advice during play, which a coach or an instructor cannot.

Houston Coca-Cola Open—April 26-29, 1984

Purse: $500,000

Woodlands CC (West Course), Woodlands, TX

Place: 69th

Score: 74-68-74-77

Made: $1,010.00

I recall getting paired with Greg Norman in the first two rounds, and I opened with 74-68, while Norman shot 68-71. My mind was completely focused on trying to implement what Clay Edwards taught me, and I knew there was going to be a period of adaptation. I went on to shoot 74-77 on the weekend in Houston.

I missed the cut at Congressional and started to prepare for the Sectional Qualifying for the US Open, which was a 36-hole one-day qualifying. The qualifying site was East Orange Golf Club in Short Hills, New Jersey. I am not able to recall the scores of my two rounds, but I do recall having to go into a sudden-death playoff for the first few alternate spots for the US Open. And I got that alternate spot. The way I figured, starting the next Monday as first alternate of the US Open, I had a good chance. Someone would likely WD, and I'd get in.

Manufacturers Hanover Westchester Classic–June 7-10, 1984

Purse: $500,000

Westchester CC, Harrison, NY

Place: T46th

Score: 71-72-71-72

Made: $1,337.14

US Open–June 14-17, 1984

Purse: $602,324

Winged Foot GC, Mamaroneck, NY

Qualifying: 1st Alternate

Nelford successfully got through the qualifying at East Orange, NJ, and we arrived to play a practice round at Winged Foot first thing Monday morning. As Nelford was registering at the registration desk, I informed the other person at the desk that I was the first alternate in the championship, and if there were any updates on a player WDing, I would be on the golf course playing a practice round. The person on the other side of the registration desk proceeded to say, "You cannot play on the course if you are not in the field." This comment completely shocked me, and I replied back to them, "As first alternate, there's a good probability that I will get into the tournament, and I will be playing a practice round. If you want to deny me from playing a practice round, you will have to take me off the golf course by force."

Nelford and I played a practice round at Winged Foot without incident, and I am pretty sure they changed the rules to allow up to five alternate players to practice on the site at future US Opens.

Tuesday and Wednesday came and went without any WDs, and all entrants had registered. I was left ready to play, sitting on the first tee at 6:45 AM, waiting. On Thursday, I arrived at Winged Foot at 6:00 AM and let the USGA official know that I was on site and ready, willing and able to go if anyone withdrew, then headed into the locker room for breakfast. I sat down at a large circular table in the men's grill with a bunch of players, including Fuzzy Zoeller. Someone asked me, "What time you teeing off?" I said, "I'm the first alternate. Are any of you guys considering not playing?" That's when Fuzzy piped up and said, "My back has been acting up on me again, and I'm

50/50. I am going to the range to see how it's feeling, and if it's bothering me too much, you can have my spot." Things were looking up! I had some breakfast and then made my way to the range to hit some balls and to see how Fuzzy was making out. After Fuzzy warmed up, he said, "Zokol, my back is feeling pretty good this morning. Sorry I can't help you out." Fuzzy went on to win the 1984 US Open, and I never got the chance to tee it up.

Georgia-Pacific Atlanta Classic—June 21-24, 1984

Purse: 400,000

Atlanta CC, Mariette, GA

Place: T15th

Score: 69-73-66-72

Made: $6,000.00

Things started to fall into place on the golf course. Clay Edwards came out for two weeks to Atlanta and then to Toronto for the Canadian Open. We started to get some real traction. In Atlanta, I finished T15th shooting 69-73-66-72 and made $6,000.00. For a period of time through that summer, my best friend Russ Jordan came out on Tour and caddied for me. It was great to have him on the bag for a few weeks.

The Canadian Open—June 28-July 1, 1984

Purse: CAD $525,000

Glen Abbey GC, Oakville ON

Place: T5th

Score: 69-74-71-70

Made: $14,050.00

When Clay came to the 1984 Canadian Open, it started a ritual at the Canadian Open with Moe Norman. On that Tuesday afternoon, we were on the range hitting balls. Clay saw Moe in the gallery and said to me, "There's Moe." So I walked over to Moe and lifted up the rope, inviting him in. Moe was a bit hesitant, then I mentioned, "Clay has come up from Texas, and we want you to come over and visit with us." Moe was always a bit reluctant. I headed back to my spot and started hitting balls again. Moe wandered up, and the next thing you know, Moe was standing next to Clay and Russ, and Clay and Moe were exchanging pleasantries. I thanked Moe for introducing Clay to me earlier in the year at Bay Hill.

After a few shots, I said, "Moe, hit a few shots for us." Moe said, "Oh no, I can't do that, they would throw me out on my ear." I said, "No, they won't," and I continued to hit a few more balls. The next thing I did was step out of the spot where I was hitting balls and simply pass my 5-iron to Moe. He automatically stepped into my spot and started hitting balls while I stepped back beside Clay and Russ and watched. Moe went into his routine, "I eat the golf course for breakfast—just like bacon and eggs." I went to get two more buckets of brand new Titleist balls and added them to Moe's pile.

I then cruised up and down the line, telling the other players in the tournament, "Moe Norman is hitting balls and you need to see this." The crowd of Tour players started to gather around Moc, who was in his element—performing in front of PGA Tour players. Everyone wanted to watch Moe hit balls.

This was the start of what became an annual happening when Moe Norman showed up at the Canadian Open at Glen Abbey and put on his little clinic on Tuesdays of the Canadian Open.

Russ Jordan, my best friend who caddied for me in the summer of 1984.

Moe Norman on the Range early in the week at Glen Abbey during the Canadian Open.

When Is a Canadian Going to Win the Canadian Open?

The 1984 Canadian Open was a big breakthrough for me with Clay in my head and Russ on my bag. Every year at the Canadian Open, the few Canadians on the PGA Tour shouldered the brunt of the questions, the most common being, "When is a Canadian going to win the Canadian Open?" Thank goodness Nick Taylor made this question go away by winning the 2023 RBC Canadian Open, at least for the time being.

At the start of the week, Jim "Shaky" Hunt who was an iconic Toronto-based sports columnist and who spent over 50 years covering the biggest events in sports including the NHL, the NFL, the Olympics, all of the golf Majors, and the Canadian Open, came out with his column in the *Toronto Star* stating, "Canadians Have Two Chances to Win the Canadian Open—Slim and None!" Hunt's article went on about how the Canadian players on the PGA Tour can't respond to the pressure of playing well in their own national title. Well that really pissed me and the other Canadian PGA Tour players off.

After the first round, Nick Price opened with a 67 and led by two shots over Larry Rinker and me with our 69s to share second place. Being in second meant a trip to the media room for the post-round press conference. So, I settled into my seat in front of the media and the first thing that came out of my mouth was, "Who said Canadians can't play well at the Canadian Open?" I look straight at Jim Hunt.

I played well that week, getting into contention. Greg Norman went on to win and denied Jack Nicklaus his first Canadian Open victory. I shot rounds of 69-74-72-70 to finish in T5th, making $14,050.00, which was the second biggest check of my career at that point. I was the first Canadian to play well in a couple of decades.

I recall playing in the third-to-last group on Sunday. Jack Nicklaus and Greg Norman, who were playing in the final group, were playing their second shots from the 17th fairway at Glen Abbey, and I was putting for birdie on the 18th green. When I rolled my birdie putt in on the 18th green, a huge roar went up in the massive partisan of Canadians surrounding the 18th green. The roar was so loud that it backed Nicklaus off his second shot on the 17th fairway. That rarely happens to Jack. Jack usually does that to others. Norman, on the other hand, hit his second shot on 17, 30 yards

Moe hitting balls at the Canadian Open at Glen Abbey in front of PGA Tour players. Clay Edwards on the right.

Zokol using Clay Edwards's custom-built T.P. Mills putter in the '84 Canadian Open.

right of the green into a temporary parking lot that had an out-of-bounds stake missing, which made his ball not out of bounds. He got very lucky in that situation and won the tournament.

A Wonderful Gesture from Payne Stewart

Finishing T5th in the Canadian Open was a real big deal, and I had Clay Edwards to thank. What we accomplished since meeting at Bay Hill earlier in the year was a monumental shift. Later that Sunday evening, while staying in the Howard Johnson in Oakville on the QEW, my little entourage of Clay Edwards, Russ Jordan, and Peter Radiuk, who came in from Vancouver for the week, went down to the bar to celebrate. We ordered drinks and were having a good time when Payne Stewart came walking in and noticed our little celebration. Payne was one of those guys who didn't like missing any reason to celebrate. He went up to the bar and purchased a couple of bottles of champagne. He then came over and plunked the two bottles down on our table, saying, "Zoke, great playing in your country's national championship. I want to buy you guys a drink. Sorry, I can't stay and join you guys, but just want to say great playing." A very thoughtful gesture on Payne's part.

Sammy Davis Jr. Greater Hartford Open—July 26-29, 1984

Purse: $400,000

TPC of Connecticut, Cromwell, CT

Place: T28th

Score: 70-74-68-72

Made: $2,720.00

Playing with Player

My game was really starting to take shape, and in the third round at Hartford I got paired with Gary Player. Player had just finished a five-year sabbatical from the PGA Tour. He was 49 years old and was preparing for the PGA Senior Tour.

Getting paired with any big name was always a great experience for younger aspiring players. Playing with Gary Player is like getting paired with Jack Nicklaus or Arnold Palmer. That day, I met Gary on the tee, and he was full of inspiration. I can assure you, top players like Nicklaus, Palmer, Player, and Trevino absolutely know how their presence impacts young aspiring players.

Gary Player was one of the most ambitious people on this planet. He always has been and always will be to his last day. It didn't matter if it was physical fitness, nutrition, or developing a better mindset—Gary Player has always been a strong advocate for improvement and was a wonderful example of physical and mental health.

For whatever reason, Gary Player took a shine to me that day. He shot 69 while I bettered him with a 68. On the back nine, Gary started to open up and ask me questions. He said to me, "Richard, I like how you play. Where did you learn the game?" When Player asked me this question, I immediately felt proud that a legend in the game took notice of my game. I could not have gotten a better compliment. I didn't have the nerve to tell him I'd been playing well for about 20 minutes and said, "My mentor in Canada was Alvie Thompson, but most recently Moe Norman introduced me to this great instructor named Clay Edwards from Texas. I went to Clay's home in Texas for a week a few months ago, and he really turned my game around." Gary Player said, "Yes, I know Alvie Thompson, he along with George Knudson, Stan Leonard, and Al Balding were great Canadian players. Tell me about the young man who has helped you so much recently—I'd like to know more of this Clay Edwards lad?"

So I go on about how poorly I was playing earlier this year and how I was looking for help from Moe at Bay Hill. I told him, "Moe said to me, 'This guy will help you,' pointing to Clay Edwards. When Moe said that, Clay was under the rope in an instant. I hit a few balls for him to look at my action, and the first thing he said to me was, 'I want you to stress the shaft—compress the ball—down your target line—as long as you can.' With those thoughts in mind, I started to flush the ball. Then I went to his home for a week to learn how to putt. He gets me out of bed at 4:30 AM, and he gets me putting before I could wake up—he wants me putting each morning as my senses were beginning to wake up."

Gary Player said, "I like the sound of this young man. Is he coming out on the road with you anytime soon?" I said, "Yes, as a matter of fact, Clay came out to the Canadian Open and is coming back out for the PGA Championship at Shoal Creek in a few weeks." Player said, "I will be at the PGA. Do you think he'd be willing to work with me at Shoal Creek?" I said, "I'm sure he would love the opportunity to work with you. Do you want me to make arrangements?" Player said, "Yes, indeed, please make arrangements for Clay to meet me on Shoal Creek's driving range at 8:00 AM Monday morning the week of the PGA."

Early that evening, I gave Clay a call to tell him, "Gary Player wants a lesson with you. You need to be on the driving range to introduce yourself to him at 8:00 AM on Monday at Shoal Creek." Clay said, "Tell Mr. Player, I will be there."

The next day, I confirmed with Gary Player that Clay Edwards would be at Shoal Creek at 8:00 AM, and I would make the introduction.

Danny Thomas Memphis Classic—August 2-5, 1984

Purse: $500,000

Colonial CC, Cordova, TN

Place: T18th

Score: 70-73-72-73

Made: $6,085.00

The Utah State Open—A Win is a Win

Before the Danny Thomas Memphis Classic, I applied to the PGA Tour commissioner for a release from the Buick Open to play in the Utah Open. All PGA Tour members sign their rights over to the PGA Tour as a Condition of Membership. If a PGA Tour member wants to play in any other event that conflicts with the dates of any PGA Tour event, they are not allowed to play unless they receive a release from Commissioner Deane Beman. Beman gave me a release from the PGA Tour's Buick Open to play in the Utah Open.

Utah State Open—August 10-12, 1984

Purse: $80,000

Willow Creek CC, Sandy, UT

Place: 1st

Score: 69-67-69

Made: $10,000 (plus a 1984 Ford Bronco, which I sold back to the dealership for $12,000)

The 1984 Utah Open was my second professional victory. Playing back in Utah was a bit of a homecoming for me. I hadn't been back to Utah for a couple of years since our 1981 NCAA Championship victory.

Name	Scores
Richard Zokol	**69-67-69–205**
Mike Reid	67-69-70–206
Tom Costello	67-69-70–206
Bob Betley	69-75-65–209
Keith Clearwater	70-70-69–209

Name	Scores
Bill Garrett	74-67-71–212
Dave Desantis	71-73-70–214
Larry Webb	72-70-72–214
Jimmy Blair	75-73-67–215
Ray Stewart	74-69-72–215
Rick Fehr	69-74-73–215

The Utah State Open was one of the bigger State Opens, along with the Colorado State Open, and it attracted many great players who weren't on the PGA Tour. Past winners of the Utah Open were Mike Reid, Jay Don Blake, Jimmy Blair, Tom Costello, Ray Arinno, Bob Betley, Mike Brannan, Mike Malaska, Dennis Paulson, and Buddy Allin before it became a Korn Ferry Tour event.

In the final round, it was a real BYU battle: I shot 69 and finished at 11 under par to fend off defending champion Mike Reid and my close buddy Tom Costello by one shot.

PGA Championship—August 16–19, 1984

Purse: $700,000

Shoal Creek CC, Birmingham, AL

Place: T39th

Score: 74-74-70-73

Made: $2,505.56

I got tied up in Salt Lake City with the obligations that come with a victory in the Utah State Open; my plans to get to Birmingham and subsequently Shoal Creek got delayed until late Monday. It meant I wouldn't be there Monday morning to introduce Clay Edwards to Gary Player at 8:00 AM on the driving range, and Clay would be on his own to get into Shoal Creek. They didn't have PGA Tour coaches' credentials in those days.

Clay Edwards and his friend, Harry Garrison, drove 792 miles, 12 hours, from Victoria, TX, to Shoal Creek in Birmingham, AL, through the night. They arrived and caught a couple hours sleep in the parking lot at Shoal Creek, and Clay met Gary Player on the putting green at 8:00 AM on Monday. Clay actually had to sneak onto the property. He approached

Gary Player, and when he shook Gary's hand, he said, "I'm here to fix your game." They spent a significant amount of time on and around the putting green on Monday.

Then on Tuesday, Clay and Gary Player worked on the driving range, then back onto the short game area. They had an instant connection.

On Tuesday afternoon, I arrived on site at Shoal Creek, fresh off my Utah Open victory, full of confidence. This PGA Championship was my first major championship, and I was excited to play. I reconnected with Clay, and we proceeded to the first tee at Shoal Creek to play a practice round. As we turned the corner to the tee, I saw Jim King by himself on the tee preparing to tee off. He didn't see me coming, and I did an immediate about-face and got the hell out of there. I said to my caddie and Clay, "Jim King on the tee, let's go play the back nine." We walked to the 10th tee just in time to find Tom Watson and Arnold Palmer, playing as a twosome, making the turn. I asked if I could join them, and they happily invited me to play along.

Before things got underway in the first round, I was able to connect with Gary Player in the locker room to ask about how things went with Clay Edwards. Gary said, "I very much liked how that young man thinks and goes about his business. He gave me some good directions with my swing thoughts and short game technique. I think he's a fine young instructor." Clay had just turned 27, and Player was 49.

Not that Gary Player needed others to help him play. Gary finished second to Lee Trevino that week at Shoal Creek, shooting rounds of 74-63-69-71—277. Gary Player's amazing major championship record saw him earn nine major wins and six runner-up finishes. Player's first and second place finishes in major championships spanned 25 years, from the 1959 British Open to the 1984 PGA Championship. Clay Edwards was thrilled to have played a small role with Gary Player. That 63 shot by Player in the second round was Gary Player's lowest score shot on American soil over his entire PGA Tour career.

T-Bird Lost My Putter in the Middle of the Bloody Round

Tommy Williams, aka "T-Bird," was caddying for me again, and we were on the sixth hole in the first round of the PGA Championship. As we approached the green after hitting the green with my second shot, I asked T-Bird for my putter. T-Bird couldn't find the putter with his one hand, so he put the bag down to get a better view. He rifled through the bag, and said, "Zoke, I can't find your putter." I said something to the effect of, "What the fuck do you mean you can't find the putter?" So now I started looking through the bag too. "Fuck T-Bird, what have you done now?"

We tried to backtrack in our minds to the previous hole when I last used the putter, but we still couldn't figure out what happened to it. I called in the PGA officials to let them know what was happening while time was ticking away, and pace of play needed to continue. After about 10 minutes, still with no idea where my putter was, my attention had to shift to my eight-foot putt for birdie that I now had to navigate without a putter. I thought, *What the hell am I going to use?* So I immediately grabbed a few clubs and started trying to figure it out . . . I pulled out my 3-iron—too long, I pulled out my 9-iron—too much loft, I pulled out my 5-iron and figured that it would have to do. I then made a stance with a few practice putting strokes, shutting down the loft and playing the ball way back in my stance, trying to find and feel for the low point of my stroke. When I got over the ball, because I played the ball so far back outside my stance, my eyes were much closer to the hole than usual in relation to my ball position. I could see the line perfectly as my eyes were between the ball and the hole. I executed this makeshift stroke with this 5-iron and made the putt for birdie.

A caddie's biggest nightmare is to lose their player's putter in a tournament, let alone in a major championship. As I handed the 5-iron back to T-Bird, he said with a big shit-eating grin on his face and in his New England inflection, "Zoke, you can make it with anything." My reply was, "Don't even think about trying to fucking weasel out of this."

By the time we got to the next hole, we still had no clue what happened to my putter, and I didn't know what to think. I needed to proceed with the same putting method using my 5-iron. On the next hole, I 2-putted for par. As I walked down to the hole after that, T-Bird was keeping his distance from me. I noticed a PGA official driving toward me in a golf cart with a golf club in his hand. He said, "Did you lose this?" I looked at it and said, "Yes, I did. Where did you find it?" The official said, "The volunteer by the fifth green found it right beside the bunker."

As I handed the putter to T-Bird, I said, "They found the putter beside the greenside bunker on 5." I thought back to the fifth green, where I had a bunker shot, which I hit to a couple inches from the hole. T-Bird handed me the putter, and I walked up and tapped it in, then gave the putter back to T-Bird before the other players in the group read their putts, and before T-Bird went back to rake the bunker. Apparently, T-Bird tossed the putter back to the bag lying beside the bunker, and I guess the putter bounced off the bag and flopped into the deep rough beside the golf bag. After T-Bird finished raking, he went back to the bag, and the length of the rough was so long, it covered up the putter. T-Bird didn't notice and walked off, leaving the putter behind.

Playing with Jack on Sunday

Saturday evening, when I called in for my Sunday tee time, it went like this: "Hello, it's Richard Zokol, and I am looking for my Sunday tee time." The person on the other line told me the time. I said, "Thank you, and can you tell me who I am playing with?" They said, "Yes, you are paired with Jack Nicklaus and . . ." I couldn't comprehend anything after I heard *Jack Nicklaus*. I thought to myself, *I am playing with Jack fucking Nicklaus in a major championship on Sunday . . . how cool is that?*

The rough at Shoal Creek that week was the highest rough I had ever seen. I can still recall my tee shot on the 18th hole that found the rough about three feet from the edge of the fairway. I had to part the grass with my hands to identify my golf ball. Once I pulled my hand away, the grass completely covered the ball. I could not see any white of my golf ball, the rough was so thick. With all of my might, using my sand wedge, I swung as hard as I could to advance my ball three feet back to the fairway.

It was great to play with Jack Nicklaus on Sunday in a major championship; the ovations the gallery gave Jack as he approached the 18th green were an amazing experience . . . and yes, Jack made birdie on the 18th hole on Sunday.

After the PGA Championship in Birmingham was over, and since we were in the neighborhood, Clay suggested we go see T.P. Mills. Clay gave

T.P. a call and he said to drop by his shop on the way back to Victoria. I jumped in the car with Clay and Harry Garrison and off we went west to Tuscaloosa. It was a real pleasure meeting and visiting with T.P. Mills and his son, and spending a little time in his workshop. I ordered two T.P. Mills custom-made putters.

Panasonic Las Vegas Invitational—September 19-23, 1984

Purse: $1,122,500

Las Vegas CC, Desert Inn CC, Showboat CC, Tropicana CC, Las Vegas, NV

Place: T66th

Score: 75-70-65-73-73

Made: $1,845.00

Southern Open—October 11-14, 1984

Purse: $300,000

Green Island CC, Columbus, GA

Place: T26th

Score: 70-69-70-68

Made: $2,355.00

Walt Disney World Golf Classic—October 18-21, 1984

Purse: $400,000

Magnolia Course, Palm Course, and Lake Buena Vista Course, Orlando, FL

Place: T74th

Score: 67-72-68-78

Made: $756.00

Hassan II Golf Trophy

Hassan II Golf Trophy—November 1984

Royal Golf Dar Es Salam, Rabat, Morocco

The Hassan II Golf Trophy was a Pro-Am played during the off-season. The King of Morocco established a close relationship with Billy Casper and the Harman family back in the late 1960s. In fact, after spending a few years in the US Army and seeing duty in Vietnam, and after Butch spent a few years trying to play on the PGA Tour, Butch Harman became the Head Pro of Royal Golf Dar Es Salam in 1973 and the personal pro to the King. That same year began a long history of PGA Tour players playing in this event.

The flight on the King's Royal Air Maroc took off from New York to Casablanca full of PGA Tour players and amateur players and their wives. The whole plane was chartered for this event, and everyone on this flight was participating in the 1984 Hassan II Trophy. I remember meeting Neil Armstrong, the first man on the moon, on the flight.

The tournament was three rounds, and Roger Maltbie won the event in a sudden-death playoff over Bruce Fleisher and me, at 3 under par. Roger won the jewel-encrusted Moroccan dagger called a Jambiya as the trophy.

After the week of playing golf and having dinner as a large group, I got to know many of the people there, and soon we all became good friends. On the flight back from Casablanca to New York a week later, the event director and his wife decided they wanted to join the Mile High Club. The director made the mistake of telling his buddy, who was part of our group. Prior to taking off, the event director's friend (I cannot remember his name) started to tell everyone the director and his wife's plans. He told everyone to keep an eye out for this, and when it happens, when they come out of the washroom, we should give them a standing ovation for joining this illustrious club.

As soon as the flight took off and levelled off at cruising altitude, the wife got out of her seat, heading for the washroom at the back of the plane. A few minutes later, the event director got up and did the same, sneaking into the same washroom as his wife. A few minutes after the door closed, the event director's buddy got on the plane's PA system and announced to all on the plane, even those in the washroom, that they were currently in the process of becoming members of the Mile High Club and that we should applaud them when they're done.

After some time, he stepped out and walked back to his seat with a grin from ear to ear, everyone giving applause. After what must have seemed like an eternity, the wife finally stepped out of the washroom, embarrassed to say the least. Her hands covered her face as she made her way back to her seat, while everyone on the flight gave her a standing ovation.

Chrysler Team Invitational—December 13-16, 1984

Purse: $400,000

Team: Jim Nelford/Richard Zokol

Boca West Resort & CC, Boca Raton, FL

Place: T7th

Score: 65-64-65-66

Made: $7,725,00

1984 PGA TOUR SEASON SUMMARY

Tournaments Entered	27
Cuts Made	14
Cut Missed	13
Top 10 finishes	2
Stroke Average	72.67
Driving Accuracy	T47th (.667)
Official Money Made	$56,605.00
Official Money List	97th on the 1984 Official PGA Tour Money List

Mike Barnett's CorpSport International

The week of the 1984 Chrysler Team Classic, Mike Barnett was in Florida watching his client Jim Nelford play. Barnett owned Edmonton-based CorpSport International and managed some of the top Canadian athletes. Mike's CorpSport International clients included Wayne Gretzky, Brett Hull, Paul Coffey, Sergei Fedorov, Jaromir Jagr, Joe Thornton, Mats Sundin, Lanny McDonald, Grant Fuhr, Marty McSorley, Alexander Mogilny, Owen Nolan, and Daniel and Henrik Sedin. In the golf world, Mike had Jim Nelford and Barb Bunkowsky. Other clients were Kurt Browning and Katarina Witt (ice skating), Willie de Wit (boxing), Matt Dunigan (football), Cody Snyder (rodeo), Steve Podborski, Brian Stemmle, Rob Boyd, and Karen Percy (skiing), and Karen Baldwin, Canada's first ever Miss Universe in 1982.

At this event, Mike asked me to join the CorpSport International Team. I felt honored to join Mike's agency, and he invited me to fly to Edmonton for a few days before flying home to Vancouver.

On December 17, 1984, I flew from Boca Raton, FL, to Edmonton, Alberta. I had only packed for warm Florida weather and had not anticipated going to Edmonton before heading back home to Vancouver. When I landed in Edmonton, the temperature was 45 below zero, and the only coat I had was a light suede jacket.

On December 18th, I walked into the CorpSport office in the LeMarchand Mansion to meet with Mike Barnett, and I was introduced to Joanie Kindrachuk, Mike's office administrator. We had an instant attraction to one another.

Later that day, Joanie invited me to her girlfriend Marea Evans's celebration of being named Model of the Year the next evening. I happily said yes, and that evening we fell in love. I had planned to only spend a couple days in Edmonton, but the more time I spent with Joanie the more I wanted to stay in Edmonton, despite the -45 degree weather. I spent four or five extra days in Edmonton.

Joanie and I committed to an exclusive long-distance relationship, with her living in Edmonton and me living on the road. Nelford and I gave up our rental property in Palm Springs, and Jim went to Scottsdale, AZ, when Mike Barnett got Nelford a representation agreement with a new golf course real estate development called Gainey Ranch.

Nelford went to Arizona, and I went back to Vancouver, BC.

CHAPTER 7

1985—Joanie Checks Out the PGA Tour—Jim Nelford's Boating Accident Almost Killed Him

At the start of 1985, things were going well. My golf game was starting to come around, and I had started this new relationship with Joanie Kindrachuk. The moment I met Joanie, I knew there was something special about her, and I was ready to establish the groundwork for a serious relationship. Joanie was just what I was looking for. She came from a small farming community outside Saskatoon, Saskatchewan, called Cudworth. She came from a wonderful loving family, and her aspirations revolved around family—she was very attractive and perfect from my perspective. We needed to see if things would work out considering my career was living on the road.

Bob Hope Classic—January 9-13, 1985

Purse: $500,000

Indian Wells, Bermuda Dunes, La Quinta, Tamarisk

Place: T31st

Score: 79-69-67-66-69

Made: $2,957.14

Joanie and I made arrangements for her to come out to a PGA Tour event for the Phoenix Open. If she was going to be the one, and I was pretty sure she was, she needed to see what this PGA Tour thing was all about. She flew from Edmonton to Phoenix on Friday, and she was scheduled to fly back to Edmonton on Sunday night. The problem was I missed the cut in the Phoenix Open. She wasn't able to see me play, but we went out to the tournament regardless so she could get a sense of what takes place at PGA Tour events.

Honda Classic—February 28–March 3, 1985

Purse: $500,000

TPC Eagle Trace, Coral Springs, FL

Place: T65th

Score: 70-71-77-73

Made: $1,040.00

USF&G Classic—March 14–17, 1985

Purse: $400,000

Lakewood CC, New Orleans, LA

Place: T11th

Score: 69-73-68

Made: $7,942.00

The Players Championship—March 28–31, 1985

Purse: $900,000

TPC Sawgrass, Ponte Vedra, FL

Place: T49th

Score: 71-75-70-77

Made: $2,199,00

Greater Greensboro Open—April 4–7, 1985

Purse: $400,000

Forest Oaks CC, Greensboro, NC

Place: T60th

Score: 73-75-73-79

Made: $848.00

Sea Pines Heritage Classic—April 18–21, 1985

Purse: $400,000

Harbour Town GL, Hilton Head Island, SC

Place: T17th

Score: 71-72-73-66
Made: $6,000.00

Houston Open—April 25-28, 1985
Purse: $500,000
TPC Woodlands, The Woodlands, TX
Place: T19th
Score: 71-72-72-69
Made: $6,060.00

Kemper Open—May 30-June 2, 1985
Purse: $500,000
Congressional CC, Bethesda, MD
Place: T39th
Score: 73-71-74-71
Made: $1,950.00

My first hole-in-one on the PGA Tour happened on the 12th hole at Congressional on the second round with a 4-iron.

Manufacturers Hanover Westchester Classic—June 6-9, 1985
Purse: $500,000
Westchester CC, Harrison, NY
Place: 75th
Score: 73-71-77-78
Made: $950.00

St. Jude Memphis Classic—June 27-30, 1985
Purse: $500,000
Colonial CC, Cordova, TN
Place: T14th
Score: 68-69-74-72
Made: $8,250.00

Canadian Open—July 4-7, 1985

Purse: CAD $480,000

Glen Abbey GC, Oakville, ON

Place: T18th

Score: 74-71-70-73

Made: $6,746.00

Even though Joanie flew down to the Phoenix Open earlier in the year, she didn't get a full sense of what it was like seeing me play in a PGA Tour event when I missed the cut, so I invited her to the Canadian Open in Oakville for the whole week in early July. Joanie accepted my invitation on the condition that she could bring her mother, Mary Kindrachuk. I thought that was a great idea; getting to know more about the Kindrachuk family, and having them learn about me, was important.

Joanie often tells the story about how her brother Brian, who was driving Joanie and her mother, Mary, to the airport to fly to Toronto, was trying to explain what some basic golf terms, like *birdie*, *par*, and *bogey*, meant. She didn't quite understand golf—yet. But after the week was over, Joanie had met a number of Tour wives in family dining and walking the golf course, which was interesting for her to say the least. There was one standout person that week that Joanie still remembers to this day: Sue Sindelar, who made Joanie feel welcomed. Tour wives can be a little standoffish to "girl friends" of single players, unless you are married—you're not in the club yet. Sue Sindelar, like her husband, Joey, just might be the two nicest people on this planet.

BC Open—August 28-September 1, 1985

Purse: $300,000

En-Joie Golf Club, Endicott, NY

Place: T35th

Score: 69-74-70-72

Made: $1,447.50

Greater Milwaukee Open—September 12-15, 1985

Purse: $300,000

Tuckaway CC, Franklin, WI

Place: T25th

Score: 74-70-71-69

Made: $2,146.67

Jim Nelford's Boating Accident

I will never forget the message I received from the PGA Tour to call Mike Barnett early that next week in Milwaukee—Jim Nelford had been in a boating accident in Scottsdale, AZ. Mike mentioned that the doctors may have to remove Jim's right arm.

> **Golfer Injured in Water Skiing Mishap**[4]
> ASSOCIATED PRESS
>
> SCOTTSDALE, Ariz.—Professional golfer Jim Nelford was listed in fair condition Monday at Scottsdale Memorial Hospital after suffering severe injuries in a boating accident a day earlier on Saguaro Lake.
>
> Nelford, 30, a native of Vancouver, British Columbia, had been water skiing and was struck by the boat when it made a pass to pick him up. Hospital officials said Nelford suffered severe cuts to his right arm, thigh and back.
>
> He underwent 2 ½ hours of surgery late Sunday night.
>
> Maricopa County sheriff's officials were investigating the accident, which happened near Burro Beach Cove.

Joanie and I had made arrangements for her to come to next week's Tour event, the Southwest Golf Classic in Abilene, TX. We made plans to travel to Scottsdale on Monday, September 23rd, to see Jim in the hospital and

4 *LA Times*, September 10, 1985.

then fly to Abilene the next day. Throughout the week, I kept hoping things would work out for Jim.

Southwest Golf Classic—September 19–22, 1985

Purse: $400,000

Fairway Oaks G&RC, Abilene, TX

Place: 4th

Score: 69-72-64-70

Made: $19,200.00

Joanie and I rendezvoused at the Phoenix airport on Monday. I flew in from Milwaukee, and Joanie flew in from Edmonton. We made our way to the hospital and met with Jim's parents, who had come down from Vancouver to be with Jim. When we walked into the hospital room Jim was in, Jim and I looked at each other. He looked horrible. I moved in to hug Jim. We embraced and held each other, and we both started to cry. We held each other for quite some time.

The mental trauma Nelford went through was significant. As he watched the speedboat coming straight at him, he tried to dunk under the boat so he wouldn't get hit, but his lifejacket resisted his efforts and kept him afloat. The boat hit him, and he got tangled up in the boat's propeller, which hit his right arm, turning it into hamburger. Luckily, the propeller missed his elbow. The propeller also tore up his lifejacket and cut into his back and right thigh. The doctors stated one of the options was to remove Nelford's arm. When Jim and I held each other, Jim kept saying, "They want to take my arm! I told my parents, 'Do not let them take my arm!'"

The doctors' biggest concern was infection once they learned the accident had happened on Saguaro Lake. Saguaro was notoriously polluted. So the first order of business was to hook Jim up to as many antibiotics as he could absorb to fight infection. His arm, and his life for that matter, depended on it.

Joanie and I flew out of Phoenix and arrived in Abilene for her first full week on the PGA Tour. Joanie got to meet Clay Edwards, who brought a whole bunch of folks up from Victoria, TX, to Abilene, TX, for the weekend. This time I made the cut.

Fairway Oaks was a really interesting property. The golf course routing had a creek running through it, and each side of the creek was in a different county. One county was dry (unable to sell liquor), and the other was wet (able to sell liquor). Since there was a large contingent in my gallery, my new Texas friends, someone in the group suggested that for every birdie I made, everyone in the group had to drink a beer at the start of the third round.

My tee time was relatively early on Saturday morning, and I shot 64—the whole group was sloshed by lunchtime; Joanie was toast for the rest of the day. That evening, the tournament put on a big Texas BBQ and Joanie and I were introduced to a person with the first name Garrett. I said to Joanie, "Let's call our firstborn male Garrett." In 1987, we did.

It was a great week all the way around in the West Texas wind. My ball-striking was effective, and I shot rounds of 69-72-64-70, finishing fourth.

Tee shot in Abilene, TX.

Texas Open—September 26-29, 1985

Purse: $350,000

Oak Hills CC, San Antonio, TX

Place: T42nd

Score: 69-71-73-72

Made: $1,190.00

Pensacola Open—October 17-20, 1985

Purse: $300,000

Perdido Bay Inn & CC, Pensacola, FL

Place: T41st

Score: 70-69-69-71

Made: $1,800.00

1985 PGA TOUR SEASON SUMMARY

Tournaments Entered	27
Cuts Made	16
Cut Missed	14
Top 10 finished	1 (4th Southwest Classic)
Stroke Average	72.01
Driving Accuracy	T24th (.701)
Official Money	**$71,192.00**
Official Money List	**102nd on the 1985 Official PGA Tour Money List**

At the end of the season, I was in the market for a new car. I had a few bucks burning a hole in my pocket. I always loved driving Nelford's BMW 535i—it was fast and stable. I walked into the BMW dealership on Burrard Street in Vancouver and treated myself to a new BMW 535i right off the floor.

By November, Joanie had spent a number of weeks on the road with me to see the life of a professional player on the PGA Tour. I learned a lot about Joanie's mother, Mary, and the wonderful mother that she was. I thought, *This is too good to pass up. Joanie has all the attributes I could have ever imagined in a partner—she is beautiful, she is sexy, strong-willed, smart, and she has strong family values. And wants to have children.*

I recall Bobby Clampett asking me what my intentions were with Joanie. I told him that I was going to ask her to marry me. Clampett asked if I had thought about a ring yet. I said, "No, can you suggest something?" Clampett told me I needed to learn a bit about diamond color and clarity, then go to Las Vegas to buy a single stone from The Jewelry Store. "Ask for Mordechai," he said. "He's a friend. I'll call him for you."

On December 17, 1985, one year exactly to the day I met Joanie Kindrachuk, over dinner at the William Tell Restaurant in Vancouver's Georgian Court Hotel, I asked Joanie to marry me.

She said, "Yes." Prior to the start of the 1986 season, Joanie and I set our wedding date for July 19, 1986, the Saturday of the Open Championship. This date fit into our schedule because I chose not to travel to the UK to qualify for the Open.

CHAPTER 8

1986—Walking the Gauntlet—Getting Married—Losing My Job—"Comfortably Numb" at Q-School

In early January 1986, I jumped into my new BMW and took off for Palm Springs. I wanted to have my car on the West Coast Swing. I was ready to have a great year in 1986—always being the optimist. I felt this was going to be the year, my fifth on the Tour.

I'd finished comfortably in the top 125 in the two previous years and felt I'd established myself. I felt I belonged. But as I started to play poorly once again, and after a string of missed cuts, my fear-based mindset locked onto what it would mean if I didn't make the top 125.

This is exactly where Henry Ford's famous quote comes from: "Whether you think you can, or you think you can't, you're right." My ego wanted to protect what I wanted, and I wanted to stay as an exempt PGA Tour player. But my ego was being threatened, and I had not developed my mindset skills enough to stop this dysfunctional thought cycle. It became a self-fulfilling prophecy as these thoughts actually increased the likelihood of missing the top 125—and this nightmare turned into my reality.

Missing the top 125 in 1986 was the furthest thing from my mind as I drove south on I-5 from Vancouver to Southern California to start my prep for the season.

Bob Hope Classic—January 15-19, 1986

Purse: $500,000

Indian Wells, Eldorado, La Quinta

Place: T31st

Scores: 71-77-64-69-65

Made: $3,480.00

AT&T Pebble Beach National Pro-Am—January 30-February 2, 1986

Purse: $600.000

Pebble Beach, Cypress Point, Spyglass Hill

Place: T35th

Scores: 76-69-73 (Tournament shortened to 54 holes due to rain)

Made: $2,649.00

1986 was the first year AT&T began its sponsorship with the PGA Tour—all contestants were happy they continued the tradition of being given decanters as tee gifts.

My West Coast Swing performance was miserable, making only two cuts in the six events I played. When I got to Florida, I went eight weeks in a row without making another cut. When I did make a cut, I was finishing in the bottom half of the field and earning small checks. Thoughts of a failed outcome began to take hold. I started to press without thinking that this would lead to a poor frame of mind. It's when you're playing poorly that you need to be the most mentally disciplined so you stop projecting forward to thoughts of the outcome. But that's exactly what I found myself doing as my poor play continued.

Greater Greensboro Open—April 3-6, 1986
Purse: $500,000
Forest Oaks CC, Greensboro, NC
Place: T61st
Scores: 69-74-78-71
Made: $1,075.00

Deposit Guaranty Classic—April 10-13, 1986
Purse: $200,000
Hattiesburg CC, Hattiesburg, MS
Place: T9th
Scores: 64-71-71-66
Made: $5,000

Houston Open—April 23-27, 1986
Purse: $500,000
TPC Woodlands, The Woodlands, TX
Place: T70th
Scores: 69-75-73-81
Made: $990.00

Prior to our wedding, Joanie and I decided to buy our first home. The plan was to purchase a town house in the False Creek neighborhood of Vancouver. Joanie would move into our new home the week before our July wedding date, and I'd move in after we were married. Buying the home presented a financial challenge, however. My year to date had not gone well. Money was tight. I needed to raise as much cash as I could for the down payment and to manage mortgage payments. Among other things, I had to bite the bullet and sell my beloved BMW, taking a big hit on the depreciation of a brand new luxury vehicle in the process. In its place, I bought a used Chevette for less than $2,000. I hated that fucking car. But it was an essential part of our next step in life together. The only good thing about the damn Chevette was how much it motivated me to do better every time I got into it. It was a valuable life lesson.

Provident Classic—June 12-15, 1986

Purse: $300,000

Valleybrook CC, Hixson, TN

Place: T50th

Scores: 69-70-66-75

Made: $716.00

Georgia-Pacific Atlanta Classic—June 19-22, 1986

Purse: $500,000

Atlanta CC, Marietta, GA

Place: T67th

Scores: 71-71-78-70

Made: $1,010.00

Anheuser-Busch Classic—July 10-13, 1986

Purse: $500,000

Kingsmill GC, Williamsburg, VA

Place: T34th

Scores: 72-66-67-79

Made: $2,471.43

Holding the 54-Hole Lead in a PGA Tour Event—Walking the Gauntlet on Sunday

The 1986 Anheuser-Busch Classic was the final Tour event I played before Joanie and I tied the knot. Despite my poor play up until this point, I played well at Kingsmill. I opened with rounds of 72-66, and then shot 67 in the third round and was alone with the lead at 8-under-par 205. Jodie Mudd and Kenny Knox were two shots behind me at 207. It would be my second time still in uncomfortable waters—Walking the Gauntlet—on Sunday with the lead of a PGA Tour event, playing in the final group on national television. Being comfortable in that environment and being able to perform and play well in a Sunday final group(s) with a chance to win is an essential and acquired skill set unto itself. There is a learning curve, and most learn from their mistakes. Even though I was playing well and leading the tournament, my confidence level was unstable. It was like I was in uncharted waters and hadn't learned how to swim yet.

I didn't have the mental discipline nor the knowledge to contain my thoughts that Saturday night before the final round. I tossed and turned all night and did not get a good night's sleep at all. My mind was constantly projecting to the future, dwelling over what might or might not happen the next day. My thoughts went back and forth, assuming that because I was playing so well that I should expect to play well in the final round, exactly like I had in the first three rounds, and win. Isn't that what you're supposed to do? Well, it doesn't work that way.

My mind was racing, then it jumped to the outcome on Sunday afternoon. I started to think about what I would write in my winner's speech and what we were going to do with the $90,000 winner's check. The first thing I'd do is get rid of that fucking Chevette. Would it make sense to buy another BMW? I'd get an invitation to the Masters. It was all going to be so great. Then my mind would flip to the other possible outcome. I found myself asking questions like, *What if I don't play well? What if I shoot 80 tomorrow? This could be embarrassing*. My confidence was unstable, and my thought processes were completely undisciplined. But that's how you learn.

The morning of the final round was especially uncomfortable. My stress level rose to a whole new level. I felt like I was cast adrift, all alone. The other difficult thing about Walking the Gauntlet in the final round(s) was that the final group tee times were in the 2:30 PM to 3:00 PM range. Waking up at my normal time of 5:00 AM meant I had hours for my mind to play games with me. The wait was excruciating.

As unsettled as I was, it was impossible for me to feel as comfortable or calm as I had for the first three rounds. This was a whole new situation I was facing. My level of anxiety affected my ability to execute shots the way I had on Thursday, Friday, and Saturday. My nightmare came true. I got off to a bad start, and things went downhill from there. I shot a final round 79. Instead of receiving a surfboard-sized check for $90,000.00, I won a paltry $2,471.00. Fuzzy Zoeller shot a final round 64 to win. After the post-round media interviews were over, I slumped back to the locker room. Tour lockers are usually organized alphabetically. That meant Zoeller's locker was next to mine. He was celebrating by buying champagne for all the locker room staff. I sat at my locker knowing what it felt like to be roadkill.

It's said, "The best lessons are learned from failure." That is exactly what Walking the Gauntlet for the first time on a Sunday afternoon on the PGA Tour teaches. Learning (or failing to learn) is the by-product of how you collect yourself and respond to the situation—good or bad—and what you decide to do about it. There are always choices to be made.

My next choice was an easy one. I got on a plane and flew home to marry Joanie on Saturday, July 19, 1986. It was a fantastic day. We got married in a stunning Ukrainian Catholic Church in Vancouver. Joanie was more beautiful than ever, and she had five gorgeous bridesmaids alongside her. I had my close friends and family, including old buddies Chris Rivers, Russ Jordan, Jim Nelford, Clay Edwards, and my cousin Neil Zokol.

Jim Nelford's arm was saved; a year after Nelford's boating accident Pat McGowan and I were with Jim when he struck his first shot, a pitching wedge at Gainey Ranch in Scottsdale, AZ. If I recall properly, I think he hit the 100-yard sign on the driving range with his first shot. The PGA Tour gave a major medical exemption but he struggled. He then went back to the PGA Tour Q-School and qualified back onto the PGA Tour with a complete different golf swing.

The International—August 14-18, 1986

Purse: $1,000,000

Castle Pines CC, Castle Rock, CO

Scores: Plus 6 (Stableford Scoring System)

Made: $6,000.00

Federal Express St. Jude Classic—August 28-31, 1986

Purse: $605,000

Colonial CC, Cordova, TN

Place: T57th

Scores: 78-72-72-73

Made: $1,363.00

BC Open—September 4-7, 1986

Purse: $400,000

En-Joie GC, Endicott, NY

Place: T16th

Scores: 69-70-72-68

Made: $5,611.00

Bank of Boston Classic—September 11-14, 1986

Purse: $450,000

Pleasant Valley CC, Sutton, MA

Place: T24th

Scores: 71-73-69-72

Made: $3,836.00

Greater Milwaukee Open—September 18-21, 1986

Purse: $400,000

Tuckaway CC, Franklin, WI

Place: T54th

Scores: 69-73-73-70

Made: $912.00

1986 Dunhill Cup—September 25-28, 1986

Missing Purse Old Course, St Andrews, Scotland

Team Canada—Dave Barr, Dan Halldorson, and Richard Zokol

Made: $16,000

1986 THE DUNHILL CUP

Canada	**2**	**Sweden**	**1**
Dave Barr	69	Mats Lanner	74
Richard Zokol	75	Ove Sellberg	72
Dan Halldorson	69	Anders Forsbrand	71

United States	**2**	**Canada**	**1**
Mark O'Meara	72	Richard Zokol	76
Lanny Wadkins	68	Dave Barr	66
Raymond Floyd	69	Dan Halldorson	70

My First Dunhill Cup

The Dunhill Cup presented me with my first opportunity to represent Canada internationally since I had been a member of the Canadian team in the 1980 Eisenhower Cup/World Amateur matches with Greg Olson, Graham Cooke, and Stu Hamilton. It was always an honor to do so. After all, how many athletes get to represent the country? In any sport! I was very proud. Along with teammates and good friends Dave Barr and Dan Halldorson, off we set to St Andrews, Scotland, to play the Dunhill Cup at the Old Course.

Having never been to Scotland, let alone played the Old Course, I was looking forward to this experience of playing links golf. I knew it was going to be a steep learning curve. We were provided rooms in the Old Course Hotel, and I remember waking up the next morning and looking over the Road Hole (the famous 17th Hole) and being totally mesmerized by the crumpled ground. The history of this place was overwhelming. I couldn't get on the course fast enough.

One of the many fascinating things about playing the Old Course was that it was such a different game than the golf played in North America. If you were left alone, without a caddie to guide you, you'd be totally lost. Then when you came back the next day to play, the wind would hit you from another direction and the holes would play completely different from what you learned yesterday—such is links golf.

After defeating Sweden in the first-round matches, we drew the US team of Mark O'Meara, Lanny Wadkins, and Raymond Floyd for our quarter-final match. Each match was head-to-head stroke play. Barr took care of Lanny Wadkins for the first point for Canada. Ray Floyd made an 18-foot putt on the 18th hole to beat Halldorson by a stroke. The overall team match came down to me playing O'Meara, Canada vs. USA. Standing on the tee of the famous 17th, the Road Hole, I had a three-shot lead on

O'Meara, and we both hit our second shots into the infamous Road Hole bunker. In hindsight, with my lead, I should have played sideways and taken my chances from there. But I fancied myself an excellent bunker player and thought, *No, I'll get it out onto the green and finish him off.*

With the chance to defeat the US hanging in the balance, I felt great as I went through my shot routine. Facing the nearly vertical face of the Road Hole bunker, I hit an excellent shot. The ball lifted almost vertically but caught the lip no more than an inch from the top—my ball popped straight up and landed back in the bunker at the base of the sod-revetted face. Now I was fucked.

O'Meara hit his bunker shot out to the side to see how I would deal with my unfolding disaster. I had no alternative with my second but to attempt to hit my ball three feet back to the middle of the bunker that would allow me to hit my next shot up onto the green. Instead, I hit the shot, and my ball went into my original footprints. That left me in a position where I couldn't even get out of the damn bunker sideways. It was now a nightmare. I took another couple shots and finally got it out, making an eight on the hole and blowing Canada's chances of upsetting Team USA. It was my own version of Tommy Nakajima's disastrous Sands of Nakajima experience in the same bunker in the Open of 1978.

The Road Hole has accumulated many ghosts in her closet over the past few hundred years.

I finished with a 76 to O'Meara's 72 and lost the match for Canada. I was devastated, feeling like I had let down my team and my country for all to see on the BBC's worldwide broadcast. Joanie and I headed back to our room in the Old Course Hotel to lick my emotional wounds. I had my head down as we got in the elevator, and when I looked up, I faced the gaze of Mark McCormack, the founder of International Management Group (better known now as IMG). McCormack was the brainchild behind the Dunhill Cup. Searching for words, McCormick said, "Hey kid, I saw what happened on 17. Bad recognition is better than no recognition. You'll do fine." As shitty as I felt in that moment, I just nodded and said, "Thank you."

Later that evening, after dinner (and a few consoling malt whiskeys), Joanie and I went back to our room and turned on the TV to find the BBC replaying the Dunhill Cup quarterfinals from earlier that day. The iconic voice of Peter Alliss rang through, and his color commentary was on point. With his versatile British accent, dry with extensive vocabulary, he documented my shot-by-shot troubles thrashing around the bottom of the Road bunker in my match against Mark O'Meara. After I finally got my ball onto the green and had climbed out of the bunker, the BBC camera panned the mess I had left in the Road Hole bunker. Allis dryly and stoically remarked, "Yes, it looks as though a couple of Shetland Ponies have been mating in there." Truer words have never been spoken. That road kill feeling happened again.

Vantage Championship—October 23-26, 1986

Purse: $1,000,000

Oak Hills CC, San Antonio, TX

Place: T46th

Scores: 68-68-71 (Rain shortened the tournament to three rounds)

Made: $2,772.00

Tallahassee Open—October 27-November 3, 1986

Purse: $200,000

Killearn CC, Tallahassee, FL

Missed Cut

When We Thought Things Could Not Have Gotten Worse—They Did

By the time the Tour got to Tallahassee, the final tournament of the year, I was in the precarious position of needing a Hail Mary week to make the top 125, or even a good week to make the top 150, and keep my PGA Tour membership. I got neither. I played poorly and missed the cut, which always makes you feel like shit, but on top of that, it meant I lost my job. A necessary trip back to PGA Tour Q-School was like rubbing salt in the wound. Resigned to what was to come, Joanie and I made arrangements to fly back to Vancouver from Tallahassee, FL, the next day.

Our routing back to Vancouver had us going through Atlanta and Chicago. It was going to be an all-day affair even if everything went perfectly. Sadly, they did not. It turned into a trip from hell.

To start the day, prior to catching our flight to Atlanta, Joanie hyperextended her knee, and we had to have the tournament doctor take a look at her. He arranged for us to go to the hospital for X-rays. Joanie emerged from her examination in pain and on crutches, but nothing was broken. Struggling with her discomfort, we pulled ourselves together and scrambled to get to the airport. The first two flight legs went fine. But when we got to Chicago, we got significantly delayed awaiting our final leg to Vancouver. We didn't get to Vancouver until 2:00 AM. Collecting our bags, we headed to Canada Customs. At that time in the early morning, the customs hall was virtually empty. We proceeded to the nearest customs officer, who directed us to another customs office for a more detailed screening. The secondary officer asked us, "Where you folks coming from?" I replied, "Florida." She responded, "Do you have anything to declare?" I said, "We have nothing to declare." She then looked at my golf bag and asked, "What's in the big bag?" I responded, "My golf bag and golf clubs." She mused, "Hmmm. Golf bag, can you lift it here? Why is it so big?" I said, "I play golf for a living in the US, and it's my equipment." By now, I was sensing an attitude, so I needed to keep my wits about me.

The customs officer started pulling my golf clubs out one by one. As she did so she asked, "Did you purchase these golf clubs in the US?" I said, "These clubs are two years old. They are not new." She snapped back, "I didn't ask you how old the clubs were, I asked you if you purchased them in the US." I could see where this was going, and I was trying to stay as calm as I could, even as my frustration started to heat up. I replied, "No, I didn't purchase them in the US. The manufacturer pays me to use them." She looked at me and, as though she hadn't heard my response, said, "Do you have the paperwork on all your equipment showing you've paid duty on them?" Joanie said something as an aside to me about how this was all going. The customs officer glared at her and said, "Did you just call me a bitch?" Joanie said, "Absolutely not." We were obviously in the middle of some kind of shakedown, and I was starting to get mad. I stated, "No, I don't have papers stating I've paid duty on this equipment."

The officer asked, "What is the value of these golf clubs?" I said to her, "I don't know. I don't pay for my golf clubs." The officer then said, "You better give me a price that says what they are worth, or I will put a value on them that you won't like." I said, "I don't know the value." She examined every club in my bag, and then said, "What's the value of all these golf balls, these golf gloves, and these golf shoes?" I responded defiantly to each question. "I don't know the value." I was not budging an inch.

The officer then went through every piece of our luggage looking for God knows what. Then she tallied everything up and, handing me a form, said, "With duty and penalties, you owe $2,000, you can pay over there." I replied, "I am not paying it—you can have it all—I don't want it." Finding nothing more she could use against us, she finally let us go. Joanie and I collected our suitcases, and I left my golf bag and all my golf contents on the table. We walked out of Canadian Customs and caught a taxi home. We just wanted to get home and fall asleep.

After being dropped off by the cab outside our town home in False Creek, we made our way through the gate entrance with luggage in hand. As we got closer to the front door, something didn't seem right. We could see the front door was ajar. We entered the house and quickly figured out that our home had been robbed. It must have been 4:00 AM when we called the police. With the kind of day we'd had, all Joanie and I could do was laugh. It was just another day in the glamorous life of a PGA Tour player. I am pretty sure the people who broke into our home were disappointed that we had nothing of value to take.

In the days that followed, I started to gather my thoughts. The season was over, and I was feeling the pain of losing my job as a PGA Tour player. I quickly needed to reset and reboot. I had to set my sights on getting my job back. This meant going back to the dreaded Q-School and hoping to play well and earn my way back. But making matters worse, finishing outside the top 150 meant I would have to get through Sectional Qualifying again before being able to advance to the final stage of Q-School.

As I was reflecting and preparing for my journey ahead, I got an unexpected call from PGA Tour Headquarters informing me that three players ahead of me on the PGA Tour Money List chose not to retain their memberships. That meant my spot at 152 moved up to 149, making my number exempt from the Sectional Qualifying after all. I caught a wonderful break. I needed to rest before prepping for another gruelling experience at the goddamn Q-School finals.

1986 PGA TOUR SEASON SUMMARY

Tournaments Entered	31
Cuts Made	14
Cuts Missed	17
Top 10 finished	1
Stroke Average	72.15
Official Money Made	**$37,888.00**
Official Money List	**149th on the 1986 Official PGA Tour Money List**

Breaking Through The Wall—"Comfortably Numb"

Joanie and I headed to California's Coachella Valley for the Q-School finals. My game was not in great form, and as a result I knew that I would need to rely on my course management and keeping my shit wired tight.

The PGA Tour Q-School is never fun. Having been through it twice before, I knew what to expect. It's a gruelling six-round competition that directly affects your dreams and life. With four of the six rounds being played on an insane course, PGA West Stadium Course, the situation puts everything you have invested into your game and life at risk—it's a case of mental discipline. The Stadium Course was just as diabolical as TPC Sawgrass when it opened. With four rounds out of the six played at the Stadium Course, every shot the player faces is fraught with danger. Any miscue could result in a catastrophic outcome on any given shot in this six-round test.

I managed my first four rounds quite well, shooting 71-73-70-69; I was pleased with the scores considering how poorly I had been playing coming into Q-School. I was in good shape with two rounds to go. If I continued to manage my mistakes. But I was in a tenuous position. I still was not stable on my shot executions—I was "leaking oil" and couldn't get to the finish line fast enough. A fifth round 75 put me on shaky ground. My mind went straight to, *If you didn't play well in the final round, you will find yourself in the death zone.* I felt like I was starting to hemorrhage with two rounds to play, fighting for my life. It was not a comfortable feeling.

Bearing witness to the aftermath of the final rounds at PGA Tour Q-Schools is to the observer the complete spectrum of human emotions.

Players who make it experience some of the happiest days of their lives—getting to the PGA Tour is truly life-changing. On the other hand, there are those whose dreams get shattered. And then there are those openly pleading with their Lord and Savior to answer their prayers. And everything in between, to put it bluntly; it's an emotional meat grinder.

I started the sixth and final round playing the same way I had the previous five, struggling hard to keep my emotional shit wired tight. Pressure was accumulating, and there's only so much you can take before something must give. As the round progressed, my performance wasn't getting better. Joanie was following me, helpless and concerned. The only thing worse than playing in the PGA Tour Q-School is being a spouse watching your loved one play, and there's nothing you can do but witness as this car accident unfolds right in front of you in slow motion.

When I made the turn, I was in the death zone with nine holes to play. Joanie was in tears and was being consoled by a good friend of our family who spent the winters in Palm Springs, Bob Keenan. With four holes to play and the finish line in sight, I could not afford to make another bogey if I wanted to regain my Tour card.

On the 15th hole, I 2-putted, making a routine par with agony on every shot. On the 16th hole, a par 5, I had to work hard and made a four-foot putt for par. I had two holes left to play. Both holes were daunting as hell. It was in this moment, I fully grasped the sadistic architectural nature of Pete Dye.

The 17th hole at PGA West's Stadium Course, a par 3 called Alcatraz, is an island green playing about 160 yards. The only thing you wanted to accomplish when standing on the tee was to hit the center of the green. It was a 7-iron shot for me in that moment. I was absolutely choking my guts out, and I executed an excellent shot. After my ball was safely on the middle of the 17th green, feeling relief, I said to myself, *Fuck you, Pete.*

Standing over my 25-foot putt for birdie on 17, I got very cautious again, which disrupted my shot routine, and I executed a horrible putt, which came up four feet short. Another scary putt for par loomed. My four-footer for par wasn't executed well either, but somehow the ball wobbled into the hole for a par 3. It could have just as easily wobbled out of the hole rather than wobbling in. I was excruciatingly uncomfortable, full of fear as I walked to the 18th tee, the final hole, thinking I needed a par to have any chance of making it, and thinking about the magnitude of possible outcomes on the next few shots and their consequences. It was pure mental torture—I was in absolute Golf Insanity.

The 18th hole at PGA West is an archetypal Pete Dye finishing hole, a man-made water hazard that runs the entire left side of the hole, from the tee all the way to behind the 18th green, designed to scare the shit out of you. Pete was good at that. There are bunkers on the right side of the fairway in the landing zone. The smart play, especially if you were choking, was a 3-wood off the tee short of the right bunkers. Gripped in fear of the water on the left, I made a tentative swing, leaking my shot into the right rough.

As I walked off the 18th tee, I was engulfed in this nightmare, absolutely hating how I was thinking and how I was feeling. As I walked to the fairway, I could feel anger starting to build, anger at me for allowing myself to feel this way. I remember thinking, *I fucking hate this—what I am doing to myself—this is crazy—this is fucking insanity—I am not going to take this anymore.*

When Bruce Berry, my caddie, and I got to the ball, we went through our calculations to figure out the shot. I looked at the pin, which was all the way back left, only a few steps from the edge of the water. The proper shot was to play to the middle of the green, short and right of the pin.

In that moment, I knew if this Golf Insanity continued, gripped in fear, I would likely hit another weak-ass shot short right just like my tee shot on 18th, which would leave me with another long and difficult pitch shot, and I would likely fail to get it up and down.

After running through scenarios in my mind right then and there—in that moment, on my final hole in the sixth round of PGA Tour Q-School—I decided there was no fucking way I was going to continue to put up with this Golf Insanity. I had to end it right here, right now, in this moment before I hit this shot. If I didn't, I'd be emotionally imprisoned, and I couldn't allow this to happen. I started saying to myself, *If I go down, I am okay with that, but I am going down swinging with dignity. There is no way I am holding on to these debilitating thoughts and feelings anymore—FUCK IT! I have to let it go right fucking here, right fucking now. And it must be done in the heat of battle, not after the round or on the driving range.*

As I was waiting for the other players in my group to hit, I continued my self-dialogue, *If this is what it's all about—I don't want any part of it—I*

DON'T FUCKING CARE. My whole perspective changed instantly. In this new perspective, I had no fear, and in some weird way, I felt like my intuition needed me to prove it to myself in this situation right now.

It was now my shot. I said, "Fuck it." I put the 6-iron back in the bag that I planned for the middle of the green, pulled out my 5-iron, and realigned my target from the middle of the green to the pin that was hugging the water hazard. I wasn't going to allow myself to be emotionally incarcerated by my own thoughts anymore. I completely let go. I took dead aim at the pin, literally not caring whether my ball went in the water or in the hole—I was either going to blow through The Wall right now or die trying.

I went through my shot routine and executed my 5-iron right on the button. When I looked up and saw my ball flight take off, the dialogue in my mind went like this: *Wow, this looks good, it's going right at the pin.* As the ball reached its apex in flight, the other voice in my mind countered, *Fuck you. I don't care where it goes.* In that moment, I had completely detached from the result of that shot; in the words of Pink Floyd, "I have become comfortably numb." It felt good.

My intuition decided *enough of this bullshit* and took control back from my fear-based ego. I had to prove to myself that if I truly let go, I'd have the freedom to fire at the pin, and I accepted this risk and the outcome, whatever happened. If I bailed out on my shot, it would mean I was still gripped in fear, still bullshitting myself.

My ball came to rest seven feet from the hole, dead pin high. It was one of the best shots of my life, given the circumstances, what was at stake, and my state of mind. In that moment on the 18th fairway on my second shot at PGA West Stadium Course, I broke through The Wall.

I felt an overwhelming sense of relief after hitting that 5-iron. Not because I didn't have to play any more holes, but relieved that I had finally let go of my emotional confinement. I pledged that I was never going to become a prisoner of my own mind again.

Pink Floyd's song resonated with me in my rookie year wearing the Walkman, and it resonated with me on that second shot on the 18th hole. I was comfortably numb in my isolation; there was no discomfort with the expectation, the risk, and the relentless exposure. To this day, every time I hear Roger Waters or David Gilmour sing "Comfortably Numb," or if I hear the music in a movie such as *The Departed* (2006), it takes me right back to those moments, and I become overwhelmed with emotion. It felt like it was some form of answer.

On the 18th green, I stood over my birdie putt without any apprehension at all. I executed my birdie putt well, but it lipped out. I still didn't care, and I tapped it in. I was proud of myself. Our group walked off the 18th green into the scoring tent to check and submit our scorecards. When I exited the tent, I was done. I didn't want to go to the scoreboard, where everyone was mingling, waiting to see what the cutoff number was going to be. I didn't want any part of this Golf Insanity whatsoever.

My caddie, Bruce Berry, turned to me and asked, "Are we going to the scoreboard?" In that moment, I still didn't care if I made it or not—I was truly detached from that extrinsic result. I replied, "No we're going to the car." I turned to Joanie and said, "Let's get the hell out of here." I just wanted to get back to our motel and go to sleep. As we left the PGA West parking lot, I said to Bruce, "Call me at the hotel later." Joanie and I drove out of the PGA West parking lot back to the hotel, and I went to sleep.

A couple hours later, the phone rang, pulling me out of a deep sleep. Joanie picked up the phone and handed it to me. "It's Bruce." I said, "Hey, Bruce." Bruce said, "We made it right on the number." I replied, "I don't fucking care," hung up the phone, and went back to sleep. There was no celebration in this.

PGA Tour Qualifying Tournament (Q-School)—December 3-8, 1986

Purse: PGA Tour Cards, 50+ ties

PGA West Stadium Course, La Quinta Hotel Golf & Tennis Resort (Dunes Course)

Place: T50th

Scores: 71-73-70-69-75-76–434

Made: $220.00

1986 PGA TOUR QUALIFYING TOURNAMENT

Ranking	Name	Score	Money
1	Steve Jones	67-65-69-67-72-75–415	$15,000.00
2	Steve Elkington	72-67-70-67-71-72–419	9,000.00
3	Philip Parkin	70-70-72-69-70-70–421	6,875.00
4	Rocco Mediate	69-69-73-71-67-72–421	6,875.00

Ranking	Name	Score	Money
5	Tom Garner	70-73-68-72-69-71–423	5,000.00
6	Bill Britton	68-69-70-69-75-73–424	3,625.00
7	Doug Johnson	76-68-66-65-75-74–424	3,625.00
8	Duffy Waldorf	73-69-73-72-68-70–435	2,853.34
9	Don Shirey Jr.	69-73-73-70-69-71–425	2,853.34
10	Loren Roberts	72-68-72-71-70-72–425	2,855.34
11	Mark Brooks	74-73-68-70-70-71–426	2,325.00
12	Sam Randolph	69-72-70-72-72-71–426	2,325.00
13	David Peoples	71-74-71-70-73-68–427	1,775.00
14	Jim Carter	70-71-70-72-75-69–427	1,775.00
15	Ted Schulz	70-71-73-71-72-70–427	1,775.00
16	Keith Clearwater	71-73-70-71-71-71–427	1,775.00
17	Ray Barr Jr.	72-69-73-70-72-71–427	1,775.00
18	Philip Jonas	67-71-71-71-73-74–427	1,775.00
19	John Inman	72-75-70-72-66-73–428	1,281.25
20	Ray Stewart	68-69-73-73-72-73–428	1,281.25
21	Brad Fabel	67-73-70-73-71-74–428	1,281.25
22	Jim Wilson	74-66-69-73-71-75–418	1,281.25
23	Perry Arthur	70-76-75-69-67-72–429	1,043.75
24	David Canipe	73-74-69-71-68-75–429	1,043.75
25	Trevor Dodds	72-69-70-72-72-74–429	1,043.75
26	John Horne	71-67-73-71-72-75–429	1,043.75
27	Jeff Lewis	74-74-71-71-72-68–430	880
28	Ted K. Lehmann	68-71-71-72-77-71–430	880
29	Rick Dalpos	70-77-69-73-69-72–430	880
30	Dave Eichelberger	72-69-68-72-74-75–430	880
31	Mike Bender	68-74-72-65-75-76–430	880
32	Jay Don Blake	74-78-75-69-78-67–431	735.71
33	Tim Norris	69-70-70-76-75-71–431	735.71
34	Bill Sander	74-70-65-71-79-71–431	735.71
35	Harry Taylor	72-73-75-69-69-73–431	735.71
36	Bruce Soulsby	75-69-71-70-73-73–431	735.71
37	Mike Smith	72-72-71-70-72-74–431	735.71
38	Vance Heafner	69-68-72-70-70-75–431	735.71
39	Brad Greer	71-70-75-70-75-71–432	625

Ranking	Name	Score	Money
40	Kenny Perry	69-70-79-71-71-72–432	625
41	John Riegger	74-70-73-70-72-73–432	625
42	Gary Krueger	72-72-71-69-75-73–432	625
43	Robert Wrenn	71-75-74-67-71-74–432	625
44	Robert Thompson	69-69-73-72-75-75–432	625
45	Aki Omachi	75-72-67-72-69-75–432	625
46	Denny Hepler	76-73-66-69-73-75–432	625
47	John MComish	70-72-74-70-68-78–432	625
48	David Hobby	70-74-74-73-76-66–433	565
49	Ed Dougherty	71-78-66-73-74-72–434	220
50	Tony Grimes	72-76-68-72-73-73–434	220
51	**Richard Zokol**	**71-73-70-69-75-76–434**	**220**
52	Mike McGee	71-70-75-70-71-77–434	220
53	Dewey Arnette	69-72-76-65-74-78–434	220

CHAPTER 9

1987—Learning the PGA Tour's Moniker—Play Better

AT&T Pebble Beach National Pro-Am—January 29-February 1, 1987

Purse: $600.000

Pebble Beach, Cypress Point, Spyglass Hill

Place: T23rd

Score: 69-75-73-69

Made: $5,190.00

There's an Old Saying on the PGA Tour: Play Better

If you play golf for a living, Playing Better solves everything. At the start of 1987, I was happy to put my 1986 playing performance in the rearview mirror. I was lucky to even have a PGA Tour card. It was sobering to think I was a whisker away from not having a job. But the new year and the clean slate of a new season never fails to inspire.

Now, the big hurdle I had to deal with was improving my priority playing position. Being way down the priority list meant I was not going to get into many Tour events if I didn't play better. Playing better was the only way out of the hole I had dug for myself. But one of the wonderful aspects of this game is that either your ball goes in the hole or it doesn't, and the PGA Tour is a meritocratic ecosystem; it's all about performance. If you play better than the others, you get rewarded.

At the start of every year, everybody starts from zero. And there are many different categories of exempt players and non-exempt players. Access to PGA Tour events is based on priority and space availability on each field. The Q-School category that I was in comes in right behind the top 125 exempt category. My calculated pecking order number coming out of the Q-School was 51st. That meant my overall priority number to gain access to Tour events was 176th (125 plus 51). Most Tour events on the West Coast had 144 players in the field because of limited daylight at that time of the year. As such, I did not draw into the Bob Hope Chrysler Classic in Palm Springs or the Phoenix Open in 1987.

The AT&T Pebble Beach National Pro-Am and the Shearson Lehman Brothers Andy Williams Open in San Diego were the only two Tour events on the West Coast Swing that I would gain access to based on my number. Both events are played on more than one golf course and had significantly larger fields than the other events on the West Coast Swing. If I wanted to survive, I would have to not only get into these two events on my number, but I'd have to Play Better when I got in them. My immediate objective was to make as much money as I could in those two events prior to the Q-School first reshuffle after the West Coast. It would allow me to gain access to more PGA Tour events after the Tour headed to Florida. If I didn't improve my position before the Tour went to Florida, I'd be stuck in a bad position for the whole year, looking in from the outside.

Sitting in the 51st Q-School category meant my back was up against the wall, with nothing to lose and everything to gain, which gave me that feeling of freedom again.

The Sunday night before the week of AT&T, I got the call from Cindy Zoller, who was a long-time administrator for the Pebble Beach Pro-Am, to let me know my number got in. They were scraping the bottom of the PGA Tour player barrel. But I was delighted, and Joanie and I flew from Phoenix, where we were staying with Jim Nelford, preparing for the upcoming season—I couldn't afford to not be ready.

I had a good week at Pebble, shooting rounds of 69-75-73-69, making $5,190.00. Making the cut achieved my first objective. Now, after the first Q-School category shuffle, my numbered position would improve. I could breathe a bit more.

The next week, my number got into the Hawaiian Open, and I played solid again, shooting 68-72-72-68, finishing T23rd, making $2,771.25, improving my position even more. Then I made the cut in San Diego, making an additional $1,301.00.

Hawaiian Open—February 5-8, 1987

Purse: $600,000

Waialae CC, Honolulu, HI

Place: T35

Score: 68-72-72-68

Made: $2,771.25

Shearson Lehman Brothers Andy Williams Open—February 11-15, 1987

Purse: $500,000

Torrey Pines GC (South), Torrey Pines (North), La Jolla, CA

Place: T47th

Score: 67-69-70-74

Made: $1,301.00

Even though I missed the cut at Riviera, I left the West Coast Swing very happy indeed. I had accomplished my goal to improve my priority number in the reshuffle. I think I jumped from 51st in the Q-School category to 10th, making $9,262.25, which basically put me in a position where I would get into all the Tour events I needed for the rest of the year.

Los Angeles Open Presented by Nissan—February 18-22, 1987

Purse: $600,000

Riviera CC, Pacific Palisades, CA

Score: Missed cut (MC)

Counterbalancing My Irons

Clay Edwards came to Riviera to look at some minor swing changes we were working on and watch me play. I liked what we were working on, as my swing improved structurally. Clay then said to me as we were hitting balls on the Riviera driving range, "You are ready to put more mass into your clubs." He stated. "Moe always said, 'mass in motion will stabilize your shots.'" My first reaction was, "What does that mean?"

Clay said, "Let's increase the mass of your irons, but not enough to slow your speed or change the swing-weight of your clubs." I said, "How do we do that?" Clay said, "Let's add eight ounces of lead on the head of your irons and eight ounces of lead into the butt end of the shaft. This added weight will put more stress on your shaft, effectively weakening your shaft, so we'll need to start with a stiffer shaft. The mass will stabilize both ends of the golf club; it's called counterbalancing."

I said, "Should we do this to my driver?" Clay said, "No, you don't want to slow down your driver."

So Clay and I headed to the Precision Shaft trailer on the range at Riviera to speak with Joe Braly. Joe Braly was often called "the father of frequency-matching golf shafts." Joe and his son Kim owned FM Precision and Rifle Shafts. I was using 7.5 FM Precision shafts in my irons. Joe was brilliant and had degrees in aeronautical engineering. His shaft designs are still embedded in shaft technology today, such as in Project X shafts.

We spoke with both Joe and Kim. They both were interested in looking at the concept of counterbalancing my irons. Within 30 minutes, they made a 7-iron and a 5-iron prototype exactly to my specifications, adding eight ounces of lead tape to the head and butt of these two clubs. Clay and I went back to my spot on the range to test these two counterbalanced clubs. As I started hitting the counterbalanced 7-iron, I noticed a significant difference in weight, particularly the mass in my hands, which slowed my hands down a bit at takeaway. It felt smoother and better. I could also feel more mass as I came into the impact zone—this increased mass in my hands and in the overall club and gave me more containment—passive hands through impact—but with more energy, making it more difficult to flip my hands. My swing motion instantly felt more stable.

After hitting just a few balls, I could feel the rhythm of my swing smooth out because of the weight. I didn't lose distance, which meant the increased mass didn't make for a net slower speed. Clay and I could see that with the added weight, my ball flight was more stable in the air, particularly in crosswinds. It was a noticeable improvement. But the biggest improvements were to those slightly miss-hit shots. Because there was more mass being delivered to the ball, even in miss-hit shots, my ball flight pattern tightened up and became more contained and consistent.

Instantly I was able to adapt to these counterbalanced clubs. After hitting about 30 balls with the prototype 7-iron I moved onto the 5-iron. I loved it, and my intuition told me not to go back to my standard clubs, but I needed to get a sense for the difference. When I went back to my old clubs, straightaway they felt too light and less stable. I didn't like the feeling.

Right then and there Clay and I took all my irons over the Precision Shaft trailer, and Kim Braly reassembled my 2-iron all the way down to my pitching wedge. The Bralys said, "You need to understand that if you increase the weight to the head, you will effectively weaken the shaft during your swing. So we will need to start with a stiffer shaft. You are currently using Precision FM 7.5 shafts, but I recommend you start with Precision FM 8.0 shafts so you maintain the proper flex that fits your swing."

From that day on the range at Riviera forward, I always counterbalanced my irons.

Even though I missed the cut at Riviera, I left the West Coast Swing enthusiastic. By the time we got to Florida, I was born again and had a lineup of events in front of me.

In mid-February, Joanie found out she was pregnant. We were delighted with this wonderful news. We both wanted children, and we were only in our second month of trying. It was such a wonderful feeling to start our family. Within the week, Joanie made an appointment with Dr. House to confirm her pregnancy and schedule an ultrasound for the first trimester of her pregnancy.

There Are Two Hearts Beating in There

Back in Vancouver, Joanie and I headed to her appointment for her first ultrasound. The technicians took Joanie into a room, and I stayed to wait in the reception area. About 20 minutes later, Joanie and the technician came out, and Joanie was in tears, emotionally upset. When I saw her, my heart sank. I jumped out of my seat, saying, "What is wrong?" I needed to console Joanie. She said, "We are going to have twins." My reaction to this news was, "Yes, we're going to have twins." Joanie was in complete shock that there were two wonderful little beings in her, and I was over the moon.

Soon after, things started to settle down, and the shock of learning and accepting that we were having twins wore off. Joanie, as she does, started planning.

USF&G Classic—March 19-22, 1987

Purse: $500,000

Lakewood CC, New Orleans, LA

Place: T61st

Scores: 70-70-71-74

Made: $1,045.00

In New Orleans, Joanie and I decided to take a stroll. When we turned the corner onto Bourbon Street—those who have been there will know—we were hit pretty hard with this foul stench of rotting beer, which smells more like puke in the hot, humid air of New Orleans. Well, Joanie got one whiff of this smell, and her morning sickness kicked in. We did an about-face and went back to the hotel. Joanie's morning sickness wasn't much of a problem, but she couldn't look at or eat chicken for a couple of years.

Hole-in-One

Saturday on the 12th hole, a 149-yard par 3, I made my second hole-in-one on the PGA Tour. Johnny Miller witnessed my ball going in the hole and told us, "It went in." I could not see the ball due to the height of the bunker on the front right of the green, but Johnny just happened to drive up to the 12th green in his golf cart in his reconnaissance of how the hole was playing for his NBC broadcast.

Deposit Guaranty Classic—April 9-12, 1987

Purse: $200,000

Hattiesburg CC, Hattiesburg, MS

Place: T3rd

Scores: 69-67-65-68

Made: $10,400.00

The Deposit Guaranty Classic remained a PGA Tour event opposite the Masters. It was a satellite PGA Tour event and did not count as an official win, but the money won in the event counted as Official Money. Playing well and winning more than $10,000 gave me a big boost. Things felt like they were really coming together.

1987 DEPOSIT GUARANTY CLASSIC

Place	Name	Scores	Money
1st	David Ogrin	66-68-69-64–267	$36,000
2nd	Nick Faldo	67-67-67-67–268	$21,000
T3rd	Richard Zokol	69-67-65-68–269	$10,400
T3rd	Bill Glasson	65-69-67-68–269	$10,400

I recall that week, April 6, 1987, Jim Nelford, Joanie, and I went to an arena in Hattiesburg to watch Marvin Hagler fight Sugar Ray Leonard. I was a big Marvelous Marvin Hagler fan and didn't like Sugar Ray Leonard much. This renowned fight was controversial, and the split decision went in favor of Sugar Ray. Hagler got robbed and walked away from boxing.

Georgia-Pacific Atlanta Classic—May 21-24, 1987

Purse: $600,000

Atlanta CC, Marietta, GA

Place: T23rd

Scores: 72-63-72-71

Made: $5,760.00

My good friend and fellow Canadian professional Dave Barr won the 1987 Georgia-Pacific Atlanta Classic. It was a great victory for Dave. He played well under the pressure of being chased in the final round by former major champions Lanny Wadkins and Larry Mize. Dave handled the difficult situation like a champion, winning his second PGA Tour event and taking home the $108,000 first prize money.

Breaking Through The Wall—Again

My second round 63 at the 1987 Georgia-Pacific Atlanta Classic was the best round of golf I ever played in PGA Tour competition. How it all came about was fascinating. My ball-striking was off-the-charts good coming into Atlanta, and it continued into the first round. It didn't matter if I had a 2-iron in my hand or a pitching wedge. My approach shots were attacking the hole. In contrast, however, my putting the entire week was off-the-charts bad. And it got to a point where the closer my birdie putts were to the hole, the worse my stroke got. In fact, because I was hitting it so good and had so many short birdie putts, my excellent ball-striking put a great deal of pressure on my putting.

I was gripped with fear when I faced short putts that I was "expected" to make. It got to the point that I wanted to avoid facing any putt between three and 12-feet—I was developing the *yips*. I shot 72 in the first round and hit so many shots close to the pin that round that 72 was a horrible score, considering I couldn't make a putt to save my life. I was frustrated, and my mind was spiralling off track when it came to putting. The closer I hit my ball to the hole, the more anxiety I built up to make the putt, which only recycled more fear and anxiety in my mind.

At the start of the second round, my fear of yipping short putts was gnawing at me like the monster that lived under my bed when I was a little boy. When I teed off for the second round, I wondered how my yipping problem was going to turn out. On the first hole, as my second shot 7-iron from the middle of the fairway was heading straight at the pin, an internal voice said, *Oh shit, it's going right at it.* I knew it was going to be close, and I worried about the ball being in my three-to-twelve-foot-foot "vomit zone." When I got to the green, I saw my ball was three feet from the hole, which only accelerated my uneasiness about my upcoming putt. I could feel the pressure mounting as I waited for the two other players in my group to play. Standing over this three-foot putt, I nervously thought to myself, *Okay, what's in store with my putting today.* I executed my putt in a jerky motion, and my ball didn't even come close to hitting the hole. I tapped in for my par and was ready to explode.

The second hole at Atlanta Golf & CC was a par 5. I set my second shot up perfectly to my favorite distance for my third shot to the hole, 115 yards. Now facing this third shot with my pitching wedge, I was afraid to shoot at the pin. I didn't want to deal with another short putt—how fucked up was that? Based on my fear of facing another short putt, I decided to aim away from the pin. I hit a perfect pitching wedge to 25 feet from the pin, precisely where I wanted it to go. I had never done that before in all my life. *You bloody chicken,* I thought to myself. I had so much control over my ball-striking, but I never thought in my wildest dreams that I would purposely aim away from the hole out of fear. My fear was now impacting my decisions. Here we go with this Golf Insanity again.

Once on the second green, facing this 25-foot putt, which I was not expected to make, my anxiety was reduced to a manageable level. I executed my 25-foot putt, the ball almost went in, and I tapped in for par.

The third hole, a par 3, I hit another great tee shot with a mid-iron that never left the flag—another great shot, five feet from the hole. My immediate reaction was, *Oh fuck, here we go again.* And I proceeded to metaphorically puke on myself in my first putt, again. In that moment, my mind reconnected with my Q-School experience on the 18th. I had again reached a breaking point and simply refused to tolerate the fear that crept back into my mind. I said to myself, *FUCK THIS BULLSHIT.* Without even knowing it, my ego infiltrated back into my mind, and once again, it took over and started to undermine my ability. The Wall got built up again by poor thought habits that revolved around future projecting to results and fear.

When I missed that short putt on the third green—I snapped—my perspective instantly changed. My anxiety reached a breaking point, and I broke through The Wall again. Starting on the fourth tee shot, from that point forward for the rest of the round, I let go of all my fears and thoughts of results and tapped into my internal freedom. I became comfortably numb—again. The freedom was beautiful, it was rhythmic, and it was easy. In my next 13 holes, I made 10 birdies and three pars. Standing on the 17th tee, I noticed Furman Bisher, the great sports columnist for the *Atlanta Journal-Constitution* and the one to dub Byron Nelson "Lord Byron," standing in my gallery. He had come out of the press room to watch this possible 59. He had no idea this round started with the yips.

Standing on the 17th tee, in order to shoot 59, I needed a birdie on the 17th, then an eagle on the 18th, a reachable par 5. I wasn't aware of the numbers in my new state of mind; I was locked in on "this shot right now."

I was totally consumed in the present moment and fearless, comfortably numb. Locking into the shot at hand, not caring about the result or the consequences of any shot, it was freedom without the "pin prick" of a needle in the song.

The 17th was a relatively short par 4. I drove the ball perfectly off the tee, leaving myself with a short iron for my second shot. The pin was back right, a few steps from the back edge of the green. I assessed my shot, chose an 8-iron, and executed another perfect shot. My ball, like all of my shots that day, was on radar-lock to the pin. I thought to myself, *This looks good.* My ball went right over the top of the pin, landing just behind the hole, took one big hop into the rough over the green. I was left with a tough up and down, which I didn't convert and made bogey. I then proceeded to make par on the last hole to shoot 63. To this day, that round holds a special place in my mind because of what I learned—I started the round with the yips, which triggered my mind to break through The Wall and shoot the best round of my life. Our minds are so psychologically sensitive—we can make a change in an instant—my yips were gone.

Canon Sammy Davis Jr.–Greater Hartford Open–June 25–28, 1987
Purse: $700,000
TPC of Connecticut, Cromwell, CT
Place: T60th
Scores: 72-69-71-71
Made: $1,653.00

Canadian Open–July 2–5, 1987
Purse: CAD $600,000
Glen Abbey GC, Oakville, ON
Place: T7th
Scores: 70-68-69-75
Made: $16,850.00

If you are a Canadian professional golfer, you absolutely love playing in the Canadian Open. Ever since I started playing at a high level, I kept an eye on the Canadian Open every summer, dreaming of winning our national championship. Glen Abbey in the late '70s and into the early '80s was still considered a challenging PGA Tour course. Golf equipment had not yet made the advances that transformed many long-standing Tour courses, including Glen Abbey, into a short track that provided birdie fests to the best players in the world.

When Is a Canadian Going to Win the Canadian Open?

Regardless of Glen Abbey's difficulty, the annual question posed from the Canadian golf media to Canadian PGA Tour players was always "When is a Canadian going to finally win the Canadian Open?" In 1987, it had been 33 years since Pat Fletcher won at the Point Grey Golf Club in Vancouver in 1954. As we now know, the victory drought would last a total of 69 years until 2023, when Nick Taylor won. At least now that question won't come up quite the same way. For a while at least!

In the first round of the 1987 Canadian Open, I played well and shot a 2-under-par round of 70. I sat two shots behind first-round leader Joey Sindelar. In the second round, I finished with a birdie on 16, a birdie on 17, and I hit my 5-wood to three feet on the 18th hole and made the eagle putt to shoot 68 and tie for the lead with David Frost at 6 under par.

In the third round, I again played well and shot 69 to tie for the 54-hole lead with Curtis Strange and Mike McCullough at 9-under-par 209. I'd started the last round Walking the Gauntlet for the third time in my career after the Anheuser-Busch tournament in 1986.

Walking the Gauntlet for the Third Time

It takes an acquired skill to Walk the Gauntlet comfortably and successfully. Pressure, as they say, should be viewed as a privilege. Every time you Walk the Gauntlet is an opportunity to learn to become more comfortable and focus on process and performance rather than outcome. My definition of Walking the Gauntlet successfully is having the lead or being close to the lead going into the final round, playing in the final two or three groups, and playing better than any of the other players who are also Walking the Gauntlet. My only experience of Walking the Gauntlet to this point was in my rookie year in Milwaukee and the 1986 Anheuser-Busch Golf Classic, where I shit the bed. Now I found myself tied for the lead and paired with the best player in the world at the time, Curtis Strange.

The night before the final round, I had a nervous sleep but managed a few decent hours of rest. The Sunday morning newspapers were asking the 33-year-old question. People in the gallery were wearing the Canadian flag and pulling for me to win. Across the country, golf fans were pinning their hopes on "the Canadian" and tuning in to the broadcast. Would this be the year?

On the first tee of that final round, Curtis knew exactly how I was feeling. He was a seasoned champion. He knew I had not won on Tour—yet. He knew the pressure of a nation was on me. The way I figured it, Curtis knew he was going to win—I knew Curtis was going to win—and Curtis knew, I knew, he was going to win.

In my personal road map to winning on the PGA Tour, I would Walk the Gauntlet successfully, but only after I learned to better handle these difficult and uncomfortable situations. To get there, I needed to feel comfortable playing in the final group with the lead. But this trip of the Gauntlet was nothing like last year's experience in Kingsmill. I was carrying the hopes of the entire country on my back this time. The difference was night and day. Anheuser-Busch was a picnic compared to what I was facing on Sunday, July 5, 1987, at Glen Abbey.

The first objective in these types of pressure situations is to execute a good opening tee shot and settle down as fast as possible into the round. But the waiting to get to that opening tee shot is where an undisciplined mind can disrupt your best intentions. When you play in the final group on Sunday, your tee time is around 2:00 PM. When you are conditioned to get up at 5:00 to 6:00 AM each morning, you have to learn how to effectively deal with the large amount of time you have before you tee off. A key to learning how to win on the PGA Tour is learning how to deal with your Sunday morning time.

On the first hole, I hit my second shot into the right green side bunker. My bunker shot left me with a six-foot putt for par. Learning how to manage your shot routine when you're unsettled is a mental skill that every Tour player must master in order to Walk the Gauntlet successfully. My shot routine with my par putt was not stable enough, and my rhythm was a bit quick. The speed of my putts was off just enough to lip out—an opening bogey. I still knew my first objective was to execute my shot routine on every shot. If I could accomplish that, I would calm myself and settle down to play well.

As the round progressed, I was able to settle down and stabilize my ball-striking. I didn't play great, but I didn't play bad. I didn't shit the bed like I had at the 1986 Anheuser-Busch, first thing's first. Unfortunately, I just could not settle down enough on the greens. Putts that had been falling into the middle of the hole in the first three rounds were now lipping out. My sense of feel for the speed of the greens was not where it needed to be. I did not make a single birdie in the final round. Instead, I made 15 pars and three bogies and shot a 3-over 75. Curtis cruised through with a 69 and won by three shots over Nick Price. For me, the round was a great learning experience. It was a valuable step forward for me in learning how to Walk the Gauntlet. Whether I knew it or not at the time, it was great progress.

Anheuser-Busch Golf Classic—July 9-12, 1987

Purse: $612,000

Kingsmill GC, Williamsburg, VA

Place: T11th

Scores: 68-71-68-69

Made: $14,076.00

The International—August 12-16, 1987

Purse: $1,115,280.00

Castle Pines GC, Castle Rock, CO

Place: T16th

Scores: Minus 3 (Stableford System)

Made: $17,000.00

Beatrice Western Open—August 21-23, 1987

Purse: $800,000

Butler National GC, Oakbrook, IL

Place: T13th

Scores: 70-73-68 (tournament shortened to 54-holes due to inclement weather)

Made: $14,133.33

Provident Classic—August 27-30, 1987

Purse: $450,000

Valleybrook G&CC, Hixson, TN

Place: T7th

Scores: 69-67-66-67

Made: $14,025.00

Greater Milwaukee Open—September 17-20, 1987

Purse: $600,000

Tuckaway CC, Franklin, WI

Place: T14th

Scores: 69-68-71-70

Made: $10,200.00

The Dunhill Cup—October 1-4, 1987

The Old Course, St Andrews, Scotland

Team Canada—Dave Barr, Dan Halldorson & Richard Zokol

Greg Norman (Australia) and Richard Zokol (Canada) waiting on first tee at the Old Course prior to the Sudden-Death Playoff Match.

1987 DUNHILL CUP

Canada	**2.50**	**New Zealand**	**0.5**
Dave Barr	71	Bruce Soulsby	75
Dan Halldorson	74	Greg Turner	74
Richard Zokol	72	Frank Nobilo	74

Australia	**2**	**Canada**	**1**
Rodger Davis	63	Dan Halldorson	73
Peter Senior	73	Dave Barr*	73
Greg Norman	71	Richard Zokol	71

* Barr won on first playoff hole over Senior. Norman won on fifth playoff hole over Zokol

The handshake on the Old Course's famous Road Hole after the fifth Sudden-Death Playoff hole.

The Dunhill Cup—Canada vs. Australia

The Canada versus Australia Match was interesting. Our first match out was Halldorson vs. Rodger Davis. Davis caught fire, shooting 63 to Dan

Halldorson's 73. Australia 1 – Canada 0. Our second group out was Dave Barr vs. Peter Senior. Both Dave and Peter shot 73, and Barr went on to beat Peter Senior on the first hole of sudden death, tying the match Australia 1 – Canada 1. The third and deciding match was going to be Zokol vs. Norman.

As Greg Norman and I were playing our second shots to the Road Hole in our regulation match, I was three shots back of Norman with two holes to play. I hit a great second shot onto the front right of the green's lower level. Norman hit his shot onto the right side of the green, and his ball ran just over the edge of the green, down the slope, and onto the road. The road is an integral part of this course, so you do not get free relief from the road. Hitting off the road is a difficult proposition at best. It's hard to know how the ball will interact off the rough on a pebbly surface. It's total guesswork.

Although I was on the green and Norman was not, I was away, facing the better part of a 60-foot putt. When I made that 60-foot putt for birdie, it took the wind right out of Norman's sails. It felt like the Golf Gods had delivered retribution for my embarrassing "Shetland pony" experience in the Road Bunker the year prior. Norman had trouble with the road and ended up making a double bogey. We were tied with one hole to play. Neither Greg nor I birdied the 18th. We finished the round with matching 1-under-par 71s and prepared for a sudden-death playoff to determine whether Australia or Canada would move on to the semi-finals.

Both Norman and I made pars on the first sudden-death hole. On the second hole, Greg got into trouble off the tee, ending up in a bunker, and was forced to play out sideways. I hit a good second shot to about 12 feet. Norman hit his third shot to the back of the green leaving him with a 25-foot putt for par. I was facing a birdie half the distance of Norman's putt for par, thinking this could be it, but Norman made his putt for par. If I made my birdie putt, the match would be over—but I missed it. Off we headed to the third playoff hole.

We both parred the third and fourth holes and continued on. Tournament officials informed us that the fifth sudden-death hole will be played on the Road Hole. We both drove the ball into the 17th fairway, and Norman hit a good second shot to the middle of the green and made a routine par 4. I hit what I thought was a great second shot just right of the pin, but just like Norman's shot an hour earlier, it went over the edge of the green and rolled down onto the road. The Golf Gods are fickle. No miraculous recovery came my way. I made bogey. Australia won the match and advanced. My teammates and I were left to wonder what might have been.

1987 PGA TOUR SEASON SUMMARY

Tournaments Entered	21
Cuts Made	13
Cut Missed	8
Top 10 finished	3 (Deposit Guaranty, Canadian Open, Provident)
Stroke Average	70.93
Greens in Regulation	T19th (.691)
Putting	T49th
Scoring Leaders	25th (70.93)
Sand Saves	38 (.518)
Official Money	**$114,406.00**
Official Money List	**89th on the 1987 Official PGA Tour Money List**

Joanie Gives Birth to Twins Garrett and Conor, October 14, 1987

Joanie being pregnant with our twins curtailed her travel. We were both concerned that the delivery would come early. Our first priority was making sure the twins got to a minimum size before labor came. We were particularly concerned that I would be caught on the other side of the globe in Scotland for the Dunhill Cup when she went into labor. The Dunhill Cup was going to be my last event of the year; I decided to skip the last four PGA Tour events of the season, Pensacola, Disney, Tucson, and the Centel Classic in Tallahassee, to be with Joanie. I was glad to get back home the first week of October.

Considering I had started the year at 179th on the PGA Tour priority list, I was delighted at how well I had dug myself out of a hole and made some dough. But the best thing was the birth of our twin sons, Garrett and Conor, on October 14th. Now we had the off-season, November and December off, which was perfect timing because learning to care for newborn twins is not for the faint of heart—it took three people to manage feeding 24 hours a day for the first couple of months.

Joanie's mother, Mary, came to Vancouver to assist us with Garrett and Conor until the end of November. We don't know what we would have done without Mary's help. The biggest challenge was feeding Garrett and Conor and allowing Joanie time to rest and recover—a difficult proposition given feeding is every hour of a 24-hour day. We soon learned that we needed to break it into three eight-hour feeding shifts. I took the night shift, midnight to 8:00 AM. Joanie took the 8:00 AM to 4:00 PM shift, and Joanie's mom took the 4:00 PM to midnight shift. This continued for the first six weeks, but Mary couldn't stay forever, and she eventually headed back home to Calgary on December 1. After that, we were all alone.

Earlier in the year, I had committed to playing in the JC Penney Mixed Team event in Largo, FL, the first week of December with Kathy Whitworth. How could I pass up the opportunity to play with the most winningest professional player of all time, with 88 professional wins on the LPGA Tour? That record still stands by the way (Tiger Woods and Sam Snead are tied with 82 PGA Tour wins). I felt privileged to play with such a legend in the game. Kathy was a wonderful lady, and we had a great time playing as a team. Nonetheless, leaving for Largo, FL, to play a tournament for the first time meant leaving Joanie and the twins. My flight to Florida left early in the morning after I'd been up the entire night handling my feeding shift. Pulling the all-nighter and then having three connecting flights to get to Largo, FL, from Vancouver was a bitch, but I managed. I slept very well that first night out of sheer exhaustion.

Once back home, we came up with a solution that would allow us both to get the rest we needed. When you're sleep-deprived, you can't tie your own shoes. On the other hand, getting good sleep assures you can take on the world. The boys still weren't sleeping through the night. So, we decided to hire a nanny to handle the midnight to 8:00 AM feedings shift. It was a brilliant move. We got the rest and recovery we needed. Once the boys were finally able to sleep through the night at three months old, we were able to get back to a somewhat normal routine. We were more than ready for it!

JC Penny Classic–Mixed Team–Richard Zokol/Kathy Whitworth–
December 3-6, 1987
Purse: $650,000
Bardmoor CC, Largo, FL
Place: T16
Scores: 70-69-69-68
Made: $4,375.00

When Garrett and Conor came into our world and given we'd be trying for a little girl in short order—our plan was to keep our kids close in age—we needed a larger home with a backyard rather than a small town house in the city of Vancouver. We put our townhome up for sale and chose to rent a single family home in Richmond, BC.

CHAPTER 10

1988—Learning to Play Better When Walking the Gauntlet

In preparation for the start of the 1988 season, Joanie and I decided to hit the road with Garrett and Conor when they were three months old. We also decided to purchase and travel in a Toyota van so we'd have all the stuff we needed within reach at all times—two cribs, toys, bottles, diapers, etc. We were a young family about to hit the road for real.

If the drive from one tournament site to the next wasn't too far, we figured we would drive—say, Phoenix to Palm Springs. But the long-haul drives, such as Phoenix to Pebble Beach or Los Angeles to Miami, I would have my caddie drive the van, and we would fly.

Joanie's mom thankfully came to help us on our first excursion on Tour with our two three-month-old babies. To get started, I drove the van by myself to Palm Springs to get the vehicle to Southern California for a week and give me time to get my game in shape for the first event—the Bob Hope Chrysler Classic. Joanie and her mother flew from Vancouver to Phoenix the following week with Garrett and Conor. I picked them up on arrival at the airport, and we started down this brand new path.

Bob Hope Chrysler Classic—January 20-24, 1988

Purse: $1,000,000

Indian Wells CC, Bermuda Dunes, La Quinta, PGA West (Palmer)

Place: MC

Phoenix Open—January 28-31, 1988

Purse: $650,000

TPC of Scottsdale, Scottsdale, AZ

Place: MC

AT&T Pebble Beach National Pro-Am—February 4-7, 1988

Purse: $600.000

Pebble Beach, Cypress Point, Spyglass Hill

Place: T69

Score: 77-65-78 (tournament shortened to 54 holes due to inclement weather)

Made: $1,358.00

Hawaiian Open—February 11-14, 1988

Purse: $600,000

Waialae CC, Honolulu, HI

Place: 2nd

Score: 66-71-65-70

Made: $64,000.00

We spent the first four weeks of the West Coast Swing on the road with the boys. I wasn't playing well. The start of our life on Tour with the twins was going to take some getting used to. As we'd planned though, following the AT&T, Joanie, her mom, and the boys flew back to Vancouver, and I flew to Honolulu for the Hawaiian Open.

After being on the road for four weeks with the family, I was able to sleep more deeply, being on my own for a week.

Walking the Gauntlet for the Fourth Time

In 1988, Waialae CC was playing firm, fast, and it was windy. Jodie Mudd and I opened with 6-under 66s and had the first-round lead, one shot ahead of Scott Simpson and Brad Bryant (a.k.a. "Dr. Dirt" or "Commander-in-Chief of all Dirt Forces" as Greg Powers had labeled him). My second round score was 71, and at 7 under par, I was sitting three shots off the 36-hole lead, held by Loren Roberts. By the third round, the course was really drying out and was getting a little treacherous. I caught fire and fired a 7-under-par round of 65 to take a two-shot lead over Loren Roberts and Mark Brooks heading into the final round. Lanny Wadkins and Tom Watson were three shots off my lead.

It was time for me to Walk the Gauntlet again—for the fourth time in my career, I'd be playing in the final group on Sunday with the lead in the tournament. I started thinking about how to handle the situation. Two years earlier, in the same situation at Anheuser-Busch, I completely shit the bed and shot 79. A year ago at the Canadian Open, I had managed to feel more comfortable, played a little better, but still didn't settle down enough to play well. I definitely found myself feeling more comfortable facing the situation in Hawaii. I suppose a good analogy might be that I was still in a dark room, but I had a pretty good idea where all the furniture was located.

Prior to teeing off for the final round, I said to my caddie, Dick Christy, the best chance for us to win was for me to not get ahead of myself and keep calm. I felt the best way for me to accomplish this was to avoid looking at the scoreboards. I had made progress over the two previous years, but I was still not completely comfortable Walking the Gauntlet. Progress is brick by brick, and my next brick was to stay present and not get ahead of myself. My best chance was staying tight with my shot routine and taking care of my business with each individual shot.

In the final group that Sunday, I was paired with Loren Roberts and Mark Brooks. Tom Watson, Fulton Allem, and Gene Sauers were the group in front of us, second to last. After getting the first few holes behind me, I settled down quickly and established the rhythm of my shot routine nicely. I wasn't looking at the scoreboard, curtailing my excitement and helping me stay in the present moment for each shot. I got off to a stable start, I was locked in, and I was not thinking about the outcome or consequences. At the turn, I felt like I had the lead, but I wasn't sure, and it didn't matter because I had work to do on the back nine.

I knew I was ahead of the guys in my group, Roberts and Brooks. Standing on the 10th tee, I watched Tom Watson 4-putt the 10th green. The large gallery following our group gave me the sense I was leading. I thought to myself, *Okay, my plan is working—this is good—I've got a handle on this. Let's keep doing this on the back nine, ignore the scoreboard.* I can deal with any situation that presents itself.

The back nine went well. I made great par-saving putts on 16 and 17. The putt on 17 was particularly good as I locked into my putt for par and executed a great stroke after making a good bunker shot. In that moment, I didn't have any thoughts about what the putt meant. I simply *assessed* and *executed* on a difficult five-foot putt to the best of my ability. The ball dove into the middle of the hole like a homesick gopher. It felt good being able to handle the situation, making that critical putt.

The 18th hole, if you've watched the Hawaiian Open over the decades, is a reachable par 5 that doglegged hard left. I hit a great tee shot, which got around the corner and set me up to reach the green with my second shot. In that moment, I felt like I had the tournament in hand, and I could handle whatever situation I was in. I turned to Dick Christy and asked him, "What do we need to make to win?" I was fully expecting Dick to say, "We need a par or a birdie to win." Instead, Dick responded, "We need to make an eagle three to tie." I was shocked. "Eagle to tie! Fuck, I thought I had the lead!" I felt a bit deflated. Lanny Wadkins had come out of nowhere to shoot 66 in the final round and got into the house at 17-under par 271. Because I hadn't been looking at the scoreboards, I wasn't aware Lanny was even a factor.

Nonetheless, in that moment, I still had a chance. There was work to do. With a clear understanding of the situation and knowing I needed to make an eagle, I refocused on the shot at hand. I chose a 2-iron for my second shot. The pin was in its usual Sunday placement for the Hawaiian Open, on the front left of the green behind the front bunker—anything left of the pin would leave me short-sided with a difficult third shot. I flushed the 2-iron to the middle of the green, and my ball ended up pin high a foot off the right edge of the green, leaving me a 25-foot chip shot for the eagle to get to 17 under par and force a playoff with Wadkins. I thoroughly assessed my situation. I was one shot ahead of third place, John Huston, who was in at 14 under par, so I wasn't worried about losing solo second if I made par. This gave me freedom to try and make the chip without worrying about getting too aggressive with it.

With the tournament on the line and the whole golf world watching, I executed the chip shot perfectly. Halfway to the hole, my ball was tracking to go in, and I thought, *This has a chance.* Speed and line looked good, but it slowed a bit, and my chip came up about one foot short dead in the middle of the hole. Lanny Wadkins won the Hawaiian Open. I finished solo second. Yes, there was disappointment; I didn't win when I thought I was going to, but I achieved my primary objective—to play well while Walking the Gauntlet.

Lessons Learned

My performance at the 1988 Hawaiian Open was a big step forward in my mental fitness development as a professional player. When I started the final round, my primary objective was to find a path that would give me the best chance to win. I climbed into my bubble and stayed there for each shot. I wasn't yet experienced enough to be looking at scoreboards without it affecting my composure. Nonetheless, my primary objective was achieved, playing well while Walking the Gauntlet.

My progress across the last three seasons of playing in the final group with the tournament lead was an excellent ascent. It reassured me that I could successfully Walk the Gauntlet from this point forward.

2nd Place Hawaiian Open trophy—Large Swarovski crystal pineapple.

Los Angeles Open Presented By Nissan—February 25-28, 1988

Purse: $750,000

Riviera CC, Pacific Palisades, CA

Place: MC

Joanie, the boys, and I flew to Los Angeles for the LA Open at Riviera. Riviera is one of my favorite courses, even though I never played it well and as much as I hated the traffic in Los Angeles.

After missing the cut, Joanie and I faced our first cross-country flight with the boys—five hours in the air with five-month-old twins. We were concerned with Garrett and Conor's comfort as well as the passengers around us. We knew we would have our hands full. But Bernhard and Vikki Langer came to our rescue as they happened to be seated nearby. They immediately recognized our situation and wanted to help us out. Even better, they took great joy in holding Garrett and Conor for most of the flight. We were grateful and we have never forgotten their kindness. It was truly lovely to watch both Bernhard and Vikki hold our babies.

Doral-Ryder Open–March 3-6, 1988

Purse: $1,000,000

Doral Hotel & CC, Miami, FL

Place: T43

Score: 71-72-71-72

Made: $3,045.00

Hertz Bay Hill Classic–March 17-20, 1988

Purse: $750,000

Bay Hill Club & Lodge, Orlando, FL

Place: 71st

Score: 73-69-79-82

Made: $1,485.00

GTE Byron Nelson Classic–May 12-15, 1988

Purse: $750,000

TPC at Los Colinas, Los Colinas, TX

Place: T41st

Score: 70-72-69-70

Made: $2,486.67

Colonial National Invitational—May 19-22, 1988

Purse: $750,000

Colonial CC, Fort Worth, TX

Place: 61st

Score: 73-71-73-71

Made: $1,635.00

The Colonial National Invitational was a short field invitational with a district tradition. Each year, former Colonial National Invitational champions selected two deserving young players, who otherwise would be ineligible to play in this tournament. They called it Champion's Choice.

Dave Stockton let me know that I was a recipient of one of their two Champion Choice Invitations. Another important part of the Colonial National Invitational tradition was honoring the history of the game by identifying and celebrating key individuals who had played a role in building their club's tradition. That year, they were celebrating Byron Nelson at the event's gala dinner.

Meeting Ben Hogan & Byron Nelson

As a native of Fort Worth and a five-time winner of the Colonial National Invitational, Ben Hogan was the tournament's unofficial host. Inside the Colonial Country Club clubhouse was a shrine of Ben Hogan memorabilia. At the cocktail reception prior to the evening's dinner honoring Byron Nelson, Hogan stood in his enclaved shrine and greeted people. As one of the Champion's Choice invitees, I was introduced to Mr. Hogan. I felt honored to meet and shake Ben Hogan's hand. I couldn't keep myself from constantly looking at Hogan throughout the dinner and the evening speeches. It was spellbinding.

The whole experience was fascinating, watching two of golf's all-time legends, Golf Hall of Fame members. Both Hogan and Nelson were "sons of Texas" and lifelong competitors starting from their childhood, in the Caddie Yard at Glen Gardens Country Club in Fort Worth. Even at their ages that evening, and long retired from their competitive careers, you could

Byron Nelson and Ben Hogan.
Getty Images: Augusta National

nonetheless still sense their competitive nature. Neither would budge an inch for each other—head-to-head competitors for life. You've got to love it.

As the evening's honoree, Byron Nelson came to the podium after dinner and spoke eloquently about his career, his competition with Ben Hogan, and how he played golf to earn enough money to achieve his goal of buying his own ranch. It was a warm and heartfelt speech by Byron. When Byron finished his talk, he received a standing ovation.

Everyone stood to honor, acknowledge, and applaud Byron Nelson, everyone except for Ben Hogan, that is. Hogan stayed in his seat and never stood up. That blew my mind.

Memorial Tournament—May 26-29, 1988

Purse: $1,000,250

Muirfield Village GC, Dublin, OH

Place: 70th

Score: 73-75-78-75

Made: $2,500.00

Beatrice Western Open—June 30-July 3, 1988

Purse: $900,000

Butler National

Place: T74th

Score: 73-73-72-75

Made: $1,710.00

Anheuser-Busch Golf Classic—July 7-10, 1988

Purse: $650,000

Kingsmill Golf Club, Williamsburg, VA

Place: T14th

Score: 71-67-68-70

Made: $10,075.00

Federal Express St. Jude Classic—August 4-7, 1988

Purse: $953,842

Colonial CC, Memphis, TN

Place: T10th

Score: 71-70-73-65

Made: $21,143.17

PGA Championship—August 11-14, 1988

Purse: $1,000,000

Oak Tree GC, Edmond, OK

Place: T17th

Score: 70-70-74-70

Made: $11,500.00

The International—August 17-21, 1988

Purse: $1,115,280

Castle Pines GC, Castle Rock, CO

Place: T17th

Score: minus two points in final round (Stableford System)

Made: $15,500.00

BC Open—September 22-25, 1988

Purse: $500,000

En-Joie GC, Endecott, NY

Place: T45th

Score: 72-69-69-71

Made: $1,600.00

Northern Telecom Tucson Open—November 3-6, 1988

Purse: $600,000

TPC at StarPass, Tucson, AZ

Place: T33rd

Score: 72-68-71-70

Made: $3,315.00

JC Penny Classic—Mixed Team—Richard Zokol/Kathy Whitworth—December 1-4, 1988

Purse: $800,000

Bardmoor CC, Largo, FL

Place: T38th

Scores: 74-65-71-74

Made: $2,162.00

1988 PGA TOUR SEASON SUMMARY

Tournaments Entered	25
Cuts Made	14
Cut Missed	11
Top 10 finishes	2 (Hawaiian Open & FedEx St. Jude Classic)
Stroke Average	71.61
Driving Accuracy	T44 (.680)
Sand Saves	10th (.562)
Official Money	**$142,153.00**
Official Money List	**83rd on the 1988 Official PGA Tour Money List**

CHAPTER 11

1989—Back to Q-School Again—Getting a Taste of Golf Course Development—Dornoch Dunes

The wonderful ups and dreadful downs continued for me—1989 turned out to be another down year. At the start of each PGA Tour season, my objective, as it is with every Tour player, was to play well and get off to a fast start. It was never any fun to have to count on a strong second half to have a successful year. The Play Better perspective is always on your mind on the Tour—and the competition year over year only gets stronger.

I had learned over the previous few years that when my back was against the wall and when I felt I had nothing to lose, whatever it was it freed me up to perform. I had no answer to the question "Why do I play my best when I have the most to lose?" From the start of the year, I struggled to perform well. I was battling to stay in the top 125 on the PGA Tour Money List for most of 1989, and I became gripped in fear again—it was not fun.

In contrast, a year earlier, I had finished second in the Hawaii Open, and getting off to that good start gave me comfort in the year-long competition to make the top 125—therefore keeping my job. Looking back on it, it is obvious that I wasn't mentally disciplined enough. Instead, I struggled to keep my thoughts contained and in the present moment. It felt like I took a step backward in 1989. I had not yet learned to maintain my mental focus and discipline the way I knew I had to. Yes, I was making gradual improvements, but I was also still letting my anxious thoughts take over when I got off to poor starts. The longer it went on, the more it snowballed and became a bigger impediment to my progression.

Things could not have started worse in 1989. I missed the cut in the Bob Hope Chrysler Classic, then made the cut in the Phoenix Open, and then proceeded to miss the cuts in the next seven events. I made the cut at the Players Championship, then missed the next three cuts. My confidence was so unstable, and my mind (my ego) was constantly saying, *You don't want to go back to Q-School.* Those terrible thoughts only served to compound my problem.

What your mind focuses on is exactly what you will get. Throughout my 1989 PGA Tour season, my mind was fixated on not going back to Q-School. And that is exactly what I got—Q-School again.

Phoenix Open–January 28–31, 1989

Purse: $650,000

TPC of Scottsdale, Scottsdale, AZ

Place: T46th

Score: 70-73-70-68

Made: $1,844.50

The Players Championship–March 16–19, 1989

Purse: $1,350,000

TPC Sawgrass, Ponte Vedra, FL

Place: T50th

Score: 71-74-72-76

Made: $3,256.20

MCI Heritage Classic–April 13–16, 1989

Purse: $800,000

Harbour Town GL, Hilton Head Island, SC

Place: 72nd

Score: 72-73-75-78

Made: $1,568.00

Kemper Open—June 1-4, 1989
Purse: $900,000
TPC at Avenel, Potomac, MD
Place: T50th
Score: 70-70-73-72
Made: $2,114.00

US Open—June 15-18, 1989
Purse: $1,049,089
Oak Hill CC, Rochester, NY
Place: T46th
Score: 71-69-76-75
Made: $5,485.00

In the third round of the US Open, I got paired with Jumbo Ozaki. Ozaki played well, shooting 68 and got into contention. After the round concluded, a member of the Japanese golf media kept hounding me, asking if I had seen or had any evidence of Jumbo cheating during the round. It struck me at the time that the reporter was dead set on turning over any rock to accuse Jumbo of fudging the rules. I kept telling the reporter I had not seen anything untoward or inappropriate. I took note that he did not like my answer.

In the fourth round, I got paired with Raymond Floyd. I loved playing with legends of the game, particularly in major championships. There was a memorable moment when Raymond missed the green on the short side on the par-3 sixth hole. His ball ended up in a shallow mud puddle. Floyd was standing in casual water since the week had been inundated with rain, and the course was waterlogged. I took a good look at the position of Floyd's ball. It was obvious he was entitled to free relief from the casual water if he wanted. However, his nearest point of relief was in deep, wet rough. He didn't have a good option. I couldn't help but watch intently, wondering how one of the greatest-ever masters of creative shot-making would manage a difficult 15-foot flop shot with his ball in mud. After considering his situation, Floyd laid the face of his sand wedge wide open, quickly picked the club straight up, and then he came straight down on the ball with full speed. His ball flew straight up as if it were in an elevator shaft and came straight down and one-hopped into the hole. It was one of the greatest flop shots I ever witnessed.

Raymond took notice of me minding his business on that shot and his predicament. I looked at him and said, "Great fuckin' shot" as he strode triumphantly past me to retrieve his ball from the hole and gave me a little smirk. In his North Carolinian accent he said, "Now, Richard, I don't want you goin' round tellin' my little secrets." It was one of the coolest situations I ever witnessed.

Canadian Open—June 22-25, 1989

Purse: CAD $900,000

Glen Abbey GC, Oakville, ON

Place: T42nd

Score: 69-70-71-71

Made: $2,895.75

Beatrice Western Open—June 29-July 2, 1989

Purse: $1,000,000

Butler National GC, Oak Brook, IL

Place: T67th

Score: 69-74-73-75

Made: $2,040.00

Buick Open—July 27-30, 1989

Purse: $1,000,000

Warwick Hills G&CC, Grand Blanc, MI

Place: T31st

Score: 66-74-70-70

Made: $5,100.00

The International—August 17-20, 1989

Purse: $1,000,000

Castle Pines CC, Castle Rock, CO

Place: T32nd

Score: +4 (Stableford system)

Made: $5,660.00

Dornoch Dunes

In 1989, my brother-in-law and I started to plan out a concept for a golf course development in the Lower Mainland of Vancouver. We identified a property for 36-holes of golf on 400 acres of farmland between Mud Bay and the Highway 91 loop in Delta, BC, which was in the province of British Columbia's Agricultural Land Reserve (ALR). At the time, golf courses were a permitted use in ALR land. We brought in a "Landman" to negotiate an option to purchase agreement with the landowners. At that time, I had always felt the Greater Vancouver area needed a state-of-the-art golf course, and I wanted to be part of a project to bring it to reality.

The plan was to build two 18-hole true links-style courses to be designed by Jack Nicklaus. At the same time, another golf course development application had also been filed in Delta on ALR land near the Boundary Bay Airport by a fascinating character named Bob Ahoy.

My brother-in-law and I pitched the development concept to my good friend Peter Bentley. Peter then reached out to his close friend Ron Cliff—being able to attract two significant and influential Canadian businessmen into the deal gave the project credibility. Peter and Ron were both appointed members of the Order of Canada and both invested in the Dornoch Dunes development as principals. We proceeded with all the necessary steps, working with the City of Delta to develop the land. We connected with Jack Nicklaus's architectural team to do the design work, and two Nicklaus Design team employees arrived in Delta to assess the site.

The thinking behind naming the project Dornoch Dunes was two-fold. First, we wanted to create a true links course—not a "faux links" course. Second, I thought the project would appeal to Jack himself. Nicklaus had chosen the name *Muirfield* for his Muirfield Village Golf Club in Columbus, Ohio. A tribute to one of the great Scottish links courses. I thought it would resonate with Jack and his team to similarly pay homage to the great Royal Dornoch in Scotland. We wanted Dornoch Dunes to deliver a true Scottish experience in a suburb of Vancouver on the Pacific Ocean.

In 1993, after the New Democratic Party (NDP) came into power in the government of the Province of British Columbia, they amended the provincial ALR zoning restriction and removed "golf as a permitted use in ALR land." The project was effectively dead in the water. There would be no golf course development permitted. Even with powerhouse partners like Peter Bentley and Ron Cliff, our development efforts were stopped in their tracks. Sadly, Dornoch Dunes was not to be.

But the provincial government's amendment to ALR land was not going to stop Bob Ahoy. "Damn the politics," Ahoy told me. "It is my land and I am going to do whatever I want to do with it—and I want to build a golf course." Bob, of course, could not get a development permit for the construction of his golf course. That didn't stop him. And without permits, he also knew he wouldn't be able to hire architects or tradespeople. So, he decided to build his golf course all by himself. "I went to the library and took out books on golf course architecture and construction," he once shared with me. Bob was neither short on money nor on courage. He acquired bulldozers and other heavy equipment, and got proficient enough to run the equipment himself and proceeded to build a golf course all by himself. The end product was more than passable, considering he was prevented from hiring professionals. Bob Ahoy opened his golf course to his friends as a private golf course. The golf course was sold to Brad Newell in 2007 and renamed Kings Links by the Sea.

Meeting Armen Suny

While working on the Dornoch Dunes project, one of my priorities was to identify the best person to help guide and oversee the agronomics for the project. I felt at the time that most of the golf course conditioning in the lower mainland of British Columbia and the Vancouver area lagged behind the top golf courses in the US. I asked myself, "Which golf course on the PGA Tour has the best putting surfaces on a year-round basis?" My answer to that question was Castle Pines, an hour south of Denver, CO, where the International was played each year. Those were the best greens I had ever seen year over year. And they weren't in peak shape just because the PGA Tour was in town; Jack Vickers, the owner of Castle Pines, insisted the greens be immaculate every day.

My new objective was to find out who the "Keeper of the Green" at Castle Pines was. So, when I got to Castle Pines for the International in August of 1989, I knocked on Larry Thiel's door. Larry was the Tournament

Director of The International. I asked him if I could meet the golf course superintendent. Larry said, "Sure, his name is Armen Suny, let me get him on the radio." Larry switched the frequency on the radio and spoke into it, "Armen Suny, come in please." The voice came back, "This is Armen." Larry responded, "Richard Zokol, a contestant in the tournament would like to meet you." Soon after, Armen met me in the clubhouse, and I explained to him what I was thinking about Dornoch Dunes. He invited Joanie and me with our kids to his home for dinner to discuss it further. Joanie and I, plus the kids, arrived at the Suny home later that evening, and Armen introduced us to his wife, Christy, and their young kids.

It was a fascinating evening. I found out what a remarkable background Armen had from working at many of America's great golf clubs. Armen was a Philly guy and had previously been the superintendent at many of the great Philly courses, such as Rolling Green Golf Club and Aronimink. In 1981, Armen was assistant superintendent at Marion when the club hosted the 1981 US Open. Armen had graduated from Penn State's renowned turfgrass management program. Armen learned from one of the greats—Joe Duich, professor emeritus of turfgrass science at Penn State. Duich was responsible for creating Penncross Bent grass—a grass that transformed golf agronomy in the United States.

By the end of the evening, Christy told Armen that someday the two of us would be business partners. Though it would not come to pass at Dornoch Dunes, we stayed in touch, our friendship became strong, and we eventually reconnected as partners 12 years later, along with Rod Whitman. We co-designed Sagebrush Golf & Sporting Club near Merritt, BC. Armen and I formed Suny, Zokol Golf Design Ltd. in 2009.

Chattanooga Classic—August 24-27, 1989

Purse: $500,000

Valleybrook G&CC, Hixson, TN

Place: T5th

Score: 68-67-65-66

Made: $17,562.50

The Oilman's Tournament—Banff Springs

In 1989, I was thrilled to be invited to participate in the 39th Annual Oilman's Tournament in Banff, Alberta. The Oilman's Tournament attracted senior oil industry executives from across North America to gather at a special place, and it alternated each year between the Banff Springs Hotel and the Jasper Park Lodge.

Byron Nelson was the Oilman's Honorary Host Professional. Each year, the tournament would invite a second PGA Tour player to participate along with the great Byron Nelson. Joanie and I were delighted to get to know Byron and Peggy Nelson. My obligations in this event were to hit shots for every group on the famous par-3 fourth hole, known as the Devil's Cauldron, and later speak at the gala dinner after Byron Nelson had addressed the large gathering.

Everything the Oilman's committee did around the event was first class. My honorarium was more than generous, and they spared no expense. The committee sent Petro-Canada's Bombardier Challenger jet to pick me up in Chattanooga, Tennessee, following the last round of the Chattanooga

From left to right: Joanie Zokol, Richard Zokol, Byron Nelson, and Peggy Nelson standing on Banff Springs Golf Course's dramatic par-3 fourth hole—a.k.a. Devil's Cauldron.

Classic. Immediately following the final round, tournament transportation drove me right up to the steps of the waiting jet with the engines running, and we took off for Calgary. Other than two pilots and a flight attendant, I was the only passenger on the flight. Having played well in Chattanooga, finishing fifth, I was already in a good mood. When we landed in Calgary, a limousine was waiting near the steps of the aircraft. Joanie was in it. The committee had flown her in from Vancouver. The limo took us to the Banff Springs Hotel, where we were put up in the honeymoon suite. It was a great way to cap what had already been a great week.

Fairmont Banff Springs Hotel.

Greater Milwaukee Open—August 31-September 3, 1989

Purse: $800,000

Tuckaway CC, Franklin, WI

Place: T33rd

Score: 70-70-70-68

Made: $3,796.37

The Dunhill Cup—September 28-October 1, 1989

The Old Course, St Andrews, Scotland

THE 1989 DUNHILL CUP, FIRST ROUND

England	**2**	**Canada**	**1**
Mark James	73	Dave Barr	74
Howard Clark	74	Dan Halldorson	72
Denis Durnian*	72	Richard Zokol	72

* Durnian won on first playoff hole over Zokol

In mid-October, Joanie was pregnant again. We were absolutely delighted, as we wanted our children to be close in age. The first thing we needed to do was find out how many babies were in there. We drew a sense of relief when the sonogram showed there was just one heartbeat. The due date was June 1990.

Our happiness was tempered by the fact that I had played poorly most of the year and finished 163rd on the PGA Tour Money List. I was going to have to face the damn Q-School again. Following the conclusion of the 1989 PGA Tour season, I had to head back to Sectional Qualifying.

1989 PGA TOUR SEASON SUMMARY

Tournaments Entered	27
Cuts Made	11
Cut Missed	16
Top 10 finish	1 (5th in Chattanooga)
Stroke Average	71.74
Driving Accuracy	T41 (.696)
Greens in Regulation	48th (.671)
Official Money	**$51,323.00**
Official Money List	**163rd on the 1989 Official PGA Tour Money List**

Sectional Qualifying at Deerwood

My memory of sectional Q-School at Deerwood is a bit foggy, other than I played well and got through easily enough. The one thing that stood out in my mind at Deerwood was seeing this new young phenom coming out of the University of Arizona, Robert Gamez.

The weather in Houston, for the finals, was cold and difficult all week. I absolutely despised the cold because it had such a negative effect on my ball-striking. My body doesn't like the cold. But once again, I managed to make it right on the number, shooting an even par round of 72, the final round to go along with an act of good luck from P.H. Horgan III. I was able to keep my job.

1989 PGA Tour Q-School Finals—November 29-December 4, 1989

PGA Tour Spots: 50+ties

The Woodlands Inn &CC, North Course, TPC at The Woodlands, The Woodlands, TX

Par: 36-36-72 Yards 7,045

Score: 73-74-71-72-73-72—435

A total of 825 applications were accepted with 11 regionals held to reduce the field to 180 players for the final tournament. After 72 holes, the field was cut to 100 players who scored 292 or better.

1990 PGA TOUR Q-SCHOOL

1. David Peoples	73-67-69-72-67-72—420	$15,000.00
2. Tommy Moore	70-71-68-69-71-72—421	9,000.00
3. Jerry Haas	69-71-69-68-73-72—422	7,500.00
4. David Canipe	71-72-67-69-71-73—423	6,250.00
5. Bob Eastwood	73-69-71-67-73-71—424	4,375.00
6. Emlyn Aubrey	72-70-71-70-68-73—424	4,375.00
7. Ray Barr Jr.	71-67-74-71-75-68—426	3,500.00
8. Jim Woodward	73-70-69-70-76-69—427	2,975.00
9. Fred Funk	74-72-66-72-71-72—427	2,975.00
10. Dennis Harrington	76-71-69-75-70-67—428	2,048.00
11. Greg Bruckner	76-69-70-74-72-68—428	2,048.00
12. Michael Allen	74-69-68-71-76-70—428	2,048.00
13. Jay Delsing	75-67-68-74-73-71—428	2,048.00
14. Peter Persons	73-73-69-69-72-72—428	2,048.00
15. Greg Hickman	71-72-64-76-73-72—428	2,048.00

16. Lee Janzen 71-71-68-69-77-72–428 2,048.00
17. Patrick Burke 70-71-68-71-73-75–428 2,048.00
18. Neal Lancaster 74-69-72-72-73-69–429 1,475.00
19. Ed Dougherty 74-71-73-73-68-70–429 1,475.00
20. Tom Eubank 75-71-73-69-74-68–430 1,065.00
21. Steve Lamontagne 75-71-70-73-72-71–430 1,065.00
22. Jeff Wilson 70-73-72-71-73-71–430 1,065.00
23. Sonny Skinner 69-73-76-69-71-72–430 1,065.00
24. Bob Wolcott 76-70-70-70-72-72–430 1,065.00
25. Grant Waite 73-72-70-69-75-72–430 1,065.00
26. Rick Todd 71-69-74-69-74-73–430 1,065.00
27. Tony Sills 73-71-70-71-70-75–430 1,065.00
28. Brian Kamm 72-70-69-74-70-75–430 1,065.00
29. Bill Buttner 73-72-66-71-72-76–430 1,065.00
30. Steve Hart 71-74-72-72-70-72–431 800
31. Kirk Triplett 76-71-68-69-75-72–431 800
32. Mike Schuchart 72-73-69-68-76-73–431 800
33. Mark Hayes 75-73-69-71-75-69–432 743.75
34. Carl Cooper 78-69-70-70-76-69–432 743.75
35. Rick Fehr 73-71-72-72-71-73–432 743.75
36. Pat Fitzsimons 70-73-70-71-73-75–432 743.75
37. Larry Silveira 76-74-71-71-73-68–433 638.64
38. Tom Silva 74-72-71-70-78-68–433 638.64
39. Dillard Pruitt 71-73-75-73-71-70–433 638.64
40. Joel Edwards 73-72-72-71-75-70–433 638.64
41. Harry Taylor 72-73-74-69-73-72–433 638.64
42. Robert Gamez 75-73-69-73-70-73–433 638.64
43. Jerry Anderson 72-72-70-73-73-73–433 638.64
44. Sean Murphy 71-70-73-70-76-73–433 638.64
45. Nolan Henke 71-72-72-73-71-74–433 638.64
46. Dewey Arnette 72-74-67-69-75-76–433 638.64
47. Mike Smith 72-72-68-67-77-77–433 638.64
48. Mitch Adcock 72-77-69-73-71-72–434 560
49. Lennie Clements 74-69-68-73-71-79–434 560
50. Ted Tryba 72-75-71-74-67-76–435 54.5
51. Paul Trittler 72-74-70-72-75-72–435 54.5

52. Jeff Hart	75-72-69-75-70-74–435	54.5
53. Jack Ferenz	74-68-72-74-73-74–435	54.5
54. Brian Claar	79-70-70-71-78-67–435	54.5
55. Clark Dennis	72-74-72-71-75-71–435	54.5
56. John Dowdall	77-73-66-71-74-74–435	54.5
57. **Richard Zokol**	**73-74-71-72-73-72–435**	**54.5**
58. P.H. Horgan, III	74-69-70-72-72-78–435	54.5
59. Brad Fabel	76-72-68-71-74-74–435	54.5

Q-School Is Hell—for Everyone

The difference between making it and not making it as a professional player is such a precarious thing. Too many people think the key to being a great player is improving your golf swing. If you're at a high performance level, to even consider the professional level, the key to success involves how well or poorly you think. If you want to perform and make a living in professional golf, you'd better have a strong and healthy perspective. This includes developing a high level of acceptance and being comfortable and accepting the risk that things may or may not go the way you want. You have to proceed forward with the highest level of acceptance you can. As renowned psychologist Dr. Raymond Prior states, "It's simple, but that does not mean it's easy."

The big drama in the 1989 Q-School came down to the final hole, the 108th. The 18th hole at TPC at the Woodlands is a difficult one, with water lurking down the right side on your second shot. P.H. Horgan III made a double bogey on his last hole, which included missing a short two-foot putt for bogey, to shoot 78 and allowed nine of us with a six-round total of 435 to tie for 50th spot to get our PGA Tour cards.

There were nine of us who were sitting on 435 and watching things unfold with P.H. Horgan on the 18th hole miss a short two-foot putt; it was really ugly, but we thought the putt P.H. missed was for par. If that was the case, P.H. would have finished his sixth round at 434, in exactly 50th, eliminating all nine of us. But when P.H. came off the 18th green, he informed everyone his missed putt was for bogey, not par. He made a double bogey and finished at 435, which allowed all of us at 435 to tie for

50th spot. P.H. Horgan III received "thank you" messages and hugs from all nine of us for the next few months. Once I finished, I wanted to get the hell out of there. I didn't like being part of the euphoria of those who made it while standing next to the suffering ones who didn't.

CHAPTER 12

1990—Playing a Practical Joke on Jack Nicklaus at Cypress Point's 16th Hole

I will always remember the 1990 AT&T Pebble Beach National Pro-Am. There is such a distinct and special feeling awakening in Carmel, California, and then driving through the scenic 17-mile drive to Pebble Beach along with the sights and smells of the Pacific Ocean and the ocean waves crashing against the coastline. Experiencing the scenery never gets old. The Monterey Peninsula is truly one of the most awe-inspiring places on our planet.

Having barely squeaked through the 1989 Q-School (T57th) once again, I was happy to put 1989 in the past and eager for 1990 to get going. I had a sense of purpose and freedom once again as I looked for a fresh start for 1990. And once again, I was in a difficult situation, sitting 57th out of the 59 players in the Q-School category. I had to perform well immediately at the start of the season to improve my position in the Q-School reshuffle after the West Coast Swing. Even with that challenge in front of me, my eagerness to "get after it" had never been stronger.

As usual, every year at Pebble Beach, Jim Nelford and I set out early Monday morning to play a practice round at Cypress Point—one of the greatest golf courses in the world. Clay Edwards came in for the week to help me out, and he was also now working with Nelford. We got to Cypress Point early, and were hitting a few putts on the practice green, when we noticed Jack Nicklaus and Howard Clark, along with their amateur partners, walking up from the parking lot toward the first tee. As Jack and Howard walked up to the first tee, I reached out to greet Howard, who I had met in several Dunhill Cup events when he was a member of England's team (Howard was also a European Ryder Cup player). This AT&T Pebble Beach Pro-Am was Howard's first PGA Tour event, and that Monday would be the first time he had ever played the world-famous Cypress Point. We chatted and were reminiscing when Nicklaus said to us, "You guys are only two, so why don't you jump ahead of us." We said, "Thank you." As we were teeing it up, the starter asked Nelford and me if one of the tournament's amateurs in the field could join us. We happily agreed. The fellow turned out to be an investment banker from New York, and off we went.

That morning the fog or marine layer rolled in off the ocean thick as pea soup. Visibility was very poor. You could follow the ball's trajectory for about 30 to 50 yards before it disappeared into the fog. After teeing off, the three of us strode down Cypress Point's first fairway, which is always a great feeling. Playing golf does not get any better than Cypress Point. I was in a euphoric mood. Playing Cypress Point in the fog was magical.

The front nine at Cypress meanders through a forest of Monterey pines before it deposits you into rolling sand dunes and, eventually, onto the Pacific coastline for a stretch of finishing holes unmatched in all of golf. We arrived at the famous par-3 16th hole—a 230-yard carry across the crashing waves of the Pacific, which might be the most spectacular par 3 in the world. Standing there, in the fog, if you hadn't played the hole before, you wouldn't have any idea where the green is or where to aim. I didn't want the day to end. Still euphoric about the day and the setting, I suddenly had an idea. The fog remained thick. In fact, we could only see halfway to the 16th green, which was completely blanketed in the fog. Nicklaus and Clark were still behind us—as usual, there was a large gallery following Jack. I thought, *Let's play a little practical joke on them*. Given the green was invisible from the tee, all you could do was guess the line and club and hope for the best. It was just like being a kid playing the last holes in the dark. You just hit it and hoped to find it. What if we used the conditions to pull a fast one on Jack Nicklaus?

I turned to Nelford, Clay Edwards, and our amateur partner and shared the idea with them. Because the gallery following Jack couldn't see the green in the fog, I figured they would stay with him on the 16th tee. I said to Nelford, Clay, and our new friend, "When Jack hits his shot on the 16th green, he won't know I will be standing on the green. I am going to put

Jack's ball in the hole." Our amateur player instantly said, "I don't want any part of this, I am out."

I said to Nelford and Clay, "After we tee off on 17, and walk off the tee, you guys occupy that marshal over by the tree so he doesn't see me walking back onto the 16th green." A smile came across our faces, but I could also sense the apprehension—this was Jack Nicklaus himself. Nobody fucks with Jack. Besides, Cypress Point's 16th hole is sacred ground.

We hit our tee shots on 17. Clay and Jim went straight to the marshals and occupied them while I walked back onto the middle of the 16th green and stood there alone in the fog. A few minutes passed. There weren't any balls landing on the green. I was getting a little anxious. As I waited, which felt like an eternity, finally a ball landed on the green 20 feet from the hole. It was a Spalding Tour Edition. Jack plays MacGregor balls and clubs exclusively. It was Clark's ball. Without any other balls hitting the green, I finally couldn't wait any longer. I picked up Howard's ball on the green, dropped it into the hole, and ran down the 17th fairway, catching up with my group with no one the wiser.

We were putting on the 17th green when we heard the roar of the gallery behind us as Clark's ball was finally discovered in the hole. This thing we had just done had suddenly become very real. Nelford, Clay, and I had a nervous laugh. *What do we do now?* we wondered. Do we say nothing and let Howard think he had made one, playing with Nicklaus on one of the most famous par 3s in the world without even being able to see the hole? If yes, we'd be including an unwitting Jack Nicklaus in our charade. After talking out a couple of different scenarios, we decided we needed to come clean. We left a note on the 18th tee. I grabbed a blank scorecard and scribbled in pencil, "Howard, nice one on 16—NOT. Signed, 'The Crazy Canucks.'"

Jim, Clay, and I finished the 18th hole and waited for Jack and Howard to arrive at the 18th green to face them. As Howard and Jack approached the 18th green, I was standing there with a big grin on my face. Howard looked at me and said, "I didn't make a one on the 16th, did I?" I said, "No, sorry to say, you did not." Howard was good-natured about it. We had a chuckle, and Jack suddenly piped in, "So, how are we going to handle our $50 game, now?" I was unsure whether Jack liked our little prank or not as Clay, Jim, and I departed the scene.

On Thursday, I was scheduled to play Cypress Point in my first round. As I was hitting a few putts on the practice putting green, I noticed Jack was working on his putting too. I began hitting a few when Jack hit a putt in my direction. I didn't know what to expect as he approached me. I held my breath. Instead, and much to my relief and delight, Jack told me he had mentioned our little prank to the large group attending the annual Golf Writers Association conference last night. Each year at Pebble Beach, during the AT&T, Jack was the keynote speaker. He looked at me with a twinkle in his eye and, chuckling, said to me, "That was a good one." I instantly felt relief that Jack gave me his approval.

Ed Dougherty 11-Putts the 17th Green at Cypress Point

The wind can blow hard off the Pacific, and it's always unpredictable at Pebble Beach in February. The wind started to really pick up during the third round of the 1990 AT&T Pebble Beach National Pro-Am. Gusts were topping up to 40 mph by midafternoon, and play had to be suspended late in the afternoon when the 17th holes at Cypress Point became unplayable. Just prior to play being suspended, Ed Dougherty was playing the 17th at Cypress. Ed's second shot came to rest just a few inches off the green—25 feet or so from the hole. His putt was directly into the strong wind. Ed's first putt stopped just short of the hole. But it wasn't finished rolling after it stopped. The wind slowly got the ball moving. It picked up speed and eventually came to rest on the spot from which Ed had just hit it, right off the edge of the green. Dougherty repeated the putt and the outcome was the same. He did this another 10 times until the wind subsided enough to stop his ball from rolling back. Dougherty 11-putted Cypress Point's 17th and made a 13 on the hole. Tour officials blew the horn after Ed finished the hole, and play was suspended for the day.

Finally—a Good Round at Spyglass Hill

I've always loved Nicklaus's quote about the courses we played at the AT&T Pro-Am (Cypress Point, sadly, is no longer part of the rota). Jack said, "Playing Pebble Beach and Cypress Point makes you want to play golf. Playing Spyglass Hill makes you want to go fishing." His view was widely shared among Tour players—including me. Playing Spyglass Hill was always a bitch.

As much as I loved Spyglass Hill as a golf course, I'd always found it difficult to play well. It was such a demanding golf course. You could never let your guard down. You were always pressed to play your best at Spyglass or suffer the consequences.

In the third round of the AT&T, I teed off early in the morning on Spyglass's front nine. It was the same day Ed Dougherty 11-putted the 17th hole at Cypress Point. Hole numbers one through five at Spyglass are exposed to the wind coming directly off the ocean, totally exposed to the wind. Players knew that surviving the first five holes that day and being able to get into the sheltered forest that starts on the sixth would be critical. By the time I got to the sixth hole, the wind was just starting to gust. I was lucky. I had managed to get to the forested part of Spyglass and escape the worst of the strong wind.

It was a tough day to score on any of the three courses in the tournament. But playing in the shelter of the Monterey Forest was a stroke of good fortune for me. On top of that, I played the best round I had ever played at Spyglass, shooting 71. Because of the wind, scores that day were uncharacteristically high. I leapt into the top 10 after three rounds. With a final round 69, I grabbed sixth place and earned $35,000. It was the start to the year I was looking for—especially when combined with a T12th in the following week's Hawaiian Open, earning another $19,000. It was a great boost to start the year to improve my Q-School category position for the reshuffle after the West Coast Swing of the PGA Tour.

AT&T Pebble Beach National Pro-Am—February 1-4, 1990

Purse: $1,000,000

Pebble Beach GL, Cypress Point, Spyglass Hill

Place: T6th

Score: 75-71-71-69

Made: $34,750.00

Hawaiian Open—February 8-11, 1990

Purse: $1,000,000

Waialae CC, Honolulu, HI

Place: T12th

Score: 73-72-69-69

Made: $19,000.00

Shearson Lehman Hutton Open—February 15-18, 1990

Purse: $900,000

Torrey Pines GC, La Jolla, CA

Place: T37th

Score: 69-68-78-71

Made: $3,339.69

My good play during the West Coast Swing reshuffled me from 57th in the Q-School category to the third spot and also got me into the Players Championship. My new number allowed me to play in most Tour events I wanted to for 1990—another testament to what Play Better can mean.

The Players Championship—March 15-16, 1990

Purse: $1,500,000

TPC Sawgrass, Ponte Vedra, FL

Place: T56th

Score: 74-72-73-75

Made: $3,375.00

My Encounter with the Head of Rules for the PGA of America

During the first round of the Players Championship I had an unusual and costly run-in with PGA of America rules official Larry Startzel. PGA rules officials are not and never have been the same as PGA Tour rules officials. Larry had been a member of the PGA of America Rules Committee since 1981 and was a previous Chairman of the PGA Rules Committee. In fact, he had officiated in numerous major championships and 11 Ryder Cups.

The incident happened on the fourth hole at TPC Sawgrass in the first round of the Players Championship. My tee shot found the right fairway bunker. The pin was tucked on the front left portion of the green. As with many holes at TPC Sawgrass, water skirts the front of the green and around the left side of the green, effectively semi-circling the left side of the green. Larry Startzel was sitting in his rules cart on the hill behind the fourth green, watching me as I played my second shot from the fairway bunker. My second shot landed on the front left side of the green, and then scooted through the peninsula of the green into the water hazard off the left side.

I proceeded straight to the drop zone circle in front of the water hazard, preparing to drop my ball. Startzel immediately started yelling from his cart about 50 yards away, "Richard, you can't take your drop in the drop zone. You must take your drop up here on the opposite side of your point of entry of the water hazard behind the green." The spot where Startzel insisted I had to drop was on a huge mound with deep rough on an extremely steep slope. It would have left me with an impossible shot, no matter how well I struck it; my ball would not be able to stop before rolling into the water in front of the green. I pushed back, saying, "No, the drop zone is right here, and since I hit my ball into the water hazard, one of my options is to drop my ball in the designated drop zone." Startzel refused to reconsider and mandated, "No, you must drop your ball up here on the other side of the water from your point of entry." Startzel was insisting that I was not entitled to use the designated drop zone. My playing competitor, Fulton Allem, joined the debate with Startzel, insisting I had the right to use the drop zone. We all really got into it, debating out loud and very publicly while still 40 yards from each other. Startzel finally ended the debate by yelling, "I am the head of rules at the PGA of America, and I insist you drop the ball on the other side of the water hazard." Larry Startzel had just pulled rank.

Begrudgingly, I proceeded to the other side of the hazard where Startzel watched triumphantly as I dropped my ball where he had insisted, on the steep slope in deep rough. I was now faced with an impossible shot. Even if I hit a miraculous Ray Floyd-caliber lob shot, nothing was going to stop my ball from running straight downhill and into the water hazard in front of the green. I was resigned to this fate. Despite hitting a great shot, that is exactly what happened—my lob shot landed on the green, it raced downhill past the pin and rolled into the water hazard. Now Startzel watched me go to the drop zone. I dropped a ball, hit a lob shot over the water hazard, and 2-putted for a triple bogey seven.

After I had completed my round and exited the scoring tent, P.J. Boatright from the USGA was waiting for me in his cart. For decades, P.J. Boatright had been one of the game's leading authorities on the rules of golf. He was legendary and had played a leadership role in reorganizing the rules book and aligning the world's two governing bodies, the USGA and the Royal and Ancient Golf Club of St Andrews, to a standard view of the rules of play. P.J. waved me down as he sat in his rules cart, saying, "Richard, get in here." I got in the cart with Boatright. We drove off, and he proceeded to tell me, "Larry gave you an incorrect ruling on the fourth hole." I responded, "He cost me two, maybe three shots, P.J. he gave me the 'I am the head of rules for the PGA of America' lecture. What can I do about it now? Can I get my three shots back?" Boatright was sympathetic to my plight but had to say, "No, you cannot get those shots back." I asked, "Where can I find Larry?" P.J. replied, "He might be having lunch in the rules office in the clubhouse."

P.J. Boatright dropped me off at the clubhouse, and I went looking for Larry Startzel. I walked into the rules office, where a large round table of PGA Tour, USGA, R&A, and PGA of America rules officials were having lunch. The moment I walked into the room, the active conversation among the group of officials instantly stopped. It became eerily silent when they saw me walking over to the table. Larry Startzel was not among the assembled group. Everyone at the table knew why I was there; it is a rules official's worst nightmare to give an incorrect ruling that costs a player shots.

As I approached the table, everyone's face was down, looking at their lunch plates. I asked, "Anyone seen Larry?" PGA Tour official Glen Tait responded, "He just left, he's on the course." All the officials had walkie-talkies, so I asked, "Glen, can you get Larry on the radio and ask him his location? I'd like to talk with him." Tait got on the radio and, with the entire table of rules officials listening in, "Come in, Larry Startzel." Larry came back, "Startzel here." Tait said, "What's your 20?" Larry's voice responded, "Right behind the second green." Tait shared, "Richard Zokol would like to meet with you. He's on his way to you." Startzel responded, "Roger that."

The second green at TPC Sawgrass is close to the clubhouse. As I made my way to confront Larry, I started to think about how best to deal with this horrible situation. I was suddenly sympathetic to his position. I thought, *This must be a nightmare for him, all right in front of his peers and players.* It would be for me, but he made his own bed. He knew he cost me two or three shots. We would both have to accept the situation, the consequences, and move on.

As I approached Larry, I could see his guilt in his body language. Before I could say a word, he sincerely stated how remorseful he was for his ruling. I felt even worse for him now, hearing his voice. How could he face his rules official peers after such a blunder? After he had finished his apology, I said, "Larry, we all have to live with our mistakes, but what I had a problem with was your God-like approach when you said, 'I am the head of rules for the PGA of America and what I say goes.' Are you fucking kidding me? Yes, I should have asked for a second opinion, but your overassertive attitude as a rules official put me off, and that attitude leaves you with no room for error." He nodded. My message landed hard. He apologized over and over again. I am sure Larry never made that mistake again.

In all my years thereafter, I never bumped into Larry Startzel again.

Nestle Invitational—March 22-25, 1990

Purse: $900,000

Bay Hill Club & Lodge, Orlando, FL

Place: T41st

Score: 71-74-73-70

Made: $3,150.00

Independent Insurance Agent Open—March 28-April 1, 1990

Purse: $1,00,000

TPC at The Woodlands, The Woodlands, TX

Place: T56th

Score: 70-70-73

Made: $2,210.00

USF&G Classic—April 26-29, 1990

Purse: $100,000

English Turn G&CC, New Orleans, LA

Place: T58th

Score: 73-75-74-75

Made: $2,210.00

GTE Byron Nelson Classic—May 3-6, 1990

Purse: $1,000,000

TPC Las Colinas, Irving, TX

Place: T68th

Score: 71-70-76

Made: $2,010.00

Southwestern Bell Colonial—May 17-20, 1990

Purse: $1,000,000

Colonial CC, Fort Worth, TX

Place: T40th

Score: 67-71-76-70

Made: $4,100.00

I took off three weeks before and a few weeks after our beautiful Hayley Elizabeth Zokol was born on June 25, 1990. Joanie and I were so happy to have such a special little girl now in our lives. As a dad, I also liked the idea that Hayley, Dad's precious little angel, was going to have two older brothers hanging around throughout the school years to watch over her.

Chattanooga Classic—August 23-26, 1990

Purse: $600,000

Valleybrook G&CC, Hixson, TN

Place: 2nd

Score: 65-66-65-66

Made: $64,800.00

Greater Milwaukee Open—August 30-September 2, 1990

Purse: $900,000

Tuckaway CC, Franklin, WI

Place: 57th

Score: 72-68-71-72

Made: $1,989.00

Las Vegas Invitational—October 10-14, 1990

Purse: $1,300,000

Las Vegas CC, Desert Inn CC, Spanish Trail CC, Las Vegas, NV

Place: T8th

Score: 69-68-66-67-70

Made: $37,700.00

Walt Disney World Oldsmobile Classic—October 17-20, 1990

Purse: $1,000,000

Magnolia, Lake Buena Vista and Palm Courses, Lake Buena Vista, FL

Place: 20th

Score: 69-67-68-70

Made: $13,000.00

1990 PGA TOUR SEASON SUMMARY

Tournaments Entered	21
Cuts Made	13
Cut Missed	8
Top 10 finish	3 (2nd Chattanooga, T6th AT&T, T8th Las Vegas)
Stroke Average	71.03
Driving Accuracy	T42nd (.694)
Greens in Regulation	11th (.688)
All Around	33rd (561)
Official Money Made	**$191,634.00**
Official Money List	**84th on the 1990 Official PGA Tour Money List**

CHAPTER 13

1991—Back to the Q-School for My Fifth Time

Now with three children in tow, Joanie and I had new challenges trying to figure out the year's schedule for 1991. How much time on the road could the family travel? How much time would I be on the road by myself, leaving Joanie with her hands full at home? We had committed to never spending more than two consecutive weeks apart—but that was predicated on me playing well.

With all that in mind, I could not have gotten off to a worse start to the season. I missed the cut in my first four tournaments (Tucson, Hawaii, Phoenix, and Pebble Beach). I then played well at the Hope, missed the cut in San Diego, and then made the cut at Riviera—that was four missed out of six events on the West Coast. It didn't get any better as the Tour headed east. I made just one cut, and with scheduled time off in the next 11 events. Our initial plan turned out to be an unmitigated disaster.

As the year unfolded, when I made the cut, I made mostly small checks. I was also wearing down; I was getting sinus infections on a regular basis. Taking antibiotics and prednisone was routine. My body was taking a beating. My state of mind was too.

Bob Hope Chrysler Classic—February 6-10, 1991

Purse: $1,100,000

Indian Wells CC, Bermuda Dunes CC, La Quinta CC, PGA West (Palmer)

Place: T13

Score: 71-72-64-66-66

Made: $18,857.14

AT&T Pebble Beach National Pro-Am—January 31-February 3, 1991

Purse: $1,100,000

Spyglass Hill, Poppy Hills, Pebble Beach, GL

Place: MC

Prior to the 1991 season, the PGA Tour had begun to pay more attention to its political interests and any public perception that could harm its brand. Among other things, the PGA Tour Policy Board decided to cut ties with golf clubs refusing to adhere to non-discrimination practices. The highest profile action resulting from this new policy was precipitated by the hardline position of Hall Thompson, the owner of Shoal Creek Golf Club in Birmingham, Alabama. Shoal Creek was a private golf club that hosted two previous PGA Championships. But the club had no Black members. When challenged about the club's obvious lack of diversity, Thompson's blunt honesty exposed his deep racism that sent shock waves through the sports world. "That's just not done in Birmingham, Alabama," he said. "We have the right to associate or not to associate with whomever we choose. The country club is our home, and we pick and choose who we want."[5]

PGA Tour commissioner Tim Finchem's response was quick and direct: "It wasn't a tough decision for us to make, at all. Either the clubs where we play our events have a non-discrimination membership policy or we don't play our events there."

That also meant the AT&T Pebble Beach National Pro-Am would have to exclude Cypress Point from future AT&T Pro-Ams for the same reason. A local public golf course owned by the Northern California Golf Association Poppy Hills would take the place of Cypress Point in the three-course rotation. Johnny Miller put it quite succinctly on the NBC telecast, "Leaving Cypress Point and going to Poppy Hills is like leaving Bo Derek for Rosanne Barr." The PGA Tour took this political stand long before Augusta National Golf Club's the Masters were pressured to react to Martha Burk's National Council of Women's Organizations. In 1991, Augusta National had zero female or Black members. In 2002, the chairman of Augusta National provided a defiant statement about the club's

---

5 Shane Ryan, "When the 1990 PGA Championship at Shoal Creek Forced Golf into a Racial Reckoning," *Golf Digest.*

privacy, "Our membership alone decides our members—not any outside group with its own agenda. We will not be bullied, threatened, or intimidated to become a trophy in their display case. There may come a day when women will be invited to join our membership, but the timetable will be ours, and not at the point of a bayonet."[6] The Masters is not a PGA Tour event, so the PGA Tour chose to have zero say in this matter. At this point, the PGA Tour just handed over a significant amount of power to Augusta National Golf Club.

Nissan Los Angeles Open—February 21-24, 1991

Purse: $1,000,000

Riviera CC, Pacific Palisades, CA

Place: T54th

Score: 70-72-70-73

Made: $2,270.00

Riviera was always a favorite course of mine, a real treat to play, even though I never played it very well. The golf course was the reason I played the LA Open every year that I could. We always had crappy weather in LA each February, though. It was cold, and we seemed to catch some type of virus every year in Los Angeles.

Every mom and dad learns that parenting has its challenges, particularly when the kids get sick. After making the cut at Riviera and completing my third round, I headed back to the hotel to my waiting family, all of whom were severely sick. Hayley, now one year old, was sick. Three-year-old twins Garrett and Conor were sick. But Joanie was the sickest of the bunch. Each had flu symptoms, vomiting, diarrhea, and fever. I was the only one still healthy and was desperately trying to stay that way as I tried to care for them all as best I could while still playing in the tournament.

Even in her ill state, Joanie was trying to do the best she could for the kids, but by the time I got back to the room, she desperately needed rest. Throughout that Saturday, the night before the final round, we had called housekeeping several times for clean replacement bed sheets and towels. It was quite the scene. We were trying our best to get the kids to sleep, but

---

6 Ron Green Jr., *Cape Cod Times*, July 15, 2002.

nonstop puking and diarrhea kept them up crying. Which, of course, meant Joanie and I couldn't rest. Our room was a pretty foul scene. Housekeeping would arrive at the door with new sheets and towels, and I would pass them the soiled ones. By the middle of the night, I was in a state of delirium. I was trying to keep my wife and kids as comfortable and calm as possible. By morning, Joanie was finally starting to feel a little better. Off I headed to Riviera to prepare to play the final round of the LA Open without having slept a wink. I didn't think I'd break 80 that final round.

I made my way down Sunset Boulevard and arrived at Riviera. I had some breakfast, drank more coffee than usual, and set out to play. My goal was to simply survive the day. You may have heard the saying, "Beware of the sick golfer." Well, I felt that way. I knew I had limitations, which meant I had zero expectations. I was surprised how well I played. I shot 73. Perhaps the greatest 73 I ever shot, given what we had gone through all night.

GTE Byron Nelson–Classic May 2–5, 1991

Purse: $1,100,000

TPC at Los Colinas, Irving TX

Place: T12th

Score: 68-70-67-71

Made: $20,900.00

Kemper Open–May 30–June 2, 1991

Purse: $1,000,000

TPC at Avenel, Potomac, MD

Place: T49th

Score: 70-66-69-72

Made: $2,560.00

Centel Western Open–July 4–7, 1991

Purse: $1,000,000

Cog Hill G&CC (Dubsdread Course) Lemont, IL

Place: T21st

Score: 73-73-69-71

Made: $9,133.14

Buick Open—August 1-4, 1991

Purse: $1,000,000

Warwick Hills G&CC, Grand Blanc, MI

Place: T55th

Score: 70-70-73-71

Made: $2,250.00

The International—August 15-18, 1991

Purse: $1,100,000

Castle Pines GC, Castle Rock, CO

Place: T25th

Score: +15 (Stableford scoring system)

Made: $8,983.34

Greater Milwaukee Open—August 20-September 1, 1991

Purse: $1,000,000

Tuckaway CC, Franklin, WI

Place: T53rd

Score: 72-66-78-69

Made: $2,293.34

Buick Southern Open—September 26-29, 1991

Purse: $700,000

Calloway Gardens Resort, Pine Mountain, GA

Place: T67th

Score: 68-75-77-78

Made: $1,442.00

Independent Insurance Agent Open October 23-26, 1991

Purse: $800,000

TPC at The Woodlands, The Woodlands, TX

Place: T18th

Score: 68-70-68-72

Made: $9,737.14

1991 PGA TOUR SEASON SUMMARY

Tournaments Entered	25
Cuts Made	10
Cuts Missed	15
Top 10 finish	0 (best 1991 finish–12th GTE Byron Nelson Classic)
Stroke Average	71.03
Driving Accuracy	T42nd (.694)
Greens in Regulation	11th (.688)
All Around	33rd (561)
Official Money	**$78,426.00**
Official Money List	**149th on the 1991 Official PGA Tour Money List**

My tough year in 1991 meant a return trip to the dreaded Q-School. This would be my fifth time in the last 10 years. I knew what to expect, and I wanted to use that to my advantage. I had to if I was again going to keep my job. I had a family to protect and feed.

1991 PGA Tour Q-School

PGA Tour Q-School–December 4-9, 1991
Grenelefe Resort & Conference Center
Haines City, FL

I was very proud of the fact that I made it through the PGA Tour Q-School each time I'd played—1981, 1982, 1986, and 1989. I guess you could say I was an expert at it. I had always tried to bring a healthy perspective to Q-School. How I reacted, including having a high level of acceptance, was key and gave me more freedom. I learned not to let Q-School situations overwhelm me. Most players at PGA Tour Q-School harbor a significant amount of fear, apprehension, resentment, and anxiety that they haven't come to terms with. Instead, they feel like they're being held captive by an unhealthy mindset based on the fear of what may or may not happen—or what may have transpired in the past. I felt I had a strong game and was well-suited with a healthy and strong mindset to deal with difficult situations.

My coach, Clay Edwards, came out to caddie for me. I felt if we ran into any problems, Clay would be there with me. We were a team.

A total of 855 applications were accepted for the 1991 Q-School. There were 12 regional trials to reduce the field to 181 players for the finals. After 72 holes—the field was cut to 93 players who scored 289 or better—we were playing for 45 spots plus ties. I played solid for six rounds, using my composure in the Q-School environment and the experience to my advantage. I tied for 23rd and held 28th ranking position on the Q-School category at the start of the 1992 PGA Tour season. I was now five for five at PGA Tour Q-School.

1991 PGA TOUR Q-SCHOOL

Grenelefe Resort & Conference Center, December 4-9, 1991

South Course	Par: 36-35	Yards: 6,869
West Course	Par: 36-36	Yards: 7,150

Ranking	Name	Scores
1	Mike Standly	67-71-67-70-69-68-412
2	Carl Cooper	67-64-68-73-73-70-415
3	Tom Byrum	68-69-70-71-69-69-417
4	Kelly Gibson	72-68-68-71-69-69-417
5	Sonny Skinner	71-66-67-69-73-71-417
6	Paul McIntire	69-74-70-67-67-71-418
7	Jon Chaffee	72-74-68-65-70-69-418
8	Steve Hart	71-69-71-68-71-71-421
9	Fran Quinn	67-69-73-69-75-68-421
10	Patrick Burke	74-69-66-73-71-68-421
11	Donnie Hammond	71-71-69-68-73-69-421
12	Emlyn Aubrey	70-77-73-66-67-69-422
13	Mike Cunning	76-73-69-69-68-68-423
14	Greg Lesher	73-68-73-67-71-71-423
15	John Ross	71-68-73-68-71-74-423
16	Greg Whisman	74-71-67-72-67-72-423

Ranking	Name	Scores
17	J.P. Hayes	73-72-70-71-69-69-424
18	E.J. Pfister	73-69-66-71-76-70-425
19	Mark Carnavele	74-72-68-69-71-71-425
20	Robert Friend	72-72-69-69-72-71-425
21	Jim Woodward	72-73-65-73-70-72-425
22	Doug Marin	72-69-70-71-69-74-425
23	John Inman	72-74-69-69-73-69-426
24	Mitch Adcock	71-74-64-70-75-72-426
25	Bruce Zabriski	76-69-72-75-72-72-426
26	David Toms	72-73-70-69-70-72-426
27	David Ogrin	66-72-72-70-73-73-426
28	**Richard Zokol**	71-70-69-71-72-73-426
29	Chris Tucker	73-73-70-69-68-73-426
30	Tray Tyner	72-70-64-73-78-70-427
31	Michael Allen	73-70-69-73-73-69-427
32	Dicky Thompson	74-70-66-74-73-70-427
33	Brandel Chamblee	71-72-74-69-73-68-427
34	John Riegger	74-71-72-68-70-72-427
35	Jim McGovern	72-66-70-67-75-76-427
36	John Elliott	73-70-70-70-74-71-428
37	Kim Young	74-71-70-69-73-71-428
38	Marco Dawson	70-69-69-68-73-69-428
39	Robin Freeman	72-74-71-67-72-72-428
40	David Peege	72-75-70-70-74-67-428
41	Greg Hickman	75-68-69-69-72-75-428
42	Dave Schreyer	73-73-69-70-72-72-429
43	Mike Sullivan	74-74-70-69-70-72-429
44	Lon Hinkle	74-71-71-71-72-70-429
45	Dick Mast	70-74-71-71-70-73-429
46	Brad Bell	76-68-71-70-75-69-429
47	Greg Kraft	73-73-68-71-70-74-429
48	Steve Lamontagne	72-70-71-73-68-75-429

But I wasn't taking my strong mindset for granted at Q-School. Continually returning to PGA Tour Q-Schools and assuming I'd get through them was playing with fire. I knew it was only a matter of time. If I stayed on the same path, I'd eventually stumble and break my perfect PGA Tour Q-School qualifying streak.

As I looked forward to the 1992 PGA Tour season, I knew I needed to make changes—but I wasn't sure what I needed to change yet. During the break, I did some self-reflection. At that point in my career, there was a lot I liked about how I played. But there was a lot I didn't like. I was determined that 1992 would be my breakthrough year!

CHAPTER 14

1992—Q1—Building a New Foundation—Full Swing Reconstruction

The only thing better than winning once on the PGA Tour is winning twice—especially in the same year!

At the start of the 1992 PGA Tour season, I had small patterns of good play, but I was frustrated, feeling stuck on my moments of poor play—it was happening again. As I faced my 10th year on the PGA Tour, I felt I was spinning my tires. I was also running low on cash again, and I had a family to support. That is not an unfamiliar position to be in as a journeyman PGA Tour player in the pre-Tiger Woods era; it's a problem many players face at some point if you play golf for a living.

There's also another PGA Tour idiosyncrasy: no one wants to hear about your shot or how you played. Out of courtesy, whenever another Tour player asks you how you played, the proper response is with the number you shot, and you end it there. You never describe the details of your round to other players. They don't want to hear it, and in the exact same way, you don't want to hear details about their round. The other saying on Tour is, half the players on the PGA Tour don't give a shit what you shot, and the other half wish you shot worse.

The only thing that matters on the PGA Tour is what you shoot, and the solution to any and all problems is crystal clear to all Tour players—Play Better. Reflecting back, at the start of my season in 1992, I liked how I played when I played well, but I needed to improve my poor play. I was simply missing too many cuts. I needed to either play better more often and raise the level of my poor play, or learn to win when I played my best.

Until I could accomplish one or both of those things, I was too susceptible to missing the top 125.

Playing better more often was the key. And when I wasn't playing well, I needed to manage my game better to make more cuts. One's stability on the PGA Tour hinges on playing well in five or six tournaments per year. The Pareto Principle applies to PGA Tour players, just as it does to many things that revolve around performance. The most successful players make 80% of their money each year in 20% of the events they play.

Lee Trevino once stated, "Two things that don't last very long are dogs that chase cars and pros that putt for par." Put another way, if you don't improve your game, it's only a matter of time before you get run over. There is always a group of players trying to take your spot on the PGA Tour. And the best way to improve, for all levels and abilities, is to change the way you think on and off the golf course.

My first tournament in 1992 was the AT&T Pebble Beach National Pro-Am. Being at Pebble Beach was always a remarkable experience at one of the most special places in the world. Even if I had missed my fair share of cuts there, and the weather was always dubious at that time of year in Northern California, I would never turn down an opportunity to play the AT&T. Once again, I missed the cut, but what happened to me early in the week would be another turning point in my playing career.

Tony Robbins's Book *Awaken the Giant Within*

When on the road, I would often find myself in the mall, browsing the self-help section in a bookstore. One of these times, I came across Tony Robbins's book *Awaken the Giant Within*. Jim Nelford had completed a fire walk at a Tony Robbins event back in 1983 to improve his belief system, and the title of Robbins's book resonated with me. I purchased it and dove into it. It immediately helped me put things together in my mind. It validated what I was doing correctly, and it opened my eyes to other important aspects of my mental framework, much of which was new to me. Robbins's book provided the framework for me to build a healthy belief system and realize the importance of understanding the decision-making process and how it affected my perspective. After each reading session, which was usually in the evening prior to going to bed, I always felt inspired—and I loved that feeling.

Each time I picked up this book, it really resonated with me. I made a series of self-empowering decisions. I particularly loved Tony Robbins's explanation of an initial investment—an idea—nurturing that idea like compound interest. For example, I decided not to just read the book *Awaken the Giant Within*, instead I made daily deposits into studying the book. Each daily deposit was a small investment into my mental fitness account to strengthen my mindset. I felt this daily mental-skill deposit would accrue and was as fundamentally important as practicing my putting or any other part of my golf swing fundamentals.

The next powerful decision I made was to stop studying the book prior to going to bed in the evenings. I decided it would be better to experience the inspirational feeling I'd get from reading at the start of each morning, so I began my studies at the start of my day. I decided to wake up at 5:00 AM and immediately begin my daily mental fitness training with this book. I set a minimum study time of at least 60 minutes for *Awaken the Giant Within*. I'd pick up in the book from where I left off the previous morning. It set the tone for me each day. I was learning and building new healthy habits. Every night before I went to sleep, I'd look forward to waking up the next morning, grabbing my coffee, and settling in to work on my mindset development for the day ahead.

When I finished the last page of the book, I'd immediately turn to the first page and start studying it all over again. I would review what I had highlighted in notations on the pages in previous studies. Each time I reread the book, I'd pick up something new and different because my perspective was changing daily. I reread the book over and over throughout the 1992 season.

My Decision to Make a Full Swing Reconstruction

The book's perspective on the power of decisions really resonated with me. In 1992 my spot on the PGA Tour coming out of the 1991 Q-School category did not get me into the Bob Hope Desert Classic or Phoenix

Open tournaments. As had so often been the case for me, the AT&T was my first tournament of the year.

I vividly recall being on the practice range at the AT&T, which was still located on a polo field that was large enough to accommodate the extended field of PGA Tour players and amateur players for the week.

On the Monday of tournament week, I was hitting balls at the far right side of the practice tee. I was not happy. I was hitting it like shit and feeling completely frustrated with a specific aspect of my golf swing. The dialogue in my head went something like, *You've been on the PGA Tour for 10 years now, you haven't won, and here you are at the back of the bus again having barely squeaked through Q-School. Your swing isn't working and it feels like shit.* Something had to change. There was an aspect of my golf swing that had not changed over the past 10 years that was a barrier in my progress, and I hated it.

The technical problem I was having with my golf swing was coming over the top in transition to my downswing. It was a habitual problem for me. It showed up too often in my game. In my frustration, I stopped hitting balls and thought to myself, *This is fucking insane, I haven't made any progress with this aspect of my golf swing.* I could not keep doing this and expect things to change—I was in Golf Insanity, and it was time to make some changes. But I had no idea what those changes would be.

Johnny Miller Showed Me the Way Without Saying a Word

Exasperated again, I looked down the practice line and noticed fellow BYU alum Johnny Miller at the opposite end. I decided to take a break and go watch Johnny hit balls. I walked the length of the practice line to watch him. In my opinion, Johnny Miller in his prime reached a higher level of ball-striking perfection than any other Tour player had ever reached. His ball-striking and performance in late 1974 and early 1975 set a new high mark on Tour and earned him the title "Desert Fox." Miller had won the last two tournaments of the 1974 Tour season by eight and seven strokes, respectively. He then began 1975 in dominating fashion, shooting 24 under par at the Phoenix Open to win by 14 shots and followed that up by shooting 25 under par at the Tucson Open and winning by nine shots. His ball-striking and shot-making were unmatched in that stretch. Miller had shot 63 in the final round of the 1973 US Open at Oakmont to come from six strokes back and win. That round is still the stuff of legend.

I'd always marveled at how Miller struck the ball. I loved his one-knuckle left-hand grip that was square with his clubface at the top of his backswing. I loved how his shaft at the top of his backswing was perfectly square to his target. I just loved how he played and the freedom he demonstrated through his ball-striking skills. Miller's ball-striking skills were so high that he and his caddie Andy Martinez acquired their distant measurements to their targets in half-yard increments. Miller's putting was another matter, though. Who knows how many Majors (he also won the 1976 Open Championship) he'd have won if his putting had been better.

As old BYU Golf Team alumni, we exchanged greetings as I approached. I pulled up a chair behind Miller and sat down. I made sure my chair was back far enough to silently reassure him I didn't want to engage in conversation and disrupt his work. I just wanted to watch him hit balls.

I settled in, watching intently, trying to glean something—anything that would help me. He was there absolutely striping 5-irons as I looked on. That in itself was not unusual. I took notice again of how perfectly structured his golf swing was. His takeaway folded perfectly on plane; his grip, the back of his left hand was perfectly square to his clubface at the top of his swing. His shaft was square to his target, and his arc was fully extended. His back rotated 90 degrees around a perfect spine angle. At impact, he compressed the ball down the line, and his ball flew perfectly straight down his line of compression. He then started alternating fades and draw shots with the 5-iron he was hitting. It was truly an exhibition of great ball-striking. But the most amazing thing was that he was swinging *with only his left hand* gripping the club. His right hand was stuffed in his pocket through all these magnificent shots. I was flabbergasted and marveled at his lead-hand strength, structure, and coordination. Right then and there, it came to me that this was the foundation of Johnny Miller's remarkable ball-striking ability.

I knew Johnny was left-handed. I took notice of just how well established his coordination, strength, and structure were with his lead left side to be able to perform the one-handed ball-striking skills. His left-hand strength had to be massive in order to handle the centripetal force[7] (club head speed) required to square his clubface with the speed he generated through his impact zone. I had never realized how truly amazing Johnny Miller's skills were until that point, and it was all automatic for him.

The more I studied Johnny Miller's swing, the more apparent it was that his left side was dominating his swing. That is what enabled his swing structure to fold and fall into proper sequence. Lead-side pulling is more stable than backend pushing. All of it suddenly became clear to me. My mind was flooded with excitement. A vehicle can only fishtail if the force comes from the back wheels. A front-wheel drive vehicle cannot fishtail. It suddenly all seemed to clear, so simple.

As I continued to watch, I started to think about players who were lead-hand dominant. What I mean by that is I set about identifying left-handed players who swung right-handed. Johnny Miller, Moe Norman, Ben Hogan, Curtis Strange, and the great Canadian ball-striker Corey Conners are all left-handed. None of these players came over the top of their proper swing plane. Their lead side pulled with their lead left side, rather than pushed with their right hand or right side. Hogan took the club back inside his plane and then came over the top onto the proper plane. When Hogan initiated his transition, he put his shaft back on his proper swing plane in the same way as George Knudson. Many other great ball-strikers had this same action, including Bruce Lietzke, Sam Snead, and even Bobby Jones back in the day.

Then there are others that do the opposite, such as Lee Trevino, Fred Couples, and Jim Furyk, who take their backswing outside their plane and then drop it inside to get back on their proper plane. Either way works; the thing every player must avoid is putting the club on the wrong plane in transition in their downswing. There are different ways to achieve what you want as long as you eventually get it back on the proper plane. This was what I needed to change.

I thought to myself, *Most golfers are right-hand dominant with a right-handed golf swing. Perhaps that was the reason so many golfers have a problem with coming over the top?* I realized this was likely my problem.

---

7 Centripetal force is the force required for circular motion. Centrifugal force is the force that makes something flee from the center.

After watching Miller hit balls with his left hand only, he then started to hit balls with both his hands on the club. I could still see his left-hand dominant structure when both his hands gripped the club in his normal swing. Miller's swing was a thing of beauty and made complete sense to my way of thinking. After watching him for a total of 30 minutes or so, all kinds of fresh thoughts were running through my mind. I thanked Johnny for putting on a clinic, and I went back to my spot on the practice tee, excited. Other than exchanging greetings when I sat down behind Johnny to watch, nothing was said. When I was done, I said, "Thanks, Johnny, have a good week," and went back to my spot.

Right-Hand Dominant Golf Swing

When I got back to my spot on the practice tee, I started to experiment. I addressed the ball with my right hand only on the club and took the club away stopping when my shaft was parallel to the ground. I looked at the structure of this position. I noticed my right-hand dominance—even though my shaft was on plane, my clubface was shut, square to the ground. My pivot point rotated around my right shoulder. This was a strong right-hand dominant position. It was not the ideal position for my golf swing, but it was a strong and comfortable position that my right-hand domination naturally went to. Then I rotated my clubface to the proper toe-up, 12 o'clock position, square to my path's clubface. This position felt extremely weak and unnatural. There was no way my right-hand dominant swing wanted to be in this weak position—interesting!

Left-Hand Dominant Golf Swing

Then, I addressed the ball with my left hand only and took the club away and stopped when the shaft was again parallel to the ground. Everything naturally fell and folded into the proper position. With this left-hand only motion, the toe of my clubface pointed naturally to the 12 o'clock position, which felt strong and square to the path. I then turned the clubface to the closed position, still with my left hand only, with my clubface square to the ground. This position felt extremely weak and unnatural. I also noticed my pivot point shifted to my left shoulder, which is centered about one foot left of my right-hand-dominant pivot point—interesting. That meant I didn't have to maneuver my center of gravity laterally to align with my ball position. The one-foot difference was significant—even more interesting.

It occurred to me then and there that if I had my druthers, I would choose to have a lead-hand/side-dominant golf swing. The best way to eliminate my come-over-the-top habits would be to change to a left-hand dominant golf swing.

I realized it didn't help that I had a short back swing to begin with. When I got anxious, I got quick and had the tendency to disrupt my swing in transition, starting my down swing before I completed my back swing, which made it even more likely to come over the top.

My First Attempt to Swing with the Left Hand Only

I pulled out my pitching wedge and gripped the club in my left hand. I put my right hand into my pocket and then addressed the ball with the intention to make a left-hand only golf swing just like Miller had been doing. As I was about to make a swing with only my left hand, I started to freak out. The voice in my mind said, *There's no fucking way I can do this.* When I took the club away, I had no coordination, spatial awareness, or strength in this motion. Swinging the golf club with just my left hand felt like I was a beginning golfer, which in this context, I was. As I got into my backswing, my left elbow collapsed because my left forearm and grip didn't have the strength to hold the weight of the golf club in the fully extended radius of my left arm. The weight of the pitching wedge felt like a sledgehammer in my left hand. There was no structure whatsoever at the top of my back swing. I came straight into my downswing and tried to make contact with the ball. I completely whiffed the ball—interesting.

It blew my mind that I was so pathetic at something so important to me. But I knew theoretically that if I was able to recondition, strengthen my lead-hand, and develop the coordination (rewire the neuroplasticity in my brain) to swing with lead-hand domination, like Miller, it would greatly improve my swing structure and also eliminate my coming-over-the-top problem. It all made complete sense to me—BINGO, I found my new path. In that moment, I made a decision to commit to this path.

My first step down my new path began with pitch shots on the range with my 9-iron or pitching wedge, left-hand only shots. I am talking about hitting shots that flew 5 yards. I felt my mind struggling to adapt, struggling to find my low spot and squaring up the clubface. Hitting shots fat and then thin. Learning from the feedback with every missed shot.

Slowly the contact quality of each shot started to get better than the pitch shot before. My brain was working to acclimate to this new task. But all these shots when I hit them well were going significantly right of my target line—these ball flights were starting right of my line of compression (path). This was an indication that my clubface was open at impact. My clubface, in relation to the path was not square. I could tell my left hand wasn't strong enough, and I did not yet have neuropathic wiring to square my clubface at impact. It was a skill, strength, and coordination thing I needed to develop. When I swung with a right-hand dominant motion, my right hand would take over, coming into my impact zone and start to flip, which gave way to my two-way miss.

After hitting the first 25 or 30 shots, my left hand, fingers, wrist, and forearm were getting fatigued. My entire left side had gone through a significant and unusual workout swinging the club this way. All these new muscles were being worked out like never before and were getting pumped up with blood like in any physical fitness workout. Which made sense to me. My right hand (and right side) had been dominant in my golf swing, and my left hand and side was just along for the ride.

Just as I'd observed Miller doing 20 minutes earlier, I finally put both hands back on the club for my next series of pitching wedge shots. I immediately sensed my left hand and side was now "in the game" and not just along for the ride. With this left-hand dominance motion, my pivot point rotated around the axis of my left shoulder rather than the axis point of my right shoulder. After hitting just a few shots, my mind was blown again. The pattern of shots with both hands on the club, with my newfound lead-hand swing, seemed to eliminate coming-over-the-top action and gave me way more depth through my impact zone. It was a brand new feeling for me. This must be the feeling Johnny Miller had experienced his entire life.

My internal dialogue accepted that my habitual coming-over-the-top golf swing problem would be resolved if I conditioned my golf swing to become lead-side dominant.

I knew what I was doing was going to put stress on and strengthen the muscles in the fingers, hands, wrists, and forearms of my left hand. More importantly, I was establishing new neural motor skill pathways (neuroplasticity) in my brain to develop this new skill to execute my new swing motion. At the same time, I knew I needed to be careful not to overdo it—this new workload could easily damage my left hand, wrist, forearm, elbow, or left rotator cuff. Each morning I'd monitor the strain and feeling of recovery from the previous day's physical workout with my left arm, wrist, and rotator cuff.

I decided I would do everything I could to expedite my left-hand redevelopment. I would start each day brushing my teeth with my left hand, and on the first attempt, I damn near poked my eye out. I turned the pages in my book left-handed. I started to mark my ball on the green with my left hand. When on the practice range, I made efforts to pull each ball from the pile of golf balls with my left hand on the club rather than my right. At first, I couldn't believe how uncoordinated my left hand was in performing a wide variety of simple, daily skills. When I stopped consciously thinking about using my left hand to maneuver a golf ball to a good lie, my subconscious reverted to using my right hand. When that happened, I'd immediately catch myself and make a conscious correction to my left hand. It was all part of my neuroplasticity training plan to rewire my brain and habits.

Forming New Habits

Every day from that point forward, I would warm up by using my left-hand-only swing. Before putting both hands on the club and starting to hit real shots, I'd hit 20 full swing pitching-wedges with my left hand only. I could feel I was getting better and better at it with each shot, each day.

This habitual shift started to generate results. I could feel the improvement in my coordination with my left-hand-only swings. I was now making good contact, and my ball position and low-point awareness improved.

With each passing day, my path got more stable. Squaring my clubface was the most difficult skill to develop. It was the last thing to come around. I struggled with it initially. The lack of left-hand strength was the major factor, given the significant force required at impact. Finally, that started to come around too. In short order, I was able to make full swings using my left hand only and being able to square the face down the line at impact; the ball started flying down the line of compression rather than starting right and fading. At that point, after just a couple days, I knew I was on the right track. The next question was how long would it take before I could take this new motion to tournament rounds? That I did not know.

From my perspective, I was really building a second golf swing. Golf Swing #1 was my old right-hand dominant swing. And Golf Swing #2 was my new left-hand dominant golf swing. It was a complete rebuild of my golf swing from what I'd been doing on the PGA Tour for 10 years. I needed to muster the courage and trust to be able to handle the risk when I pulled the trigger and launched Golf Swing #2 in tournament play.

Through my Golf Swing #2 transformation, I continued preparation for the AT&T in just a few days. I had no problem going back with Golf Swing #1 for the time being. I really had no choice. I certainly wasn't prepared to bring Golf Swing #2 into play so quickly, even as I continued working on Golf Swing #2 before and after each competitive round. I knew that Golf Swing No #1 was the only one conditioned for tournament golf. Golf Swing #2 was not—not yet.

With each passing day, I made rapid progress. My enthusiasm grew, and I looked forward to seeing more progress with each passing day. Even though I missed the three-round cut at the AT&T, I worked hard every day that week on my new path. I accepted the difficulty and risk of heading down this path, and I believed I was on the right track and was 100% invested in my plan. On Sunday, I flew to Honolulu for the Hawaiian Open.

According to *Awaken the Giant Within* each day I was making big deposits into my Golf Swing #2 investment account, and I could feel the compound interest growing in my golf swing. I'd already realized I had established a different mindset than I'd had just six days earlier. It was a monumental shift.

Playing with Celebrities at AT&T

Clint Eastwood, Joanie Zokol, and John Denver behind the 18th green at Pebble Beach, February 1992. John Denver passed away on October 12, 1997, when his plane crashed in Monterey Bay.

My AT&T Pro-Am partner in 1992 was John Denver. It was the second time John and I had been partnered together at the AT&T. The first time was in the late '80s when John was a relatively new golfer. From the beginning, I recognized John had the ability to focus in on the task at hand. And John had the wonderful gift of not being self-conscious about his golf ability. Both are unusual and important characteristics that most golfers can easily struggle with, especially while playing in front of thousands of spectators. Even though he hadn't developed his golf skills the way he wanted yet, he was present-minded and had freedom in his pursuit to improve his golf game. It was impressive to watch him deal with situations so foreign to him while on national TV. By 1992, the second time we were paired together, John had significantly improved his golf skills. I marveled at him.

Clay Edwards often came out to Pebble Beach. Over the years, Clay became somewhat of a fixture on Tour. Clay periodically worked with Tour players other than me and Nelford. Clay was also a significant help to Mike Weir, both on and off the golf course, when Mike was trying to get on the PGA Tour. That week Clay also made a big impact on John Denver's game; Denver was over the moon when Clay's advice helped him win the celebrity shoot-out.

The Saturday of the AT&T was always the big CBS broadcast day. That was when the celebrity amateurs did their entertainment thing. Denver and I were paired with Clint Eastwood and Fulton Allem for the first three rounds. On Saturday, an especially hilarious moment occurred as our foursome walked onto the 15th tee at Pebble. The crowds that came out to see the celebrities were enormous, and it was the celebrities' job to entertain them. As we approached the large gallery standing behind the 15th tee, Denver addressed the crowd in his best Dirty Harry voice, saying, "Why don't I get Clint Eastwood to sing 'Rocky Mountain High,' and I will pull out my .44 magnum and start shooting." The crowd went nuts.

John told me he enjoyed playing golf, but his big passion was flying. He spoke about flying his Learjet, but he said, "There wasn't much fun in that, those jets fly themselves." He spoke passionately about the freedom he

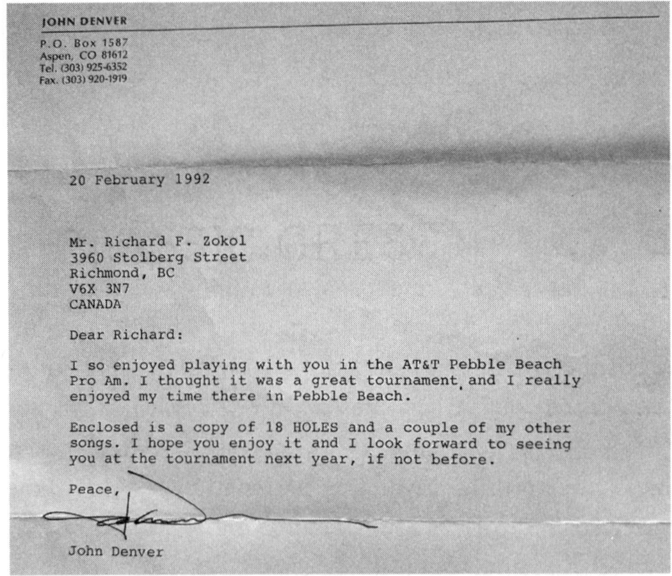
JOHN DENVER

P.O. Box 1587
Aspen, CO 81612
Tel. (303) 925-6352
Fax. (303) 920-1919

20 February 1992

Mr. Richard F. Zokol
3960 Stolberg Street
Richmond, BC
V6X 3N7
CANADA

Dear Richard:

I so enjoyed playing with you in the AT&T Pebble Beach Pro Am. I thought it was a great tournament and I really enjoyed my time there in Pebble Beach.

Enclosed is a copy of 18 HOLES and a couple of my other songs. I hope you enjoy it and I look forward to seeing you at the tournament next year, if not before.

Peace,

John Denver

felt in the maneuverability while flying his biplane and other lightweight experimental aircraft he owned. He was a passionate aviator.

As we all know, John Denver lost his life in a plane crash while flying one of his aircraft over Monterey Bay, California, on October 12, 1997. He was a remarkable person. I am one of the millions of fans who miss him every time I hear his songs.

I looked forward to working on my new discovery every day, and I was eager to get to Waialae and into the warm, clean ocean air of Hawaii. My ability—strength, coordination, and spatial awareness—to execute Golf Swing #2 was improving with each passing day. Despite the workload I was putting on my hands, wrists, forearms, elbows, and rotator cuff, I was recovering overnight without any problems at all. I was pleased that I didn't have any issues with hurting myself. My confidence continued to grow. Based on my daily progress, and even though it had only been one week since the revelation with Johnny Miller at Pebble Beach, I was all in. I said to myself, "Do it!" and decided to implement my new left-hand dominant swing on Thursday during the first round of the Hawaiian Open. During the practice rounds, I had no problem with my left-hand dominant swing. I also knew practice rounds were not the same as tournament rounds. The real test would be how my mind would hold up using Golf Swing #2 when the gun went off in tournament golf. I'd soon have my answer. The best way to learn how to swim is to jump into the deep end.

That first round at Waialae was another inflection point for me. Prior to teeing off, I told myself, *You will not be successful if you're not fully committed to executing this new swing. Otherwise, it will all have been a waste of time. If you bail out on this, you will be sentenced to Golf Insanity for life.* A voice inside responded, *Okay, let's do this.* During the first round, I did struggle with the new swing on most shots. But I never bailed out on it. I struggled through each shot and shot 79. I walked off the golf course elated, triumphant that I refused to bail out on my objective. I could have easily gone back to Golf Swing #1 at any moment during the round in an effort to save my score. But hell no! I held the line all the way to the clubhouse. I was proud of myself—this was a major step.

The second round of the Hawaiian Open was a "Eureka, I struck gold!" moment. Golf Swing #2 was fantastic and performed beautifully. Because I hadn't broken my commitment to myself in the first round, I had permitted myself the freedom to let it go. My new swing felt powerful, stable, and I felt I could rely on it. I shot 68 in the second round, but still missed the cut.

I was extremely excited about this progress. It truly was a victory for me, and in that moment, Golf Swing #2 instantly turned into Golf Swing #1, and there was no looking back. I no longer had two golf swings; I only had one. And it was my new left-hand dominant swing. I hadn't realized it at the time, but upon reflection, I was able to detach emotionally from the results, the score, in the first round of the Hawaiian Open. That was the breakthrough. I refused to get down on myself because I had shot 79. Instead, I kept my focus on executing my new golf swing the best I could and accepted any result it delivered. I spent the week working on my new swing.

After missing the cut in the Hawaiian Open, we flew to San Diego. On the Monday of San Diego, two significant things happened. One involved my good friend and agent Mike Barnett. The other was being introduced to a brand new putter manufacturer that nobody had ever heard of at the time called Odyssey Golf.

Michael Barnett

In 1988, Mike Barnett merged his Edmonton-based sports management company, CorpSport International, with Mark McCormick's International Management Group (IMG), and Mike became president of IMG's Hockey Division in Los Angeles. Mike had been my agent since 1984. I gave him a call early in the week after arriving in San Diego for the 1992 Buick Invitational to tell him I was broke.

My poor play and weekly expenses over the previous year had depleted my financial resources. Our boys, Garrett and Conor, were four, and beautiful Hayley was two. We were traveling as a family on Tour as much as we could because we didn't want to be apart. It was expensive. Each week, my after-tax cash burn rate was high: two hotel rooms per night and five airline tickets were costly. My poor play meant more cash was going out than coming in. I had run out of money and was thinking I needed to arrange a group to sponsor me to help alleviate my financial pressure. Mike had significant influence, and I thought he'd be able to help assemble a group of businessmen who might like to get involved. Either way, I needed his advice. After our conversation, Mike said, "I have some people in mind who might want to help."

The next day, I received a FedEx package with a personal check from Mike Barnett for $25,000.00. There were no new investors. Instead, Mike had reached into his own pocket to write the check. To this day, I have never heard of an agent reaching into his or her own pocket for a client. I will never forget that moment. That is someone who has your back. It not only gave me some breathing room, Mike's gesture gave me inspiration. It was a key that helped me turn 1992 around for me. I am grateful to this day to Mike Barnett for his friendship, support, and belief in me.

Odyssey Putters

When I got to Torrey Pines for a practice round and stepped onto the practice putting green, I noticed an equipment representative displaying his new product called Odyssey Putters. On Tour you get to know equipment reps, or at least recognize them, as part of the weekly traveling circus that is the PGA Tour. But this new product on display at the edge of the green caught my eye. It was a mallet putter from a company I'd never heard of. This Odyssey Stronomic Rossie 1 putter was named after Bob Rosburg (Rossie)—then a network broadcaster but also a notable Tour player who had won the 1959 PGA Championship. The Odyssey rep introduced himself to me as Michael Magerman. He was the Founder and CEO of this start-up company called Odyssey Sports Inc. Their product was strictly putters.

This Odyssey Putter won PGA Tour Win No. 1 & No. 2—both in 1992.

I hit a few putts with the Odyssey mallet. The ball felt great coming off the face of this putter. Magerman, in the process of selling me on his product, told me what differentiated the Odyssey Putter from others was its soft feel—the result of being manufactured with a metal called *stronomic*. I didn't care what it was made from—I only cared if it improved my putting. I gave it a good workout on the putting green, hitting all kinds of putts. I loved it. I asked him, "Can I keep the one?" He said, "Of course you can." He then handed me a one-page agreement stating that if I win a PGA Tour event using an Odyssey Putter, the company would pay $1.00 for every Odyssey Putter sold in North America in the one year following the win.

Shortly after meeting Michael Magerman, I found out that Brad Adams was Sr. VP at Odyssey Golf. I knew Brad through his father, Gary, the founder of TaylorMade Golf, the manufacturer of metalwoods. I was a TaylorMade player in my rookie year and got to know Gary Adams and his family.

Later in the 1992 PGA Tour season I would win both the Deposit Guaranty Classic and the Greater Milwaukee Open. The agreement that Magerman gave me stated I was entitled to $1.00 for every Odyssey Putter sold in North America for one year from the date of winning the 1992 Deposit Guaranty Classic. But I had won twice. The agreement had an accelerator clause that committed the company to paying me $2.00 for every putter sold for the year following the date of my first win until the 1993 Deposit Guaranty Classic, then $1.00 until the date of the 1993 Greater Milwaukee Open.

At the conclusion of the 1992 PGA Tour season, Mike Barnett reached out to Magerman to calculate and process the payouts. Even with my two wins, Odyssey was still a fledgling start-up company, and the company didn't have the cash on hand to fulfill the terms of the contract. Instead, Magerman offered me a significant equity position in Odyssey Sports Inc. The equity offer was around 10% if I recall properly. I chose not to accept the equity offer, and we instead settled on a smaller cash number—I cannot recall the exact amount, but it was a sizable amount for me.

Fast-forward six years, in July 1997, Callaway Golf acquired Odyssey Sports Inc. for $130 million. Today, the Odyssey brand is one of the most recognizable putter brands on the PGA Tour and in pro shops and golf retail outlets around the world. Not long after the sale, I ran into Magerman at the PGA Merchandise Show in Orlando, FL. By then, Magerman had become president of Tommy Armour Golf. He looked at me and said, "Richard, you should have taken the fucking stock." No shit, Sherlock!

My hard work was clearly paying off. My ball-striking had dramatically improved. My game was trending in the right direction. I felt like I was on the right track and my confidence was reaching new heights. My game was getting stronger with each passing week.

Nissan Los Angeles Open—February 28–March 1, 1992

Purse: $1,000,000

Riviera CC, Pacific Palisades, CA

Place: T50th

Score: 69-72-69-72

Made: $2,365.50

After the West Coast Swing, I had only made one cut. On paper, it looked like any other year I had to date. But I had laid down the foundation for a new future with my new swing. Normally, making just one cut on the West Coast would have triggered a downward spiral, but my ball-striking investment was growing with interest each passing day. I felt confident that I was on the right track.

Dunhill Cup Qualifying

Dunhill Cup Qualifying—March 26–30, 1992

Royal Hong Kong Golf Club, Fanling, Hong Kong

Canada sent a three-man team to Hong Kong to qualify Canada for the Dunhill Cup being played later in the year in Scotland. Joining me on the Canadian team were my good friends Rick Gibson and Ray Stewart. We played well and qualified Canada for the finals in October. The qualifying format in Hong Kong was Medal Play. We (Canada) were paired in the first two rounds with South Africa. As chance would have it, I played with a young Ernie Els for three days. Nobody in North America knew about Els at the time. I had never heard of him, but after watching him up close for those three days, I came away more impressed than I'd ever been with a young player's ability. I told Rick and Ray that this Ernie Els kid from South Africa will become the best player in the world within five years. That, of course, was prior to Tiger Woods bursting onto the PGA Tour scene a few years later and setting a new bar for performance at the highest level of the game. Nonetheless, Els ended up having a tremendous career, winning four Majors. He remains one of only six players to win both the US Open and the Open Championship twice.

CHAPTER 15

1992—Q2—My First PGA Tour Win was an Unofficial Win

After Rick Gibson, Ray Stewart, and I played for Canada and successfully qualified Canada into the Dunhill Cup, I flew from Hong Kong to New Orleans to play the Freeport-McMoran Classic. I've always had a fondness for New Orleans culture and food. Strolling down Bourbon Street was always entertaining, if not a bit sketchy. But the food was always worth any risk in downtown New Orleans. My favorite restaurant was the Bon Ton Café on Magazine Street. Their Bon Ton Red Fish and Bread Pudding with Whiskey Sauce was to die for. I could have it every night.

Freeport-McMoRan Golf Classic—April 2, 1992
Purse: $1,000,000
English Turn G&CC, New Orleans, LA
Place: T18th
Score: 73-71-71-69
Made: $12,600.00

My new golf swing was getting more stable day by day, week by week, and I placed T18th in New Orleans, making $12,600. The week after New Orleans was the Masters, and I figured my invitations must have gotten lost in the mail because I didn't receive one. So I drove from New Orleans to Hattiesburg, MS, to play the PGA Tour's satellite event, the Deposit Guaranty Classic or as others called it, the Mississippi Masters.

Deposit Guaranty Classic—April 9-12, 1992

Purse: $300,000

Hattiesburg CC, Hattiesburg, MS

Place: 1st

Score: 67-67-66-67

Made: $54,000.00

Walking the Gauntlet for the Fifth Time—and Winning

The Deposit Guaranty Classic did not count as an official PGA Tour win until 1994 since it was played opposite the Masters—but money won in the event counted as official on the PGA Tour money list. For me though, the 1992 win validated everything I'd been working so hard to change in my game. I was ecstatic.

The best way to learn is through the struggle of failure. Whether it's learning to walk as a toddler or standing at a podium and becoming an eloquent public speaker, nobody is born with these inherent skills. That's especially the case with golf. The skills required to perform at a high level in golf are learned. And, like anything worthwhile, it does not come easy. Only through struggle and perseverance do golfers learn. That includes learning what it takes to perform at the peak of your abilities in pressure-filled situations and difficult playing conditions. Learning to play well while in contention during the final round of a PGA Tour event is an acquired skillset unto itself.

To win on the PGA Tour, you need to learn to feel comfortable in difficult situations in order to play well while being in contention and on national television. That includes being able to outperform everyone else and successfully Walk the Gauntlet. This is not easy to do when the golf world's eyes are upon you and you are competing against the best players in the world who are also playing their best at that moment.

On The Tee with Harry C

At the start of 1992, I went through a period of rotating through a few caddies. Too often, I found that player/caddie relationships get stuck. When

Harry Caddell (a.k.a. Harry "C").

in sync, the player/caddie relationship can be powerful; there is a rhythmic flow with the duty to acquire each shot assessment and shot execution as a team. I liken it to the military's sniper/scout team that requires both to perform specific duties in order to achieve the objective. I expect my caddie to range in the target and Kentucky windage and gather other information that may be involved in strategizing each specific shot, such as how the ball may react when it hits the ground, etc.

I was a player who did not like to have my caddie involved in reading my putts. I only called my caddie in to read my putt if I couldn't get a good read myself. The reason why is if I read my putt a certain way and my caddie reads the same putt a different way, it could cause confusion or possibly leave me second-guessing my own read, which could easily disrupt my commitment to assess or execute the putt.

I felt like I was an excellent reader of the greens—except when it came to Common Bermuda greens. Though over the decades, technology on certain strains of Bermuda greens, such as TifEagle, has improved, making them much easier to read, and they are now some of the best putting surfaces.

I first met Harry C in 1982 in Greensboro, NC, and Harry was on my bag in Hattiesburg the following week in the 1982 Magnolia Classic, my rookie year. It was 10 years later that Harry first worked for me. A couple of weeks prior, Harry had noticed I had turned my game around. He approached me to ask if he could work for me in Hattiesburg on our 10-year anniversary, as well as later in the year at the Canadian Open in September. Harry knew I would not hire him on a full-time basis. From our previous time working together, he was aware I could only take so much of him. Harry loved the game, and he wanted to help everyone. He had a wonderful heart and loved giving advice, whether you wanted to hear it or not. He couldn't help giving unsolicited advice, and he just didn't quite know where the line was. He couldn't help himself; he wanted to be in charge. Despite our rocky history, we did have a better player-caddie relationship than was the norm on Tour. I really liked Harry, but our time together wouldn't last long or end well. But Harry knew I would be gearing up with a specific focus on the Canadian Open later in the season, so he wanted to work for me later in the year in Canada.

Harry C was an exuberant, passionate, and knowledgeable caddie. I loved the guy and had fired him on a number of occasions. But we got along great off the golf course. I had a soft spot for Harry and once told him sincerely, "Harry, if I had my druthers, I would want you on my bag for my first PGA Tour win." In the end, that's the way it turned out. But it almost didn't because of what happened on the back nine on Sunday at the Deposit Guaranty Classic. I almost fired Harry C on the 16th hole with the tournament win in sight.

As my game was dramatically improving week by week, I felt good about my chances. Standing with Harry on the first tee of Thursday's opening round, I turned to him and said, "Harry, as good as I am playing right now, if we eliminate all mental mistakes this week, we will win this tournament." Harry responded in his classic North Carolinian accent, "You got it, Pro—you are on the tee with Harry 'C.'" I looked at him and said, "Shut the fuck up with all that bullshit, Harry. Let's focus in here." Harry gave me a big shit-eating grin right back. And so, the week began.

Harry and I did a great job of minimizing our mental mistakes across the first three rounds. I opened with 67-67-66, which got me in contention to win going into the final round. On Sunday, we played in the second-to-last group. It was my fourth time preparing to Walk the Gauntlet and the first time with Harry C. I had made progress becoming more comfortable with each successive Gauntlet Walk experience. I no longer got anxious seeing my name near the top of the leaderboard; in fact I liked it. I didn't need my Sony Walkman to distract me. Whether this event was an official PGA Tour win or not—a win was a win—and I was ready to finally walk through the door in Hattiesburg in 1992. Still, it would be my first time Walking the Gauntlet since the Hawaiian Open in 1988.

The final round began with Mike Donald in the lead at 13 under par. Bob Eastwood, Mike Nicolette, and Greg Twiggs were two shots back at 11 under. I was at 10 under par.

As well as I was playing, I was still struggling to pick up on the grain of the Common Bermuda greens at Hattiesburg CC. On the other hand, Harry was a brilliant green reader, particularly on those grainy Common Bermuda greens he had grown up with his entire life.

We got off to a strong start in the final round. Standing on the 10th tee, I found myself tied for the lead. I wanted to get in front of Harry as he was already showing signs of getting a bit too excited for my liking. I turned to Harry and said, "Harry, on the greens, if I call you in to read my putt, all I want you to do is tell me which direction the grain is going, that's it, nothing more. I don't want any other information. All I want is the direction of the grain, okay?" Harry responded with his standard, "You got it, Pro."

Waking the Gauntlet on the back nine in a final round gets intense when you're around the lead. I had my hands full striving to keep my emotional shit wired tight. I'd never been in contention with Harry C on my bag, and I had no idea how excited he might get. I didn't want to have to worry about him. Instead, what I needed most was his eye to figure out the grain on the greens. When we got to the 13th green, and I found myself trying to read a putt, I found I couldn't pick up the grain. I called Harry over, "Harry, have a look at this putt." Harry was on the putt like a German shorthaired pointer getting after quail in the bush. If Harry had a tail, it would have been wagging like a son of a bitch. He looked at the putt carefully from a couple of angles, and having completed his assessment, he stood next to me behind the ball and went, "Pro, I need you to put this thing eight inches off the left edge of the cup with firm pace, and I want you to drill it in the back of the hole." I said, "Fuck Harry, I don't want to hear what you think I should do with this putt. I want you to tell me which way the grain is going! That's it." Harry said, "The grain is going hard from 8 o'clock to 2 o'clock, Pro." I responded with a very terse, "Thank you."

When it was my turn to play, I went through my shot routine, pulled the trigger, and made the putt. As I picked the ball out of the hole, I looked over at Harry on the back of the green, and he was giving me fist pumps, beaming ear to ear. I could see he was jacked up to the max and trying to pump me up, too. Up to that point, I had been doing a great job keeping my thoughts and emotions focused on being calm. Now all of a sudden I had to calm Harry C down. I barked, "Harry, calm the fuck down, we've got holes to play."

As we played the 14th and 15th holes, I could sense Harry was chomping at the bit like a thoroughbred at the gate; he was amped up and wanted to run. I was desperately hoping I wouldn't need to ask him anything that would trigger him more. I feared Harry wouldn't be able to calm himself. I hit a good tee shot on 16 right down the middle of the fairway. As we walked toward my second shot, out of nowhere, Harry blurted out, "Pro, you can win this." I thought to myself, *Geez, he's back trying to pump me up.* I reminded him, "Harry, don't say anything unless I bring you in and ask you." We arrived at my ball and went through our pre-shot routine to confirm the yardage and figure out the shot I needed to make. I was between clubs. I asked him, "Harry, do you think 7-iron is too much?" Harry was beyond jacked up by now and said, "Pro, I need you to go right at the pin with a hard draw with your 8-iron." Annoyed yet again, I responded, "Harry, the only thing I want to hear from you is 'Yes, it's too much' or 'No, it's not.' That's it." Harry said, "Yes, 7-iron is too much." It validated my own thoughts. I said, "Thank you." I pulled my 8-iron, went into my shot routine, and executed another great shot. After I handed the club back to Harry, he went right back to giving me praise, saying that I've got this. I stopped him mid-stream, "Harry, you are really pissing me off, you need to just shut up unless I ask you for something." By this point, our playing contestants and caddies were noticing that Harry C and I were quarreling. They were looking at us, wondering what the hell was going on. Harry didn't stop. He muttered more encouragement, still not listening to me—thinking I needed to be encouraged when I needed the exact opposite. I needed to stay calm.

As we approached the green, I'd had enough and needed to get my message through to Harry, so I shouted at him, "HARRY, SHUT THE FUCK UP. IF YOU SAY ANOTHER FUCKING WORD WITHOUT ME ASKING YOU A FUCKING QUESTION, I AM GOING TO FUCKING FIRE YOUR ASS RIGHT HERE RIGHT NOW." Harry went silent. I made par on the 16th hole.

The 17th hole was a long par 5. A strong third shot with a pitching wedge left me with a 10-foot putt for birdie. I wasn't sure where I was in the standings—I could have been tied for the lead or have the lead, I wasn't sure. All my efforts were going into making this putt, and once again, I couldn't pick up the grain. Once again, I had to bring Harry in to look at the putt. I said, "Harry, what's the grain doing here, Pal?" Harry's tail started to rapidly wag. After Harry looked at the putt, he said, "It's going from 11 o'clock to 5 o'clock, Pro." I made the putt. As it turned out, I took a one-shot lead into the 72nd hole. I looked at Harry. He had the biggest shit-eating grin I'd ever seen on his face. I couldn't help but smile back at him. I made par on the last hole to shoot 67 and won my first PGA Tour event with Harry C beside me every step of the way.

Winning felt weird. I thought there would be fireworks of excitement, but there weren't. Instead, I felt a deep sense of gratification and great validation in what I believed and the decision to make such a massive swing change to lead-side domination. It was tremendously fulfilling.

THE 1992 DEPOSIT GUARANTY CLASSIC

Place	Name	Scores	Money
1st	Richard Zokol	67-67-66-67-267	$54,000.00
T2nd	Mike Donald	68-62-67-71-268	19,800.00
T2nd	Bob Eastwood	67-65-69-67-268	19,800.00
T2nd	Mike Nicolette	71-64-64-69-268	19,800.00

Place	Name	Scores	Money
T2nd	Greg Twiggs	65-69-65-69-268	19,800.00
T6th	Frank Conner	69-66-66-68-269	9,712.50
T6th	Marco Dawson	67-68-70-64-269	9,712.50
T6th	Jack Renner	68-69-69-63-269	9,712.50

With the 1992 Deposit Guaranty Classic trophy.

GTE Byron Nelson Classic—May 14–17, 1992

Purse: $1,000,000

TPC at Las Colinas, Irving, TX

Place: T21st

Score: 68-70-66

Made: $10,326.25

Southwestern Bell Colonial—May 21-24, 1992

Purse: $1,300,000

Colonial CC, Fort Worth, TX

Place: T16th

Score: 70-67-71-66

Made: $17,073.00

Federal Express St. Jude Classic—June 11-14, 1992

Purse: $1,100,000

TPC Southwind, Memphis, TN

Place: T64th

Score: 70-69-71-69

Made: $2,200.00

US Open—June 18-21, 1992

Purse: $1,000,000

Pebble Beach GL, Pebble Beach, CA

Place: T33rd

Score: 72-72-72-80

Made: $10,531.09

Next up was the 1992 US Open at Pebble Beach. There is something special about US Opens being played at Pebble Beach. It's akin to the Open Championships being played at the Old Course in St Andrews, Scotland. Both venues are cathedral-like when US Opens and Open Championships are played there.

US Opens are intended to be brutally difficult. Russ Jordan, my best friend, was caddying for me as he usually did in US Opens. Russ always loved the US Open and was instrumental in how I looked at US Open completion as well. Russ helped me embrace US Opens. The purpose of all US Opens is to subject all 156 players in the field to extremely difficult situations in order to identify the champion. In most cases, the victor is the last man standing. But the final round of the 1992 US Open at Pebble Beach set a new high bar for most difficult US Open rounds. Winds were gusting to 45 mph. It was a brutal test all day.

After 54 holes, I was feeling good, having shot three consecutive rounds of even par 72. Playing the first three rounds of the US Open without shooting over par would typically find you in contention. With 18 holes to go, I was just three shots off the lead. Paul Azinger and I were paired together in the final round. I will never forget how I felt standing on the first tee that Sunday. It was the most nervous I had ever felt at any point in my career. My friend Ron Read from the USGA was the starter, and I had the first tee honor. As we stood on the tee nervously waiting for the announcement, Ron turned to me and said, "Richard, the telecast is coming out of commercial in 45 seconds, and then I will call you to the tee." In that moment, I turned and walked straight into the starter's tent and began to hyperventilate. I immediately started taking deep breaths, trying to calm myself to a controllable level. I said to myself, *This is why you have a shot routine: trust and execute your routine.* The moment felt surreal. I stepped out of the tent to Ron Read's voice shouting from the PA system, "On the tee from Vancouver, Canada, please welcome Richard Zokol."

Breathing deeply, I teed my ball, which was not an easy task, trusting that if I executed my shot routine properly I'd be able to handle the situation. From behind the ball, I took my first step into my shot routine and took my stance. I went through my normal rhythmic practice swing with my 2-iron, with a glance at my target, I took my breath in, exhaled smoothly, felt the Drop, took one last glance at my target, and with my target in mind, I pulled the trigger. I crushed it down the middle of the fairway. I had never struck a better 2-iron shot in my life. As I picked up my tee, my pulse rate was exploding out of my chest. I couldn't believe how fast my pulse rate had gone up the moment after impact.

Walking down the first fairway at Pebble Beach in contention on Sunday at the US Open was as exhilarating as hell. I felt alive at that moment, focusing on my breathing mantra, trying to calm myself and settle into the round. I knew it would take a few holes. My primary objective was to establish my rhythmic shot routine and keep my shit wired tight—I kept saying to myself, *Breathe motherfucker breathe.*

I was less nervous on my first hole's second shot than I had been on my tee shot, but not by much. Russ and I went through our assessment procedures for the shot. I pulled my 7-iron, went through my shot routine once more, and flushed it perfectly; my ball came to rest eight feet below the hole.

On the first hole, I had a great look at birdie. I assessed the putt, went through my shot routine and made an excellent Execution. The putt went right into the middle of the hole for an opening birdie 3. I could not have possibly handled the start of this hyper-pressured round any better than those three shots I executed on that first hole. At this point, I was at 1 under par for the tournament, two shots off the US Open lead with the final round in front of me. In one of the highest-pressure situations I had ever faced, it was the stability of my shot routine that allowed me to perform well. I thought, *Okay, focus on your shot routine—trust it—and let it go.*

When Azinger and I got to our second shots on the third hole, the atmosphere suddenly changed, and it really started to get windy. Tremendous gusts were blowing directly off the Pacific. There was nothing to stop the wind, and gusts were hitting 45 mph. Playing golf in a US Open in that type of wind was bizarre to the extreme. If you had a four-foot putt in a crosswind, you had to factor the influence of a gust while the ball was rolling. If you guessed wrong and the wind didn't gust, you could easily miss the hole of a four-foot putt by a foot. These were unbelievable and surreal playing conditions.

The groups that teed off in the less blustery wind in the early part of the day scored significantly better than those in the latter half of the field on Sunday. The final round produced 20 rounds of 80 or higher, almost all of which were from players with later tee times. Scott Simpson, the US Open Champion five years earlier at Olympic Club in San Francisco, shot 88. Nick Faldo started the final round one shot off the lead in second place, shot 77, and dropped only two places to finish T4th. This was the case for all players Walking the Gauntlet: we were subjected to the day's toughest conditions. Both Azinger and I shot 80. We finished T33rd. Colin Montgomerie, who had played in the early wave in significantly easier conditions, shot 70 and got into the clubhouse at 288, even par. Jack Nicklaus, speaking on the network telecast when Montgomerie finished, as conditions were worsening, predicted Monty would win—believing Mother Nature's fury was still coming and would be too much to handle for those still on the golf course.

Tom Kite was on the front nine as Nicklaus made his bold prediction. Jack could not have foreseen that Kite would pull off a series of near-miraculous shots across the final nine holes. Kite was Houdini-like at dealing with these near-impossible conditions under the most intense pressure possible. He prevailed and won his first and only Major, and he did so playing in conditions that were like golf on another planet.

CHAPTER 16

1992—Q3—My Desperation Created My Inspiration

With a win under my belt and my game stronger than it had ever been, my mind was on the upcoming Canadian Open. I wanted to answer that preverbal question "When is a Canadian going to win the Canadian Open?" with my golf clubs. Having Walked the Gauntlet successfully earlier that year, I felt ready to make this step.

And because winning the 1992 Deposit Guaranty Classic was not an official PGA Tour win, I was motivated to walk through this door.

Buick Open—August 6-9, 1992

Purse: $1,000,000

Warwick Hills G&CC, Grand Blanc, MI

Place: T48th

Score: 75-67-72-73

Made: $2,442.22

The International—August 20-23, 1992

Purse: $1,200,000

Castle Pines GC, Castle Rock, CO

Place: T39th

Score: -1 + 8 + 4 = 11 points (Stableford system)

Made: $4,800.00

Jim Freedman

During the International at Castle Pines in Castle Rock, CO, PGA Tour caddie Jim Freedman, with whom I'd always had a good friendship, approached me on the practice range and asked me if I had made arrangements for a caddie in Milwaukee in a couple of weeks. In that moment, I was still platooning a few caddies. I said, "Absolutely, let's give it a go in Milwaukee." I always liked Jim Freedman. I received a text message from Jim's brother recently, on June 8, 2025, telling me that Jim had passed away that morning from cancer.

Back on Tour in '92, I went back and forth platooning caddies—Bruce Hauchan, Richard "Jelly" Hansberry, Dick Christy, Russ Steib, Andy Leno, Ed Malkus, or Charles "Grady" Williams. But Jim and I made arrangements to meet at Tuckaway CC the Monday of the GMO.

The week after the International was the NEC World Series of Golf, which was a limited field event, and I was not eligible to play. So I had a week off and I flew back home to Vancouver.

My Desperation Created My Inspiration—They Don't Stand a Chance

My game was peaking, and my sights were fixed on the upcoming Canadian Open. My strategy was to play in Milwaukee the week before, in an effort to sharpen my game and have a full tank for the Canadian Open at Glen Abbey. Joanie decided she and the kids would pass on Milwaukee, and instead they'd fly to Toronto from Vancouver and meet me Sunday night after I finished up in Milwaukee.

The day before I was scheduled to fly from Vancouver to Milwaukee, I got a call from the landlord of the house we were renting in Richmond, BC. He gave me formal notice that he was selling the property and that we'd need to be out of the house in three months—this was the third time in five years that we'd been evicted from a house rental because the property was being sold. I was upset when I hung up the phone. I felt like I was not performing my basic duty of protecting my family, being a good provider, and literally putting a roof over my family's head. I felt I was failing in my responsibilities. The more I thought about it, the more furious with myself

I became. I came down the stairs, and Joanie immediately looked at me, sensing something. "What's wrong?" she asked. I responded, "We're being evicted again, we've got three months to be out." After telling Joanie, I felt even more incompetent as a provider. In that moment something changed. My next words to Joanie were, "Fuck this, I am going to win this week. I am not going to fucking wait for it, I am going to fucking take it right now." Once I'd said it out loud to Joanie, everything changed. I felt empowered like never before. I went on, "All the players in the field this week in Milwaukee are in the way of me achieving what I want. They don't know they don't stand a chance. I am going to fucking win." It wasn't wishful thinking; it was a certainty.

It was truly the most powerful feeling I had ever felt. From my perspective, all the other 155 players in the GMO field were blocking my path to put a roof over my family's head. In that moment, I had a new perspective. I said to myself, "They won't see me coming, they have no idea, they don't stand a chance." I not only kept on saying it to myself, I had complete conviction about my new perspective.

When I got to Milwaukee, I didn't share my convictions with my new caddie, Jim Freedman. We were in the start-up stage of the player/caddie arrangement. The only person I shared my thoughts with was Joanie. Jim was a highly intelligent guy who had a calm demeanor. Immediately, Jim and I clicked in tournament play. We were in sync right from the start.

Throughout the week in Milwaukee, my conviction did not diminish one bit. In fact it only got stronger. All I needed to do was say to myself, *All these other players in this tournament are standing in the way of me providing for my kids and family.* Each time I said it, the more it empowered me. I kept repeating it to myself over and over during the week.

On Thursday, I opened with a solid 67 and then followed up with 71 in the second round on Friday. After that second round 71, I said to myself, *Okay, you got your highest round out of the way.*

On Saturday morning, having just finished breakfast, I was heading out of the locker room and getting ready to prep for my third round, when my good friend Ray Stewart asked me, "Who you playing with today?" I responded, "Duffy Waldorf and John Adams." Ray remarked, "Have fun being 25 yards behind those boys all day." Waldorf and Adams were considered long drivers. It never bothered me when anyone hit it past me. The only thing at the top of my mind was, *They don't stand a fucking chance.* I shot 64 in the third round.

The Final Round—Walking the Gauntlet

Jim Freedman and I entered the final round of the GMO at 14 under par, one shot behind Mark Brooks, who was the defending GMO champion. We were paired together in the final group. Jay Hass was one shot behind me at 13 under par, playing in the second-to-last group. All the media attention, including on ABC Sports, which was handling the network telecast, had the storyline fixed on Mark Brooks, as he was the defending champion. I am sure "Brooksy" himself believed he had the upper hand. But I still had this superpower feeling as I stepped onto the first tee that Sunday, having this conversation with myself, *Everyone around here is thinking Brooks is going to win, and I am sure Mark is thinking this too. But none of them know what I know; they don't know they are standing in the way of me providing for my family. And I am not about to let that happen. They don't know they don't stand a fucking chance.* I knew exactly what was going to happen. My mind was absolutely made up—I wasn't going to knock on the door, I was going to kick the fucking door off its hinges. And there was nothing they could do about it.

Mark Brooks and I teed off. I set the tone on the first green by making an eight-foot putt for par, and when that putt went in, it settled me down. I made pars on the first five holes. I 2-putted birdie on the par-5 sixth hole, and then hit my second shot on the seventh hole to a foot, and tapped in for another birdie. I missed a good birdie opportunity on the long par-3 eighth hole and then dropped a 12-foot birdie putt on the ninth hole, making the turn with the lead.

On the tough 10th hole, I made par, then hit a wedge to two feet on the 11th for another birdie. After pars on 12 and 13, I made birdies on 14 and 16. Standing on the 17th tee, I held a two-shot lead over Mark Brooks with two holes to play. The 17th hole was a long par 3, and I struck my 3-iron perfectly. My ball flew right over the pin, leaving me a 20-foot downhill putt. The down-hiller got away from me and went five feet past the hole. I missed my par putt coming back. It didn't matter; I had a one-shot lead over

Brooks with a hole to play. That's all I needed. As I tapped in my bogey on the 17th, there was a little murmur coming from the crowd; a little smirk came over me and I thought, *This is for my family—I will not be denied.*

The 18th hole at Tuckaway was a long par 4 with an uphill second shot to an elevated green. Brooks had the honor off the 18th tee and pull-hooked his tee shot deep into the left junk. I went straight to my 3-wood to optimize my chance to hit the fairway. I crushed it down the middle of the fairway, leaving me with a 4-iron for my second shot. Brooks's second shot didn't get out of the rough—leaving himself in deep trouble. I hit my 4-iron perfectly to the middle of the green, and it was all over. Brooks finally got it on the green and 2-putted for a triple bogey. I lagged my 25-foot putt close to the hole and tapped it in to win the Greater Milwaukee Open by two shots over Dick Mast.

I cannot explain the inspiration I had to even think the way I did, not only going into the tournament all the way through to winning the Greater Milwaukee Open that week. When I explain it to others, it sounds like that folktale where the mother lifts the back of the Volkswagen to free her child from under the car. The only thing I can think of is, when I hit that breaking point, I changed the way I thought and felt.

Greater Milwaukee Open—September 3-6, 1992

Purse: $1,000,000

Tuckaway CC, Franklin, WI

Place: 1st

Score: 67-71-64-67

Made: $180,000.00

GREATER MILWAUKEE OPEN

Place	Name	Scores	Money
1st	Richard Zokol	67-71-64-67-269	$180,000.00
2nd	Dick Mast	67-69-71-63-271	108,000.00
T3rd	Mark Brooks	70-66-65-72-273	52,000.00
T3rd	Dudley Hart	69-67-69-68-273	52,000.00
T3rd	Tom Lehman	68-67-72-66-273	52,000.00

Place	Name	Scores	Money
T6th	Larry Mize	70-67-69-68-274	33,500.00
T6th	Nick Price	69-71-65-69-274	33,500.00
T6th	Payne Stewart	68-72-67-67-274	33,500.00

As I went into the scorer's tent, I said to Jim, "Let's make sure we get this scorecard right." I went through my scorecard, Jim went through my scorecard, and then I asked the PGA Tour official to go through my scorecard once more. Then I handed the scorecard in. After it was all over and I won, I felt the deepest sense of gratification I had ever felt. All the work, all the sacrifice from my family and particularly from Joanie, who had to not only put up with everything as a golf pro's wife, but truly was the architect of our family, even when things got difficult in life. I thought about my parents, my brother and sisters, how proud we all felt. I thought to myself, *now I can put a roof over my family's head and own it.* Then I thought about the Masters. It was a great feeling to earn my way into playing the Masters next year.

At the ceremony on the 18th green, I was presented with a surfboard-sized check for $180,000 on national TV. After saying a few words of thanks to the tournament staff, volunteers, grounds crew, and sponsors, I was waltzed into the media room to answer questions. I was a PGA Tour winner for the second time, but this time it was an official win.

Jim Freedman was with me in the locker room, helping me get all my gear packed up. Jim came right to the point and said, "Richard, being that we won, I need to ask you, do I automatically get the jobs caddying for you in all the tournaments next year that come with this win? Such as the Tournament of Champions, the Masters, the World Series of Golf, etc.?" I said to Jim, "You earned it, you got it." I wrote Jim a check for $20,500. The caddie deal was $2,500 for the week, plus 5% of the money made, 8% for a top 10, or 10% on a win.

After completing my media and sponsor obligations at Tuckaway, I was rushed to the airport by tournament transportation to catch the last flight of the day from Milwaukee to Toronto. The only thing I wanted to do was to be with my family to share this special moment with Joanie. Joanie and the kids were on route to Toronto from Vancouver and I wanted to be with them that night. Joanie found out I had won when they landed in Toronto;

On the 18th green with the GMO sponsors and executives.

she was told by the transportation people as they were picked up and delivered to the house we rented for the week in Oakville.

I barely made the flight to Toronto. When I got on board, the plane was, of course, full of Tour players headed to the Canadian Open. As I made my way down the aisle to my seat, they began to applaud. There's nothing better than being respected by your peers. I sat down beside my old buddy Dan Halldorson, and we took off to Toronto.

The flight to Toronto seemed to take forever. Then the drive from Pearson Airport to Oakville was surreal. I couldn't get there fast enough. Everything was happening in slow motion. All I wanted to do was to hold Joanie and the kids. When I got to the house, I saw that my Honda Canada sponsors had already delivered an Acura NSX and an Acura Legend, which were in the driveway. I knocked on the door, and when Joanie opened it, we hugged, held each other tight, and we cried together. It was a beautiful moment. The kids were already in bed for the night. Joanie and I couldn't sleep. We thought to ourselves, *Holy shit*—that feeling of desperation I had a week ago created some serious inspiration.

The Chairman's Day at the Canadian Open

The next morning was the Chairman's Day during the week of the Canadian Open, an annual Monday offsite event hosted by the tournament sponsor, Imperial Tobacco. Imperial Tobacco spared nothing to host the biggest names on the PGA Tour at this all-day golf affair followed by an elegant dinner. They paid enormous honorariums to the top players to play this one event, making it convenient for players to remain and play in the Canadian Open since they were already in town. You could look at it as a way of circumventing the "no appearance fee" rules on the PGA Tour.

A limousine picked me up at 8:00 AM and we arrived at St. George's Golf Club for breakfast and then shuffled out to the practice range to hit a few balls. There was already a large gallery watching the line of top PGA Tour players warm up. I felt validated as a Chairman's Day invitee after having won in Milwaukee the day before. I took the spot beside Greg Norman and started hitting balls. Norman took notice and stepped toward me and reached out and shook my hand in congratulations for winning in Milwaukee.

I began warming up with my now set routine of hitting balls with only my left hand. By now, having reconditioned my skill level, I was very proficient. Norman turned around to watch me hitting 7-irons with only my left hand. Playing to the Canadian crowd Norman barked, "For Christ's sake Zokol, are you going to beat us with one hand now?" It was a very thoughtful gesture; he knew exactly how it would resonate with the Canadian fans.

Chairman's Day was always a special event. Imperial Tobacco, despite the difficult position they were in as a business (tobacco company sponsorships was being prohibited by law in Canada), gave generously to golf, supporting both the PGA Tour and LPGA Tours. Don and Deanna Brown—Don Brown was president of Imperial Tobacco—and Rick and Maurine Matias—Rick Matias ran the Ontario operations—became good friends. Prior to dinner they served champagne in crystal flutes and toasted my victory the day before. I was on cloud nine and I appreciated the gesture.

Canadian Open—September 10-13, 1992

Purse: CAD $1,000,000

Glen Abbey GC, Oakville, ON

Place: T68st

Score: 73-74-73-78

Made: $2,030.00

Clay Edwards flew up from Houston to join us for the week as he did every year for the Canadian Open. He wanted to both check in on my game and stay in touch with Moe. When Clay arrived on Tuesday, we had an emotional embrace. Clay and I had both invested so much into our climb to win on the PGA Tour. Now it had all come to pass. I know I would not have been able to learn how to win on the PGA Tour without Clay Edwards. We will both take this to our graves, this deep sense of gratification we both felt, and feel to this day, about what we accomplished together.

One of the most meaningful notes of congratulations came from Byron Nelson—mailed the day after my first official PGA Tour victory:

September 7, 1992

Dear Richard

"Congratulations."

So glad to watch you play so well.

We went to the Oilman's at Jasper this year. Had fun. Weather cold.

Will be my last year, I think. Keep going.

Byron

The note I received from Byron Nelson after winning the Great Milwaukee Open.

Arriving at Glen Abbey for the Canadian Open

As was the case each year, Canadian players playing in the Canadian Open would immediately be faced with the barrage of usual questions about when a Canadian would finally win the Canadian Open.

My win two days before had stirred things up to a new level, triggering the Canadian golf media into an emotional frenzy. Headlines in the newspapers read, "Zokol Crashes Winner's Circle." All hell broke loose in my world when I finally got on site at Glen Abbey on Tuesday and Wednesday. My PGA Tour victory a few days prior gave the Toronto media new fodder to throw on the bonfire of a Canadian not winning the Canadian Open. I wasn't ready for the firestorm. It was an all-encompassing high-energy burn, and I was not prepared.

The 1992 Canadian Open.

Had the next week's Tour event been any event other than the Canadian Open, I would have had the opportunity to breathe and settle down after my win in Milwaukee, but the whole week was absolutely overwhelming. I was tired and delirious. On Tuesday and Wednesday, media demands were off-the-charts crazy. Plus, I was still jacked up from my *they don't stand a chance* energy rush of the prior week. I couldn't calm down enough to even sleep.

The first round of the Canadian Open on Thursday was a real treat. Not only was being behind the ropes a sanctuary from the media, but the ovation I received at my introduction on the first tee was one I will never forget. It was truly overwhelming. I never felt so proud to be a Canadian. By the time Thursday's first round began, I was already exhausted from the emotional tsunami I'd been riding for the previous week. My mental state was a mix of adrenaline intoxication, elation, and exhaustion all at once. By the time I got to the final round, I had nothing left. I staggered to the finish line, shooting 78 on Sunday.

Buying Our First House

As they say, be careful what you wish for, because it may come true. It was just 16 days after we received an eviction notice from our landlord, but man, how things had changed over those 16 days. Now we were financially in a position to buy our first single-family home in the Vancouver market.

Joanie, the kids, and I flew back to Vancouver after all the excitement of Milwaukee and the emotional roller-coaster ride in Toronto. We walked back into our rental home, and the first thought that went through my mind was, *Adios, motherfucker.* We were going to buy our own home. With the winner's prize money, plus the bonus clauses triggered in my contracts for winning a PGA Tour event, in US dollars, our net worth had significantly increased over the past two weeks.

Joanie and I were eager to immediately start house hunting, but I had already committed to a road trip into the interior of British Columbia with my brother-in-law, Brian Kirby, to watch grizzly bears feeding on spawning salmon. We decided I'd still do the road trip with Brian while Joanie began house hunting with my best friend since our grade four fight, Chris Rivers, who was a Vancouver realtor.

Brian and I took off through Whistler, BC, up over the mountain pass headed north into the high plateau of BC's South Chilcotin. We figured we'd head to Bella Coola—a two-day drive to where rivers flowed into the Pacific Ocean and where the salmon were spawning and the bears were feeding.

By the end of our first day drive, on mostly backwoods logging roads, we decided to camp near Gold Bridge, BC. Brian was a camper, and I was a hunter. I had my 12-gauge shotgun with me. I wasn't about to face anything that could eat us unprotected, like grizzlies sniffing around our tent in the night. That shotgun stayed by my side the entire night. We got up early in the morning, a bit sore from sleeping on the ground in sleeping bags, and exhausted from keeping one eye open for bears. We headed north toward Gang Ranch.

Me and my brother-in-law Brian Kirby.

The Gang Ranch

Two brothers, Jerome and Thaddeus Harper, who came to British Columbia for the Gold Rush in 1865, established the Gang Ranch. The Gang Ranch was the largest cattle ranch in the world, at one million acres, or so they claimed. Stan Kroenke, who owns the Douglas Lake Ranch, acquired the Gang Ranch in 2021. One time, I asked my friend Joe Gardner, who was the GM of the Douglas Lake Ranch for 40 years, how large the Gang Ranch is. Joe said, "They claimed a million acres, but it was never that big."

When Brian and I got to the Gang Ranch, I found a public pay phone and made a collect call home (they didn't have cell reception in the wilderness). Joanie had already found our home! She had immediately fallen in love with a unique house in Richmond's Steveston community that Chris showed her. Joanie was so excited about the house. And it was in our price range. There was already a written offer on the property, but the offer was subject to the sale of the purchaser's home. Joanie really wanted the home; she told me everything was perfect—the house, the yard, the neighborhood, and the elementary school for our kids. My response? "Honey, if you like it, I will love it." I didn't need to see it. I said, "Let's make them a full price cash offer with only a 'subject to inspection' clause, a Subject Removal Date in five days, and a Closing Date in two weeks."

By the next day, Brian and I were still heading north on the back roads. We finally popped out of the bush at Highway 20 (the Chilcotin-Bella Coola Highway) at Riske Creek when the sun was going down. We saw a greasy spoon restaurant called the Road Kill Café. It had a crappy old motel right beside it. I looked at Brian and said, "Brian, a bed in that shitty motel, breakfast in the greasy spoon, and being able to take a shower, is a lot more inviting than sleeping on the ground in a tent, cooking on an open fire, not taking a shower, and shitting in the bush with bears around us. Let's spend the night there."

Brian concurred. We checked into the motel, slept great, awoke the next morning, and immediately had breakfast at the Road Kill Café. We then took off east to Bella Coola. By the end of day, we had settled into a log cabin at the Anahim Lake Resort. I called home from a telephone booth outside the office to see how everything was going with the possible purchase. Joanie picked up the phone and immediately screamed, "They accepted our offer!" That was fast! It also meant we had a binding sales agreement before Brian and I would get back from our road trip and before I had even looked at it.

I couldn't wait to see our new home.

CHAPTER 17

1992—Q4—A Day Like No Other in the History of the Old Course, St Andrews

1992 Dunhill Cup–October 15–18, 1992

The Old Course, St Andrews, Scotland

Team Canada: Danny Mijovic–Brent Franklin–Richard Zokol

I flew from Vancouver to Edinburgh, Scotland, on the Saturday prior to the week of the Dunhill Cup. I wanted to get there early and settle in to have an extra day to help me get over the jet lag before the tournament started. I had no idea what was about to happen.

A Day Like No Other in the Ancient History of the Old Course

My caddie for the Dunhill Cup in 1992 was Richard (Rick) Mackenzie. Rick Mackenzie previously worked for Dan Halldorson and was the caddie master at the Old Course. He had also written a book called *A Wee Nip at the 19th Hole*. He knew the Old Course perhaps better than any man alive. We made arrangements to play a practice round on the Old Course on the Sunday prior to the tournament week.

Many people may not be aware that the Old Course at St Andrews is on Common Land held in trust by the St Andrews Links Trust under an Act of Parliament. On Sundays, the Old Course is closed for golf, and the public enjoys the land like a park. People walk their dogs, have picnics, or just go for a stroll across the links. Golf on the Old Course is prohibited on Sundays except when the Open or the Dunhill Cup is played.

The agreement in place to play the Old Course stipulates that only contestants in the countries playing in the Dunhill Cup tournament are permitted to play the Old Course from the Sunday prior to the event to the following Sunday of the Championship's final round. With only 16 countries playing and three players per country, only 48 players participate in the Dunhill Cup. The Open, on the other hand, has a 158-player field.

After my Sunday morning breakfast in the Old Course Hotel, I was eager to get going. Rick and I met in the lobby at the agreed time. We made that glorious walk to the first tee. The area around the tee was deserted. There were no other players in sight. I took some time to work on my putting prior to teeing off, sensing there wasn't the normal urgency around the first tee that one was accustomed. After finishing my putting, Rick and I finally walked over to the first tee. As usual, Ivor Robson, the long-standing first tee announcer with his distinguished voice was standing post.

As we approached Ivor, he said, "Gentlemen, it's a beautiful day, there is not a cloud in the sky today, the wind is down, and you can tee off as you wish. The two of you will have the Old Course to yourself today. No other contestants are scheduled to arrive in St Andrews until later in the evening."

It didn't hit me until Rick and I were walking down the second fairway, and I glanced across the Road Hole (the 17th hole) at the Old Course Hotel, which had a large sign on the side of the hotel that read, "Carpe Diem." The magnitude of the moment dawned on me. We had the entire Old Course to ourselves—just the two of us—for the whole bloody day. I turned to Rick and said, "Has there ever been a time at the Old Course where only one golfer and caddie had the golf course to themselves for the entire day?" Rick thought for a moment and replied, "I've never heard of such a thing." We let it sink in for the entire day—October 11, 1992. Rick Mackenzie and I had the Old Course all to ourselves. We spent more than eight hours on the golf course, alone. In the past 200+ years that the Old Course has been around, I wondered if it had ever happened. Or, if it ever will again.

The Links Wedge

We spent a great deal of time working on bump-and-run shots using my TaylorMade 19-degree Tour Cleek, which basically was my 5-wood. It was an exceptional tool in windy conditions. I found that employing it to bump-and-run shots along the ground was extremely effective—even up to 100 yards, given the firm and fast conditions of the seaside turf. Rick remarked at one point, "I've never seen this type of shot being played with a fairway metal before." Rick couldn't believe how effective the shot was. He started to call it the "Links Wedge." Today, it's not unusual to see players using some type of fairway metal or hybrid club in lieu of conventional chipping. But in 1992, in Scotland, it was a new concept.

Historically, bump-and-run shots had been executed with mid-iron clubs, not fairway metals. However, the perimeter weighting of the fairway metal allowed the player to have a significantly greater margin for error with this club. It became apparent to me that a poorly struck bump-and-run shot with a fairway metal had a far better result than a missed conventional chip, particularly as the length of the shot increased. I also employed this shot when on the double greens at the Old Course, such as the fifth and 13th greens, where you could be on the green and have a putt of more than 80 yards. Using a putter on an 80-yard putt is an extremely difficult shot. A putt of that length needs more of a swing than a stroke, and there is a significant difference in how the ball rolls when struck solidly with this Links Wedge versus a missed shot with a putter.

I recall using my Links Wedge for my second shot on the 18th hole during the first round. My tee shot got past the road that bisects the 18th and first fairways (Granny Clark's Wynde). I had about 80 yards to the hole, and the wind was blowing hard into my face. I knew if I got my second shot too much in the air, the wind would stand my ball up, and it would not cover the Valley of Sin in front of the green. So I took out my Links Wedge, made a half swing, and clipped the ball perfectly. The ball started to roll immediately off the clubface, and it appeared to onlookers on the road that I had topped my shot. Someone in the gallery yelled, "Come on, man," as though I were a beginner. The ball bounced, rolled, and slipped its way over the sways and crooks of the turf, finally scooting into and through the

Valley of Sin, stopping 12 feet from the cup. It was a magnificent shot. The gallery standing along the road and in the stands thought I made a poor shot and got lucky when it was, in fact, a great shot.

The next day, I was playing Andres Forsbrand from Sweden. We were on the ninth hole, and the wind was gusting so hard you couldn't keep a hat on. I must have had 100 yards to the hole facing gale force winds. I took out my Links Wedge, hit the shot perfectly, and watched the ball trundle across the turf as though it were being held down by a magnet the entire way before it settled right next to the hole. I blew Forsbrand's mind with that bump-and-run shot. Later, other players told me that they heard Forsbrand say he could not get over that he got beat by a guy "who chips with his 3-wood."

Team Canada finished T5th in the 1992 Dunhill Cup.

1992 DUNHILL CUP

Scotland	**3.00**	**Canada**	**0**
Gordon Brand Jr.	75	Danny Mijovic	81
Colin Montgomerie	71	Bent Franklin	72
Sandy Lyle	71	Richard Zokol	74
Sweden	**0**	**Canada**	**3**
Robert Karlsson	75	Brent Franklin	71
Anders Forsbrand	74	Richard Zokol	72
Per-Ulrik Johansson	75	Danny Mijovic	74
France	**1**	**Canada**	**2**
Jean van de Velde	75	Danny Mijovic	73
Marc Farry	76	Brent Franklin	73
Thomas Levet	73	Richard Zokol	75

At the end of the 1992 season, I looked back at my performance with pride. It was a breakthrough year. From where I started the 1992 PGA Tour season, from the middle of the pack in the Q-School category, to where I ended up were two completely different worlds. I finished in 48th place on the PGA Tour Official Money List. With two wins under my belt, and one of them unofficial, I was poised to play a complete schedule in 1993, including the Masters. I was on my way. My transformation during the year was a powerful personal experience.

The desperation created my inspiration. What a year it was—thank you, Clay Edwards, and thank you, Tony Robbins.

1992 PGA TOUR SEASON SUMMARY

Tournaments Entered	23
Cuts Made	12
Cut Missed	11
Number of Wins	2 (Deposit Guaranty & Greater Milwaukee Open)
Top 10 finish	2 (Deposit Guaranty & Greater Milwaukee Open)
Stroke Average	71.06
Driving Distance	T62 (263.6)
Driving Accuracy	33rd (73.6)
Greens in Regulation	14th (70.5)
Putting	T87th (1.787)
All Around	51st (624)
Total Driving	9th (95)
Hole-in-one	1 (Freeport-McMoRan 12th hole)
Official Money	**$311,909.00**
Official Money List	**48th on the 1992 Official PGA Tour Money List**

The Battle Over the Marine Drive Clubhouse

As I have shared previously, the Marine Drive Golf Club (MDGC) played a significant role in my and my family's lives. Growing up across the street from the club's entrance made for convenient and easy access. I loved the club's culture and, from my earliest days, I wanted to follow in the shoes of so many great MDGC players of the past. From the day I joined as a junior member in 1970 to being an honorary member today, I always felt proud of my association with MDGC, the club of champions.

In September of 1992, Marine Drive and Capilano Golf Club in Vancouver jointly hosted the World Amateur Championship (for the

Eisenhower Trophy), a four-person International Team Championship that I had competed in for Canada in 1980 with Greg Olson, Stu Hamilton, and Graham Cooke. Many of the game's great players played in this wonderful event prior to turning pro. In 1992, Michael Campbell and Phil Tataurangi from New Zealand won the Eisenhower Trophy, defeating, among others, Team USA, which included David Duvall and Justin Leonard. Annika Sorenstam played for Sweden in the 1992 event.

However, on August 9, 1992, just before the World Amateur, a fire broke out in the Marine Drive's clubhouse in the club storage area. The blaze was extensive and devastating. But the good news was nobody was hurt. However, a new clubhouse would have to be built.

By September 14, 1992, just six weeks after the fire, the board of directors had already crafted a proposal for presentation to the membership outlining a special general resolution with a confirmed budget for construction of a mid-century modern-design clubhouse. A special general meeting of the membership and vote was held. Pat Cash, the club president at the time, summarized in his President's Report after the meeting, "It's a Yes. President Pat Cash reported: A momentous decision to proceed with the construction of a new clubhouse was made at the special general meeting of members on September 14, 1992. The decision by members is one of the major happenings in the history of the Club."[8]

A week later, I got a call from my good friend and fellow MDGC member Marty Zlotnik. Marty said, "Dick, I'd like to talk to you about our new clubhouse that was passed by the membership." I replied, "Sure, I am excited that we're getting a new clubhouse." Marty replied, "Yes, everyone is excited that we're getting a new clubhouse, but have you seen the plans and the architectural style of the clubhouse yet?" I said, "No, I haven't." Marty shared, "You've been around many of the great classic golf clubs in the US and seen their clubhouses, and I'd like to get your thoughts on ours, predominantly on the architectural style of the clubhouse that is going to be built." I said, "I'd be happy to take a look at the clubhouse renderings and floor plans."

Marty and I met at MDGC soon after our conversation. He brought the floor plans and renderings of the new clubhouse. We went through

---

8 Mike Riste, *Champions Attract Champions: Marine Drive Golf Club Centennial 1922–2022* (Marine Drive Golf Club, 2022), 209.

the floor plans. Then Marty showed me the architectural renderings of the exterior design. I was shocked. The rendering showed a flat-roofed mid-century modern clubhouse with floor-to-ceiling glass windows. My reaction to Marty was, "This is awful—it looks like a Shell gas station. It doesn't fit our club's characteristics or architectural style at all."

The entrance to the MDGC is on the corner of Vancouver's 57th Avenue and Southwest Marine Drive, and it is situated between two mansions, owned by two prominent and renowned Vancouver families—homes that had been designed and constructed in classic Tudor style some 70 years prior. It would only be fitting to retain the architectural integrity of the neighborhood in the new clubhouse. A mid-century modern-style clubhouse was clearly incongruent for this historic community.

Marty was hoping I'd react negatively to the design. My next comment was, "The members won't like this." Marty remarked, "The members approved this plan at the September 14th meeting by passing the special general resolution. But I don't think many members were even given the time and opportunity to comment on the new clubhouse. Members were so excited to get a new clubhouse that they passed the budget without scrutinizing the architectural style. The style of the clubhouse has been totally overlooked. These plans were submitted to the club's board of directors by the McMahon Group, the club's consultants, and the membership approved this plan."

I asked Marty, "What can we do about this?" Marty was excited that I used the word "we." He said, "We can organize and form an ad hoc group to gain enough signatures from the membership base to put forward an extraordinary resolution at the annual general meeting in December to overturn the September 14th resolution." I said, "Count me in." Even though my honorary membership had to be approved by the MDGC's board of directors on an annual basis, I was prepared to risk it on this matter. Marty and I went to work calling members and getting signatures. Along with signatures, we were asking members for $200 to cover the cost of hiring a design firm to draw up Tudor-style renderings as an option to show the membership. Marty also received estimated costs from Dominion Construction that fell within the previously approved budget.

We had an uphill climb. Both the club president and the board met us with resistance. The issue split the club. Nonetheless, we had the required signatures and followed procedures to put an extraordinary resolution on the agenda at the MDGC's 1992 AGM. We needed at least 75% of the votes to pass the extraordinary resolution to overturn the September 14th special general resolution. Would we get the votes?

The MDGC's 1992 AGM was held on December 14, 1992, with our extraordinary resolution to overturn the September 14, 1992, special general resolution on the agenda. Arguments for and against the project were opened up on the floor before the vote was put to the membership. The extraordinary resolution passed with a 92% consensus to overturn the September 14, 1992, resolution to build a modern clubhouse.

In the January 1993 edition of *The Marine Driver*, the Club's news publication, the newly elected President Blake Cook in his report stated, "The December vote of the membership left no doubt; a sizable majority of the membership wanted a Tudor-style building, and it is the mandate of a new building committee to blend the two proposals into a new Tudor design that meets our functional requirements. I suspect we are quite close to final design and layout, but further architectural and committee input will be required . . . Marine Drive Golf Club is very fortunate to have so many members who believe passionately in our club."[9]

Following the AGM, my dear friend Peter Bentley congratulated me for sticking my neck out for what I believed to be in the best interest of our club. "You stuck your neck out and it could have easily been cut off," he said. I took Peter's comments as a badge of honor.

In the MDGC's 100-year anniversary book is the following entry: "Following the approval of a new building, a group of members, unhappy with a new building design [referring to Marty Zlotnik and me] that was based upon a renovation proposal, lobbied the board and membership to reconsider the design in favor of a Tudor-style building. This design change was approved at a special general meeting held December 14, 1992."[10]

This entry is not an accurate representation of what actually happened. Marty and I did lobby the board and the president Pat Cash. As a matter of fact, the president and most of the board were personal friends of mine. But the board and president tried to stymie our efforts. We had to go to war

9 "The President's Report," *The Marine Driver*, January 1993.

10 *Marine Drive Golf Club: 100 Years—Champions Attract Champions*, 209–210.

with both the president of the club and the board. Members were forced to choose sides. Our goal was to overturn the September 14th, 1992, special general resolution to build a modern-style clubhouse. In the end, the right thing was done. The clubhouse that stands today is a testament to our hard work and passion for the club. I'm reminded of this and proud to look at the MDGC clubhouse whenever I return to MDGC.

CHAPTER 18

1993—My Visit With Byron Nelson at the Masters

After having my best year on the PGA Tour in 1992 and enjoying the financial benefits it delivered both on and off the golf course, it was great to start the 1993 PGA Tour season at the Tournament of Champions. It sure beat every one of my starts to the season up to that point—hoping my number would get me into an early-season tournament based on my Q-School category. Being able to play in the Tournament of Champions at the La Costa Resort was a great feeling.

Infiniti Tournament of Champions–January 7-10, 1993
Purse: $800,000
LaCosta Resort & Spa, Carlsbad, CA
Place: T22nd
Score: 70-72-73-73
Made: $13,825

Having a PGA Tour victory under my belt was a wonderful new feeling. As they say, nobody will ever be able to take it away. I'd always be known as a winner on the PGA Tour. Many PGA Tour players finish their careers never being able to say, "I've won on the PGA Tour." The deep feeling of gratification was its greatest reward. The feeling of accomplishment—that all the work, the sacrifice, the practice, the dreaming, and the assistance from family, coach Clay Edwards, my caddies (Jim Freedman, Dick Christy, and

Harry C), and particularly from Joanie, who walked every step of the good, the bad, and the "scared shitless" with me, made it all so worth it.

At La Costa during the 1993 Tournament of Champions, as it happened, I met the great left-handed player Bob Charles (Sir Robert Charles, Order of the British Empire). Bob was playing in the Infinity Senior Tournament of Champions that was held in combination with the regular Tour's Tournament of Champions. Bob had won the 1963 Open Championship and was universally renowned as one of the great putters in the history of the game. I had often focused on and studied Bob's putting stroke. My theory about why Bob Charles had for so long been such a great putter hinged on the low point of his stroke—it was consistently in the same spot at impact. I had always suspected Bob was right-hand dominant, and because he played left-handed, I felt this structure played a significant part in him being such a great putter.

When I saw Bob at La Costa, I went over to him and introduced myself. We had a pleasant conversation, and I put the question to him, "Bob, I've had a theory that may help answer why you have always been such a great putter." Bob expressed, "Okay, let's hear it." I asked him, "Are you right-hand dominant?" Bob smiled and replied, "Yes, I am." I nodded as I said, "I thought you would be." I explained my theory to Bob, how I had started to implement lead-hand dominance in my swing and told him that it had turned my game around. I was delighted to hear he agreed with my theory.

United Airlines Hawaiian Open—January 14-17, 1993

Purse: $1,200,000

Waialae CC, Honolulu, HI

Place: T22nd

Score: 72-71-68-72

Made: $12,000

Hole-in-One

In the third round, I made my third hole-in-one on the PGA Tour. It happened on the fourth hole at Waialae. The fourth green at Waialae is a long

Biarritz template design par 3 that Seth Raynor, the designer of Waialae, loved to build. A Biarritz green is narrow in width but very long in length, with a significant "chasm" in the middle of the green, which was intended to test a player's long game.

That day, the pin was in the very back right portion of the green. The green was close to 50 yards deep from front to back. The wind was blowing hard left to right and into us. The shot must have been playing in the 225-yard range. I struck a beautiful, hard and low 2-iron with a draw into the wind that landed on the front left edge of the green and took off running perfectly through its length, through the chasm in the middle of the green, all the way through the 50-yard length of the green, before it went in the hole. It was one of my all-time greatest golf shots.

Phoenix Open—January 18-31, 1993

Purse: $1,000,000

TPC of Scottsdale, Scottsdale, AZ

Place: T57th

Score: 69-72-70-77

Made: $2,110

AT&T Pebble Beach National Pro-Am February 4-7, 1993

Purse: $1,250,000

Pebble Beach GL, Spyglass Hill CC, and Poppy Hills GC, Pebble Beach, CA

Place: T70th

Score: 72-76-70

Made: $2,350

Doral-Ryder Open—March 4-7, 1993

Purse: $1,400,000

Doral Resort & CC, Miami, FL

Place: T38th

Score: 71-71-74-68

Made: $5,740

Honda Classic—March 11-14, 1993
Purse: $1,100,000
Weston Hills CC, Ft. Lauderdale, FL
Place: T48th
Score: 70-73-74 (rain shortened it to three rounds)
Made: $2,734

Freeport-McMoRan Golf Classic—April 1-4, 1993
Purse: $1,000,000
English Turn G&CC, New Orleans, LA
Place: T20th
Score: 75-74-70-73
Made: $10,833.33

After the final round of the Freeport-McMoRan Golf Classic, all attention quickly shifted to the Masters. It began Sunday evening with a chartered flight from New Orleans to Augusta, GA, that took players, families, caddies, and PGA Tour administration to the Masters. It was all very exciting.

The Masters—April 8-11, 1993
Purse: $1,700,000
Augusta National GC, Augusta, GA
Place: MC
Score: 75-79

Like many professional players, I was one of those players who refused any opportunity to play Augusta National Golf Club (ANGC) until I had earned my way into playing the Masters. Like many others, I had always tried to take that view to increase my motivation to qualify for the Masters. I wanted to get to Augusta by "earning it." I am not sure it worked out in my case, but I went with it regardless.

You know you're going to get an invitation to the Masters the moment you win an official PGA Tour event, even though you don't get the formal invitation in the mail until early January. When you earn your Masters invitation, you learn about the interesting perks that come with the invitation. You are allowed to play practice rounds—they don't say how many but typically it's a couple. And you can bring one guest with you when you do, but only you can play the golf course. I didn't know this until I played my second practice round, about a month before the event. Once I qualified, I knew I wanted to play Augusta a couple of times before the tournament.

I was unaware that players who qualified for the Masters could call the Augusta National pro shop and make arrangements to play. Instead, to get practice in at Augusta before the end of 1992, I called my good friend Peter Bentley to ask him if he knew anyone who was a member of Augusta National and, if so, might they be gracious enough to accompany me in a practice round as their guest. Peter told me he sat on the board of directors of CAI Capital in Montreal and that the chairman of CAI Capital, David Culver, was a good friend and member of Augusta National. Peter gave him a call.

The Masters Contestant Dinner Plate.

Peter introduced me to David Culver, who was more than happy to host me at ANGC. We decided to meet and play in early December 1992 (the course is only open from November to early May) to play a round, have dinner, spend the night in the Eisenhower Cabin, and play a second round the next day. David's son Mark joined us for the two days. It was a pleasure getting to know the Culvers, and I was appreciative of their gracious invitation to join them and play at Augusta National.

I played another practice round at Augusta in March of 1993 and invited James Deacon to be my guest and walk the practice round with me. James wrote for *Maclean's* and was doing a story on my first Masters.

By the time tournament week came around, the weather had turned cold and wet. The course was playing long. Like every player competing in their first Masters, I was excited; it is difficult to settle down when you are realizing this lifelong dream. I certainly hoped to play more Masters, but it is hard to play well in your first one. Not only is it a challenge to master the nuances of Augusta National from tee to green, the excitement of playing in the tournament for the first time made it all a bit overwhelming. Settling down enough to play well when the gun went off was difficult.

In the cool and damp weather in the first round, I shot a 3-over-par 75. To make the cut now I had to play well in the second round. My first objective in my first Masters was to play all four rounds, as every round played in the Masters is valuable experience for first-timers. Friday's second round dawned cold and wet weather. I was not playing great, but I was grinding and right on the cut line standing on the 12th tee still 3 over par for the tournament, even par for the day. The 12th hole at Augusta, the shortest hole on the course, is one of the world's greatest par 3s. It can be the most intimidating hole a player is ever confronted with—and that's at the best of times. But when conditions worsen, this short hole turns into a real bitch. Two-time Masters Champion Ben Crenshaw once famously said, "The 12th hole eventually makes you look like a fool. Because of the swirling wind there are times when you hit it and hope."

My caddie, Jim Freedman, and I found ourselves standing on 12th tee on that Friday trying to figure out what the hell the wind was doing. We were not getting any answers we liked. The more we tried to figure it out the more confused we became. We'd look back at the flag on the 11th green. It was blowing the opposite direction of the flag on 12. Not a good thing. I finally settled on a 7-iron, but I was still unsure. I hesitated just a little during the Execution of my shot—also not a good thing—and my shot took off right of my intended target line. It also got caught up in the wind, and I came up short and splashed into Rae's Creek. I chose to hit my second ball from the tee instead of the drop zone circle because I thought I could get on the green more easily, now knowing how the swirling wind would affect my shot. When my second shot from the tee also found Rae's Creek, I was completely befuddled. I walked down to the drop zone circle in front of Rae's Creek—no easy shot either—and knocked it on the green from there, then 2-putted for a seven on the 12th hole. My chances of making the cut and playing the weekend vanished. With three holes left to play in my second round, heavy rains came in and suspended play for the day. I would have to return to finish my second round early on Saturday morning before closing my first Masters tournament experience.

The second round resumed early Saturday morning. It was no fun getting up that morning at +9 just to play a few holes, knowing I had no hope to make the cut. If it were at a regular PGA Tour event and I were in the same situation, like most players, I would have found a reason to WD. But I wasn't about to do that in my first Masters.

The cold and damp weather made playing Augusta National difficult. I recall playing the 17th hole that Saturday morning, after hitting a good tee shot into the cold wind, standing in the fairway with over 200 yards to the pin with a 3-iron in hand, hitting into one of the most perilous greens at ANGC. Through all my years of watching the Masters on TV, I can't ever recall anyone hitting long irons into the 17th green. I finished my second round shooting 79. After shooting 75-79 (+10), I had missed the cut at +3 by seven shots.

My Visit with Byron Nelson

After finishing my second round Saturday morning, I went back to the clubhouse, changed my shoes, went into the grill room, and noticed Byron Nelson sitting at a table by himself. I went over to greet him. Byron invited me to sit down. I did and ordered some breakfast. Byron asked me how I played. I said with a disappointed expression, "I shot 79, the tee shot on number 12 got me. I hit two balls in Rae's Creek and made seven."

Byron of course knew the challenges players faced with assessing the proper club and shot on the 12th hole's tee shot. He said, "The 12th is a very tricky shot to figure out. What's the wind doing?" He went on, "Whatever you do, don't look at the flag on 11. It will mislead you because the wind swirls around the trees at the back of both the 11th and 12th greens." I said to Byron, "Yeah, I did that." Byron went on. "The proper shot on 12 is always a right-to-left shot over the right side of the bunker, nothing more. A draw is most effective in the wind. Second, to figure out the wind direction, look at the Spanish moss hanging in the tree branches right off the 12th tee, nothing else. Figure out your draw shot to the middle of the green." I took in each word Byron said to be better prepared for my next Masters—but it would never come.

Sitting down with Byron Nelson in the Augusta National clubhouse was a special moment for me. Byron was well known for his graciousness. He would share his advice with younger players, including a young Tom Watson and Hal Sutton. I decided to open up and share my lead-side domination swing theory with Byron. I explained to Byron my swing's over-the-top issue and then described my discovery while watching Johnny Miller. I told him how I restructured my swing, which had helped me win twice last year.

Ken Venturi and Byron Nelson.
Getty Images: Bettmann

Byron's reply was fascinating. Firstly, he said, "Richard, I absolutely believe in lead-side dominant structure in the swing." Byron went on, "Let me tell you the story involving Ken Venturi. It runs along the line you are talking about. In those days Kenny came to both Ben Hogan and me for swing advice. I would tell Kenny to do this with his swing or that with his swing, and he'd go away and work on what I said. Then he'd come back and say, 'How does this look?' He'd hit a few balls, I'd watch, and then I'd give him something else to work on. He'd go away and come back a little later, and we'd repeat the process." Listening to Byron Nelson tell me this story was blowing my mind. I was getting a close inside look into the deep history of one of the greatest players of the game inside the clubhouse at Augusta National Golf Club at the Masters. No longer was I thinking about my missed cut at the Masters. Instead, I reveled in Lord Byron describing how he and Ben Hogan went about teaching Ken Venturi.

Byron went on, "Kenny was really looking for Hogan's and my approval. That's what he wanted more than anything. He worked hard on his swing. He would incorporate the things I wanted him to work on, and he'd come back to show me his progress. He started hitting shots, and he was striking it great. But Kenny had such a strong right-side dominant golf swing. It was quite noticeable. I told Kenny to swing exactly the way he was currently swinging, but do so with a dominant lead-side rather than your right side and right hand."

I was absolutely thrilled. Byron Nelson had validated my theory. Having this conversation with Byron in the clubhouse at the Masters was a great moment for me.

MCI Heritage Classic–April 15–18, 1993

Purse: $1,125,000

Harbour Town GL, Hilton Head Island, SC

Place: T39th

Score: 71-71-70-74

Made: $4,275.50

Sprint Western–Open July 1-4, 1993

Purse: $1,200,000

Cog Hill G&CC (Dubsdread Course), Lemont, IL

Place: T64th

Score: 72-70-70-77

Made: $2,532

Anheuser-Busch Golf Classic–July 8-11, 1993

Purse: $1,100,000

Kingsmill GC, Williamsburg, VA

Place: T60th

Score: 67-71-74-72

Made: $2,365

PGA Championship–August 12-15, 1993

Purse: $1,700,000

Inverness Club, Toledo, OH

Place: T14th

Score: 66-71-71-70

Made: $25,000

The PGA Championship at Inverness

I fell in love with Inverness the moment I set foot on the property. It was a classic major championship golf course with deep history. Inverness was incorporated in 1903. The course designer was Donald Ross. Construction on the course began in 1916 and was completed in 1919. Inverness then hired Byron Nelson as its first head professional in 1940 when Byron beat out Ben Hogan for the job (no wonder they were so competitive). Nelson worked at Inverness for four years before deciding to devote himself to playing full time. In 1945, his first full year as a playing professional, Byron Nelson won 18 PGA Tour events, including an astounding 11 in a row. It is a record for the ages—one that will never be equaled.

I played with Hale Irwin in the third round. We were both playing well. Sometimes when two players in the same group are playing well, they can get into a rhythm and feed off each other. This doesn't always happen, but it did for us that round. Hale Irwin, obviously, was one of the greatest major championship players in the game. Not too many players could keep pace with Irwin in his prime in a major championship. This day I could. I loved the feeling of playing well in a major alongside one of the legends of the game.

Coming down the last few holes on Sunday I was trying to finish in the top 10, which would get me an invitation back into the Masters next year. I holed out a bunker shot on the 18th hole, thinking I just might do it, but even with that I missed finishing in the top 10 by one shot.

NEC World Series of Golf—August 26-29, 1993

Purse: $2,000,000

Firestone CC, South Course, Akron, OH

Place: T14th

Score: 73-71-71-72

Made: $37,100

Like Inverness, I looked forward to playing Firestone South the first time with great anticipation. We flew into Akron Sunday night after the final round of the PGA Championship. I started to feel sick that night. I woke up Monday morning and could not get out of bed. Tuesday morning was no better. I was getting a bit concerned about playing a tough course like Firestone without even seeing it. I thought I'd be better by the Wednesday Pro-Am. But when Wednesday morning came, I still wasn't able to get out of bed and was forced to WD from the Pro-Am. By this time I was weak from three days in bed.

I was doing everything I could to feel better, hoping to wake up Thursday morning feeling well enough to play. When Thursday morning came, I did start to feel better. I decided to try to play; I didn't want to WD. I left for the course, but I had never played Firestone. I wasn't exactly sure how to get there and had to stop and ask directions. It had been a tough three days. Not the ideal way to get ready to play an important event.

I wasn't anywhere near 100%, but I felt good enough to play. As they say, "Beware of the sick player." Trying to conserve energy, I had no expectations; I performed quite well and shot 73 in my first round, not too bad for having spent three miserable days in bed and never having seen the golf course.

Greater Milwaukee Open—September 2-5, 1993

Purse: $1,000,000

Tuckaway CC, Franklin, WI

Place: T4th

Score: 67-68-68-68

Made: $44,000

Defending my PGA Tour Championship

Heading back to the Greater Milwaukee Open this time as the defending champion was a first for me. Historically, I played Tuckaway really well, and it turned out to be a thrilling week as my good play continued. I felt proud of a gallant effort and fell a single shot short of getting into a four-man playoff.

1993 GREATER MILWAUKEE OPEN SEPTEMBER RESULTS

Place	Name	Scores	Money
1	Billy Mayfair	67-66-69-68-270	180,000
T2	Mark Calcavecchia	72-64-67-67-270	88,000
T2	Ted Schulz	69-67-68-66-270	88,000
T4	Bruce Lietzke	69-66-69-67-271	44,000
T4	Richard Zokol	67-68-68-68-271	44,000

Having put up a solid effort to successfully defend my championship, I looked forward to the next week's Canadian Open. Unfortunately, good play ran out, and I missed the cut at Glen Abbey. We flew back home to Vancouver for some needed rest.

Frosty Wins the Canadian Open

After missing the cut at Glen Abbey, I watched the final round of the Canadian Open from the comfort of my couch. I was delighted my good friend from South Africa, David Frost, won the Canadian Open. Frosty played well and hit some courageous shots to edge out Fred Couples by one shot to win. It's interesting how some PGA Tour players, particularly those from countries in the British Commonwealth, like Australia, New Zealand, South Africa, Fiji, and Canada, considered the Canadian Open a national championship. Players such as Sir Bob Charles, Peter Oosterhuis, Gary Player, Greg Norman, Vijay Singh, Nick Price, Nathan Green, Tim Clark, and David Frost. Most other Tour players think of the Canadian Open as just another PGA Tour event.

The next week, I called Blake Corosky, my agent at IMG, to touch base. Blake told me, "You are not going to believe what fucking happened at Redtail this past Monday." Blake was talking about Redtail Golf Club in St. Thomas, ON. He said, "We booked David Frost (an IMG client) for a corporate outing on the Monday after the Canadian Open (Blake was a roundtable member of Redtail). When Frosty wins at Glen Abbey on Sunday, this becomes a significant bonus for this Monday corporate group. We had a great day at Redtail, and later that evening, long after dinner was over and everyone had cleared out, Gregg Gladstone (the Director of Golf at Redtail), David, and I were sitting at the Redtail bar having a few more drinks. It's about 1:30 AM when Frosty says, 'Good night, boys, I am heading upstairs to bed.' Gregg and I said good night to David, and we poured ourselves another drink."

Gregg Gladstone lived on the property, and Blake was staying in one of the Redtail's guest bedrooms.

Blake continued, "About half an hour later, here comes Frosty walking down the stairs from his bedroom wearing nothing but his tighty whities. Frost says to us, 'It's 2:00 AM and you fuckers are still up?' Gregg then says to David, 'Frosty, I want to get a picture of you drinking wine in your underwear at the bar.' Frosty says, 'Go get your camera, I'll give you a photo.' Gregg runs over to the pro shop just around the corner from the bar, gets his camera, and returns in short order. Frost proceeds to climb up onto the bar and says, 'Take a photo of this!'—Frost stands up on the bar, clenching both fists with his best Gary Player victory expression and says, 'I just fucking won your National Open!'" So Gregg took the photo of Frosty in this pose on the bar at Redtail in his underwear, adding to the many interesting stories that happened at Redtail.

Las Vegas Invitational—October 20-24, 1993

Purse: $1,400,000

TPC at Summerlin, Desert Inn, and Las Vegas GG, Las Vegas, NV

Place: T6th

Score: 68-67-68-69-70

Made: $46,900

Dunhill Cup—October 14-17, 1993

The Old Course, St Andrews, Scotland

1993 DUNHILL CUP RESULTS

Australia	1	Canada	2
Player	**Score**	**Player**	**Score**
Peter Senior	77	Richard Zokol	70
Rodger Davis	71	Jim Rutledge	71
Craig Parry	73	Dave Barr	73

Sweden	2	Canada	1
Player	**Score**	**Player**	**Score**
Jesper Parnevik	72	Richard Zokol	71
Joakim Haeggman	71	Jim Rutledge	73
Anders Forsbrand	69	Dave Barr	71

Canada	2	Japan	1
Player	**Score**	**Player**	**Score**
Dave Barr	74	Tetsu Nishikawa	76
Jim Rutledge	81	Tsuyoshi Yoneyama	75
Richard Zokol	72	Yoshi Mizumaki	77

World Cup of Golf by Heineken—November 11-14, 1993

Purse: $1,200,000

Lake Nona GC, Orlando, FL

Place: T11th

Score: Dave Barr: 74-70-70-71–285

Score: Richard Zokol: 76-71-70-72–289

Made: $7,000

1993 PGA TOUR SEASON SUMMARY

Tournaments Entered	25
Cuts Made	15
Cut Missed	10
Top 10 finish	2 (Greater Milwaukee Open & Las Vegas Inv.)
Stroke Average	71.36 (T105)
Driving Distance	252.3 (T153)
Driving Accuracy	T70th (70.3)
Greens in Regulation	151st (62.9)
Putting	T61st (1.787)
All Around	1,005 (132)
Total Driving	223 (143rd)
Official Money	**$214,418.00**
Official Money List	**80th on the 1993 Official PGA Tour Money List**

CHAPTER 19

1994—Golf Insanity—My Ego—I Didn't See It Coming

United Airlines Hawaiian Open–January 13-16, 1994
Purse: $1,200,000
Waialae Country Club, Honolulu, HI
Place: T27th
Score: 72-67-72-69
Made: $8,520.00

David Feherty Can Say Some Bizarre Things

At the 1994 United Airlines Hawaiian Open, on Wednesday, the Pro-Am day that I was not playing, I decided to take a stroll on Waikiki Beach and bumped into David Feherty by himself getting some sunshine on his pasty white skin. I had gotten to know David from playing in the Dunhill Cup over the years when he was representing Ireland and I was representing Canada. Feherty was brand new to the PGA Tour, but he already had established his reputation as a good player, having a strong wit on the European Tour.

I greeted David and welcomed him to the PGA Tour. He said, "Pull up a chair, you crazy Canuck." I sat down and we had a good visit. I inquired what his intentions were relating to coming over from the European Tour. Feherty stated he moved to Dallas and was fully committed to moving and playing in the US. I said, "That's wonderful." The next words that came out of his mouth were, "I had a circumcision last week." It set me back a bit. I said, "I'm sorry, what did you say?" David repeated himself, "I had a circumcision last week." I said, "Really, why in hell would you want to do that at your age?" Feherty then told me his wife insisted he get it done. I looked at Feherty and all I could say was, "How's that working out for you?" From my perspective, it was pretty bizarre, but it set the tone of David Feherty's character and impact on the PGA Tour.

The Los Angeles Earthquake

The infamous Northridge earthquake struck at 4:31 AM on Monday, January 17, 1994, at the precise moment our PGA Tour charter flight from Honolulu en route to Tucson was touching down at LAX to refuel. Our red-eye flight was transporting PGA Tour players, player families, caddies, and tournament officials to the Northern Telecom Tucson Open. The earthquake was centered in the San Fernando Valley region west of Los Angeles and measured 6.7 on the Richter scale. It was devastating. The death toll was 57, with more than 9,000 injured. Damage estimates approached $50 billion.

My friend Ed Dougherty and I were sitting together on the flight. Everything had been fine and uneventful as we descended to LAX on time to meet our scheduled 4:30 AM arrival. It was of course still dark as we approached the Southern California coastline. The lights of Los Angeles seemed to go on as far as the eye could see. The captain announced we were cleared to land as he began the final approach. Ed and I were both transfixed looking out the window, struck by the immensity of greater Los Angeles. As we were a few hundred feet and descending, we noticed massive quadrants of city lights shutting down in sequence. Everything in the city of Los Angeles just went black. I said to Ed, "Look at that! What the fuck is going on? The lights of LA are turning off." About 10 seconds or so later, we felt the wheels of our aircraft touch down.

As it turned out, we had landed mere seconds after the start of the initial earthquake. In real time it was too late for air traffic control to know exactly what was happening to order our pilot to abort the landing. We later learned our flight was the last flight to land before LAX was closed to all air traffic. Our plane taxied off the main runway and stopped well before the terminal. Everything was now black outside. We all wondered what the hell was going on.

We sat for what felt like forever. The captain finally announced that we had landed during an earthquake and would have to stay in place until the taxiways could be inspected at sunrise.

Sunrise came, airport officials were able to inspect the taxiway and determined it was safe, and our plane was given a green light to taxi to our gate where we were offloaded. When we got into the terminal building, we could see signs of damage from the earthquake. We all had more questions than answers, but one of the first things we learned was that LAX was completely closed. All commercial flights coming in and taking off had stopped. We were not going to Tucson anytime soon. In hindsight, given the structural damage wrought by the quake across the LA Basin, we realized how lucky we had been that no significant damage had occurred on our runway as we touched down.

A few hours later, we got some good news. Because we were a chartered flight and not a commercial flight, we were told that after the runways were inspected and confirmed as "safe" (they literally had people walking the length of each runway to inspect them), our flight would be allowed to depart for Tucson.

During this period on Tour, I was collaborating with the *Vancouver Sun*'s golf writer Brad Ziemer on a weekly article. Every Monday, Brad and I would speak, Brad would transcribe and ghostwrite "'Tour Talk' by Dick Zokol," which was published on Tuesdays in the *Vancouver Sun*'s Sports section. Later that Monday after we had finally arrived in Tucson, I called Brad. We of course talked about the earthquake. The next day's "Tour Talk" wasn't in the Sports section. Instead, the article made the front page of the *Vancouver Sun*.

Nissan Los Angeles Open—February 10–13, 1994

Purse: $1,000,000

Riviera Country Club, Pacific Palisades, CA

Place: T40th

Score: 69-75-71-72

Made: $3,800.00

As well as I had played in both 1992 and 1993, ascending into the winner's circle and performing as consistently as I ever had in my career, in sharp contrast, 1994 was a Kamikaze dive straight down.

Doral-Ryder Open—March 3-6, 1994
Purse: $1,400,000
Doral Resort & CC, Miami, FL
Place: T69th
Score: 76-71-74-72
Made: $2,800.00

Honda Classic—March 10-13, 1994
Purse: $1,100,000
Weston Hills CC, Ft. Lauderdale, FL
Place: T39th
Score: 72-74-73-70
Made: $3,864.00

Freeport-McMoRan Classic—March 31-April 3, 1994
Purse: $1,200,000
English Turn G&CC, New Orleans, LA
Place: T51st
Score: 76-70-74-70
Made: $2,862.00

The Vancouver Canucks' Hyperbaric Oxygen Chamber

In 1994, at the age of 36, I figured I needed to step up my level of physical fitness and began a cardiovascular regimen and a very golf-specific training program. My program didn't involve lifting heavy weights to gain strength, but rather lighter weights, which were designed to tone, stretch, and strengthen for stamina; the program was outlined by Jackson Sayers. Jackson would run me through his program after analyzing my specific requirements. My routine with Jackson was a couple of hours per day, three days a week.

After these workouts, in particular the next day, my body felt sore. I understood recovery from the workout was a key aspect for improvement. At the same time, I was watching and listening to Vancouver Canucks' trainer Larry Ashley talk about how successful the Canucks were at recovery from injury using their hyperbaric oxygen chamber. I thought to myself, *What's the difference between recovering from injury and recovering muscle tissue from hard exercise?* Both require oxygenated blood.

I gave my pal Glen Ringdal a call. Glen was the VP of marketing for the Canucks at the time, and Glen gave me Larry Ashley's number. So I gave Larry a call. Larry and I connected, and we spoke about the process of tissue recovery. I asked Larry if I could test this theory by going into the Canucks' hyperbaric oxygen chamber immediately after a hard workout. Larry thought the idea was good, but before he would give me permission, he insisted I get clearance to do so from a dive-certified physician. I reached out to my physician, Dr. Peter House, who happened to be dive-certified, and he gave me the green light to do so.

Once I got the green light to climb into the oxygen chamber, I purposely went hard on a workout and then drove to the Pacific Coliseum, and Larry put me into the chamber where I breathed in 100% pure oxygen at a pressure depth of 100 feet below the surface for about 20 minutes. The next day, I was fully recovered and ready for another workout. I used this process to recover and get into physical shape. I used the chamber about half a dozen times.

GTE Byron Nelson Classic—May 12-15, 1994

Purse: $1,200,000

TPC at Las Colinas, Irving, TX

Place: T65th

Score: 72-68

Made: $2,304.00

Anheuser-Busch Golf Classic—July 7-10, 1994

Purse: $1,100,000

Kingsmill GC, Williamsburg, VA

Place: T19th

Score: 69-69-69-71

Made: $14,300.00

Deposit Guaranty Golf Classic—July 14-17, 1994

Purse: $700,000

Annandale GC, Madison, MS

Place: T62nd

Score: 73-71

Made: $1,435.00

In 1994, the PGA Tour finally designated the Deposit Guaranty Golf Classic as an official win on the PGA Tour. I petitioned the PGA Tour Policy Board to grandfather all past Deposit Guaranty Golf Classic victories as official wins. Historically, all money earned in this event counted as Official Money, but the victory did not. My petition to the PGA Tour Policy Board was not accepted.

Buick Open—August 4-7, 1994

Purse: $1,100,000

Warwick Hills G&CC, Grand Blanc, MI

Place: T56th

Score: 72-70-76-71

Made: $2,486.00

PGA Championship—August 11-14, 1994

Purse: $1,750,000

Southern Hills CC, Tulsa, OK

Place: T30th

Score: 77-67-67-73

Made: $8,458.34

The Sprint International—August 18-21, 1994

Purse: $1,400,000

Castle Pines GC, Castle Rock, CO

Place: 25th

Score: 9-5-5 (+19) (Stableford system)

Made: $12,320.00

Greater Milwaukee Open—September 1-4, 1994
Purse: $1,000,000
Brown Deer Park, Milwaukee, WI
Place: 69th
Score: 69-71-70-74
Made: $2,020.00

Buick Southern Open—September 29-October 2, 1994
Purse: $800,000
Callaway Gardens Resort, Pine Mountain, GA
Place: T19th
Score: 67-70-74
Made: $7,733.33

Texas Open—October 13-16, 1994
Purse: $1,000,000
Oak Hills CC, Sam Antonio, TX
Place: T33rd
Score: 70-67-70-69
Made: $5,171.43

Golf Insanity—When Your Ego Drives the Bus

Looking back to 1994, in hindsight, I could see the ego in my mind was driving my bus, and it took me straight into another thought shear. I had a change of thought—dysfunctional thought—when I played. The thoughts that ran through my mind in '92 and '93 were not the same as my thoughts I had in 1994. It was like I was a completely different player.

My ego took me down a rabbit hole, and I didn't see it coming. Instead of having freedom to pursue, my mind shifted and went into protecting my identity as a PGA Tour champion—my ego caused this thought shear. Our egos have an insatiable appetite for *results* that can never be satisfied, which turns into a fear-based threat.

Instead of progressing forward, being in pursuit of my next step as I had since junior golf, I went straight into protective mode. I stopped thinking the way I did when I played my best. My ego was emotionally attached to the result of being a PGA Tour winner, and it wanted to protect that identity. I became consumed with *results* and put pressure on myself to get these results. When I didn't achieve the results, my ego felt more threatened. If my results didn't reflect that of a PGA Tour winner, then my personal identity of being a PGA Tour winner was being challenged with every shot of every tournament I played. I felt that if I didn't perform as a PGA Tour champion, I was less of a player and less of a person. This insane vicious cycle is what happens when players go down this rabbit hole. I didn't know what to do about it at the time.

Another thing that added to my unhappiness, beyond my poor play, was our family unit was changing. Garrett and Conor started school in 1994. Because they were born late in a calendar year, Joanie and I had decided to hold them back a year from starting kindergarten, which allowed us to stay together on the road one year more and meant the boys would be even better prepared to start school a year older. So, now Joanie and the kids would be staying home during the school year while I traveled on my own, until we could travel together during their summer holidays.

But there was more to it than simply being unable to travel as a family. As I reflected on my season, I just couldn't wrap my mind around what was happening. Why had I suffered through such a poor season after playing at a high level for the two previous years? I knew my perspective was shit, but I had such a difficult time getting it back on track. It was like I had to hit rock bottom first and I had a little more distance to fall before I hit bottom and bounced back.

A key factor in my dysfunctional mindset in 1994 was that I had failed to prepare a next set of goals after winning on the PGA Tour. Not setting a new series of goals was my big mistake. After achieving my goal of winning a PGA Tour event, the next logical step should have been to pursue multiple wins, learn to get comfortable contending in major championships, and learn to successfully Walk the Gauntlet in major golf championships. But I didn't do that. With the benefit of hindsight, I realize I hadn't laid down goals in the same manner I had when I won on the PGA Tour. My next goal should have been to pursue winning a major championship—it wouldn't guarantee a major championship victory, but the pursuit is the key.

Not establishing my next aspirational goals was a mental mistake for my continued forward progression. My growth mindset turned into a fixed mindset, and I had unwittingly allowed my ego to take control trying to protect my personal identity as a PGA Tour winner. Our egos have our best interests in mind, but they don't have the ability to drive a healthy perspective, especially when ego becomes attached to your personal identity.

It took me 10 years on the PGA Tour to establish a level of comfort and skill, both mentally and physically, to win. I worked hard to build a belief system to win. Winning twice on the PGA Tour in one year (even if one of my wins was non-official) fed my ego. I had achieved what I had always wanted, but I had not created a vision past winning on the PGA Tour, a critical mental mistake. What my mind now wanted was to protect what I had achieved. This mindset is similar to the hockey mindset when teams get a two-goal lead—when the team collectively changes the way they think and play—they stop the pursuit and cut off the mindset that got them the two-goal lead; they start to play defensively and, ironically, allow the opposition the opportunity to get back in the game. This type of thought shear is a common problem with all players, even PGA Tour players.

My dysfunctional mindset put me in a death spiral—my Golf Insanity was growing.

My caddie, Jim Freedman, could see it all too well. He noted that I had become a different player. I knew I was a different player in 1994, but could not crawl out of my situation. I had become emotionally interred in my own mind. My failures on the golf course were making me feel lessor as a person. It was developing like cancer.

The exit ramp off the PGA Tour was looming. Missing cuts and calling home every night to see how school had been for the boys only reinforced that I wasn't doing my job well on the road—nor was I at home for my family.

The year ended with a massive void inside. I finished 169th on the Official PGA Tour Money List and had my ticket punched back to Q-School for the sixth time. I didn't like where I was and didn't like what I was doing. Nonetheless, I set out to the regional PGA Tour Q-School at Kingwood, Texas, Deerwood Course. My coach, Clay Edwards, caddied for me that week. We had a tough week.

Over the years, I had come to expect that when my back got up against a wall, it triggered me to become highly motivated, and I would always find a way to play well. But a new version of Lee Trevino's original saying kept coming to me: "There are two things that don't last—dogs that chase cars and golf pros that have to keep going back to PGA Tour Q-School."

A Crazy Story Playing with Friend Steve Flesch

It was at this sectional Q-School qualifying in 1994 where I met a young, aspiring touring professional named Steve Flesch. Steve Flesch and I got paired together in the sectional PGA Tour's Q-School round at Deerwood. Flesch was a young, left-handed player from Kentucky trying to make it onto the PGA Tour for the first time. On the other hand, I was trying to stay on the PGA Tour after 12 years. Flesch had turned professional in 1993. He scrambled around for a few years before eventually winning on the Korn Ferry Tour in 1997 and gaining his PGA Tour membership in 1998. He would go on to have a wonderful career as a PGA Tour player, winning four times as well as four times on the Champions Tour. But in 1994, at the Sectional PGA Tour Q-School at Deerwood in Kingwood, Texas, he was as desperate to get on the PGA Tour as I was trying to keep my job and stay on it. It didn't turn out well for either of us.

The Deerwood Course was the golf course where the movie *Tin Cup* was filmed. In fact, the fourth hole at Deerwood (now Deerwood's 13th hole) was the scene for the 18th hole in the movie where the character Roy McAvoy, played by Kevin Costner, famously hits shot after shot into the pond in front of the green.

It was obvious to me that Steve Flesch was a good player, but he wasn't playing well that day. It was also apparent he had a feisty personality. In either the third or fourth round, Flesch's second shot on the fourth hole carried the water in front of the green but then rolled back down the false front of the green into the pond, just like it had in the movie.

I was keeping Flesch's scorecard. As such, I had to attest and sign his scorecard after the round, so I had to pay attention to what he was doing. After his ball rolled back into the hazard, Steve had to find the proper spot to drop his ball, not nearer to the hole, between the pond and the front of the green. Standing next to him, I concurred with the spot he identified to drop his ball. He did so, and it came to rest a few inches outside the red hazard line. All was good, and I walked away to tend to my shot. Flesch then called me back, and as he was reaching down to pick his ball up, simply said, "I need to re-drop my ball." I quickly alerted him, "Don't touch that ball—that ball is in play." He straightened up and looked at me and said, "I need to take full relief, and my stance [his left foot] is now inside the hazard line." I replied, "There's no problem if your stance is in the hazard, as long as the ball is not. You are confusing the 'needing to take full relief' rule that deals with relief from ground under repair or having to take full relief from a cart path. Your ball is in play." He immediately disputed what I was saying, claiming he was entitled to re-drop his ball in a spot where his stance was completely outside the hazard. I repeated, "Your ball is in play. It doesn't matter if your stance is in the hazard or not." We went back and forth with a "yes, I can" and "no, you can't" debate before I finally said in exasperation, "Go ahead and do whatever you want, but I am stating you will be breaching the rules if you pick up that ball." Flesch didn't budge an inch from his position. He picked up his ball and re-dropped it. I proceeded to my ball and my business, and our group finished the hole.

As our group walked off the fourth green toward the fifth tee, PGA Tour official Frank Cavanagh happened to be driving by. I waved Frank down. Without breaking stride to the fifth tee, I said, "Frank, you need to have a conversation with this guy regarding the drop he took on the last hole." Clay and I kept walking to the fifth tee.

Cavanagh pulled Flesch aside and asked him to explain what had happened. Clay and I continued with our other playing competitor to the fifth tee leaving this rules situation between Steve Flesch and Frank Cavanagh. We proceeded to hit our tee shots while Flesch and Frank Cavanagh figured things out. The next thing we see is Flesch walking toward the clubhouse rather than joining us on the fifth tee. Cavanagh drove up to us and said, "It looks like you guys will be playing as a twosome the rest of the way. The other guy in your group decided not to continue and WD'd after receiving a penalty on the last hole."

My perfect run of making it five for five successful PGA Tour Q-Schools came to an end at the Sectional Qualifying in 1994. For the first time, I did not successfully advance through the PGA Tour Q-School. My access to play the 1995 PGA Tour now fell into "spots availability" to fill the field in smaller Tour events from the Past Champions category. The Past

Champions category priority followed that of the previous year's top 125; the next 50 players and ties coming out of the Q-School; and then, after members who finished 126th to 150th from the previous year's Money List. At best, that meant I'd likely get into eight to 10 starts in the lower-quality and smaller-purse Tour events.

On the plus side, it meant I would be spending more time at home in 1995. I can't deny having a sense of relief after how miserable I had been on the road in 1994. But there was also a massive feeling of failure at the same time.

1994 PGA TOUR SEASON SUMMARY

Tournaments Entered	26
Cuts Made	14
Cut Missed	12
Top 10 finish	0
Sand Saves	60.3 (8th)
Official Money	**$78,074.00**
Official Money List	**169th on the 1994 Official PGA Tour Money List**

CHAPTER 20

1995—The PGA Tour Comes to Vancouver

The beginning of 1995 was an interesting time for me. For the first time as a professional player, not being on the road at the start of the year gave me a feeling of relief. Spending time around the house was like expressing a giant exhale. It was a sabbatical from feeling the pressure to perform. Watching the Tour from the sidelines was a bit weird, but I needed a break. I wasn't happy with myself on Tour.

Early in the year, I received a call from my good friend Marty Zlotnik to inform me that a new PGA Tour event was coming to Vancouver; The Greater Vancouver Open (GVO). Zlotnik was putting together the tournament organizing team and asked me to become involved as a steering committee member. Marty was the founding chair. His tenacious personality was perfect for the job.

Marty told me about a new, young, dynamic individual in town, Tod Leiweke. Tod had been hired as executive vice president of Orca Bay Sports & Entertainment, owners of the NHL's Vancouver Canucks Hockey Team and the NBA's new expansion team, the Vancouver Grizzlies, and had been working behind the scenes to bring a PGA Tour event to Vancouver. On Tod's impressive resume, he held a position of VP marketing for the PGA Tour. As a result, he had a direct line to the PGA Tour's commissioner, Tim Finchem. Tod reached out to Finchem to ask if there was a window for a PGA Tour event in Vancouver.

The GVO's Dilemma—Shaughnessy or Northview?

One of the pressing issues the steering committee had to quickly resolve was to identify a golf course suitable for this PGA Tour event in the Greater Vancouver area. Marty reached out to the president of Shaughnessy Golf & Country Club to see if the membership would have any interest in being the site of Vancouver's first PGA Tour event. I was particularly excited about the possibility of Shaughnessy being the venue from a player's perspective. Marty and his executive team, my good friends Mike Carroll and Len Dodson, were also engaging with Chick and Marilyn Stewart, the owners of Northview Golf & Country Club in Surrey, Vancouver's largest suburb, to gauge their interest in hosting the event as well.

Marty reported back to the steering committee that the Stewarts were very enthusiastic about the possibility that Northview could become the host course for the GVO. Simultaneously, and to my delight, Shaughnessy said they too would be interested to host the inaugural event, and with a possible two-year extension after the first year. I knew my fellow PGA Tour players would absolutely love Shaughnessy, and I thought to myself, *This is a no-brainer.* The last PGA Tour event played in Vancouver was at Shaughnessy in 1966, won by Don Massengale. Other greats who played were Jack Nicklaus, Billy Casper, Tom Weiskopf, Gene Littler, Chi-Chi Rodríguez, Doug Sanders, and Al Balding. Shaughnessy's history was strong.

However, Marty became fixated on the significant revenue capability of Northview's 18th fairway area, a length that ran the distance paralleling the whole 18th fairway and connected with the clubhouse. I agreed the corporate hospitality opportunity was exceptional at Northview, but the golf course itself was not inspiring by any meaningful measure. Even worse, transporting PGA Tour players from downtown Vancouver to Surrey would be a logistical nightmare for players. The Northview in Surrey versus the Shaughnessy in Vancouver decision was a key issue from my perspective—a PGA Tour player's perspective.

I argued my case in support of Shaughnessy to Marty and the steering committee. We only had one first impression opportunity with PGA Tour players—we needed to put our best foot forward. Playing Northview, in my opinion, would assure the GVO would be viewed by the Tour players as a lower-tier PGA Tour event—a step in the wrong direction for an inaugural tournament fighting for a place on the PGA Tour schedule. I stated Northview would not attract top Tour players, which in turn would diminish corporate sponsorship value and the sponsor's ROI.

At the time, there was another significant obstacle—the value of the Canadian dollar against the US dollar. Both the Bell Canadian Open and the GVO generated sponsorship revenue in Canadian dollars while spending a minimum of $1,500,000 in US dollars for the purse. The GVO's costs were significantly reduced because it played up against the NEC World Series of Golf, which meant it didn't have to cover the network TV production costs in US dollars. In contrast, the Bell Canadian Open had to cover a significantly larger cost, in US dollars, associated with its CBS Sports coverage. If you wanted to be a title sponsor of a televised PGA Tour event, you had to cover the purse and the network production cost in US dollars. Because Bell Canada didn't do business in the US, Bell's days sponsoring the Canadian Open were numbered.

Then the $CDN/$US exchange rate, paying out $1.45 per US dollar, was akin to having a fistfight with one hand tied behind your back while having to stand on one leg. Like any PGA Tour event, finding a path to success on the PGA Tour was contingent on attracting the top PGA Tour players, and Shaughnessy was the only golf course in the Vancouver market that would give us the best chance to succeed.

The two primary criteria Tour players use to plan their playing schedule are 1) purse size and 2) the appeal of the golf course. From a PGA Tour player's perspective, the GVO started with two strikes—it had a relatively small purse, being paired with an inferior golf course. Furthermore, most PGA Tour players are based in the south eastern part of the US. Flying to Vancouver for a small purse is not ideal. Once word got around that Northview was not a great course, the decision to take that week off to be with their families would make sense for most players.

I also explained to the steering committee that the Bell Canadian Open field was suffering significantly because of the growing player dislike of Glen Abbey. And Northview couldn't even compare with Glen Abbey. I also pointed out that because the inaugural GVO would be scheduled opposite the NEC World Series of Golf that the big names would not be coming the first year. Given that reality, it was even more important that we provide the best golf course to attract top players in the future. The top PGA Tour players love playing great courses, and Northview would not pass the "sniff test." Shaughnessy would pass with flying colors. Comparing the two clubs was no contest from my perspective.

Despite my arguing otherwise, the steering committee ultimately chose Northview. But my perspective on this would be bolstered later on: after the 2005 Bell Canadian Open was played at Shaughnessy, PGA Tour players rated Shaughnessy their number one favorite golf course on the PGA Tour that year.

Regardless, the Monday Pro-Am was a massive success. Zlotnik and Leiweke had the brilliant idea to invite Vancouver Canuck head coach Pat Quinn and his entire 1996 NHL All-Star Team lineup to play in the Monday Pro-Am. It was a brilliant move. The Pro-Am set a PGA Tour Monday attendance record with over fifty thousand people coming through the gate that day. It showed there was huge pent-up demand for a PGA Tour event in Vancouver.

United Airlines Hawaiian Open—January 12-15, 1995

Purse: $1,200,000

Waialae Country Club, Honolulu, HI

Place: T47th

Score: 71-72-70-72

Made: $2,960.30

Buick Classic—May 18-21, 1995

Purse: $1,200,000

Westchester CC, Harrison, NY

Place: T40th

Score: 71-72-73-72

Made: $4,320.00

Having lost my exempt status in 1995, I was in that unenviable position that so many Tour players found themselves in, having to write letters to each PGA Tour event's executive directors asking (more like begging) for one of the sponsor exemptions into their tournament. I had a 10-year exemption into the two PGA Tour events I won in 1992, the Deposit Guaranty Classic and the Greater Milwaukee Open. I knew I was in a hole and had to figure out how to get myself out.

Anheuser-Busch Golf Classic—July 13-16, 1995

Purse: $1,100,000

Kingsmill CC, Williamsburg, VA

Place: T40th

Score: 65-75-72-70

Made: $4,290.00

Greater Milwaukee Open—August 31-September 3, 1995

Purse: $1,000,000

Brown Deer Park GC, Milwaukee, WI

Place: T17th

Score: 65-70-73-70

Made: $11,800.00

1995 PGA TOUR SEASON SUMMARY

Tournaments Entered	10
Cuts Made	4
Cut Missed	6
Top 10 finish	0
Official Money	**$23,371.00**
Official Money List	**234th on the 1995 Official PGA Tour Money List**

CHAPTER 21

1996—Eaglequest Golf Centers Inc.

In March 1996, my neighbor and good friend Bob Garnett approached me and asked if I would be interested in getting involved in a new start-up golf business called Eaglequest Golf Centers.

Bob explained he and his friend Rob Safrata had identified the driving range and small golf course business as a fractured market, dominated by independent mom-and-pop operations. They saw it as a business opportunity to consolidate this aspect of the golf industry in North America. Garnett, as a former CFO of the Loewen Group, had significant expertise, having played a key role in consolidating the funeral home business in North America.

Bob invited me to attend the initial meeting on April 1, 1996, with individuals whom he and Rob Safrata had invited to consider joining the founding group of Eaglequest Golf Centers.

The founding group emerged out of the initial meeting:

- Rob Safrata, President
- Bob Garnett, Chief Financial Officer
- Maria Alalyan, VP, Finance
- David Fergusson, VP, Marketing
- Richard Zokol, Director of Golf
- Jason Monteleone, Marketing Manager

I was excited to move forward with the Eaglequest team. It would give me some real-world business experience. Looking back, this experience laid the foundation that enabled me to launch a start-up called Sagebrush Golf & Sporting Club Ltd. 10 years later.

After the founding team was identified, the Eaglequest Golf business plan was completed soon thereafter. Eaglequest's business plan explained the company in detail, how we planned to raise the necessary capital through debt and equity financing in pursuit of a growth-through-acquisition strategy. The company's first step was to raise investor capital. Rob and Bob asked me to join them on the initial road show to Toronto for the company's first equity raise. Bob had a carry-on suitcase with wheels packed with Eaglequest Golf Center Inc.'s business plans fresh off the printer. Rusty Goepel, a friend who was on the board of governors of the Business Council of BC, got us a 15-minute meeting at Altamira Investments with legendary money manager Frank Mersch. At the time, Frank Mersch was The Man on Toronto's Bay Street. Rob and Bob gave the pitch while I sat with my ears open, mouth shut, as the "golf guy." At the end of our 15 minutes, Mersch said, "Okay, I am in for $1 million"—an amount that included his personal investment as well. Bob immediately whipped out a subscription agreement and said, "Sign here."

These are Bob Garnett's memories of that meeting: "The other key memory of Frank is him saying I have no way to evaluate this investment, but I love the concept and management team, and I am in for $1 million." We also met with another investment banker named David M. Beattie at Gordon Capital, and he came in with another $1 million as soon as we told him Frank Mersch was in for a million. Bob and Rob had raised the company's first $2 million in short order, and we had not even finished our Toronto roadshow. The next day, we met with other firms that included Griffiths McBurney and Sprott Capital.

Over the next two years, Eaglequest built Eaglequest Coquitlam while acquiring another six driving range operations in BC and Alberta. We then expanded to the United States, acquiring operations in the Seattle/Tacoma area and another four in the Houston, TX, area. In just two years, Eaglequest rapidly grew from a start-up to the second largest driving range and short golf course consolidator in North America.

The Greater Vancouver–Open August 22-25, 1996

Purse: $1,000,000

Northview G&CC, Ridge Course, Surrey, BC

Place: T18th

Score: 69-73-67-69

Made: $13,040.00

The Inaugural Greater Vancouver Open

Marty Zlotnik tells a great story about the inaugural Greater Vancouver Open. On August 16th, the Monday of the inaugural GVO, we held an on-site Pro-Am. Marty and all the other committee chairs were standing in the parking lot fields at 5:00 AM waiting to greet the professional players and amateur players participating in the Pro-Am, as well as golf fans themselves. NHL All-Stars playing that day included Wayne Gretzky, Mark Messier, and Bobby Orr. As Marty stood there reflecting on the journey and the work that went into getting to this day, he suddenly thought to himself, *After 18 months of effort and planning for this PGA Tour event, what if nobody shows up?*

That Monday, a thick fog had settled in early in the morning and would not lift for some time, until later in the morning. PGA Tour player Andrew Magee arrived at Northview for the first time in the fog, looking forward to experiencing the smell of the Pacific Ocean air and the vista of a Pacific Northwest mountainscape. When the fog lifted, Magee couldn't believe his eyes. As he surveyed power lines in front of Surrey's high-density residential neighborhood he remarked, "When the fog lifted and I looked around, it didn't look like Vancouver to me. I thought I was in Kansas."

It was also a little weird to play a PGA Tour event while sleeping in my own bed at home. I was very excited and determined to play well. Every Canadian contestant in the field of any PGA Tour event in Canada has an inherent sense of pride to perform well while playing in their home country and flying the Canadian flag.

Greater Milwaukee Open—August 29-September 1, 1996

Purse: $1,200,000

Brown Deer Park GC, Milwaukee, WI

Place: T22nd

Score: 68-70-66-66

Made: $11,520.00

The 1996 Greater Milwaukee Open was Tiger Woods's inaugural PGA Tour event as a professional. Hughes Norton of IMG already delivered Tiger three contracts to sign before Tiger famously stood at the podium in Milwaukee and announced, "Hello, World." Tiger signed a player representation agreement with IMG, a player representation agreement with Nike for $50 million, and a player representation agreement with Titleist for $10 million.[11] He was set for life without having struck a single golf shot as a professional player.

Most Tour players were already aware of Tiger's potential and had their eyes on him before he turned professional. Still, there were some that had not. Former Open and Masters champion Sandy Lyle was one. Before Tiger's professional debut in Milwaukee, Lyle was asked by a member of the golf media, "So what is your impression of Tiger Woods?" Lyle thought for a second and then, seriously, replied, "I've never played that course. Where is it?"

The week of the 1996 Milwaukee Open was also the week of the infamous Curtis Strange interview with Tiger. Strange asked Tiger what his goal was for the week, and Tiger replied, "A victory." Curtis braced and shot back, "To me that comes off as a little cocky or brash when you come out here [on the PGA Tour] on your first day as a pro and you say, 'I can win.'" Tiger then went all in, "Second place sucks and third place is even worse." Strange shook his head and snickered, "You'll learn." As the golf world would eventually realize, Strange and most everyone else had wildly underestimated the young Tiger Woods. To be fair, it was unimaginable to think one person could be so good and so quickly separate themselves from the rest of the players on the PGA Tour. Woods was that person. Nobody realized it yet, but the world of golf, and most

11 Hughes Norton, *Rainmaker* (Atria Books, 2024).

importantly, the PGA Tour and its members, was about to go for a long ride on the Tiger Woods bullet train.

Hole-in-One

During the Sunday final round of the 1996 GMO, I made my fourth and what would be my last hole-in-one on the PGA Tour on the fifth hole when I sank an 8-iron from the tee. That same round, Tiger holed a 6-iron on the 14th for his first hole-in-one on the PGA Tour in his first professional tournament.

PGA TOUR

NAME	1	2	3	4	5	6	7	8	9	OUT	10	11	12	13	14	15	16	17	18	IN	TOTALS		36	54	72
PAR	4	4	3	5	3	5	3	4	4	35	4	3	4	4	3	5	4	4	5	36	71				
TOMS,	4	4	3	4	3	4	3	4	4	33	4	3	4	4	3	4	3	3	5	33	66	68 71	139	205	273
	4	4	3	5	2	6	3	4	4	35	4	3	4	3	2	5	5	3	4	33	68				
WADKINS,	4	4	4	5	3	4	3	4	4	35	4	4	4	4	3	5	4	3	4	35	70	69 69	138	208	276
	4	5	3	4	3	4	3	4	4	34	4	2	4	4	3	5	4	4	4	34	68				
WALDORF,	4	5	3	4	2	5	3	5	4	35	4	2	4	5	3	4	5	4	4	35	70	65 65	130	200	268
	4	4	3	5	3	4	3	3	4	33	5	3	4	4	2	5	4	4	4	35	68				
WOOD,	4	3	3	4	3	5	3	4	4	33	4	2	5	3	3	5	4	4	5	35	68	66 68	134	202	278
	5	5	3	4	3	4	3	4	3	34	5	4	4	5	3	6	4	6	5	42	76				
WOODS,	5	3	3	5	3	5	4	4	6	38	5	3	4	4	3	4	4	4	4	35	73	67 69	136	209	277
	4	4	3	3	4	4	3	4	5	34	4	3	4	4	1	5	4	4	5	34	68				
ZOKOL,	4	5	3	4	1	5	3	4	4	33	4	2	4	4	3	4	4	4	4	33	66	68 70	138	204	270
	5	3	2	4	3	5	2	6	4	34	4	4	3	4	2	4	3	4	4	32	66				

The original scoreboard at the 1996 Greater Milwaukee Open.
If you look closely you will notice on the final round both Tiger and I made Hole-In-Ones that day. Tiger's was on the 14th hole and mine was on the fifth hole.

In the 1960s, Arnold Palmer's swashbuckling style and go-for-broke courage took professional golf to new levels of popularity. But this was different. Starting with his "Hello, World" moment at the GMO, Woods single-handedly put the golf world on his shoulders and took the PGA Tour to extraordinary heights. Nobody in professional golf had ever brought more eyeballs or value to the PGA Tour. Tiger was responsible for the industry's golf boom. Suddenly, it was cool to play golf. Millions of new golfers would be awed by Woods from that day forward and use him as inspiration. Starting that week in Milwaukee, every member of the PGA Tour should have gladly paid an annual tithe of 10% of their earnings to Tiger for the massive expansion of sponsorship dollars flowing to the PGA Tour that he generated. Tiger Woods was primarily responsible for making many professional players millions upon millions of dollars over the next 30 years and beyond.

Bell Canadian Open–September 5-8, 1996

Purse: CAD $1,500,000

Glen Abbey GC, Oakville, ON

Place: T57th

Score: 71-72-75

Made: $3,300.00

Quad City Classic–September 12-15, 1996

Purse: $1,200,000

Oakwood CC, Coal Valley, IL

Place: T69th

Score: 71-71-75-66

Made: $2,400.00

1996 PGA TOUR SEASON SUMMARY

Tournaments Entered	7
Cuts Made	4
Cut Missed	3
Top 10 finish	0
Official Money	**$30,260.00**
Official Money List	**221st on the 1996 Official PGA Tour Money List**

CHAPTER 22

1997—The Emperor Has No Clothes

Quad City Classic—July 10-13, 1997
Purse: $1,350,000
Oakwood CC, Coal Valley, IL
Place: T71st
Score: 70-69-70-70
Made: $2,632.50

Deposit Guaranty Classic—July 17-20, 1997
Purse: $1,000,000
Annandale GC, Madison, MS
Score: 68-WD
Made: $0

Food Poisoning

It's not often you withdraw from a tournament after opening with a good round. A bout with food poisoning the night after the first round in the 1997 Deposit Guaranty Classic was a first for me. I was staying with my good friends Mike and Janie Jarvis in Madison, MS. On Thursday, I'd played well and posted an opening round of 68. In the middle of the night, I abruptly woke up to something terribly wrong. I was up all night wearing out the bathroom toilet from both the food entrance and exit portals of my body, suffering for hours, not able to keep anything, even water, down.

I hadn't gotten much sleep, but when it was time to get ready for my second round, I was determined to play even though I was delirious from dehydration. I couldn't hydrate myself as needed because I couldn't keep water down without throwing it up. I was not thinking straight, still believing I'd be able to play. Mike drove me to the course, where I was able to stumble to the driving range with little time to spare before my tee time. My caddie was waiting for me at the range with a spot to hit balls. I asked him, "How much time we got?" He replied, "We've got 20 minutes." I responded, "I am going to lie down for a bit." I proceeded to lie down right there on the driving range. I said to my caddie, "Let me know when we've got 10 minutes." Players were walking by and looking at me on the ground, no doubt wondering, *What the hell is going on with Zokol?* Right on cue, my caddie looks down at me on the ground and said, "Okay, we've got 10 minutes." I staggered to my feet and grabbed my 9-iron. It felt like a sledgehammer in my hands as I struggled to make a backswing. I couldn't. I looked at my caddie and said, "We are done. I can't make it."

I made my way back to the locker room, and someone who knew better than I called for the tournament doctor. The doctor came into the locker room, looked at me, asked a few questions, and immediately put me on the couch to stick an IV in me. I was on that couch in the locker room for six hours, going through numerous bags of IV fluid as I fell in and out of sleep. The next day, I felt perfectly fine and flew back to Vancouver.

TV Broadcasting

In 1997, I had the opportunity to be part of a TSN telecast team for the Canadian Skins Game played at Nicklaus North in Whistler, BC, as the reporter and interviewer walking with the players. I recall getting word from the producer that Ben Hogan had passed away that day, and I informed Jack and the group about this sad news. The producer of the broadcast directed me to interview Jack Nicklaus on the eighth hole, and I asked Jack what Ben Hogan meant to the game. Jack was gracious as usual.

Jack Nicklaus, Joanie, and Dick Zokol.

Greg Norman won that Skins Game against Fred Couples, Jack, and Nick Faldo.

1997 CANADIAN SKINS GAME

Name	Earnings
Greg Norman	$275,000
Fred Couples	$50,000
Jack Nicklaus	$35,000
Nick Faldo	$0.00

Greater Vancouver Open—August 21-24, 1997

Purse: CAD $1,500,000

Northview G&CC, Ridge Course, Surrey, BC

Place: T12th

Score: 67-64-70-71

Made: $27,642.85

In 1997, I was still enjoying not playing full-time on Tour. I welcomed the change of patterns in my life and being around my kids as they grew. Driving to the Eaglequest Golf office in downtown Vancouver during the morning rush hour was a refreshing change. Rob Safrata and Bob Garnett were great and gave me the freedom to play on Tour as much as I wanted.

I got into Tour events based solely on the Past Champions category. When I did play, I was eager to do so, excited, and I played well. I considered myself a part-time player and I was enjoying playing once again. That year, 1997, was the second year for the GVO, and I opened with a 67 in the first round and followed it up with a 64 in the second round. Len Mattiace, Steve Pate, and I shared the 36-hole lead at 11 under par, one stroke ahead of Curt Byrum and Payne Stewart.

The Emperor Has No Clothes

In the post-round media gathering after I shot 64 in the second round, I was asked how I liked Northview as the course for the Greater Vancouver Open. In my stoic reply, I said, "Speaking as a PGA Tour player, Northview wouldn't be my first choice as a site, nor is it the best course for the GVO." Well, Chick Stewart, the owner of Northview, lost his mind when he read my comments in the Saturday morning *Vancouver Sun* article. That morning, before I left home to play my third round, I got a call from Mike Carroll telling me that Chick Stewart had become so outraged by my comments in the newspaper that he was making efforts to ban me from entering his golf course for the third round of this PGA Tour event. I said to Mike, "Has he lost his fucking marbles? Doesn't he know he can't do that?" When the PGA Tour officials told Chick Stewart he didn't have the authority to ban any player from his golf course, apparently, it infuriated him even more.

A few weeks prior to the event I had met and gotten to know Chick and Marilyn Stewart and found them to be wonderful people. In fact, I found them to be delightful. Chick and Marilyn may have owned the golf course, but they didn't have much knowledge of golf course design. Chick, in my mind, had been blinded by the Arnold Palmer charisma and influence, and the Stewarts commissioned Palmer to design Northview. Like

Jack Nicklaus, Palmer leveraged his celebrity, and rightly so, to "seduce" susceptible golf course developers. In the Stewarts' minds, Northview was the best course in the world simply because Arnold Palmer (a.k.a. "the King") designed it. I felt bad that I had so upset and offended Chick with my comments. Shortly after the tournament, I reached out to him to make arrangements to meet and discuss the situation. Our meeting took place in Chick's office. The meeting only confirmed my suspicion that Chick had been spellbound by Palmer's allure and graciousness, enthralled by the King's influence and warm friendship.

The entire episode reminded me of Hans Christian Andersen's fairy tale "The Emperor's New Clothes." Nobody else was brave enough to say out loud to Chick Stewart what everyone knew. It was left to me to proclaim that Northview wasn't the best golf course for a PGA Tour event in Vancouver. Not even close. Chick's last words to me during our conversation were deprecating: "Son, if you don't like my golf course, why don't you go out and build your own golf course?" I replied to him, "I look forward to that day when I do."

Bell Canadian Open—September 4-7, 1997

Purse: $1,500,000

Royal Montreal GC, Ile-Bizard, Quebec

Place: T13th

Score: 71-71-66-75

Made: $23,430.00

Brad Pelletier

Brad Pelletier and I became close friends in the 1990s when he was put in place to run the Canadian Tour's BC Tel Pacific Open at Mayfair Lakes in Richmond, BC. Brad was a great "idea guy" working for Caleb Chan's Burrard International. Brad reached out to both Ray Stewart and me as local PGA Tour players to help promote the event. With each passing year, our friendship with Brad became closer.

The 1997 Bell Canadian Open was played at Royal Montreal. In the third round of the tournament on the 17th hole, I saw my buddy Brad with two International Management Group (IMG) agents. Brad was so excited that I was playing well. The previous week, Brad had given me a call, letting me know IMG had been headhunting him, and, knowing I had left IMG as a client, Brad wanted my perspective on IMG. My reply was, "You don't want any part of them. They are the biggest sharks in the ocean, and their culture doesn't have the best reputation." Brad responded, "I am aware of their reputation, and I plan on changing it." Immediately upon hearing Brad's plans and goals at IMG, I said, "Wow, if you go to IMG, I will go back on the condition that you are my agent." Brad said, "That's a deal."

Over the next 14 years, Brad worked his way through IMG hierarchy and ended up in Toronto as IMG Canada's managing director. The private investment firm Forstmann Little & Co. acquired IMG for $750 million in cash in 2004. With Ted Forstmann now at the helm of IMG, the company went into a tailspin. Most of their talented people, including Brad, scrambled out like rats off a sinking ship. Brad and his family moved back to BC and settled in Kelowna in 2010. In July 2011, Brad was approached by Wesbild Holdings Ltd. and became their senior VP, Okanagan. Wesbild Holdings acquired Predator Ridge Resort in Vernon, BC, in 2007.

In 2011, Brad was tasked to oversee Predator's 1,400-acre development—one that had already built 600 homes so far in their master planned community that had a total of 2,100 homes projected. Brad hired me in March 2012 as executive director, golf development. Though my initial focus was selling golf memberships, in 2014, Brad suggested that a better use of my value would be in selling real estate at Predator Ridge. I left the golf operations side of Predator Ridge and began to work with Claire Radford, who had been a legend in selling Predator Ridge real estate since 2000.

1997 PGA TOUR SEASON SUMMARY	
Tournaments Entered	6
Cuts Made	4
Cut Missed	2
Top 10 finish	0
Official Money	**$53,705.00**
Official Money List	**201st on the 1997 Official PGA Tour Money List**

CHAPTER 23

1998 & 1999—Climbing Out of the Mental Hole I Dug For Myself

At the start of 1998, all hands were on deck to figure out Eaglquest's next step now that our path to an initial public offering came to an abrupt end.

The Eaglequest plan was to go public after securing a large private placement with Catterton-Simons Partners, a New York private equity firm (now L. Catterton Investments). Our plans abruptly changed when the powerful El Niño weather phenomenon hit North America in the fourth quarter of 1997. This serious weather disruption was something nobody could control, and it hammered our revenue projections, which caused Catterton-Simons to pull back on their investment. Timing is everything, and Eaglequest Golf started running out of cash—the vultures started to circle.

The industry's leading small golf course and driving range consolidator, Family Golf Centers Inc., which traded publicly on the NYSE, swooped down and acquired Eaglequest Golf Centers Inc. in April 1998 in a stock swap valued at $104 million. Initial investors in Eaglequest received a return of up to 300% during the short period of their investment.

For me, going through the steps with the Eaglequest team from initial start-up to rapid growth and then operating a consolidation plan and eventual exit all within two years was a powerful learning experience.

Family Golf Inc.'s acquisition of Eaglequest Golf Centers Inc. closed in May or June, and all Eaglequest shareholders were paid out in unrestricted Family Golf shares. I chose to sell all the Family Golf shares as soon as I held them. Family Golf Inc., a public company that traded on the

NYSE and owned and operated 119 golf courses in North America, filed for Chapter 11 bankruptcy in May 2000.

Deposit Guaranty Classic—July 16-19, 1998

Purse: $1,200,000

Annandale GC, Madison, MS

Place: T39th

Score: 68-72-73-68

Made: $4,560.00

CVS Charity Classic—July 23-26, 1998

Purse: $1,500,000

Pleasant Valley CC, Sutton, MA

Place: T59th

Score: 68-70-76-69

Made: $3,285,00

Shell's Wonderful World of Golf Telecast

One of my fondest memories was pairing up with one of the great sports broadcasters Jack Whitaker on the telecast for *Shell's Wonderful World of Golf* at Nicklaus North between Ernie Els and Fred Couples. I was absolutely delighted when Terry Jastrow, the renowned TV producer/director, asked me to be part of the two-man broadcast team with Jack, a member of the Sports Broadcasting Hall of Fame. Jack Whitaker painted a portrait when he spoke. He was the Ernest Hemingway of sport broadcasters.

Jack Whitaker was gracious, and his vocabulary was deep. His delivery was spot on, smooth as velvet. Jack was also the first broadcaster to get banished from the Masters telecast. During his first Masters broadcast in 1966, Jack referred to the crowd coming up the 18th hole on Sunday as a *mob*. He had no idea he was going to be condemned by the powers that be—Clifford Roberts, the chairman of Augusta National Golf Club—for that comment. One month before the 1967 Masters, CBS told Frank Chirkinian, the producer of the telecast, that Whitaker would not be working the 1967 Masters telecast.

A few years later, when the great CBS broadcaster Henry Longhurst took ill, Frank Chirkinian, a CBS producer, wanted to bring Jack Whitaker back to the Masters telecast and put him to work on the 16th hole. But before doing so, they needed to go down and meet with Clifford Roberts, face-to-face. Roberts, the bigoted chairman of Augusta National, was the person who banned Whitaker in the first place and the man who called all the shots at Augusta National.

Jack Whitaker could not have been nicer to me. Everything was shot on tape, and Joanie and I flew to New York to do the voiceover for the telecast. They put us up in the Waldorf Astoria. For two days, Jack Whitaker and I sat side by side in the studio voicing over the entire show. It was a marvelous experience.

This *Shell's Wonderful World of Golf* can be viewed online.

Greater Vancouver Open—August 27-30, 1998

Purse: CAD $2,000,000

Northview G&CC, Ridge Course, Surrey, BC

Place: T28th

Score: 69-69-71-68

Made: $12,200.00

The 1998 Greater Vancouver Open was won by my friend Brandel Chamblee. Brandel shot rounds of 67-64-68-66 to beat out Payne Stewart by three-shots.

Westin Texas Open—September 24-27, 1998

Purse: $1,700,000

LaCantera GC, San Antonio, TX

Place: T31st

Score: 69-70-69-71

Made: $9,860.00

1998 PGA TOUR SEASON SUMMARY

Tournaments Entered	7
Cuts Made	4
Cut Missed	3
Top 10 finish	0
Official Money	**$29,905.00**
Official Money List	**231st on the 1998 Official PGA Tour Money List**

1999

In 1999, I wanted to rededicate myself to playing, and the best path for me to get back to the PGA Tour would be to play on a weekly basis on the Nike Tour. The PGA Tour created its minor league program initially called the Ben Hogan Tour (1990-1992), then it was renamed the Nike Tour (1993-1999), then the Buy.com Tour (2000-2002), then the Nationwide Tour (2003-2012), the Web.com Tour (2013-2019), then the Korn Ferry Tour (2013-present).

The Nike Tour, now the Korn Ferry Tour is the primary feeder Tour to get onto the PGA Tour. The PGA Tour's Past Champions category gave me access to the first six Nike Tour events at the start of the season. My plan was to enter, play well in those first six Nike events, and then reshuffle my position on the Nike Tour for the rest of the season events.

Full-time playing meant going back and forth between Nike Tour events and PGA Tour events, when spots came available. I made the commitment to start playing full time, and my first step was accepting my rightful place in golf's minor leagues—the Nike Tour.

Nike Tour South Florida Classic—January 7-10, 1999

Pompano Beach, FL

Place: T31st

Score: 72-68-72-74

Nike Tour Lakeland Classic—January 14-17, 1999
Lakeland, FL
Place: T16th
Score: 70-68-72-74

Nike Tour Florida Classic—February 4-7, 1999
Gainesville, FL
Place: T14th
Score: 69-68-69-71

Nike Tour Monterrey Open—March 18-21, 1999
Monterrey, Mexico
Place: T11th
Score: 71-66-66-73

Nike Tour Louisiana Open—March 25-28, 1999
Layette, LA
Place: T3rd
Score: 67-69-74-70

During the Easter holidays, while I was on the road, Garrett and Conor's grade six class went on a camping trip into the BC Interior for an extended weekend. It was during this trip, while the teachers and students stayed in cabins at a provincial campsite, that Conor's appendix burst. Not being near a hospital was a big problem. A burst appendix could easily cause infection (peritonitis) that could lead to death if it wasn't dealt with properly, but the group was a four-hour drive outside Vancouver. The teachers, to their credit, immediately recognized the gravity of the situation, and one of them rushed Conor back to a hospital in Vancouver. Other than having to spend a couple of days in the hospital, Conor recovered well.

Nike Tour Shreveport Open—April 15-18, 1999
Shreveport, LA
Place: T11th
Score: 71-66-66-73

Nike Tour South Carolina Classic–April 21-25, 1999

Charleston, SC

Place: MC

Score: 74-73

Nike Tour Upstate Classic–April 29-May 2, 1999

Greer, SC

Place: T63rd

Score: 74-72-76

Nike Tour Dominion Open May 13-16, 1999

Richmond, VA

Place: T18th

Score: 71-72-70-72

Nike Tour Knoxville–Open May 20-23, 1999

Knoxville, TN

Place: T10th

Score: 69-73-69-70

US Open–June 17-20, 1999

Purse: $3,500,000

Pinehurst Resort & CC, Pinehurst, NC (Pinehurst No. 2 Course)

Place: MC

Score: 75-74

Nike Tour Lehigh Valley Open–June 24-27, 1999

Center Valley, PA

Place: T19th

Score: 69-71-70-69

Nike Tour Ozarks Open–August 12-15, 1999

Springfield, MO

Place: T38th

Score: 71-69-69-74

Nike Tour Fort Smith Open—August 19-22, 1999

Fort Smith, AK

Place: MC

Score: 70-71

Another Harry C Classic

Earlier in the book, I wrote about Harry C and the escapades we had together when I won the 1992 Deposit Guaranty Classic. Well, Harry asked me if he could caddie for me again in the Fort Smith Open. After our ordeal years ago, I wasn't worried about Harry; he promised me he would follow procedure.

This Harry C story was one for the ages. We were playing in the Nike Tour events' Wednesday Pro-Am with three amateurs paying good money to play with pros. Part of Harry C's purpose in this world was to help golfers improve. Harry loved helping amateurs in Pro-Am events. I've always enjoyed playing with amateurs, but it can make for some long days on the golf course—in this round, it was mid-August in Fort Smith, Arkansas, with temperatures exceeding 100+ degrees. At the start of the round, Harry asked me for permission to engage with the amateurs in our group. I said, "Absolutely, Harry, knock yourself out."

Our Pro-Am team was playing the eighth hole (our 17th hole for the day), a par 3. It was hot, sticky, and the humidity was making the heat index reach record levels. I couldn't get into the clubhouse fast enough to cool down. I hit my tee shot on the eighth hole, then Harry and I walked up to the tee right as one of the amateurs was teeing up his ball, going through his procedure to hit his shot. All of a sudden, Harry blurts out, "STOP—HOLD UP—DON'T HIT THAT SHOT." Harry C called this guy off his tee shot. The amateur looked up in shock as if he was doing something wrong. And I immediately thought, *Oh my God, what the fuck is Harry doing now?* We were all standing there looking at Harry, wondering the same thing. Harry started in, "Hey partner, let's move you from the left side of the tee box way over here to the far right side of the tee box." I thought, *Holy shit, I can't believe what he's doing,* but I was not about to say a thing. This amateur, who was about an 18 handicap, was only doing what he was being told by Harry. Harry went on and said, "If you tee it up on the far right side of the box and aim to the left side of the green, your natural slice and the left-to-right slope of this green will be perfect for you. A good shot will feed right to the hole on the right side of the green." This amateur player did exactly what Harry told him. I stood there flabbergasted that Harry called this guy off his shot in the first place, while Harry stood off to the side, knowing all too well that if he came back to me, he'd catch some grief. I have never seen a caddie do anything like that ever before on Tour.

The amateur went through his shot all over again in his new location on the far right of the tee box. He hit his shot with a big slice, and it headed toward the left side of the green just as Harry predicted. His ball landed on the green and took a left-to-right kick and started rolling toward the right side of the green. It rolled right into the hole for a hole-in-one. I couldn't believe my eyes. I said to myself, *You've got to be fucking kidding me—that didn't just happen.* I looked at Harry, and he looked at me with that big shit-eating grin, and our group exploded in celebration. The amateur ran over to Harry C and gave him a big bear hug.

It was one of the most remarkable things I've ever seen. Harry C never let me forget it.

Air Canada Championship (formerly Greater Vancouver Open)—September 2-5, 1999

Purse: CAD $2,500,000

Northview G&CC, Ridge Course, Surrey, BC

Place: T35th

Score: 67-68-74-71

Made: $11,803.57

While playing in the Wednesday Pro-Am in the Air Canada Championship I was approached by PGA Tour officials and was informed that my son Garrett was having an appendix issue and was in the hospital. In that moment, there wasn't enough information to know if his appendix had burst like his twin brother's had. I immediately apologized to my amateur partners, saying I had a family emergency to deal with and had to immediately head to the hospital. Garrett had complained about stomach pain in his belly, and Joanie instinctively put together that it could be a twin thing between Garrett and Conor. Luckily, we got Garrett to the hospital to get his appendix removed before it burst like his twin brother's had.

Bell Canadian Open—September 9-12, 1999

Purse: CAD $2,500,000

Glen Abbey Golf Club, Oakville, ON

Place: T29th

Score: 73-72-72-72

Made: $15,218.75

Nike Tour Oregon Open—September 23-26, 1999

Junction City, OR

Place: T5th

Score: 74-70-70-69

Nike Tour New Mexico Classic—October 7-10, 1999

Santa Ana Pueblo, NM

Place: MC

Score: 80-73

Nike Tour Championship—October 21-24, 1999

Dothan, AL

Place: T10th

Score: 69-74-70-76

Payne Stewart's Death, Monday, October 25, 1999

The morning after the final round of the 1999 Nike Tour Championship in Dothan, Alabama, was one of those moments in life when you recall the exact place you were when a significant event or tragedy—such as the first step on the moon, JFK's and MLK's assassinations, or Elvis's death—occurs. That Monday morning, I was in the Dothan Airport at Gate 1 waiting to board a flight to Jackson, MS, to play in the Southern Farms Bureau Classic, when PGA Tour official Jim Duncan came over to me and told me that Payne Stewart and all on board the Learjet Payne had chartered had died when the cabin depressurized during flight. They were still on the aircraft, which was flying on autopilot as we spoke. I went numb in disbelief.

That week, the PGA Tour family of players, wives, caddies, and PGA Tour staff came together to mourn the loss of Payne Stewart, Robert Fraley, Van Arden, and Bruce Borland and the two pilots of the aircraft. It was a significant loss not only for golf, but for Tracy and their two children and all the families of those who lost their lives on the flight that day. The golf world lost a great golf person that day.

1999 PGA TOUR SEASON SUMMARY	
Tournaments Entered	6
Cuts Made	2
Cut Missed	3
WDs	1
Top 10 finish	0
Official Money	**$27,022.00**
Official Money List	**246th on the 1999 Official PGA Tour Money List**

1999 NIKE TOUR SEASON SUMMARY	
Tournaments Entered	16
Cuts Made	12
Cut Missed	4
Top 10 finish	4
Official Money	**$63,937.00**
Official Money List	**42nd on the 1999 Official Nike Tour Money List**

CHAPTER 24

Year 2000—Overcoming My Golf Insanity—Learning to Putt—the 2000 US Open at Pebble—the Liberating Power of Acceptance

At the end of 1999, I was in a full court press to discover the Holy Grail—accessing This Present Moment with each golf shot. Over the years, I had engaged with various sport psychologists and performance-coaching experts, such as Dr. Saul Miller and Dr. Richard Lonetto; worked with a specialist in ancient Chinese meditation; read all of Bob Rotella's golf books, as well as many self-help books from the likes of Dr. Wayne Dyer (*Your Erroneous Zones*, 1976) Napoleon Hill (*Think and Grow Rich*, 1937), Tony Robbins (*Awaken the Giant Within*, 1992); Don Miguel Ruiz (*The Four Agreements*, 1997), Viktor Frankl (*Man's Search for Meaning*, 1946), and Stephen Covey's (*The 7 Habits of Highly Effective People*, 1989). They all had wonderful meaning and helped me to identify healthy and poor thought habits that hold most golfers back, but I hadn't come away with a way to access This Present Moment.

Over the past year, I had tried to will myself into This Present Moment in competition, but I found my conditioned response was so ingrained that when I was in those intense situations, I defaulted right back to it. I needed a system that would help me recondition myself out of my dysfunctional conditioned response.

It became very clear that if I carried thoughts from my past or had thoughts that projected into the future to possible results, or feared the possibility of a bad outcome, it would instantly pull me out of This Present Moment and disrupt my ability to *assess* and *execute* my shot.

Reverse-Engineering the Shot to Find the Answer

The light bulb came on as my ball was in flight during a competition, immediately after I executed a perfect 7-iron from the fairway to a well-bunkered green. I loved the shot I just struck—I could not have struck the shot any better. As this shot peaked to its apex, my immediate thought was, this could go in the hole, or at least it's going to be real close. In that moment, if I were given the option to take the shot over, I would not have taken that option. In the next moment, as my ball touched down, it didn't cover the distance over the lip of the front bunker. My shot came up a couple of feet short and plugged under the lip of the bunker. A moment later, that result triggered anger—my conditioned response. I said to myself, *Fuck! I just executed the most perfect shot, and now I am buried under the lip of a bunker.*

As it turned out, I knew the Execution of that shot, a key factor, was excellent, but my Assessment, the other key factor of the shot, was unsatisfactory, by my own standards. My discovery—it's not good enough to make an excellent Execution if the shot's Assessment was unsatisfactory. I didn't get it up and down from the plugged lie in the bunker, and I made a bogey on the hole. Both the shot's **Assessment** and the shot's **Execution** are critical—so I declared them **Key Performance Markers** (KPMs).

With my new perspective, I started to put my full attention on evaluating both KPMs for each shot. It became my new performance measurement system. It not only simplified my process—but it immediately freed me up, allowing me to access This Present Moment. I felt an uncoupling from results and from the performance anxiety of the shot. It simplified the situation, and I began to evaluate and measure both KPMs on a three-point Likert scale: Excellent-Satisfactory-Unsatisfactory. This led me to start assigning **Shot Lost Events** and **Shot Gained Events** to the KPM that caused them. I assigned a 1-Shot Lost Event to the Assessment of that 7-iron shot.

The **Key Performance Marker** (KPM data) capture of each golf shot is:

- The **club** used;
- Your **Assessment** of the shot (the Assessment of the shot is subjectively measured on a three-point Likert scale—Excellent-Satisfactory-Unsatisfactory);

- Your **Execution** of the shot (the Execution of the shot is subjectively measured in a three-point Likert scale—Excellent-Satisfactory-Unsatisfactory)*;* and
- **Shot Lost Event** and **Shot Gained Event** data capture of each shot and attached to the KPM that caused it.

The Problem

In my own self-analysis, over four decades of playing competitive golf, I had become conditioned to react emotionally to the result of the shot—a common problem among most golfers. Things were not going to change for me until I took a more granular look at *why* that 7-iron shot came up short. And just how critical both these KPMs are for every golfer.

In one moment, I went from loving the shot to anger. The outcome of the shot triggered me emotionally—and I recognized this was my problem. I discovered in that moment that my thought and emotional structure were tied to my outcome and results, *extrinsic* objectives. I realized I had become hard-wired to react this way. And if I wanted to get out of repeating this over and over again, like I had for decades, I needed to break my Golf Insanity cycle by detaching my emotional connection from extrinsic results and then reattaching my attentional focus and emotional connection to intrinsic results—my two KPMs. This was the Holy Grail discovery—it gave me freedom to play.

Looking back, my dysfunctional mindset took hold when my ego was trying to protect my identity as a PGA Tour winner. It dawned on me in that moment of clarity that my dysfunctional thoughts caused me to actually think myself right off the PGA Tour in 1994, right after my best two years because of where I placed my attentional focus.

I discovered when I shifted my attentional focus off of my result and onto my two KPMs, something changed internally—in this mindset, I didn't feel anxious. Each shot situation got simple. All I needed to do was ask myself, *Are you able to successfully assess and execute this shot?* My answer was always a resounding and emphatic, *Yes*.

Immediately, I felt I was onto something, and I called my new operating system **Units-of-Execution** (which became MindTRAK Golf years later).

It was a significant step toward being able to detach emotionally from results, outcomes, and stop myself from future projecting.

Looking Back to 1994

I turned the microscope back on myself in the 1994 season, when I lost my freedom to play and my fear and ego took over. Our egos have an insatiable appetite for results and have expectations, and when our egos don't get what they want, they feel threatened. My anxiety grew with every step down this godforsaken path, with every shot in every event. I could sense my ego insisted on instantaneous gratification in the form of results. I was living in and suffering on the emotional tightrope walk of results. My missed cut numbers were rapidly growing. My ego ultimately drove the "Richard Zokol PGA Tour player bus" right into the ditch at the end of 1994. I didn't see it coming and needed to find a way to avoid this conditioned response—by the end of 1994, I was deep into Golf Insanity.

Golf Insanity—Your Thoughts Can Be Your Worst Enemy

Most golfers aren't even aware that Golf Insanity can creep into their minds and take root. But every golfer feels it. Golf Insanity is the condition response that is fueled by poor thought habits, repeating thoughts over and over again and expecting different results—which then triggers anger when results are not able to feed your ego. It's a vicious cycle.

The best performance in all sports happens when the player enters The Zone, when their subconscious mind (our intuition) takes over and the player performs freely without interference or disruption from their analytical mind (and ego). Golfers occasionally and unexpectedly enter this rarefied mindset, not knowing how or why they got there, or when it might happen again.

The Hypothesis

Because I wasn't taught how to think properly or to deal with my hyperactive thoughts effectively—nobody really is—I, like almost all golfers, became conditioned to be results-oriented. When we become emotionally attached to either good or bad outcomes, it is a problem; you become motivated by extrinsic results—scores, outcomes, wins, money, etc. Our egos get locked onto this extrinsic motivation and the result of the shot. My new measurement system shifted my attentional focus onto my two Key Performance Markers, intrinsic results of the golf shot. This system freed me up and allowed me to become intrinsically motivated rather than extrinsically motivated. This way of thinking started to break my emotional connection to results. It was a huge discovery. I was looking to free myself from the mental incarceration of having my personal identity connected to the results—I found my path.

It dawned on me that my past, hitting millions of golf shots and playing competition golf with this perspective, was the source of my problem. My thought framework set me on a path for my ego to take control and head down the rabbit hole—like most golfers. This only confirmed to me that I had constructed an unhealthy mindset.

In the year 2000, at the age of 42, I was in the second year of my comeback as a full-time player. At the end of 1999, the Nike Tour sponsorship ended, and the Buy.com Tour sponsorship began. In 1999, I played in a combination of 22 events between the Nike Tour and PGA Tour events. I told myself that if I wanted to make a successful comeback as a full-time player, I needed to change three things:

1. **Stop the Golf Insanity**: Stop my ego from taking charge and stop being emotionally attached to results, outcomes, or the score. My strategy was to transfer to my new KPM performance measurement system.
2. **Develop a High Level of Acceptance**: Accept where I am, in the minor leagues of golf on the Buy.com Tour, rather than being a winner on the PGA Tour. The moment I accepted this perspective, a huge weight was lifted, helping me play with freedom with every shot.
3. **Become a Better Putter.**

The Liberating Power of Accepting Who and Where I Am

As mentioned in 1994, my ego took control, and I struggled to accept my poor performance, which relegated me off the PGA Tour as an exempt player. My ego-led perspective made me feel embarrassed and ashamed. It did not want to accept this new position—it actually refused to. My personal identity had been compromised. At the start of the year 2000, I looked into the mirror and said to myself, "You are not only exactly where you deserve to be, you are exactly where you need to be. The sooner you accept this, the sooner you will be able to climb out of this position." Bingo, I found my acceptance path.

> "Accept whatever comes to you in the
> pattern of your destiny, for what could
> more aptly fit your needs?"
> —MARCUS AURELIUS

Poor thought habits include having a low level of acceptance. Having a high level of acceptance is the framework for healthy thought habits. Developing a high level of acceptance is essential to optimizing performance. There isn't a player in this game who doesn't have to deal with poor results. How you choose to deal with your poor results is fundamental to your performance. As a player when you fully accept this risk of playing this game, you increase your ability to play with freedom. The higher the level of acceptance you have as a player, the more it will help you detach emotionally from the results, and the more you increase your ability to play with freedom.

The Origins of My Key Performance Indicators (KPM) Measurement System

At the start of the 2000 Buy.com Tour year, I committed to putting all my attentional focus onto my KPM performance. I really wanted to get good at this. The only performance measurement that mattered was my KPM data on the golf course. My goal was to simply look at each golf shot independently and perform both KPMs the best I could, then capture my KPM data on each shot in every tournament round I played on the golf course.

It's Simple—but That Doesn't Mean It's Easy

Remember, at the start of each golf shot, your objective is to ask yourself: *Are you capable of making an excellent* Assessment *and an excellent* Execution *of this shot right now?* The answer to this question should be a definite, *Yes, I absolutely can make an excellent Assessment and Execution of this shot.*

With these thoughts in mind, your immediate objective is to proceed to making an excellent Assessment and an excellent Execution of this shot. Then, after you hit the shot, you capture its KPM data. When you go through this procedure with each shot, if you have a growth mindset, your perspective and objective will start to change. You will adapt to this simple method. When you get to your next shot, you do the exact same thing—your objective is to reboot this process over and over again with each and every shot you make, all with the intention of making an excellent Assessment and Execution of the shot in front of you. This is how you play. It's that simple. When you settle into this mindset, the game becomes simple. Moreover, you rid yourself of *Golf Insanity.*

The barrier that many golfers and coaches struggle with, which is at the core of the problem, is not being able to distinguish the difference between the *Execution* of the shot and the *result* of the shot. If this happens to you, it is evident you are conditioned to results. Those who struggle with this have not yet reconciled the difference between these two aspects of the shot. This is a critical aspect that needs to be defined and fundamentally accepted and understood. Too many coaches and players simply combine these two aspects as the same thing and label the results as good or bad. This is where many get stuck and stay on the wrong path.

In 2000, at the start of the Buy.com Tour season, after every round, when I got back to my hotel room, I opened my laptop and entered my KPM data into an After Action Report (AAR). I created a template charting holes 1 to 18 on a vertical axis, and on the horizontal axis, I had the number of shots on each hole. I entered my KPM data on each hole—club used and my subjective evaluation of my Assessment and Execution of each shot. After entering my subjective evaluation per shot, I then started to attach my Shot Lost Events and Shot Gained Events to the KPM of each shot that caused them.

At the end of the AAR, I'd look at how many Shot Lost Events I made and how many Shot Gained Events I made in that round. The easiest way to improve is to reduce the amount of Shot Lost Events on a per round basis.

After going through this AAR exercise, it became clear to me I was making far too many Shot Lost Events per round. I was astonished by how many shots I pissed away each round in every tournament. At that point, I knew if I eliminated a decent amount of these Shot Lost Events, it would be very meaningful. My best path to improvement was to shore up my Shot Lost Events, and wherever the highest number of Shot Lost Events showed up in my KPM data was where I'd need to put my attention.

It made complete sense to me, and immediately I was able to gain traction, supported by the notion that results are simply a by-product of my KPM performance. This was the path to being able to detach emotionally from results, and I dove into the process.

At the start of the year 2000, with my new operating system in mind, stopping my Golf Insanity hinged on how well I shifted my attentional focus onto my KPMs in every shot in every round. Of course, as a player, you will find yourself in difficult situations on the golf course and become overwhelmed. When this happens, all you can do is let go of the last shot (whether it was good or bad) and do a full reboot on your attention toward the shot you have right now.

Once again, you need to ask yourself the question, *Are you capable of making an excellent Assessment and Execution of this shot right now?* The answer to this question should be, *Yes.* Then go into the shot with 100% commitment to perform an excellent Assessment and Execution.

No process will guarantee you will make an excellent Execution, nothing can, but it gives your attentional focus a system to rely on. The more you do, the better you will get at it. The better you get at it, the greater the freedom you will receive.

Moving forward into 2000, my new operating system on a per shot basis was:

Shot Assessment (decisions) → Commitment → Shot Execution (performance) → Measure KPM → Enter KPM Data into App in AAR

At the start of 2000, I set out to play a full schedule between the Buy.com Tour and the few PGA Tour events that I'd gain access to from my Past Champions category and maybe the odd sponsor exemption.

Just as a note, regarding the records below: I was not able to find a record of the amount of money won at each event, but I was able to find out the scores I shot and whether or not I made the cut.

Buy.com Tour Florida Classic—February 3-6, 2000

Gainesville, FL

Place: T26th

Score: 70-72-68-73

Buy.com Tour Lakeland Classic—February 10-13, 2000

Lakeland, FL

Place: T25th

Score: 69-70-71-71

Buy.com Tour Monterrey Classic—February 16-19, 2000

Monterrey, Mexico

Place: T36th

Score: 71-69-70-72

Buy.com Tour Louisiana Open—February 30-March 2, 2000

Layette, LA

Place: T40th

Score: 69-70-75-69

Buy.com Tour Shreveport Open—March 13-16, 2000

Shreveport, LA

Place: MC

Score: 77-73

Buy.com Tour South Carolina Classic–March 27-30, 2000

Charleston, SC

Place: MC

Score: 72-74

Buy.com Tour Knoxville Open–April 4-7, 2000

Knoxville, TN

Place: MC

Score: 71-75

Learning to Putt

My ball-striking performance was making fantastic traction, but my putting was causing me some serious trouble as I missed three cuts in a row in Shreveport, Charleston, and Knoxville, all due to my poor putting. I was feeling great about establishing my new operating system, but it was now time to turn my attention to solving my putting problems.

My putting discovery happened during the Buy.com Tour event in Knoxville when I got paired with Don Pooley in the first two rounds of the event. Don Pooley was not only regarded as a terrific person by his peers, he was also regarded as one of the best putters on the PGA Tour. Don was playing the Buy.com Tour in preparation for his PGA Tour Champions debut when he turned 50.

After a first-round putting disaster, and having missed my two previous cuts due to my poor putting, I approached Don on the practice putting green after our first round and asked him if he would help me with my putting. Don graciously agreed. I said to Don, "I am having trouble with my putting." Don is a no-nonsense guy and said something to the effect, "I noticed." He went on, "You don't look very comfortable over your putter. What are you trying to do?" I said, "I am trying to match the low point of my stroke with my ball position." Don said, "Okay, that's good, but when I watch you putt, you're not doing that." He goes on, "I can see the low point of your stroke is not aligned with your ball position, that's a problem. If you want to match the low point of your stroke with your ball position, you will need to either move your ball position back in your stance to correlate with the low point or move your low point (and center of gravity) to the left to align with your ball position." That made complete sense to me.

I thanked Don for the help, and I then spent the next two hours practicing with my ball position moved back to align with the low point of my stroke. I liked the theory, but I still did not feel good when I was over the ball in this new ball position—this is not unusual when making a change, so I decided to push through with it.

The next morning, we teed off for the second round, and I was doing my best to implement my new ball position. Right from the start, I could not get comfortable over the ball whatsoever. Looking down and seeing my ball position so drastically to the right in my stance freaked me out. As much as I had committed to the theory, alarms were going off in my mind when I got over the ball. My intuition was telling me this isn't going to work, and I started missing—yipping—short putts. I shot 75 and missed my third cut in a row.

After my poor second round and having missed the cut for three consecutive weeks, the usual thing to do was get the hell out of Dodge and head home for a day or two, but when you live in Vancouver, that's not a viable option. I went back to the practice green that afternoon looking to figure things out. I concluded that moving the ball position back in my stance to align with the low point of my stroke did not correlate with my eye position over the ball.

Okay, plan B—I took account of my putting stance, and noted I had approximately 60% of my weight on my left foot. Then I moved my ball position square off my left foot and stacked more than 90% of my weight over the ball of my left foot, which pulled my eyes right over my ball position—perfect. From this position, my perception naturally settled into a right angle between my left foot and the start line of my putt. My eyes were now over the ball; my center of gravity had shifted onto my left foot. In my mind, I felt like how the great Bobby Locke looked over the ball when putting. The only thing that felt out of place in this stance was my right dominant hand, which controlled my stroke.

Because I was right-handed, I had a right-hand-dominated putting stroke, and the pivot point of my stroke hinged in my right shoulder. This meant my pivot point and my low point were *not* stacked vertically over each other. The low point of my stroke and my pivot point would be right of the vertically stacked alignment that I was trying to achieve.

The Vertical Stack Putting Stance

1. My ball position was square off my front left foot.
2. My center of gravity was stacked over my left foot.
3. My eye position was pulled directly over the ball.
4. The low point of my putting stroke was still right of my ball position, which is determined by my right-hand dominance and pivot point in my right shoulder.

The only thing missing was I needed to shift my stroke's low point left to align with the vertical stack. It meant I needed to shift to lead-hand dominance to control my stroke, not my right-hand dominance.

Then I thought to myself, *I changed to a left-hand dominant golf swing in 1992; changing to left-hand dominance in my putting stroke would surely be easier than changing my whole golf swing structure.* I put my putter in my left hand and addressed the ball. I put my right hand in my pocket. My left shoulder pivot point aligned perfectly, and everything fell into place in the vertical stack. The only issue was I didn't feel comfortable with the lack of coordination in my left hand. My immediate objective was to rehabilitate my left hand to dominate my stroke. (Another way to force your left hand to take over or stay structured through the impact zone is to incorporate the claw, the saw, or the pencil grip.) This ensures the left hand stays structured through the stroke.

Over the next two hours, I decided to putt with my left hand only with my new vertically aligned putting method. Even though I hadn't yet developed the coordination in my left hand for it to be dominant yet, I felt comfortable over the ball. I noticed the ball came off my putter face rolling better with my left-hand dominant stroke than with my right-hand dominant stroke.

The next day after a major practice session on the practice putting green, I saw Don Pooley in the locker room and informed him that I decided to

This image of Matt Wallace is an example of a Vertical Stacked Putting Stance.
Getty Images: Orlando Ramirez

The Vertical Stack Putting Stance Method stacking 90% of center of gravity over left foot—ball position and start line is on a right angle off my left foot stacking over low-point of my stroke—eyes stacked over the ball with left-hand domination putting stroke.
Getty Images: Dave Sandford

change my ball position, the low point of my stroke, the center of gravity, and my eye alignment over my left foot. Don said, "Yes, I was watching you work on the practice putting green, you looked much better over the ball putting that way." I thanked Don for his help.

The same way I initiated my left-hand only golf swing on the practice range in the 1992 AT&T Pro-Am, I planned to develop, coordinate, and strengthen my left-hand dominance to align all five key factors of my putting stroke. This wasn't going to be difficult.

I made a committed effort to drill my new putting method as much as possible. In my hotel room, I left one of my backup putters beside my bed, and before I went to sleep every night, I committed to making 100 strokes with my left hand only in my new putting stance. I did four sets of 25 strokes, each stroke from the initial starting position. Then first thing the next morning, when I got out of bed, I'd make another 100 strokes (try it—you will feel a burn in your last three fingers and lower forearm muscles after 25 strokes). When I got to the golf course before I hit my first putt on the practice putting green, I made another 100 strokes with my left hand only before I would hit my first putt on the putting green. Then I'd putt with one ball using my left hand only for about 10 minutes before I put both hands on my putter. I repeated this regimen every day. It changed my world.

In the next event, my putting had stabilized, and I could feel my putting improve with each passing day. I was thrilled with my new operating system, and now my new method of putting; things were falling nicely into place.

Buy.com Tour Richmond Open–April 11-14, 2000
Richmond, VA
Place: T20th
Score: 69-68-70-72

Buy.com Tour Steamtown Classic–June 1-4, 2000
Moosic, Pennsylvania
Place: T10th
Score: 70-71-73-66

Sectional US Open Qualifying

After my final round in the Steamtown Classic, I drove down to Washington, DC, for the 36-hole Sectional Qualifying for the 2000 US Open. I was scheduled to play at Woodmont Country Club in Rockville, Maryland, on Monday, June 5th. The field was playing for 36 spots. After 36 holes were completed—I shot 67-70—I found myself in a sudden-death playoff with 13 other players. A decision was made that the playoff would begin the next morning at 8:00 AM. The next morning came, and I made a par on the first hole, as did 12 other players; my buddy Don Pooley was the lone man out in the sudden-death playoff with a bogey on the first hole. Pooley became the first alternate for the 2000 US Open, and fortunately for Don, Paul Lawrie withdrew, and Pooley got paired with David Gossett and Jack Nicklaus in the first two rounds.

Buy.com Tour Dayton Open—June 8-11, 2000

Dayton, OH

Place: MC

Score: 76-72

US Open—June 15-18, 2000

Purse: $4,500,000

Pebble Beach GL, Pebble Beach, CA

Place: T32nd

Score: 74-74-80-69

Made: $28,247.00

The 2000 US Open at Pebble Beach

There's nothing like US Open golf, and at the top of the list are the US Opens played at Pebble Beach. The year 2000 was a special year, with the US Open being played at Pebble Beach and the Open Championships being played at the Old Course in St Andrews, Scotland.

There was something very special about the 2000 US Open. It was not only the 100th US Open being played at Pebble Beach; Tiger was doing his thing against the rest of the best players in the world. It was truly historic. Not only did Tiger win by 15 shots over Ernie Els and Miguel Ángel Jiménez, but Tiger's performance was looked at as the greatest performance in major golf history, and it was at one of the great cathedrals of the game.

Tiger's 2000 US Open victory was the first leg of his four consecutive major championship wins—Tiger won the 2000 US Open at Pebble Beach; the 2000 Open Championship at the Old Course, in St Andrews, Scotland; the 2000 PGA Championship at Valhalla; and the 2001 Masters—the Tiger

Slam. On top of that, Tiger won the 2001 Players Championship making him the only person to have won all four major championships simultaneously and the Player Championship.

The day before the first round of the 2000 US Open, I played a practice round with my former BYU teammates Bobby Clampett, Rick Fehr, and Keith Clearwater. The course was playing so bloody difficult, and Bobby in particular was playing bad. I was truly worried for him, about what he might shoot. Also on that day, on the 18th tee, we all teed up a ball and struck it in the Pacific Ocean as a tribute to our friend Payne Stewart, the defending US Open Champion. I wasn't able to make the long procession of players gathering together by the USGA late on Wednesday to make the shot in the formal tribute to Payne Stewart, but I did my own personal salute to Payne on Pebble Beach's 18th tee.

As I was driving through 17 Mile Drive to Pebble late in the morning to prepare for my afternoon tee time, I looked at the leaderboard to see how the morning wave of players were making out, and I saw Clampett's name right at the top. I said to myself, *Bobby, you have never ceased to amaze me—you've got the courage of a lion.*

The coastal marine layer often rolls in on the Northern California coast in June, and in the first round, there were on-and-off fog delays. When the fog rolled in, it was quite fortunate for me as it allowed me to work on my game. I wasn't playing too well, but I was managing my mistakes. I shot 74 in the first round.

The second round was more of the same, with the fog rolling in and out, and my game wasn't getting any better. On one of the fog delays, when I had finished playing the 11th hole, I recall walking back to the par-3 12th hole. As I was walking on the 12th green and looking back to the tee, I could see the tee shot I needed to make. The 12th green underfoot felt like freshly paved concrete, and I thought to myself, *This tee shot on 12 is playing over 200 yards into the cold fog, and I need to hit some kind of 3-iron just to carry the front bunker.* But even my best shot was going to land hard, and I wouldn't be able to stop before it ran through the green into the deep rough surrounds. I didn't have a shot in my bag that could keep my ball on the green, given the club and trajectory I needed to hit for the tee shot. Yet, Tiger could launch his 6-iron straight up, covering the distance without any problem and making his ball come straight down to land softly. The thought that came to mind was, *I am bringing a knife to a gunfight.*

With two holes to play in my second round, I was right on the cut line, standing on the 17th tee at 7 over par. I couldn't afford to make a bogey in the last two holes. The pin on the 17th hole was on the back of the front portion of the green. I hit a great shot off the tee, and my shot landed hard on the front of the green, slightly right of the hole. My shot took one big hop and ran through the green about a yard over into the deep rough between the green and the bunker. My ball was about 15 feet from the hole in extremely deep, thick rough. Because the green slopes from back to front, and my ball was so deep in the rough, the type of shot I needed to make to extract my ball would likely not stop on the green. It was one of the most difficult shots I've ever faced. I accepted my fate and got in there with my 56-degree sand wedge, opened the face up and ripped through this thick rough, trying to get underneath the ball with as much speed as I could muster to pop the ball straight up and hope for the best. I executed the shot the best I could, and the ball came out exactly as I hoped, going straight up and down with a first big bounce and then into what I thought would be the second bounce, but it jumped straight into the hole for a two. I am not one to get too excited, but I was on that shot. I made par on 18 and shot a second consecutive 74 for a total of 148, making the 36-hole cut by one shot.

The third round was an absolute slaughter for those whose games weren't sharp. If you weren't on top of your game in round three, it would absolutely pry open your weaknesses. It was the epitome US Open round, designed to be hard on everyone, even those who were playing their best. I had a hard day, still focusing on my KPMs on every shot. I did my best and shot 80.

Sunday at the US Open

Heading into Sunday's final round, I said to myself, *Look at where we are. It's Sunday at the 100th US Open at Pebble Beach and my best friend Russ Jordan is on the bag with me. Russ loves everything the USGA stands for. Tiger is making history. Let's go out there, have some fun, and focus strictly on how good I do on my two KPMs on each shot. Let's have some fun!*

Russ and I were on the driving range, warming up for the final round. I was in a giddy mood and saw Colin Montgomery and his caddie walking down the practice tee with a bag of balls in hand. Colin's head was down, ignoring everyone and giving off body language that said, *Do Not Disturb.* It appeared Colin was not at all pleased with his early Sunday tee time—meaning he wasn't in contention. I recognized this situation, and I said to Russ, "Here comes Monty, he looks pissed, watch this." I waited for Colin to stroll right beside me, head still down, looking at his feet, and I blurted out rather loudly for all to hear, "Good Morning, Colin!" Monty's head snapped up a bit, startled as I disrupted his mood, and he said in his distinct English accent, "Yes, yes, it is, good morning." Russ and I had quite the chuckle together at Colin's expense, and it set the tone for one of the best days on the golf course in our lives.

I have always loved playing US Opens, particularly US Opens at Pebble Beach—a very playable golf course. Even in US Open difficulty, it gives you options to play it.

Standing on the first tee at Pebble Beach that Sunday at the 2000 US Open was magical. I accepted I was struggling to play well—but in that moment, it didn't matter. The 80 I shot in the third round didn't matter either. Russ was there, and Clay Edwards, and Tiger Woods was making history. How could you think this wasn't special? The other player in our twosome was Keith Clearwater, my former BYU teammate.

My efforts over the previous five months to emotionally detach from results and redirect my attachment onto my KPM were going well, and I could feel a sense of letting go and being free. In this moment, both aspects of my game were making progress, with my attention always on my KPMs in each round. I was truly detaching from both my good and my bad results, like the 80 I shot the day before. This is key; you cannot segregate being emotionally attached to good results while being detached from bad results. Results are results, and detaching from good results helps you detach from bad results. My putting was making progress with each passing day. My acceptance was at its highest level the moment my third round 80 didn't discourage me or threaten my ego—everything seemed to be falling into place. I didn't feel I *needed* to play well. I wanted to play well, and I was in pursuit of what I wanted—freedom.

After being announced off the first tee by Ron Reed, the USGA starter, Keith Clearwater and I set out to play the final round. Another factor that impacted my state of mind that day was I always loved and seemed to play well at Pebble Beach. Who knew I was about to tie a nine-hole USGA record for all US Opens played at Pebble Beach? I shot 30 on the front nine that day. (I even kicked Tiger's ass by five shots, but let's not talk about the seven other nine hole scores that week.) Needless to say, it was the best nine holes I had ever played.

MY FRONT NINE ON SUNDAY'S FINAL ROUND OF THE 2000 US OPEN AT PEBBLE BEACH

1st Hole	**Par 4**
Tee Shot:	2-iron–in fairway
2nd Shot:	7-iron–to 5 feet above the hole
1st Putt:	ran my birdie putt 6 feet past the hole
2nd Putt:	made my par putt
Score:	4
2nd Hole	**Par 4**
Tee Shot:	driver–in fairway
2nd Shot:	3-iron–to green
1st Putt:	30 feet
2nd Putt:	tap in
Score:	4
3rd Hole	**Par 4**
Tee Shot:	3-wood–in fairway
2nd Shot:	9-iron–to green
1st Putt:	made 20-foot putt
Score:	3

4th Hole	**Par 4**
Tee Shot:	5-wood–in fairway
2nd Shot:	sand wedge–to green
1st Putt:	made 25-foot putt
Score:	3
5th Hole	**Par 3**
Tee Shot:	5-iron–to left side of green
1st Putt:	25-foot tap in
Score:	3
6th Hole	**Par 5**
Tee Shot:	driver–in fairway
2nd Shot:	5-wood–to green
1st Putt:	30 feet
2nd Putt:	tap in
Score:	4
7th Hole	**Par 3**
Tee Shot:	pitching wedge–to green
1st Putt:	made 5-foot putt for birdie
Score:	2
8th Hole	**Par 4**
Tee Shot:	3-wood–in fairway
2nd Shot:	5-iron–to green
1st Putt:	made 8-foot putt for birdie
Score:	3
9th Hole	**Par 4**
Tee Shot:	driver–in fairway
2nd Shot:	3-iron–over green into deep rough
3rd Shot:	chip shot to 30 feet
1st Putt:	made 30-foot putt for par
Score:	4

Scotty Bowman Inside the Ropes

As Russ and I stepped onto the ninth green Russ said, "Look there's Scotty Bowman." I looked to the gallery, thinking how cool it is that Scotty Bowman was watching. I couldn't see him in the gallery. Russ said, "No, he's over there," pointing to the side of the green. "He's inside the ropes and has a USGA blazer on with a USGA arm band." Scotty Bowman was a buddy of the president of the USGA from Detroit. Before walking with Tiger Woods's group for the entire 18 holes Scotty had come out to watch a little golf for himself.

Scotty was greenside as I sized up my 30-footer putt for par that must have had at least 12 feet of break. I assessed the speed and break as best I could. And in the moment, I literally had no idea how far under par I was, and more importantly, my score didn't matter—just my KPMs. I went through my shot routine and executed the shot with the sense of speed and break to the best of my ability. My putt took off on the line I wanted, and when my putt reached the apex point of the break, then began to break hard left on this side hill putt. When the ball rolled perfectly into the middle of the hole, Scotty gave out a roar. I thought, *That's Scotty Bowman getting excited for my putt. How cool is that?*

After teeing off the 10th tee and walking down to the fairway, I looked over to my right and made eye contact with Scotty, and he yelled out at me, "Go get 'em, Richard." I was over the moon that Scotty Bowman gave me his exciting encouragement.

My Aha Moment

After my tee shot on the 10th, Russ and I were walking to the 10th fairway and he asked me, "Do you know what you just shot on the front nine?" My reply was, "No, I don't know." I hadn't given any thought to my score or results the entire front nine. All I cared about were performing my KPMs, and my Assessment and Execution of each shot. As I look back, with every Excellent Assessment and Execution I made with a shot, I felt like I was receiving dopamine bumps. It felt great—I became comfortably numb again. I loved that feeling of being detached form the score. Russ said,

"You shot 30 on the front nine!" I gave it a moment and then said to Russ, "I still don't care about the fucking *score*." In that moment, I felt completely free. I didn't care after becoming aware of this amazing score; that was my Aha Moment. It happened right there and then on the 10th hole at Pebble Beach on Sunday at the US Open.

When Russ told me I shot 30 on the front nine—I truly didn't care. When I made double bogey on the 10th hole because of a poorly executed second shot into the ravine, I still didn't care. At that moment, I felt completely detached emotionally from score and result. I just moved on to the next shot—I felt freedom—tapping into and staying in my This-Present-Moment mindset—the Holy Grail—it was a kundalini awakening.

2000 Bell Canadian Open–September 7-10, 2000

Purse: CAD $3,300,000

Glen Abbey Golf Club, Oakville, ON

Place: MC

Shot: 147 (my 2 day total, missed the cut)

The 2000 Bell Canadian Open was won by Tiger Woods, which really turned out to be a two-man battle over the last few holes between Tiger and Grant Waite. Tiger won with that famous 6-iron shot on Glen Abbey's 18th hole from the right fairway bunker that carried over the entire body of water.

Tiger Woods Meets Moe Norman–Moe Norman Meets Tiger Woods

That week, the legendary Moe Norman and Tiger Woods met for the first and only time. This special moment in golf history happened because of Clay Edwards's fast thinking.

The story unfolded on a rain delay when the players were warming up on the range and on the practice putting green, waiting to get the word to head back out on the course to resume play. The practice tee and putting green were heavily congested with players warming up at the same time. Tiger was on the putting green, head down, working on his putting and blocking everything else out. Clay Edwards was watching me putt, and he saw Moe at the edge of the fence at the putting green with his eyes locked on Tiger. Moe was about 20 feet from Tiger, and Tiger was in his own world, oblivious to Moe Norman standing about 20 feet from him. Clay absolutely recognized that nothing was going to happen here unless he did something about it—these two great historic players of the game were about to pass each other by without ever knowing, if not for Clay Edwards. Clay thought to himself, *This can't happen!* It would be a shame if these two legendary players never met when they were physically so close to one another. Moe's focus was still locked onto Tiger, and Tiger's head was not coming up at all. Clay knew Tiger wouldn't pick up his head unless there was a good reason for him to do so. Then all of a sudden, Clay yelled out, "TIGER WOODS MEET MOE NORMAN—MOE NORMAN MEET TIGER WOODS." Tiger's head popped up and swiveled around, intently scanning the fence. Clay lifted the ropes and walked Moe toward Tiger Woods on the putting green, and they greeted each other with a handshake. Moe's good friend Gus Maue took this photo.

The photo was taken in 2000 and did not surface until some 15 years later. Clay Edwards was responsible for this significant moment for both Tiger Woods and Moe Norman.

From left to right—
Clay Edwards, Moe Norman,
and Tiger Woods at the 2000
Canadian Open at
Glen Abbey.

Greater Milwaukee Open—July 13-16, 2000

Purse: $2,500,000

Brown Deer Park GC, Milwaukee, WI

Place: T35th

Score: 71-68-69-69

Made: $11,546.00

BC Open—July 20-23, 2000

Purse: $2,000,000

En-Joie Golf Club, Endicott, NY

Place: T5th

Score: 70-67-70-68

Made: $70,250.00

John Deere—July 27-30, 2000

Purse: $2,600,000

TPC at Deere Run, Silvis, IL

Place: T12th

Score: 68-71-69-64

Made: $42,356.37

SEI Pennsylvania Classic—September 14-17, 2000

Purse: $3,200,000

Waynesborough CC, Paoli, PA

Place: T66th

Score: 71-70-72-78

Made: $6,592.00

Michelob Championship at Kingsmill—October 5-8, 2000

Purse: $3,000,000

Kingsmill G&CC, Williamsburg, VA

Place: T41st

Score: 68-69-73-73

Made: $10,500.00

2000 PGA TOUR SEASON SUMMARY

Tournaments Entered	11
Cuts Made	6
Cuts Missed	5
Top 10 finishes	1
Official Money Made	**$169,492.00**
Official Money List	**172nd on the 2000 Official PGA Tour Money List**

2000 BUY.COM TOUR SEASON SUMMARY

Tournaments Entered	10
Cuts Made	4
Cut Missed	6
Top 10 finish	1
Official Money	**$27,534.00**
Official Money List	**116th on the 2000 Official Nike Tour Money List**

CHAPTER 25

2001—Winning the 2001 Samsung Canadian PGA Championship on the Buy.com Tour—Welcome Back to the PGA Tour

My 2000 season was another major inflection point in my golf career. I made significant improvements in all three of my objectives. Number 1: my level of *acceptance* significantly improved. Number 2: my ego was no longer driving the bus, which stopped my Golf Insanity and my need to defend or make excuses for playing on the Buy.com Tour. I accepted and felt I deserved to be exactly where I was—it was such a liberating feeling. Number 3: my putting significantly improved. I felt I had not only improved my putting, but that I was becoming a great putter—I had freedom to roll my rock.

In 2000, I played:

- 11 events on the PGA Tour, making $169,492.00.
- 10 events on the Buy.com Tour, making $27,534.

Now at the age of 43, having made these three significant discoveries in 2000, I was playing the best golf of my life. I was looking forward to 2001. I was ready to play my way back to the PGA Tour.

At the start of 2001, I decided to stop splitting my time between the PGA Tour and the Buy.com Tour. In 2001, if you finished in the top 15 on the Buy.com Tour Money List, you qualified for the next year's PGA Tour, and as it was, I was only getting into 11 PGA Tour events from my Past Champions category, and they were dispersed all over the place, making it difficult to know when and where I'd get into events. To get back to the

PGA Tour, I felt it would be better to focus entirely on the Buy.com Tour path. Splitting my time would only dilute my efforts.

Buy.com Florida Classic—March 8-11, 2001

Gainesville, FL

Place: T36th

Score: 70-68-67-73

Made: $2,176.50

The Power of Now & Eckhart Tolle

Then I came across the book *The Power of Now* by Eckhart Tolle. I thoroughly enjoyed diving into Eckhart Tolle's story. The simplicity and power one can gain from being present resonated with me, and how I wanted to restructure the way I thought. I incorporated my own mantra, "I am I—here and now" into my daily meditation. I would also use my mantra to ground me anytime I started to get anxious or ahead of myself on the golf course, or if my mind wandered off to places when I needed to focus or when I was having a difficult time going to sleep.

Reading *The Power of Now*, and then rereading it, validated the path I was on and the system that I was using to access This Present Moment. Eckhart Tolle calls this "The Power of *Now*."

> "The power for creating a better future is contained in the present moment—you create a good future by creating a good present."
>
> —ECKHART TOLLE

Eckhart Tolle's book helped fortify my mental foundation. Immediately, I felt the path and the system that I had created for myself, which I called Units-of-Execution, was a significant step toward being able to detach emotionally from results and outcomes and future projecting to results.

The primary messages in *The Power of Now*, and I am paraphrasing Eckhart Tolle, is "the past is gone forever and the future never comes. The only thing we have and the only thing we will ever have is the Now." These words in Eckhart Tolle's book, which has sold over 12 million copies, have helped so many people with mental health challenges and their daily anxious existence. They also speak to the perception that "the most important shot in golf is the one you have right Now."

Buy.com Monterrey Open—March 15–18, 2001

Monterrey, Mexico

Place: T18th

Score: 68-71-72-67

Made: $5,287.50

Buy.com Louisiana Open—March 29–April 1, 2001

Lafayette, LA

Place: T14th

Score: 72-70-65-69

Made: $7,875.00

Buy.com Arkansas Classic—April 19–22, 2001

Little Rock, Arkansas

Place: T33rd

Score: 68-75-69-77

Made: $2,655.00

Buy.com Charity Pro-Am the Cliffs—April 26–29, 2001

Travelers Rest, SC

Place: T25th

Score: 66-66-72-75

Made: $3,814.28

Buy.com Carolina Classic—May 3-6, 2001
Charleston, SC
Place: T12th
Score: 70-71-69-69
Made: $8,550.00

On Sunday June 3rd I flew to Memphis for the USGA's Sectional Qualifying for the 2001 US Open at Southern Hills in Tulsa. The qualifying was played at Colonial Country Club, the course where Al Geiberger shot 59. I played well in the 36-hole qualifying and got one of the 29 spots out of 135 players in the field without incident. Then I caught a flight from Memphis to Toronto that night to prepare for the Buy.com Tour's Samsung CPGA Championship.

Winning the PGA of Canada's P.D. Ross Trophy

The P.D. Ross Trophy was first presented to the Canadian Professional Golf Association (CPGA) Champion in 1912. In 2001, the CPGA, now called the PGA of Canada, partnered with the PGA Tour to host the Buy.com Tour's Samsung CPGA Championship. The CPGA Championship is rooted in some remarkable history. Back in the early 1960s, the CPGA Champion received an invitation to play in the Masters. My mentor, Alvie Thompson, punched his ticket to play in the 1963 Masters when he won the 1962 CPGA Championship at the Mississauga Golf & CC. Other past champions of the CPGA Championship are Stan Leonard (1940, 1941, 1950, 1954, 1957, and 1959); Al Balding (1955, 1956, 1963, and 1970); Bob Panasik (1972, 1973); Moe Norman (1966 and 1974); George Knudson (1964, 1967, 1968, and 1977); Lanny Wadkins (1978); Arnold Palmer (1980); Ray Floyd (1981); Jim Thorpe (1982); Lee Trevino (1983 and 1979); Jim Rutledge (1984); Dave Barr (1985); Dan Halldorson (1986); Jerry Anderson (1987); Rick Gibson (1990); Steve Striker (1993); and Tim Clark (1998).

I had my eye on this tournament from the start of the year when it was announced that the PGA of Canada had merged its championship with the Buy.com Tour. The only previous opportunity to win this event was the 1990 CPGA Championship that was held at Quilchena Golf & Country

Club, in Richmond, BC. That year, I finished second to Rick Gibson. This event had gone through many different variations since it was established in 1912. It also meant this 2001 version of the CPGA Championship had a stronger field, being a Buy.com Tour event, than it had in recent history as a Canadian Tour event.

With my acquired skill to stay present on and off the golf course, I felt comfort in having no desire to get ahead of myself like I had before. As a result of this, I felt calm and the freedom of having zero expectations. Canadian golf scribes and writers were asking the usual questions, "What do you think the winning score will be?" I'd reply, "Well, that depends on a number of factors out of our control, such as weather, and we won't know until we see what happens with the weather." How are you feeling about your game?" "I've never felt better." I could sense being in This Present Moment when I was talking to the media. My answers were getting shorter, and I didn't feel the need to explain myself.

When the tournament got underway, all I wanted to do was get into performing my KPMs as best I could—that's it. As a result of my newly founded mindset, I opened with a solid 67 in the first round and was two two-shots behind first round leaders Joel Kribel and Jeff Sanday. I followed up with another solid round, 68, to take the 36-hole lead, one shot ahead of Brian Hull and Kevin Burton. In the third round, I shot 70 and still managed to hold on to a share of the lead with Tim Petrovic at 11 under par. Petrovic and I were one shot ahead of Gary Hallberg and Pat Perez. Rod Pampling and Omar Uresti were a couple shots back of second place at 8 under par. I felt the 70 I shot in the third round was going to be my highest round given how I was playing. I do recall someone from the media asking me, "What would it mean to you if you were able to win this event?" Because I had been working on not projecting to what may or may not happen in the future my answer to the question was, "At this moment, I don't know. If you ask me that question tomorrow if I do win, I hope I will be able to answer it."

A Healthy Mind Doesn't Mean You Always Have to Be Present

A healthy mind doesn't mean you must stay in the state of being present all the time. It's critically important to look back and learn from your mistakes as well as your successes. Looking to the past has its benefits. And it's also important to project forward to set goals and make plans for your future that you can aspire to.

All young aspiring players dream of playing and winning the Masters, US Open, or winning on the PGA Tour—this future projecting is a key element in developing your belief system. And it's best to make visits to the past and the future as much as you need to—but you don't want to stay in the past or in the future during play. You need to flip that switch off when it's time to play and know how to access This Present Moment.

The night before the final round, as I went to bed, I felt comfortable allowing my mind to wander. I had no fear—I knew how to get back to This Present Moment when I wanted to. That evening, I looked back to the first time I held the 54-hole lead in a PGA Tour event, the 1986 Anheuser-Busch Classic, where my mind the night before the final round activated to what may or may not happen in the final round and what it would mean to me, not knowing how to handle those thoughts and how they disrupted my ability to perform. Those thoughts wired me up that night and triggered anxiety, and I shot 79 in that final round Walking the Gauntlet. But that was a long time ago. I thought to myself, *I've come a long way since then.* I was playing with these thoughts of the past like a cat toying with a mouse. I recognized in that moment that I had reconditioned my mind with the work I'd been doing. I was able to change my thoughts and access This Present Moment with my mantra, by simply changing the way I thought. "I am I—here and now." I fell asleep and slept like a baby.

Walking the Gauntlet in the Final Round

Heading into the final round tied with Tim Petrovic for the lead, it was time to Walk the Gauntlet again. I felt comfortable being tied for the lead. My mind was in pursuit of what I wanted—to perform my KPMs of each shot to the best of my ability. I had no expectations. My final round score would simply be a by-product of how well I performed my KPMs, and I accepted whatever I shot. I felt comfortably numb in The Zone. This time it wasn't triggered by anger; everything just flowed, everything was beautiful, and I was in control of myself.

I settled into the final round quickly. My KPMs were on point; the flow working with my caddie and my shot routine were in sync. I made the turn with the lead and was still locked in on my KPMs, which kept me in This Present Moment for the entire back nine. I felt freedom and Walked the Gauntlet flawlessly, shooting a 66 and winning by three shots over my good friend Gary Hallberg.

Buy.com Samsung Canadian PGA Championship—June 7-10, 2001

Richmond Hill, ON

Place: 1st

Score: 67-68-70-66

Made: $81,000.00

2001 SAMSUNG CANADIAN PGA CHAMPIONSHIP FINAL RESULTS					
1	Richard Zokol	67-68-70-66	-17	271	$81,000
2	Gary Hallberg	71-67-68-68	-14	274	$48,600
T3	Pat Perez	70-69-67-69	-13	275	$26,100
T3	Tim Petrovic	67-72-66-70	-13	275	$26,100
T5	Tjaart Van Der Walt	70-70-71-65	-12	276	$16,425
T5	Omar Uresti	69-70-69-68	-12	276	$16,425
T5	Rod Pampling	67-71-70-68	-12	276	$16,425
T8	Sonny Skinner	69-72-69-67	-11	277	$13,050
T8	Bob Heinz	71-70-69-67	-11	277	$13,050
T8	David McKenzie	71-71-68-67	-11	277	$13,050
T11	Steve Haskins	71-72-69-66	-10	278	$10,350
T11	Mike Small	72-69-69-68	-10	278	$10,350
T11	Tommy Biershenk	69-72-66-71	-10	278	$10,350
T14	Jeff Sanday	65-75-72-67	-9	279	$7,650
T14	Brian Hull	69-67-74-69	-9	279	$7,650
T14	Joel Kribel	65-75-69-70	-9	279	$7,650
T14	Stiles Mitchell	66-72-71-70	-9	279	$7,650
T14	Patrick Burke	66-75-68-70	-9	279	$7,650
T15	Scott Gump	70-70-71-69	-8	280	$5,265
T15	Jay Delsing	71-66-73-70	-8	280	$5,265

T15	Danny Briggs	71-71-68-70	-8	280	$5,265
T15	Brian Fogt	68-72-68-72	-8	280	$5,265
T15	Chad Wright	72-71-65-72	-8	280	$5,265
T15	Richard Johnson	66-73-67-74	-8	280	$5,265
T25	Brendan Pappas	73-69-70-69	-7	281	$3,870
T25	Jason Enloe	71-72-68-70	-7	281	$3,870
T27	Brian Bateman	68-75-72-67	-6	282	$3,082
T27	D.A. Points	68-73-73-68	-6	282	$3,082
T27	Eric Johnson	70-71-72-69	-6	282	$3,082
T27	Jay Hobby	66-71-75-70	-6	282	$3,082
T27	Scott Hebert	71-69-72-70	-6	282	$3,082
T27	Geoffrey Sisk	71-70-71-70	-6	282	$3,082
T27	Pat Bates	68-74-70-70	-6	282	$3,082
T27	Joe Daly	68-72-70-72	-6	282	$3,082
T35	John Wilson	68-73-76-66	-5	283	$2,295
T35	Morris Hatalsky	71-72-72-68	-5	283	$2,295
T35	Darron Stiles	70-72-72-69	-5	283	$2,295
T35	Steve Alker	72-71-71-69	-5	283	$2,295
T35	Mike Grob	69-71-72-71	-5	283	$2,295
T35	Chad Campbell	67-72-73-71	-5	283	$2,295
T35	Chris Wollman	70-71-70-72	-5	283	$2,295
T35	Kevin Burton	66-70-69-78	-5	283	$2,295
T43	Tom Carter	70-73-74-67	-4	284	$1,702
T43	Nick Napoleon	68-75-71-70	-4	284	$1,702
T43	Andy Morse	68-69-76-71	-4	284	$1,702
T43	Jim Rutledge	71-70-72-71	-4	284	$1,702
T43	Eric Meeks	69-72-70-73	-4	284	$1,702
T43	Ryan Howison	69-72-70-73	-4	284	$1,702
T43	Gary Webb	72-70-69-73	-4	284	$1,702
T43	Jason Caron	70-69-71-74	-4	284	$1,702
T51	Keoke Cotner	74-68-73-70	-3	285	$1,530
T51	Mark Johnson	68-72-73-72	-3	285	$1,530
T51	Michael Long	68-71-71-75	-3	285	$1,530
T54	Pete Morgan	69-73-74-70	-2	286	$1,530
T54	Rob McKelvy	66-76-73-71	-2	286	$1,530
T54	Todd Rose	70-73-70-73	-2	286	$1,530

T54	Bob Lohr	72-71-70-73	-2	286	$1,530
T54	Anthony Rodriguez	72-69-70-75	-2	286	$1,530
T59	David Kirkpatrick	70-72-73-73	-1	285	$1,530
T59	James Sullivan	71-72-72-72	-1	287	$1,339
T59	Matt Kucher	73-66-75-73	-1	287	$1,339
T59	John Elliott	74-69-71-73	-1	287	$1,339
63	Derek Gillespie	73-67-77-71	E	288	$1,282
T64	Jason Hill	69-74-75-71	1	289	$1,282
T64	Bobby Kalinowski	68-73-76-72	1	289	$1,282
66	John Drewery	71-70-74-75	1	290	$1,215
67	Simon Cooke	69-73-72-81	7	295	$1,192
68	Robert Gaus	70-72-76-78	8	296	$1,192
69	Bret Waldman	71-70-77-83	13	301	$1,148

2001 US Open–June 14-17, 2001

Southern Hills Country Club Tulsa, OK

Purse: $5,000,000

Place: T62nd

Score: 72-71-74-76

Made: $11,442.50

Buy.com Dayton Open–June 21-24, 2001

Dayton, OH

Place: T6th

Score: 65-67-71-66

Made: $14,237.50

Buy.com Wichita Open–July 12-15, 2001

Wichita, KS

Place: T21st

Score: 67-68-71-70

Made: $4,420.00

Buy.com Siouxland Open—July 19-22, 2001

Sioux City, IO

Place: T46th

Score: 73-67-69-75

Made: $1,505

Buy.com Omaha Classic—August 2-5, 2001

Omaha, NE

Place: MC

Score: 74-70

Buy.com Fort Smith Classic—August 9-12, 2001

Fort Smith, AR

Place: 75th

Score: 75-69-76-71

Made: $956.25

Buy.com Permian Basin Open—August 16-19, 2001

Midland, TX

Place: T58th

Score: 70-66-73-72

Made: $1,296.25

Buy.com Utah Open—August 30-September 2, 2001

Salt Lake City, UT

Place: T51st

Score: 70-68-67-73

Made: $1,370.63

Buy.com Tri-Cities Open—September 6-9, 2001

Richland, WA

Place: T38th

Score: 71-72-73-69

Made: $1,955.00

Buy.com Oregon Classic—September 13-16, 2001

Eugene, OR

Place: CNL (September 11 Terrorist Attack)

The 9/11 Terrorist Attack

On Monday, September 10, 2001, I drove from my home in Vancouver down to Eugene, Oregon, for the Oregon Classic. It was the first time I drove my own car into the US to play since 1983, my second year on Tour. The next morning, I recall waking up in something like a Comfort Inn and going downstairs to get my morning coffee when I noticed everyone's full attention was fixed on the TV, watching the news and trying to figure out how a commercial flight crashed into one of the World Trade Center buildings. It didn't occur to us that this was a terrorist attack until the second plane kamikazed into the other tower. I grabbed my coffee, headed back to my room, and turned on the TV.

Like everyone else, I couldn't pull away from what was happening on the news. It wasn't until lunch that I got dressed and drove to the golf course, still in shock. The next day, Commissioner Tim Finchem cancelled all PGA Tour and Buy.com Tour events. The entire airspaces of the United States and Canada were closed (a "ground stop") by order of the FAA national operations manager. Once the event was canceled, nobody could move for a few days. I got in my car and drove back home to Vancouver.

Buy.com Albertsons Boise Open—September 6-9, 2001

Boise, ID

Place: T9th

Score: 70-69-66-69

Made: $15,568.00

A Little Help from My Friends

The next event was in Boise, ID, and the FAA had not allowed commercial airlines to operate yet. I reached out to my good friend Chan Buckland, who had his own private plane, a twin-engine Cessna 441 Conquest II. I called Chan and asked him for a favor, to fly me to Boise for the Buy.com Tour event. Chan said, "Let me call my pilot and see what the government restrictions are." Chan kept his plane in Bend, Oregon. He got right back to me and said, "The FAA and Canada won't allow flights to cross the border yet." My pilot will fly up to Bellingham, WA, and you can cross the border by car in Blaine, WA, and meet him at the Bellingham airport, and he'll fly you to Boise and pick you up and fly you back on Sunday. This was a huge help for me in trying to make the top 15—thank you, Chan.

The Albertsons Boise Open was played on Hillcrest Country Club. The executive director was my buddy Jeff Sanders, who had run this event for 25 years. It was great to see Jeff that week.

Pulling Pat Perez Aside in Boise

I got paired with Pat Perez in the first two rounds in Boise. I thought it was a bit strange that we hadn't gotten paired together the entire year, as we had both played well in the season. It was quite obvious to me that Pat, a young player from Arizona, had a great deal of talent—he was a strong ball-striker—and he didn't play with fear. There was no doubt in my mind that he was going to do very well in professional golf despite his temperament and attitude.

During our first round, it was evident that Pat had a pretty foul mouth on him. The problem I had with him wasn't the language; it was how loud he was. Hillcrest CC is an old, tight golf course, and the ropes that divide the players and spectators in many cases are a few feet away from tee boxes. Being so close, spectators can hear conversations between the players and caddies, and verbal outbursts do happen from time to time.

Well, when Pat Perez hit a poor shot, his verbal expression didn't have a filter or volume gauge. It was always loud and foul. He doesn't pull back when he's next to families, women, or children. I cringed when I first experienced it. Now, I am no choirboy when it comes to foul language—I can swear with the best of them. But I always tried to be aware of who was around me in earshot when I went off with foul language. As a professional, you know exactly where the microphones are and how they pick up sound.

On the PGA Tour, there were old-school ways of policing conduct unbecoming a professional, and when a young player crosses the line, the veteran players will typically pull the young player aside and have a chat with them. I absolutely recall Peter Jacobsen pulling me aside in Pleasant Valley during my rookie year, letting me know that the player's line extended through to the other side of the hole—the through line—and proper player conduct was respecting the player's through line until he holed out his putt. Peter let me know this in a very respectful manner.

After the second round with numerous examples of Perez cursing like a drunken sailor in the presence of families with young children, it was pretty clear he just didn't give a flying fuck about who heard him. And there was nobody else in the veteran category but me. I felt it was my duty to give a little advice to this young player who acted out like a petulant adolescent.

After the round, in the locker room, I approached Perez and I said, "Pat, I need to have a chat with you." Pat's eyes lit up, and he said, "Sure." I said, "Let's go over here." Walking back to a secluded part of the locker room, I said to him, "You are a great player, I like you, and your game is going to fit nicely on the PGA Tour, but you need to do something about your conduct on the golf course—your foul language, how loud it is for spectators to hear. I don't care what comes out of your mouth personally, but I do care what comes out of your mouth when it relates to spectators, women, children, and families who pay to come watch us play. I don't know if anyone has made a formal complaint, but I am letting you know you need to do a better job with it! If you don't, I will make a formal complaint."

Perez just stared at me in shock. It seemed to me this might be the first time anyone had ever said, "No" to him. There wasn't much said after our little talk.

Buy.com Inland Empire Open—September 27-30, 2001

Rancho Cucamonga, CA

Place: T11th

Score: 64-68-69-69

Made: $8,712.50

Meeting Eckhart Tolle

As it turned out, my wife Joanie and I were fortunate to meet Constance and Howard Kellough, the principals of Namaste Publishing in Vancouver, and the publishers of *The Power of Now*, who invited us to a reception at their home after Eckhart Tolle presented to a sold-out audience on stage at the Orpheum Theatre in Vancouver.

At the Kelloughs' home, Howard introduced me to Eckhart Tolle. I was thrilled to have the opportunity to express to Eckhart Tolle personally just how significant his ideologies were to me, helping me solidify the importance of being present or "being in the Now" with each golf shot, and in many aspects of life, for that matter. I thanked Eckhart for writing a book that helped me restructure the way I thought, which helped me win the Samsung PGA of Canada Championship a few months earlier.

Buy.com Monterey Peninsula Classic–October 4-7, 2001

Monterey, CA

Place: T32nd

Score: 73-74-74-73

Made: $2,700.00

Buy.com Gila River Classic–October 11-14, 2001

Chandler, AZ

Place: MC

Score: 69-71

Buy.com Shreveport Open–October 18-21, 2001

Shreveport, LA

Place: MC

Score: 71-73

Buy.com Tour Championship–October 25-28, 2001

Dothan, AL

Place: T39th

Score: 72-79-74-73

Made: $3,120.00

2001 BUY.COM TOUR SEASON SUMMARY

Tournaments Entered	21
Cuts Made	18
Cut Missed	3
Top 10 finish	3
Wins	1
Official Money	**$167,192.00**
Official Money List	**13th on 2001 Official Buy.com Tour Money List**

The Top 15 Buy.com Tour Players Matriculating to the 2002 PGA Tour Season

1. Chad Campbell (USA)
2. Pat Bates (USA)
3. Heath Slocum (USA)
4. Rod Pampling (AUS)
5. Deane Pappas (RSA)
6. John Rollins (USA)
7. Tim Petrovic (USA)
8. Jonathan Byrd (USA)
9. Jeff Gove (USA)
10. Brenden Pappas (RSA)
11. Bo Van Pelt (USA)
12. Matt Peterson (USA)
13. Richard Zokol (Canada)
14. Jason Hill (USA)
15. Michael Long (New Zealand)

PROGRESSION IN WALKING THE GAUNTLET IN FINAL ROUNDS

Experience Walking the Gauntlet	PGA Tour Tournament	Final Round Group	Score	Place
1st time	1982 Greater Milwaukee Open	final group Sunday	shot 75	T5th
2nd time	1986 Anheuser-Busch Classic	final group Sunday	shot 79	T34th
3rd time	1987 Canadian Open	final group Sunday	shot 75	7th
4th time	1988 Hawaiian Open	final group Sunday	shot 70	2nd
5th time	1992 Deposit Guaranty Classic	2nd to last group Sunday	shot 67	1st
6th time	1992 US Open	5th to last group Sunday	shot 80	T31st
7th time	1992 Greater Milwaukee Open	final group on Sunday	shot 67	1st
8th time	2001 Buy.com CPGA Championship	final group on Sunday	Shot 66	1st

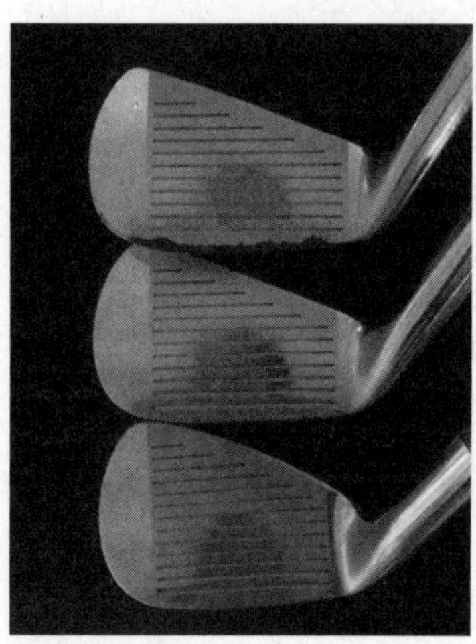

The set of Mizino MP-33 I used in 2000 and 2001.
From top to bottom: my 5-iron, 7-iron, 9-iron.

CHAPTER 26

2002—Back on the PGA Tour

Finishing 13th in the 2001 Buy.com Tour season's Money List punched my ticket back to the PGA Tour—for my sixth time. Finishing 13th gave me a tremendous sense of performance, pride, and accomplishment, having obtained the goals I set out two years ago—and the conditions I set in my comeback to playing.

My outlook toward the upcoming 2002 PGA Tour season was one of great optimism and enthusiasm. My game at that time was the strongest it had ever been. I significantly improved my putting over the past two years and created a method to reconstruct my mindset to detach emotionally from results, which contributed immensely to my improved putting. Everything seemed to be falling in place—it only took me 20 years of hard slugging through the ups and downs on the PGA Tour, getting through five Q-Schools and a couple Buy.com Tour campaigns to figure things out. At 44, I had never been more ready and eager to go.

I cannot express how happy I was to earn my way back to the PGA Tour at my age and against the youngsters. The first event of the year was the Sony Open in Hawaii, a place I love and played well in the past. It was good to see the same people volunteering for the better part of 20 years. There was such a warm feeling walking back into the locker room. The locker room guys, who'd been working there for decades, gave me a warm reception: "It's great to see you back, Richard." It felt wonderful to be back.

These feelings I had about getting back to the Tour caught me off-guard. Sure there were many new and younger faces on Tour, most of them looked as petrified as I was in my rookie year. On the practice range, Fred Couples came out to hit a few balls. He noticed me and walked over. As I looked up, Fred extended his hand and said, "Welcome back, old-timer."

On Thursday's first round, I was out in the afternoon wave, and the first tee announcer yelled out, "On the first tee, give a big welcome back, from Canada, Richard Zokol." The ovation they gave me was heartfelt, before and after I hit my tee shot. As I walked off the tee, someone from the gallery yelled out, "Welcome back on Tour, Richard." The emotions hit me really hard, and I began to tear up.

The weather and the Hawaiian air felt good. It's so easy to feel grounded in Hawaii. At the end of the day, on my way back to Waikiki, I stopped off at the Rainbow Drive-in, ordered up a BBQ Steak Plate Lunch ("two scoop rice") and sat with the locals enjoying the Hawaiian soul food. I recalled the many times over the past 20 years Nelford and I stopped for a bite to eat at the Rainbow Drive-in at the end of the day.

Sony Open—January 10-14, 2002
Purse: $4,000,000
Waialae CC, Honolulu, HI
Place: 60th
Score: 71-67-73-70
Made: $8,520

After Hawaii, it was back on the mainland to play the rest of the West Coast events, and I started to struggle again. I did not like the contrasting warm weather in Hawaii with the relatively cold weather in California and Arizona in January and February. My ball-striking started to deteriorate immediately once we got back on the West Coast. My back started to tighten up, and then lock up shortly after teeing off each round. My right hip was giving me problems.

After warming up prior to teeing off, my body felt great and was ready to go, but soon after playing the first few holes, tightness would set in, and I had a difficult time with my ball-striking. If the weather stayed warm, I was okay, but when it rained or if the weather cooled off or when the marine layer rolled in off the coast at Pebble Beach, Riviera, or San Diego, I had a problem.

AT&T Pebble Beach National Pro-Am—January 31-February 3, 2002

Purse: $4,000,000

Pebble Beach GL, Spyglass GC, Poppy Hills GC, Pebble Beach, CA

Place: MC

Score: 221

Buick Invitational—February 7-10, 2002

Purse: $3,600,000

Torrey Pines Golf Club (North & South Course)

Place: MC

Score: 147

Nissan Open—February 14-17, 2002

Purse: $3,700,000

Riviera CC, Pacific Palisades, CA

Place: MC

Score: 147

Touchstone Energy Tucson Open—February 21-24, 2002

Purse: $3,000,000

Omni Tucson National GC, Tucson, AZ

Place: WD

Score: DNF

Made: $0

In Tucson, my good pal Ian Leggatt won his first PGA Tour event on the same day Canada won the Gold Medal in hockey at the Salt Lake Olympics. It was a big day for Canadian sports and Leggo. My right hip really started to show signs of being a problem. At the end of the second round, I was literally limping the last few holes and WD'd from the tournament.

After Tucson, which was the last event on the West Coast, the Tour shifted over to Florida, and I went back home to Vancouver to attempt to figure things out again. My right hip needed to be dealt with, and I reached out to my friend Bill Reichelt. Bill spent 42 years as a trainer for the CFL's BC Lions Football Team. Bill recommended I hook up with Alex McKechnie.

I'd heard of Alex McKechnie; he was a legend in Vancouver, the real OG of core stabilization. Bill called Alex to see if he'd be able to take a look at me.

Alex fit me into his schedule, and he began helping me understand the proper muscle-firing patterns that lead to core stabilization. The proximal to distal muscle-firing patterns starts with our Multifidus group of muscles on our pelvic floor and extends up and into our lumbar spine. I was having a serious problem with mine. McKechnie stressed to me that the key was being able to fire these muscles in proper sequence (Alex used the term *keying up*) to disassociate and stabilize my hip and lower spine mobility (seeds of the core) from my upper body during my swing motion.

Alex McKechnie was great, and he introduced me to Rick Celebrini, who worked with Alex in Vancouver. Both became renowned physiotherapists for many professional athletes. Alex went on to oversee health and performance with the Toronto Raptors, and Rick Celebrini had great success with the LA Lakers and the Golden State Warriors. Both Alex and Rick played a role in helping Steve Nash obtain a fitness level that helped him become one of the great NBA players of his time.

At 44, I felt I was playing the best golf of my life, and now that I was getting back to being a full-time PGA Tour player, I thought I was going to have a few more great years ahead of me. It only made sense to accelerate my fitness level; an important step at 44 was to increase my fitness level to counteract my aging body.

In this moment I did not realize my 2002 year would be only a step toward my last season as a professional player.

The Honda Classic—March 7-19, 2002

Purse: $3,500,000

TPC at Heron Bay, Coral Springs, FL

Place: MC

Score: 147

Bellsouth Classic—April 4-7, 2002

Purse: $3,600,000

TPC at Sugarloaf, Duluth, GA

Place: T65th

Score: 71-73-73-81

Made: $7,942

Greater Greensboro Chrysler Classic—April 25-28, 2002

Purse: $3,800,000

Forest Oaks CC, Greensboro, NC

Place: MC

Score: 151

Compaq Classic of New Orleans—April 2-5, 2002

Purse: $4,500,000

English Turn G&CC, New Orleans, LA

Place: MC

Score: 151

In the spring of 2002, I met Rick Provost over a meal in the clubhouse. Rick was new on Tour and was working with a few Tour players as their personal fitness trainer. Rick brought his knowledge and services to PGA Tour players. After spending some time asking him about how he could help me with my performance, I agreed to hire Rick.

Rick Provost put me on his program, which involved a 50-minute gym warm up every morning before stepping on the golf course. The daily warm up began with 20 minutes of cardio, followed by a series of exercises to fire up key swing-related movements. The daily morning gym work added an hour to my morning routine before my tee time. Everything started at least three hours before my tee time. That means I was up at 3:45 AM to 4:00 AM in my first- or second-round morning wave tee time.

Immediately after the round, I liked to get a meal in first, then practice on the range and putting green before heading back to the fitness trailer, where Rick put me through an alternating-day workout plan. The gym work was designed to build strength and stamina. After the gym work and practice, it was time to "ice down." I'd come to love icing down at the end of the day. I'd have a garbage bag full of ice and plop it on my back for 20 minutes. Then I'd shower up and head out for dinner before climbing into bed. The daily routine I was on never seemed to give me enough time to squeeze everything in and relax. At the end of each day, I was exhausted.

Kemper Insurance Open—May 30-June 2, 2002

Purse: $3,600,000

TPC at Avenel, Potomac, MD

Place: MC

Score: 149

Buick Classic—June 6-9, 2002

Purse: $3,500,000

Westchester CC, Harrison, NY

Place: T50th

Score: 73-70-70-72

Made: $8,442

By the time the Tour was getting into summer, I hit a physical wall. I wasn't playing well. Each morning when I woke up and got out of bed, I felt exhausted. I felt like I had not recovered from the previous day. Throughout the season, I'd go out on the road for two or sometimes three weeks at a time and every time, I came home from the road exhausted. Not being able to recover from the work of the previous day was taking its toll. It was kicking my ass.

My body didn't respond well to the workload I was putting on it. I was feeling tired on the course and I was wondering what was going on. It was a feeling I had never felt before—not feeling fresh to start the next day, which was never the case in the past 20 years.

Cannon Greater Hartford Open—June 20-23, 2002

Purse: $4,000,000

TPC at River Highlands, Cromwell, CT

Place: MC

Score: 142

FedEx St. Jude Classic—June 27-30, 2002

Purse: $3,800,000

TPC at Southwind, Memphis, TN

Place: MC

Score: 143

Advil Western Open–July 4-7, 2002

Purse: $4,000,000

Cog Hill G&CC, (Dubsdread No. 4), Lemont, IL

Place: MC

Score: 146

Greater Milwaukee Open–July 11-14, 2002

Purse: $3,100,000

Brown Deer Park GC, Milwaukee, WI

Place: T68th

Score: 70-67-71-72

Made: $6,293

John Deere Classic–July 25-28, 2002

Purse: $3,000,000

TPC at Deere Run, Silvis, IL

Place: T64th

Score: 68-70-76-67

Made: $6,240

International Presented by Quest–August 1-4, 2002

Purse: $4,500,000

Castle Pines GC, Castle Pines, CO

Place: MC

Score: -6

Buick Open–August 8-11, 2002

Purse: $3,300,000

Warwick Hills G&CC, Grand Blanc, MI

Place: MC

Score: 149

Reno-Tahoe Open–August 22-25, 2002

Purse: $3,000,000

Montreux G&CC, Reno, NV

Place: MC

Score: 151

Air Canada Championship–August 29-September 1, 2002

Purse: CAD $3,500,000

Northview G&CC, Surrey, BC

Place: MC

Score: 146

Bell Canadian Open–September 5-8, 2002

Purse: CAD $4,000,000

Angus Glen GC, Markham, ON

Place: T38th

Score: 72-67-75-68

Made: $16,000

What's with All the Tim Hortons in Canada?

As usual each year at the Canadian Open, particularly early in the week, the golf media focused on the Canadians in the field and their chances to win. This question has been asked every year over the past five decades. And often our American PGA Tour colleagues would take notice while reading the local papers and then comment to Dave Barr, Dan Halldorson, Nelford, or me that our golf media puts a great deal of pressure on us Canadians. This challenge was then passed on to the new generation of players, such as Mike Weir and Ian Leggatt. Weir reached a new high water mark for Canadians by winning the 2003 Masters. This gave the next generation of Canadian players, such as Nick Taylor, Adam Hadwin, Mac Hughes, Corey Conners, and Taylor Pendrith the belief they could do it too.

I recall Roger Maltbie, a good friend and player who became a full-time NBC roving reporter, commented on how, "Canadian golf writers put some pretty high expectations on you guys." We'd all reply with, "It comes with being Canadian." Then Roger followed up, commenting, "And what's with all these Tim Hortons up here in Canada? Damn, they're on every corner, and some corners have more than one." Maltbie goes on, "You Canadians are a bunch of doughnut-eating motherfuckers." I thought to myself, *Yeah, I could see how American visitors to Canada could come to that conclusion.*

It was Saturday after the third round of the 2002 Bell Canadian Open, and I had finished practicing and had a good workout. But my right hip was really giving me problems. Particularly on the back nine, my limp was getting worse. I thought I needed some form of alignment or adjustment, and I'd be good to go. So I headed into the fitness trailer.

In the fitness trailer, there are typically three or four PGA Tour staff to take care of players' needs relating to physiotherapy before and after rounds of play. I jumped up on the table and began to explain my issue with my right hip to the physiotherapist who was attending to me. Before he looked at my hip, he began to go through all the structural mobility ranges with my knees, ankles, feet, and toes to see if there were any issues. In the fitness trailer there was a row of tables where other players were being attended to for all types of physiotherapy requirements.

As my attending physiotherapist was going through these preliminary steps, we were having pleasant locker room–type banter with other players and physiotherapists, and everything was going fine until he got to the mobility of my right big toe. In mid-conversation the physiotherapist pushed on then pulled back on my right big toe, and I let out this blood-curdling scream. It felt like I just got my big toe chopped off. After the pain subsided, he started to focus on the limitations on the range of motion of my toe. He said, "You've got turf toe. Let me see how you walk?" I got off the table and walked up and down the aisle, and I could see my right foot flaring out to the right, compensating for my big toe, which didn't want to hinge properly, therefore affecting my gate. My physiotherapist said, "Your turf toe is likely the cause of your hip problem. How long have you had this hip problem, and how long has your toe been hurting?"

The week after the Bell Canadian Open, I made an appointment with my family doctor, Dr. Peter House, to see a podiatrist to diagnose my toe. Dr. House recommended me to Dr. Scott Russell, a podiatrist at the Seymour Medical Clinic. After looking at X-rays of my toe, Dr. Russell diagnosed my right big toe as severely arthritic with bone spurs affecting its mobility.

Because my right big toe wouldn't hinge properly, I'd been compensating by flaring my right foot to avoid pain in my big toe joint with every step I took. My compensated gate, flaring my right foot out to avoid the pain, caused a chain reaction up my right side. When my right toe flared right, my right knee had to flare left to compensate. This chain reaction then had a dysfunctional effect on my right hip and lower back. After Dr. Russell made his diagnosis, he told me I needed surgery to clean up the joint and remove bone spurs in order to get proper functionality of the toe. Surgery on my big toe happened the following week.

The 2002 Bell Canadian Open was the last event of the year. I applied to the PGA Tour and was granted a Minor Medical Extension for 2003. This Medical Extension would allow me to combine my 2002 earnings ($53,437) with eight events in 2003 to equal or exceed the Official Money made in the 125th spot in the 2002 Official PGA Tour Money List ($515,445) to be elevated to the Major Medical Extension category for the remainder of 2003.

2002 PGA TOUR SEASON SUMMARY

Tournaments Entered	20
Cuts Made	6
Cut Missed	15
Top 10 finish	0
Official Money	**$53,437.00**
Official Money List	**215th on the 2002 Official PGA Tour Money List**

Despite my poor ball-striking due to my hip issue, the path I took to improve my putting over the past two years really started to show up. Below are the PGA Tour's ShotLink putting statistics for the 2002 season.

STATISTICS » PUTTING » GIR PUTTING - 10-15'

PRINT

GIR PUTTING - 10-15'

SHOTLINK POWERED BY CDW

Season: 2002 | Time Period: Year-To-Date through | Tournament: THE TOUR Championship presented by Coca-Cola

RANK THIS WEEK	RANK LAST WEEK	PLAYER NAME	ROUNDS	%	ATTEMPTS	PUTTS MADE
1	1	Richard Zokol	53	56.52	23	13
2	3	Scott Simpson	61	48.15	27	13
3	4	Donnie Hammond	60	46.51	43	20
T4	T5	Corey Pavin	78	46.15	39	18
T4	T5	Duffy Waldorf	90	46.15	52	24
6	7	Greg Chalmers	94	44.68	47	21
7	8	Mark Calcavecchia	84	44.19	43	19
8	9	Pat Perez	89	43.18	44	19
T9	T10	Fred Couples	64	42.86	28	12
T9	T10	Jesper Parnevik	85	42.86	21	9

CHAPTER 27

2003—Stick a Fork in Me—I Am Done

Hindsight is 20/20

Malcolm Gladwell hypothesizes in his book *Outliers* that one needs to rehearse a required skill daily for 10,000 hours, or 10 years, in order to achieve world-class expertise. Looking back over my last 30 years, this resonated with me. My first 10-year phase of skill development began with my six-year period playing junior and amateur golf at Marine Drive Golf Club in Vancouver (1972–1977), moving on to my four-year investment in the environment of top NCAA collegiate golf at Brigham Young University (1978–1981). The culmination of our team's great play in 1981, being ranked no. 1 through the entire year, then winning the 1981 NCAA Championship at Stanford prior to winning the 1981 Canadian Amateur Championship gave me the belief I could make it on the PGA Tour.

My development in this initial 10-year period enabled me to think and feel that I could have a career in professional golf. I then entered the 1981 PGA Tour fall Q-School. My second 10-year skill development stint (1982–1992) was in the frontline trenches on the PGA Tour, where I struggled mightily, then eventually learned not only how to survive but also how to win.

My third 10-year investment was from 1994 to 2003, when I experienced a disastrous year in 1994, crashing and burning after reaching new heights. My goal was to figure out this massive psychological gap in the golfer's mind, where I was the guinea pig.

The Discovery—Removing the Psychological Barriers

When golfers learn to recondition themselves to detach emotionally from results or outcomes during play, it removes a significant mental barrier out of the way that blocks access to This Present Moment. This Present Moment is the state of mind all players need to strive for. It is The Zone or the Holy Grail that allows the golfer to gain their freedom to pursue and perform. Through trial and error, I discovered you cannot just will yourself into This Present Moment no matter how hard you try. You need a system, a new thought protocol that changes the way you measure performance. Your thought protocol needs to shift your attentional focus onto your two Key Performance Markers (KPMs) that allow you to break away from extrinsic motivation and extrinsic result-oriented outcomes.

Over my last four-year period on the PGA Tour (2000–2003), playing with my new operating system validated to me that the golfer's mind provides the greatest opportunity for growth and improvement for all levels of players—even for the best players in the world. Now looking back over my last 50 years in pursuit of my golf performance, a couple of hit songs still resonate with me every time I hear them: "Life Is a Highway," written and performed by my good friend Tom Cochrane about life on the road. Rod Stewart's song, about wishing what I know now when I was young.

Surgery on my right big toe was successful in the fall of 2002, and it healed nicely over the winter. Heading into the 2003 season with my Minor Medical Extension from the PGA Tour enabled me to access eight events. If I were able to earn enough money in these eight events in 2003, along with the combined earnings I made in 2002, to crack the top 125 earners from the 2002 Official Money List, I'd earn my exempt status back.

The 2003 PGA Tour season was my 21st year on the PGA Tour. I was 45 years old with a hip and back that were giving me problems. I'd played in 412 PGA Tour events, and my intuition was telling me, *I am done.* My body was tired. I was worn out, having difficulty recovering from each day's work. With each passing year, I was falling a bit further behind in relation to the average PGA Tour player. Compound interest was now working against me. The writing was on the wall. I was giving it everything I had to get back to the PGA Tour, but I felt my body's ability to recover on a daily basis was now my weak link, and it just gave way. I didn't struggle at all with my realization that my time as a PGA Tour player was pretty much done. When I told my father I was done, he asked, "What are you going to do?" I said to my father, "I am going to build a great golf course."

AT&T Pebble Beach National Pro-Am—February 6-9, 2003

Purse: $5,000,000

Pebble Beach GL, Spyglass GC, Poppy Hills GC, Pebble Beach, CA

Place: MC

Score: 231

Buick Invitational—February 13-16, 2003

Purse: $4,500,000

Torrey Pines Golf Club (North & South Course)

Place: MC

Score: 147

Touchstone Energy Tucson Open—February 27-March 2, 2003

Purse: $3,000,000

Omni Tucson National GC, Tucson, AZ

Place: MC

Score: 147

Bellsouth Classic—April 3-6, 2003

Purse: $4,000,000

TPC at Sugarloaf, Duluth, GA

Place: MC

Score: 150

Shell Houston Open—April 24-27, 2003

Purse: $4,500,000

Redstone GC, Humble, TX

Place: MC

Score: 148

HP Classic of New Orleans—May 1-4, 2003

Purse: $5,000,000

English Turn G&CC, New Orleans, LA

Place: MC

Score: 143

FBR Open—June 5-9, 2003

Purse: $4,500,000

TPC at Avenel, Potomac, MD

Place: MC

Score: 151

Buick Classic—June 19-22, 2003

Purse: $5,000,000

Westchester CC, Harrison, NY

Place: T52nd

Score: 73-69-75-71

Made: $10,650

Greater Milwaukee Open—July 10-13, 2003

Purse: $3,500,000

Brown Deer Park GC, Milwaukee, WI

Place: MC

Score: 143

BC Open—July 17-20, 2003

Purse: $3,000,000

En-Joie GC, Endicott, NY

Place: MC

Score: 147

Reno-Tahoe Open—August 21-24, 2003

Purse: $3,000,000

Montreux G&CC, Reno, NV

Place: T46th

Score: 72-71-69-75

Made: $8,505

Bell Canadian Open—September 4-7, 2003

Purse: CAD $4,200,000

Hamilton G&CC, Hamilton, ON

Place: MC

Score: 147

Southern Farm Bureau Classic—October 2-5, 2003

Purse: $3,000,000

Annendale GC, Madison, MS

Place: MC

Score: 144

2003 PGA TOUR SEASON SUMMARY	
Tournaments Entered	13
Cuts Made	2
Cut Missed	11
Top 10 finish	0
Official Money	**$19,155.00**
Official Money List	**240th on the 2003 Official PGA Tour Money List**

My Next Chapter—the Vision of Sagebrush

The reality that I was bumping up against the end of the PGA Tour line wasn't a struggle for me. Over a few years, my side hustle had been trying to identify property to build a golf course. I wanted to design a golf course. But how would this ever come about? The way I figured it, the only way I'd be able to design or co-design a golf course would be to get myself in the position to be the one who made the decisions.

The vision I had was to build a golf course and golf club that captured the intimacy of a clubhouse like Redtail Golf Club in St. Thomas, ON. To create the first modern minimalist links-style design in Canada, similar to the golf being played at Bandon Dunes and Pacific Dunes.

Modern Minimalist Design

In 2002, the day I stepped foot on and played Bandon Dunes and Pacific Dunes, my perception of golf course design instantly shifted. Ben Crenshaw showed me photos of the golf course he was working on—the first modern minimalist design, Sand Hills, in Nebraska. This set the tone; I knew this direction in golf course design was my new path. This was what Ben Crenshaw had been so passionately saying over the past 10 years, and it finally made sense to me—it was a path that I wanted to be on. This was going to be my next chapter in golf.

I reached out to Ben to see if he and his design partner, Bill Coore, would like to be part of designing this golf course.

My next 10-year chapter began (2003–2012). I set out In Search of Sagebrush.

Sagebrush 17th and 18th holes.

BEN D. CRENSHAW

November 13, 2003

Richard Zokol
Sagebrush Project
Richard Zokol Enterprises, Ltd.
13663 23A Avenue
South Surrey, BC
Canada, V4A 9V1

To Whom It May Concern:

It is my pleasure to recommend highly the expertise of Rod Whitman. My partner, Bill Coore, and I have known and worked with Rod for almost two decades now. He is thoroughly versed in golf course building, in terms of planning, construction, and implementation of many golf courses in varied settings.

Rod's artistic sense, as well as practiced matters pertaining to golf courses, has made him a desirable asset to Coore & Crenshaw. We have always enjoyed working with Rod and will continue to do so in the future. I am extremely happy to know that he and Richard Zokol, a long term friend of mine, will collaborate on "Sagebrush" and I am certain that it will be a resounding success.

Sincerely,

Ben D. Crenshaw

BDC/hh

GolfDigest | GolfWorld Established 1947

December 2, 2009

Mr. Dick Zokol
Chief Executive Officer
Sagebrush Golf & Sporting Club
5A-6280 Merritt Kamloops Highway
Quilchena, British Columbia, Canada V0E 2R0

Dear Dick:

Congratulations on being ranked as the No. 1 Best New Canadian Course in *Golf Digest's* 2009 survey of America's Best New Courses.

The new ranking appears in the January 2010 issue of *Golf Digest*, on newsstands December 8. Enclosed is an early copy.

This survey marks the 27th anniversary of *Golf Digest's* annual ranking of America's Best New Courses. Our judging panel includes more than 900 panelists who evaluate candidate courses on five criteria: Shot Values, Design Variety, Resistance to Scoring, Memorability and Aesthetics.

Please extend our congratulations to your course superintendent and to the entire staff.

Cordially,

Jerry Tarde
Chairman & Editor-In-Chief

Ron Whitten
Senior Editor, Architecture

CONDE NAST PUBLICATIONS | 4 TIMES SQUARE | New York, NY 10036 | TEL 212.286.6265 | FAX 212.286.3142

CHAPTER 28

The Golfer's Mind and MindTRAK Golf®

MindTRAK Golf

MindTRAK Golf distills player performance skills down to two Key Performance Markers (KPMs)—the *Assessment* and the *Execution* of each golf shot, no matter the skill level of the player. The player's objective is to make an excellent Assessment and an excellent Execution, relatively speaking, with each shot. These two KPMs and the club used make up MindTRAK Golf's KPM data.

This thought protocol technique was designed to be used on the golf course, not on the driving range. Golfers always want to bring their driving range skills to the golf course—this is a flawed notion to begin with, as one's performance on the driving range simply doesn't matter because the risk, the threat, and the consequences of hitting a poor shot on the range don't exist, as they do on the golf course. Too often hitting it well on the range only serves to increase player *expectations.* Hitting it great or poorly on the driving range is not indicative of how you will play on the golf course, so trying to take your driving range game to the golf course is a futile objective.

Swing Coaching on the Range—Shot Coaching on the Golf Course

Over the course of my career, I have come to realize that our coaching industry has not discovered the degree of significance and importance that a healthy mindset has for every player. Our golf instruction industry has fallen short in this regard, as it still focuses mostly on the golf swing. Swing coaching on the driving range is important. But the next step includes shot performance on the golf course; an effective system should take the trainee down this path. Far too many golfers place their attentional focus on golf swing technique when playing on the golf course.

Execution Is Only Half of the Key Performance Marker (KPM) Requirement

Most PGA Tour players and coaches constantly say, "It's a matter of *Execution.*" But Execution is only half of the Key Performance Marker requirement. Most golfers give short shrift to the shot's *Assessment* as a KPM. MindTRAK Golf separates these two key aspects of performance and measures them independently. The bottom line for all levels of players, including PGA Tour players, is the player's ability to properly assess the shot and Execute the shot. And these two KPM must work together.

From a conventional perspective, when the player makes a poor shot on the golf course, they tend to ask themselves what went wrong with their swing or stroke. They don't look at it in the framework as an unsatisfactory Execution. They look at it as a bad golf swing. Then they go back to the range and try to turn a "bad swing" into a "good swing" to feel good about themselves. The player goes to the golf course and focuses on their swing rather than executing the shot, and they get stuck.

Of course, when the player needs to make swing changes, there is a gap that needs to be bridged to be able to make these swing changes subconscious and automatic, and eventually be able to take the changes to the golf course. But the coach and the player should work on these two things separately.

The MindTRAK method reconditions the player and coaching perspective; it helps the player play *golf shots* rather than *golf swing* on the golf course. I felt I discovered something missing in the industry and how the game is being taught—something fundamental that has been overlooked, something important from a mental health and mental fitness perspective.

I was most proud of how my new operating system affected my putting. Along with the technical changes I made to my putting method in 2000, this system reconditioned my mindset to stop only "trying to make the putt" (an extrinsic result and motivation) by shifting my attentional focus to perform and measure my Assessment and Execution of each putt to the best of my ability (an intrinsic result and motivation).

This discovery changed my perspective and allowed the result to find its proper place—as a by-product of my two KPMs of each putt. This system reconditioned my mindset and gave me the freedom to pursue what I wanted.

At the age of 44 at the end of 2002, the PGA Tour's ShotLink statistics in the Greens in Regulations Putting (GIR) category 10–15' showed my conversion rate to be 56.52%. This was a massive improvement.

STATISTICS » PUTTING » GIR PUTTING - 10-15'

PRINT

GIR PUTTING - 10-15'

SHOTLINK

Season: 2002 | Time Period: Year-To-Date through | Tournament: THE TOUR Championship presented by Coca-Cola

RANK THIS WEEK	RANK LAST WEEK	PLAYER NAME	ROUNDS	%	ATTEMPTS	PUTTS MADE
1	1	Richard Zokol	53	56.52	23	13
2	3	Scott Simpson	61	48.15	27	13
3	4	Donnie Hammond	60	46.51	43	20
T4	T5	Corey Pavin	78	46.15	39	18
T4	T5	Duffy Waldorf	90	46.15	52	24
6	7	Greg Chalmers	94	44.68	47	21
7	8	Mark Calcavecchia	84	44.19	43	19
8	9	Pat Perez	89	43.18	44	19
T9	T10	Fred Couples	64	42.86	28	12
T9	T10	Jesper Parnevik	85	42.86	21	9

I developed this system before the mobile phone revolution launched with the iPhone in 2007. But when the time came to write the book, I realized my system would make for a perfect mobile platform and app. I assembled a team and we changed the name of my system from Units-of-Execution to MindTRAK Golf, and we launched a start-up company—MindTRAK Golf Inc. Our plan was to raise investor capital and build a beta version of the app—it was delivered in 2019.

The MindTRAK Golf Concept

MindTRAK Golf is a mobile app and platform designed to condition, or recondition, the user's (the golfer's) mind into a healthy and proper perspective. It's a tool to help golf coaches expand their teaching curriculum by inviting them to be directly involved with their client's on-course performance.

This system has been approved by the USGA and conforms to the rules of golf.

MindTRAK is an on-the-golf-course system that trains the user/player to subjectively evaluate the Assessment and Execution of each shot on a three-point Likert scale—Excellent—Satisfactory—Unsatisfactory—as well as the golf club used. This is the KPM data capture.

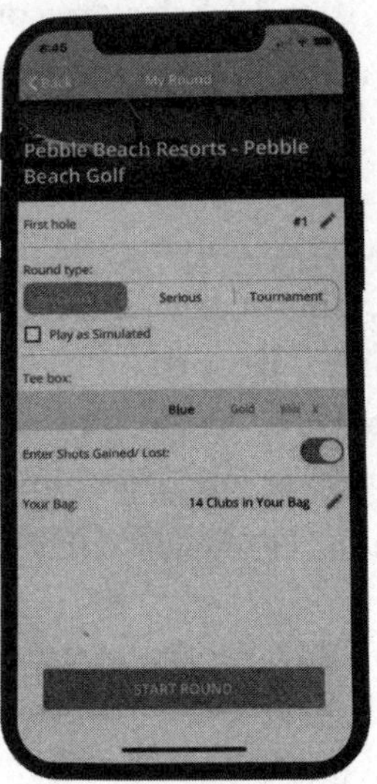

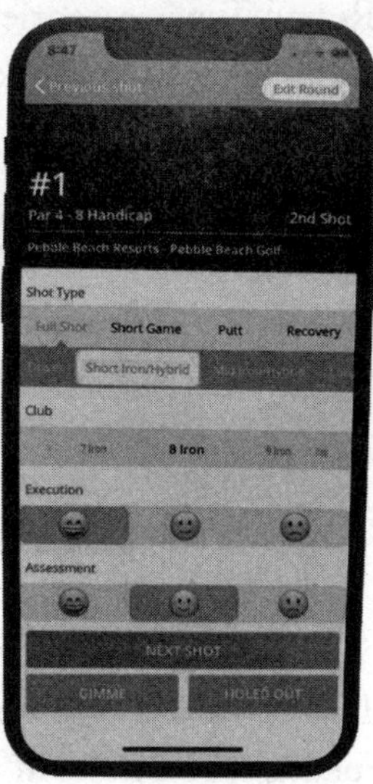

The standard operation procedure involves capturing this KPM data and entering it into the app either during play or in an After Actions Report (AAR) after the round is completed. The system also directs the user to enter the number of Shot Lost Events and/or Shot Gained Events caused by which KPM.

After three rounds played using the MindTRAK platform, the user will then have established their own KPM Baseline Standard. Each round thereafter will be compared to the player's Baseline and the KPM Trend Graph will show percentage loss/gains after each round.

MindTRAK Golf does not compare KPM performance to PGA Tour players. We think this comparable, as interesting as it may be for those who geek out in data, is not relevant for game improvement purposes.

Prior to all rounds, the user is asked to enter the type of round being played today: A Casual Round, a Serious Round, a Tournament Round, or a Simulated Round. Different round types have different psychological effects on a player's perspective—simply look at the high scores being shot in your Club Championship each year by some of the best players in your golf club. They typically shoot scores significantly higher than their handicap would indicate. In these tournament rounds, the only thing that changed is the player's psychological perspective. By playing in a formal tournament, the situation intensifies and increases the threat, the risk, and anxiety on each player.

Also, this system does not cross-contaminate data in each of these four Round Type categories. After 18 holes are complete, the platform generates three post-round reports for the player and coach to review. These three reports are:

1. **Scorecard Report**: identifying where Shot Lost and Shot Gained Events occur.
2. **KPM Trend Graph Report**: KPM % change per round.
3. **Round Summary Report:** performance in club type—driver, fairway woods, long irons, mid-irons, short irons, chipping, pitching, bunker, first putts, and second putts.

The MindTRAK Golf Mission is to rehab golfers out of their Golf Insanity affliction—and prehabilitate golfers to stop going down these mental rabbit holes in the first place.

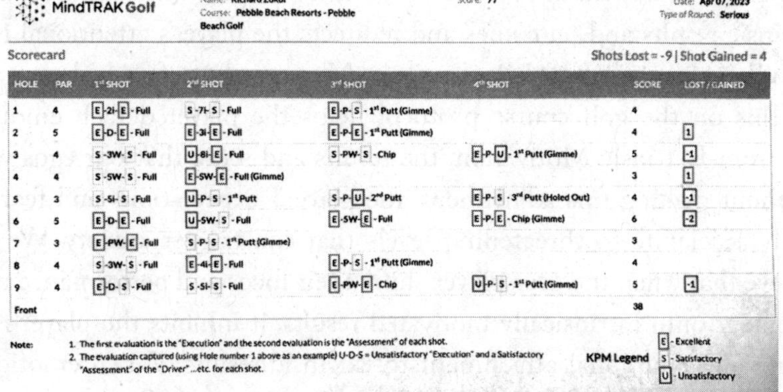

MindTRAK Golf

Name: **Richard Zokol**
Course: **Pebble Beach Resorts - Pebble Beach Golf**
Score: **77**
Date: **Apr 07, 2023**
Type of Round: **Serious**

Scorecard — **Shots Lost = -9 | Shot Gained = 4**

HOLE	PAR	1st SHOT	2nd SHOT	3rd SHOT	4th SHOT	SCORE	LOST / GAINED
1	4	E-2i-E - Full	S-7i-S - Full	E-P-S - 1st Putt (Gimme)		4	
2	5	E-D-E - Full	E-3i-E - Full	E-P-E - 1st Putt (Gimme)		4	1
3	4	S-3W-S - Full	U-8i-E - Full	S-PW-S - Chip	E-P-U - 1st Putt (Gimme)	5	-1
4	4	S-5W-S - Full	E-SW-E - Full (Gimme)			3	1
5	3	S-5i-S - Full	U-P-S - 1st Putt	S-P-U - 2nd Putt	E-P-S - 3rd Putt (Holed Out)	4	-1
6	5	E-D-E - Full	U-5W-S - Full	E-SW-E - Full	E-P-E - Chip (Gimme)	6	-2
7	3	E-PW-E - Full	S-P-S - 1st Putt (Gimme)			3	
8	4	S-3W-S - Full	E-4i-E - Full	E-P-S - 1st Putt (Gimme)		4	
9	4	E-D-S - Full	S-5i-S - Full	E-PW-E - Chip	U-P-S - 1st Putt (Gimme)	5	-1
Front						38	

Note:
1. The first evaluation is the "Execution" and the second evaluation is the "Assessment" of each shot.
2. The evaluation captured (using Hole number 1 above as an example) U-D-S = Unsatisfactory "Execution" and a Satisfactory "Assessment" of the "Driver" ...etc. for each shot.

KPM Legend
E - Excellent
S - Satisfactory
U - Unsatisfactory

Scorecard Report.

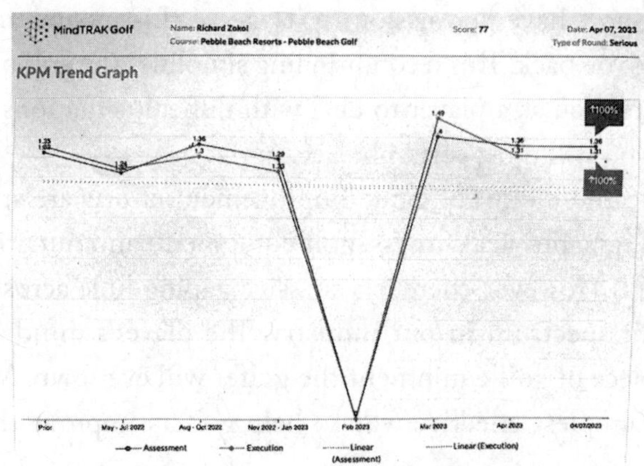

Key Performance Marker (KPM) Trend Graph.

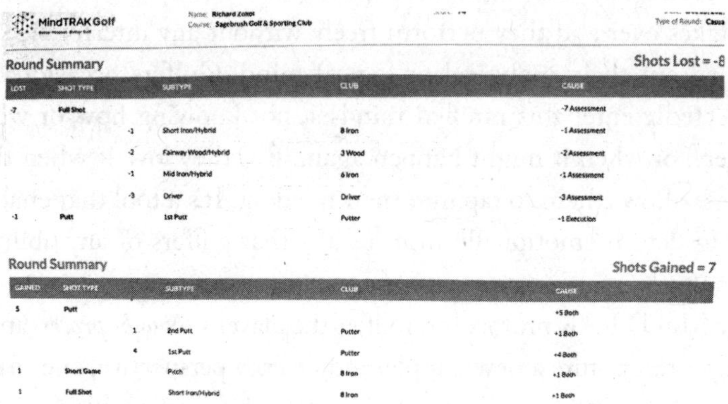

MindTRAK Golf

Name: **Richard Zokol**
Course: **Sagebrush Golf & Sporting Club**
Type of Round: **Casua**

Round Summary — **Shots Lost = -8**

LOST	SHOT TYPE		SUBTYPE	CLUB	CAUSE
-7	Full Shot				-7 Assessment
		-1	Short Iron/Hybrid	8 Iron	-1 Assessment
		-2	Fairway Wood/Hybrid	3 Wood	-2 Assessment
		-1	Mid Iron/Hybrid	6 Iron	-1 Assessment
		-3	Driver	Driver	-3 Assessment
-1	Putt		1st Putt	Putter	-1 Execution

Round Summary — **Shots Gained = 7**

GAINED	SHOT TYPE		SUBTYPE	CLUB	CAUSE
5	Putt				+5 Both
		1	2nd Putt	Putter	+1 Both
		4	1st Putt	Putter	+4 Both
1	Short Game		Pitch	8 Iron	+1 Both
1	Full Shot		Short Iron/Hybrid	8 Iron	+1 Both

Round Summary Report.

MindTRAK's thought protocols shift the player's attentional focus off extrinsic results and outcomes and redirects the player's attentional focus onto their Intrinsic KPM Performance Measurement of each shot.

This on the golf course protocol helps the player detach emotionally from Extrinsic Motivation, the results and score that our egos want. Without making this adjustment, the player's expectations and fear can easily accelerate to threatening levels that can trigger anxiety. We also believe that when the user/player shifts their focus and performance measurement onto intrinsically motivated results, it inhibits the player's ego, decreasing emotional attachment to extrinsic results. When emotion is disconnected, the path toward accessing This Present Moment with each golf shot is opened—it breaks the Golf Insanity cycle in the player's mind. It's like you now have permission to let go of this mental anchor that's been holding you back. This reconditioning simplifies the golf objective and better prepares you as a player to deal with difficult situations on the golf course that you will most certainly face.

A significant amount of game improvement efforts are spent on golf swing technique, physical fitness, golf equipment, and nutrition. And all are important. However, there is a massive gaping hole across that game improvement spectrum in our industry. The player's mind is the most important piece of golf equipment the golfer will ever own. MindTRAK Golf is the simplest effective way to help golfers improve their playing perspective.

Peak performance in any sport occurs when the athlete finds themselves in The Zone. This state of mind happens when the player's subconscious mind takes over and they perform freely without any interference or disruption from their analytical or logical mind. Golfers occasionally and unexpectedly enter this rarefied mindset, not knowing how or why they got there, or when it might happen again. But they love it when they are there—it allows them to tap into their freedom. It's a tool that enables the player to detach emotionally from results that golfers of any ability level can employ.

The MindTRAK protocol simplifies the player's *thought process* and helps the player restructure a new, simple, and healthy perspective, one that helps the golfer from getting on the Golf Insanity path to begin with. Nonetheless, many of the best players in the world still struggle with this affliction.

The MindTRAK Golf Story—The Start-Up

With the assistance of my close friends and co-founders Dave Coombs and Ken Fisher, and my sons Conor and Garrett, we met with Vancouver lawyer, investor, and financier David Raffa in 2017. David Raffa became a co-founder in MindTRAK as well. I first met David Raffa in 1996, during the Eaglequest Golf Centers start-up days. David practiced corporate finance law for 20 years, representing a number of BC-based tech companies, later transitioning to providing corporate finance and M&A expertise and service to a portfolio of early-stage companies with an objective to drive growth and generate lucrative exit events for investors.

THE MINDTRAK GOLF TEAM

Executive Team

Richard Zokol, CEO, Director

Conor Zokol, Co-COO

Josh Lai, Co-COO

Greg Olson, CMO

Rick Lambrick, Growth

External Directors

Dave Coombs, Director

Sean Foley, Director

Professional Advisors

Michael Manzo, Chief Product & Tech Officer

Dr. Raymond Prior, Professional Advisor

In 2018, we finalized the organizational structure of MindTRAK Golf Inc. and began to raise money. Through our initial Friends & Family round, we raised CAD $400,000, which funded development of our alpha prototype (minimally viable product, MVP). No one in the company got paid a salary, and all money went into product development. An iOS prototype was completed and delivered in 2019, and we made it available as a free download on the Apple App Store to begin beta testing.

Reaching Out to Golf Canada with Our MVP

With the MindTRAK prototype in hand and available to test, I set out to introduce MindTRAK to Golf Canada. In May 2019, I connected with Golf Canada's CEO Laurence Applebaum and explained to him that my team had created a product and service that could significantly help Golf Canada's Long-Term Player Development Program (LTPD) objectives. Laurence appreciated my efforts and put me in touch with Jeff Thompson, Golf Canada's chief sport officer at the time. After speaking with Jeff, we made arrangements to meet and discuss MindTRAK at the 2019 RBC Canadian Open at Hamilton Golf & CC the first week of June.

On the Tuesday during the tournament week of the 2019 RBC Canadian Open, Jeff and I sat down in a quiet section of the players' dining room in the Hamilton Golf & CC clubhouse. I explained to Jeff that MindTRAK was a tool to help build the player's thought fundamentals, addressing the mental gap that holds most players back from achieving their goals. I further explained to Jeff that I had created this method and tested it in the heat of battle, to get back to the PGA Tour, and we had now "productized" this thought technique into a mobile app and platform. I walked Jeff through the methodology and functionality of the app and explained how the platform generated three post-round reports for the player and the player's coach to review after each round played.

Jeff was receptive and suggested that a good way to test MindTRAK would be with Golf Canada's Young Pro Squad. I was delighted with Jeff's suggestion. Jeff also thought it was essential that Derek Ingram, Golf Canada's national men's head coach, and Tristan Mullally, Golf Canada's national women's head coach at the time, validate the MindTRAK Golf concept and protocol. I agreed.

At this point, I let Jeff know that I had already been keeping both Derek Ingram (Golf Canada) and Michael O'Donnell, who was working on the framework for the PGA of America's Junior Player Development Program, informed about MindTRAK Golf right from the beginning of the concept and over the previous years of development.

I welcomed having Golf Canada's two head coaches look at and come to understand the MindTRAK concept. At the same time, however, I did have some concerns knowing neither Derek nor Tristan had ever really fought it out in the golf trenches themselves at the highest level or had first-hand experience in struggling to overcoming barriers and finding solutions to those mental obstacles. Though Derek did play a couple of years on the Canadian Tour before he transitioned to coaching.

I mentioned to Jeff that Derek had received the MindTRAK Golf prototype in our beta-1 test program in May. I asked Jeff to introduce me to Tristan Mullally—which he did a short time later.

Steeped in the golf coaching industry, most golf coaches are typically players who "washed out" as professional players themselves. Not all, but most. And in all likelihood, they fell short on the mental side of performance. As such, most golf coaches remain fixated on teaching golf swing technique and have not yet grasped the significant importance of, and how to develop, a proper mindset.

Back in 2008, I was thrilled to be hired by Golf Canada as a special adviser to player development efforts. I informed Golf Canada that I had this mental-game improvement concept that I thought Golf Canada's Player Development Program would rally around because it dealt with this missing psychological gap in the game. But I was not able to get any traction with Golf Canada to help develop this product back in 2008.

My passion to help mold young minds for the rigors of professional golf was strong. I wanted to help those young minds have the courage and aspiration to play the game for a living and succeed. And I felt, given my battles in the trenches on the PGA Tour, I knew exactly where and why these young players' minds were so off track. Moreover, I wanted to be part of the solution to help develop and shape these young minds.

Golf Canada's Young Pro Squad

Golf Canada's National Team program was designed to help elite young amateurs, male and female, on their path to playing professional golf. These young professional players are striving to launch successful careers as touring pros. The program provides individualized training and competition support with an objective to help 30 Canadian athlete-golfers launch careers on the LPGA and PGA Tours by 2032.

After my meeting with Jeff, I reached out to Derek Ingram. Derek and I connected to discuss beta testing the MindTRAK app with the Young Pro Squad, who were playing on PGA Tour Canada at the time. We decided to invite a small group—Jared du Toit, Hugo Bernard, and Taylor Pendrith—to meet with me the following week at the PGA Tour Canada's Golf BC Championship in Kelowna, BC, where I live. I invited Jared, Hugo, and Taylor to meet me the following week at Predator Ridge, where I worked.

My Message to Golf Canada's Young Pro Squad

Once face-to-face with Jared, Hugo, and Taylor via phone, I said to all of them, "You each have the game to play and win on the PGA Tour or you wouldn't be sitting here right now. There isn't a golf shot you cannot hit—but that's not good enough to make it to and win on the PGA Tour. What is going to determine whether you make it or not on the PGA Tour are the thoughts that run through your mind, on and off the golf course every day." I went on, "Your thought-skill development will shape your belief system and your mental ability to get into and stay in This Present Moment when you face stressful situations. Your mindset will determine whether you will make it or not—your future as a professional player hinges on this."

We spent the next hour or so talking about what MindTRAK was designed to do with their coach, how it works, what it will enable them to do, and what they would need to do to succeed playing professional golf. They were all eager to get going with MindTRAK. We got them to download the TestFlight app in order to then be able to download the MindTRAK Golf prototype app on their iPhones. Off they went to the following week's PGA Tour Canada event in Lethbridge, AB.

The next week, after the first round of the Lethbridge Paradise Canyon Open, I reached out to Derek Ingram to review each of the players' reports with him. Derek told me only Taylor had completed the After Action Report (AAR) that was required to generate the three reports for Derek to review.

At the conclusion of the Lethbridge event, I called each of the three players to get a sense of where they were with the MindTRAK program.

Taylor Pendrith shared, "I like the app's use of emojis," when entering the KPM data after the round. Taylor instantly got the concept and applied it to his game. He made the cut and finished T46th that week in Lethbridge.

When I spoke with Jared, he told me, "It helped me get into my Think Box and Play Box," which is Vision 54's method and terminology. Vision 54 is a wonderful program founded by Lynn Marriott and Pia Nilsson, based in Scottsdale, AZ. Their program teaches the player to think in terms of their Think Box, Play Box, and Memory Box. Jared was clearly engaged in the Vision 54 program. He was also using the shot-by-shot method when he told me he had a "27-foot" putt on a specific green during our conversation. Shot-by-Shot is an analytical program that has the player collect many data points during the round. I asked Jared how he knew he had a 27-foot putt on the 16th hole. He told me he paced off the distance of the putt. I told him that during completion, your focus should be only on your two Key Performance Marker data points and not on capturing any other types of data points if you want the program to work. It needs to be simple. It was apparent Jared's head was full of other programs and he wasn't really committed to the MindTRAK program.

In the second week of this beta test was the Windsor Championship, and Taylor took to MindTRAK Golf like a fish to water. He connected with the simplicity of performing his two KPMs with each shot. He got traction and started to detach emotionally from results. He started to play golf the way he knew he could. MindTRAK gave him the thought protocol and path to free himself from internal struggles. He started to tap into his potential. In his second week implementing MindTRAK Golf's concepts, Taylor finished T16th.

I called Jared again. I caught him on the range hitting balls, and he sounded overwhelmed as I again inquired as to how things were going. He said, "I'm having a hard time taking the club away—you know, the same problem Kevin Na is having." Jared was trying to tell me without saying it that he has the yips. Picking up on this, I told Jared I had the yips with my driver and putting and stated that he can overcome this problem, then I asked him if he'd been using MindTRAK. Jared said, "No," and said he'll get to it next week in the next event. It was obvious to me Jared's attentional focus was fractured. He was lost and searching for something but wasn't committed to giving MindTRAK a go. I explained to him that the anxiety he was experiencing was due to his long-standing emotional connection and conditioning to results, outcomes, and fear, which in turn cause an involuntary reaction during the shot Execution. The medical community refers to it as task-specific focal dystonia, which is code for having no idea what it is or how to solve it.

From my perspective, Jared was showing a reinforced result-oriented conditioned response from fear that had evolved into anxiety and metastasized into the yips. He sounded defeated. Not long after, we had another discussion where he told me he had too many things going on and that he was no longer going to commit to MindTRAK. I thanked Jared for his time and wished him the best. I knew exactly where Jared was in his mind—having been there a few times myself.

Fixed Mindset vs. Growth Mindset

The thing I always look for in any player—young, old, elite, or beginner—is whether they possess a fixed mindset or a growth mindset. In my experience, those with a fixed mindset struggle more with letting go. In my opinion, I also find them to be more logic-dominant thinkers. Some are hard-wired in the belief that improving their golf swing is everything. They work to improve their golf swing their whole life. Their thoughts become so strong that they lose focus on executing golf shots on the golf course. Players with a fixed mindset don't know what they don't know. On the other hand, those who have a growth mindset are more receptive to new ideas and open to new concepts. They can make a leap of faith more easily and comfortably if it makes sense to them; they allow their intuition to drive their bus. In contrast with the others, Taylor Pendrith had a growth mindset!

Taylor Pendrith

When I first spoke with Taylor, he had recently gotten over struggling with shoulder issues that had negatively impacted his performance. He had been knocked off the Korn Ferry Tour due to his poor performance and was now back on PGA Tour Canada trying to turn things around. Taylor was also in the awkward position of being labeled by many in Canada as the next Mike Weir. That is not a comfortable position for any young player emerging from amateur and collegiate golf who is yet to make it to the PGA Tour. He had an entire country's expectations on him as he was struggling in golf's double-A and triple-A leagues.

After my initial conversation with Taylor in Kelowna, I explained to him that I'd stay in touch on a weekly basis to see how things were going. Taylor, in turn, committed to the MindTRAK Golf protocol—and immediately got traction. In fact, he went on an impressive performance run. His seven consecutive weeks of performance on the PGA Tour Canada using the MindTRAK system is listed below. The shift was an instant turnaround for Taylor.

Taylor Pendrith's Seven Weeks on PGA Tour Canada Using MindTRAK

Week	2019 Tournament	Date	Place in Competition
1	Lethbridge Canyon Open	June 17-23	T48
2	Windsor Championship	July 1-7	T16
3	Osprey Valley Open	July 8-14	2nd
4	HFX Pro-Am	July 15-21	T3rd
5	1932byBateman Open	July 29-Aug 4	**WIN**
6	Players Cup	Aug 12-18	MC
7	Mackenzie Investments Open	Sept 2-8	**WIN** (won by 8 shots)

The top five players at the end of the 2019 PGA Tour Canada season's Order of Merit:

1. Paul Barjon
2. Taylor Pendrith
3. Jake Knapp
4. Lorens Chan
5. Patrick Fishburn

As the season ended, Taylor sent me this quote after I asked him if MindTRAK Golf played a role in helping him get his mindset right.

> "MindTRAK Golf absolutely helped my performance. It got me back to the way I think when I play my best. I don't get attached to my bad shots anymore. I am super excited to have finished second on the Mackenzie PGA Tour Canada and hopefully I have a great year on the Korn Ferry Tour in 2020. I will go out there with a different mindset and hopefully continue my good play."
>
> —TAYLOR PENDRITH

Taylor's good play did not end with the 2019 PGA Tour Canada season. Over the following five years, Taylor sustained his ascent—in fact, it accelerated:

- 2019—2nd on PGA Tour Canada (graduating him to the Korn Ferry Tour)
- 2020—2nd on Korn Ferry Tour Season Point List
- 2021—5th on Korn Ferry Tour Season Point List (Covid—combined two years on the Korn Ferry Tour to graduate to the PGA Tour)
- 2022—56th on PGA Tour Official Money List as a PGA Tour rookie ($2,330,840)
- 2022—Captain Trevor Immelman picked Taylor Pendrith for International Team's Presidents Cup
- 2023—93rd on the PGA Tour's Official Money List ($1,880,027)
- 2024—T14th on the PGA Tour's Official Money List ($4,797,854)

- At the end of June 2025, Taylor was in the 33rd spot on the PGA Tour's FedEx Cup point list, having earned $3,296,030 on the 2025 PGA Tour's Official Money List

In May 2024, Taylor won his first PGA Tour event, the CJ Cup Byron Nelson, along with the $1.74 million that was wired into his bank account at 9:00 AM the next morning. Taylor won by one shot over Ben Kohles and two shots over Alex Noren. Taylor was chosen by International Team captain Mike Weir to represent the International Team for his second in the President's Cup.

Below is a screenshot of the text thread I had with Taylor immediately following his first PGA Tour win in 2024.

Taylor used MindTRAK Golf's platform as a tool to simplify his thought protocols on the golf course and it lead improved performance. Those who are left to their own devices to develop their own mindset will likely continue to wander aimlessly. To succeed at your highest level, whether it's on the PGA Tour or on a $5 Nassau, if your mind isn't in the proper place, you will fight a battle that you will likely lose.

There are endless numbers of supremely talented players who fall short of their dreams of making it to the PGA Tour because they have not developed a proper mindset. The same applies to most serious players as well. Your mind will make you or break you on the golf course.

CHAPTER 29

Golfer's Perspective & Perception—Expectations—Acceptance—Confidence—the Process—the Yips

One's Perspective, Expectations, and Acceptance

Developing a high level of acceptance is critical when playing golf if you want to optimize performance. It serves Scottie Scheffler well. It's a significant asset that complements Scheffler's ability to hit great shots. It also helps Scheffler deal with his poor shots effectively. The quote, "You are only as good as your worst shot," which is attributed to Ben Hogan, emphasizes the importance of minimizing one's mistakes. The purpose of having a high level of acceptance is to help the player stop wasting shots.

A good example of a player who appears to have a low level of acceptance is Tyrrell Hatton. Hatton has been given the nickname "Terrible Tyrrell" due to his proclivity for loud foul language on the golf course. How he has spoken to his driver that was caught on live TV would make a sailor blush. It's safe to say Hatton has a low level of acceptance *and* a high level of expectations. In golf, even if you are a great player like Hatton, if you are constantly frustrated with poor outcomes, your perspective will likely keep you in emotional turmoil.

Your perspective will determine what headspace your mind will occupy. Yet, Hatton's perspective in the 2025 Ryder Cup was noticeably different—significantly improved—in the heat of battle. Tyrrell never seemed to lose his mind when he hit poor shots. Perhaps the European's use of Virtual Reality training for the hostile New York fans. allowed Hatton to improve his perspective dealing with difficult and frustrating situations, or perhaps, Hatton felt greater responsibility beyond himself.

Let me ask you, if you had the choice of having Scheffler's perspective or Tyrrell Hatton's, what would you choose? Scheffler's perspective gives him peace of mind and freedom to perform. Hatton's keeps perpetuating a cycle of frustration.

Developing a high level of acceptance is a skillset acquisition that is too often overlooked. One thing that is absolutely certain in this game, you will hit far more bad shots than you will hit good shots. It stands to reason that how you choose to deal with poor shots and bad results is a key factor in success in this game. You don't have to like your poor results—you just have to accept them.

Expectations can be used in general terms or very specific terms. Expectations can help you and they can also hurt you: it depends on your perspective. In general terms, having expectations of success is a good thing. But in specific terms, having expectations that you must make every four-foot putt you face can easily become a problem if you were to miss one.

Too many so-called experts think you need to "manage your expectations." I am of the opinion that it's more important to develop the thought skill to have zero expectations. You want to eliminate any of those thought habits that can trigger a threat.

The human mind has been evolving for millions of years. Our mind alerts us and reacts to any perceived threat. Our fight, flight, and freeze response is at the core of our survival instincts. The problem with our mind as it relates to playing golf (if you are a serious golfer) is that our internal response cannot distinguish the threat of being attacked by a saber-toothed tiger from the threat of embarrassment if you were to miss a short putt.

Many serious players often establish poor thought habits. Problems occur when the player attaches their personal identity to the scores they shoot. You do not become a better person if you shoot lower scores. From this perspective, players find themselves in a mental and emotional battle they cannot win.

> **ASAP Sports 2025 Ryder Cup** September 23, 2025 Team USA Media Conference.
>
> **Q. Should the expectations of you be any different than any other player on the team? And whatever your answer is, if**

you could elaborate as much as you can I would really appreciate it.

SCOTTIE SCHEFFLER: Should the expectations of me be different than any other player? I mean, I don't really think about that kind of stuff. If that's something you want to write about, then more power to you. I don't think I have any—I don't think about expectations. I don't bother with that kind of stuff because it's unimportant to me. I truly don't think about expectations or anything like that. That's wasted space in my brain.

Developing a healthy perspective empowers the player, giving them freedom. A healthy perspective helps alleviate internal struggles and frustration that will develop when you don't meet those expectations, results, or outcomes on the golf course. In my opinion, a healthy perspective is one that eliminates expectations. Our expectations are connected to results and can set the tone for a poor perspective. Our egos create the expectations, and they also feel the threat of those same expectations.

Perspective & Perception—Is a Choice

When a player possesses a healthy perspective and perception, like Scottie Scheffler and Tommy Fleetwood have developed on and off the golf course, it's a significant asset. Scheffler and Fleetwood are consummate models of having "no ego." Fleetwood is the same person today as he was prior to winning his first PGA Tour event,the 2025 Tour Championship where he earned $10 million. Another reflection of Scheffler's and Fleetwood's perspective is how they treat other people. The proof is in their actions; despite their success, they don't think they're superior to others.

In contrast to Scheffler and Fleetwood, another example of a top player with a remarkable game who has a less-than-healthy perspective—who exhibits an inflated sense of entitlement—is Collin Morikawa. Morikawa's issues were on full display during his press conference on Tuesday, March 11th at the 2025 Players Championship. Two days prior, Morikawa finished second to Russell Henley in the final round of the 2025 Arnold Palmer Invitational in Orlando. In the final three holes that Sunday, Henley flipped the script on Morikawa when he chipped in for eagle on Bay Hill's 16th green. Henley then closed Morikawa out by performing extremely well on the final two difficult holes to win Arnold Palmer's tournament in outstanding fashion.

After the final round that Sunday afternoon, Collin Morikawa rejected requests to engage with the golf media or answer any of their questions.

Two days after Morikawa snubbed the golf media, he was scheduled to appear at the pre-tournament press conference for the Players Championship. One of the questions in that interview revealed something interesting.

> **ASAP Sports**
>
> **Q: You seem to have rationalized what happened Sunday to a great extent, but in the moment you didn't. I want to understand a little better what you were feeling, why you didn't stop to talk or anything?**
>
> COLLIN MORIKAWA: Yeah, just heated. Just pissed. Like I don't owe anyone anything. No offense to you guys, but for me in the moment of that time, I didn't want to be around anyone. Like, I didn't want to talk to anyone. I didn't need any sorries. I didn't need any good playings. Like, you're just pissed.
>
> Honestly, if it was an hour later I would have talked to you guys, but an hour later I was on my way out to here [Ponte Vedra Beach], because I didn't want to be in Orlando anymore. But I just felt like I put everything I did into the, let's call it, seven hours of my time being there, right, a few hours before showing up, physio, workout. Look, my entire routine, right. I was just drained.
>
> I get it. Like you guys are there to figure out how we played and how things went, but in my perspective, like I just didn't want to talk to anyone, and I think that's fair to myself, you know.[12]

---

12 The Players Championship Collin Morikawa Press Conference, *ASAP Sports*, March 11, 2025.

Morikawa is a two-time major champion. Being "pissed," and blowing off media requests is one thing. In fact, Morikawa has no obligation to speak to the media. But he said, "I don't owe anyone anything," and it echoed through the world of golf. His perspective is not one of high character with other past major champions—rather it's reminiscent of a petulant adolescent.

When Morikawa proclaimed, "No offence to you guys," it didn't make it less offensive. His comments are an affront to the PGA Tour and those sponsors who collectively invest billions of dollars into the PGA Tour, which is the source of the millions of dollars that stream into Collin Morikawa's bank account on a weekly basis.

Justin Thomas's Call to Action

In January 2025, just a couple months before Morikawa's comments, Justin Thomas sent a letter to all PGA Tour players. The purpose of Thomas's letter was to remind his peers just how fortunate they are, and hopefully they will be more enduring to fans in this tumultuous period of the PGA Tour's restructuring since a number of top players are jumping over to the LIV Tour. Thomas wrote:

> We're incredibly lucky to have many passionate people tuning in to watch us every week . . . But let's be honest—this game can feel a little distant at times . . . At the end of the day, we're all owners in this Tour. So, the bigger and better we make it not only benefits us financially, it benefits our fans and creates the ability for us to do bigger things down the road. Anybody who has any ideas or thoughts, please reach out to me or any of the Tour staff to get the ball rolling on ways we can make OUR Tour the best we possibly can.[13]

When Morikawa said, "I don't owe anyone anything," most people were absolutely stunned. My first thought on Morikawa's conduct at Arnold

---

13 Sean Zak, "Justin Thomas calls PGA Tour players to action with impassioned letter," *Golf*, January 21, 2025.

Palmer's home—in light of Arnold Palmer's legacy and what professionalism meant to him—Arnie would have pulled him aside, by the scruff of his neck, and held him accountable for what he said. Arnold Palmer would have torn him a new asshole for his lack of respect, lack of humility, and lack of professionalism.

From the start of the 2025 PGA Tour season through to the end of the 2025 Players Championship, in just those three months, Collin Morikawa played in five PGA Tour events and earned a total of $5,558,964. The PGA Tour provided him the platform to cash flow, based on his performance, an averaged $1.23 million per week. One would think he would show more appreciation, more respect, or at least work on appearing less entitled.

Collin Morikawa's comments were abhorrent. The golf media is a conduit to the fans who watch PGA Tour golf. The media is an integral part of the PGA Tour sponsorship model that provides sponsors a return on their investment.

We don't know what's going on in Morikawa's mind, but his perspective seems to be based on a result-oriented mindset. Morikawa was pissed because he didn't like his result at the Arnold Palmer Invitational. Do you think Morikawa would have snubbed the media after the round if he had won? Absolutely not. But as we all know, that is golf and that is life. And there's no place to hide.

Unbeknownst to Morikawa, he will only hold himself back if he doesn't improve his perspective. His result-oriented mindset will likely keep him in his own cycle of frustration, heated and pissed when things don't work the way he wants. Don't get me wrong, Morikawa is a remarkable player. But if he really wants to reach his full potential, he will need to improve his mental perspective by learning to detach emotionally from results.

Rocco Mediate jumped on Collin Morikawa on his SiriusXM podcast the day before the 2025 Players Championship's first round. Rocco, who developed a close personal relationship with Arnold Palmer, stated, "That's the biggest bunch of horseshit you could ever say, period. I mean, that is the dumbest, most selfish garbage you could ever say. Mr. Palmer would've hunted him down. Trust me on that one because Mr. Palmer told me one thing that stuck with me. [He said] 'You know what, Rock, it's real easy to go in and talk to somebody when you won or when you've played well, but can you do it when you don't? That's the key.' Obviously, he can't."

“Mental toughness is not just
about being tough. It’s about doing
what you know you have to do,
even when you don’t want to do it.”
—BEAR BRYANT

When It’s Over, Morikawa Doubles Down

Three days later, on Friday, March 14, 2025, after Morikawa shot a spectacular 65 in the second round of the Players to move into T4th place, in his post-round interview, the golf media had already moved on and did not bring up any further questions on this matter. Morikawa couldn’t leave it alone; he doubled down after there were no more questions from the golf media, saying:

> I just want to add one more thing. I might bite my tongue after saying this, but to the Brandel Chamblees, to the Paul McGinleys, to the Rocco Mediates of the world, I don’t regret anything I said. You know, it might have been a little bit harsh that I don’t owe anyone, but I don’t owe anyone.
>
> I respect the fans. I’m very thankful for them. I’m grateful. It makes me emotional, but it’s just—it hurts to hear people say this, and especially you guys, because I finished the round and I went to go sign for 10 minutes, 15 minutes for all the people after. Not a single person from media went to go follow me because, I don’t know. But that’s me.
>
> So for people to be calling me out is—it’s interesting. It just, it doesn’t show anything. I mean, look, I get what you guys are saying. But I was there. I was signing for every single person right after the round, whether they wanted it or not. I finished second. They could care less. But yeah, I’m going to leave it at that, all right? So thank you guys.[14]

---

14 Collin Morikawa, The Players Championship Press Conference, *ASAP Sports*, March 14, 2025.

After everything appeared to be over, Morikawa not only started digging again, he played the victim card: "It makes me emotional, but it just—it hurts to hear people say this, and especially you guys." He's gaslighting the media he snubbed for asking questions. "So for people to be calling me out—it is interesting." He gives a false cry of victimization.

Collin Morikawa is one hell of a player, and he is a great asset to the PGA Tour. And hopefully his perspective will change as he matures. When Morikawa said, "I might bite my tongue after saying this," at the start of his premeditated statement, that was his subconscious mind trying to advise that what he was about to say could very well backfire. But I think his ego overruled his intuition. If he had a healthy perspective or a decent amount of situational awareness, he would have stopped digging. But no, he fired things up again. He couldn't let it go. And by the way, that 77 Morikawa shot the next day on Saturday's third round of the 2025 Players Championship? That's called karma.

After telling the world, "I don't owe anyone anything," then digging his heels in as a follow-up back in March 2025, Morikawa's self-inflicted internal battles affected him through the rest of his season. And the 2026 PGA Tour season didn't get off to a great start either. As they say—Karma is a bitch.

But there seemed to be evidence that his perspective was beginning to change. He played magnificently in the 2026 AT&T Pebble Beach Pro Am, shooting 62, 67 on the weekend to win. Morikawa appeared to be playing with a sense of freedom. His ball striking was remarkable. That weekend, Morikawa spoke about his team, including Dr. Rick Sessinghaus, an excellent and knowledgeable sport psychologist.

After Morikawa birded Pebble Beach's 15th and16th holes in the final round to take the lead, my former PGA Tour colleague Frank Nobilo stated on the CBS Telecast, with the camera fixed on Morikawa standing on the 17th tee, "It's the change of attitude—that could happen that quick for Morikawa."[15]

Immediately after he birdied the final hole to win, Morikawa answered Amanda Balionis' question, "What does this win mean to you?" He said, "It's hard to think that you're still the same person, just a little bit wiser—a little bit more mature." Balionis then asked Collin, "When you think about

---

15 Frank Nobilo, CBS Broadcast, final round of the 2026 AT&T Pebble Beach Pro Am

what is next for you on this journey, is this just the beginning of Collin Morikawa 2.0?" He replied, "I hope so, I am going to try and stay in the moment as much as I can, I think. I look back to when I was first turned pro when I had some wins . . . I just looked too far ahead. Sometimes it's great—sometimes it's not. I think I am going to change that perspective."

Rory Started Working with Bob Rotella

At the behest of Brad Faxon, Rory McIlroy's putting coach, Rory started working with Dr. Bob Rotella. After years of trying to figure out Rory's putting issues, such as the two short putts Rory missed on the 16th and 18th holes to lose the 2024 US Open at Pinehurst to Bryson DeChambeau, it became clear Rory didn't have a problem with his putting mechanics, he had a problem with his attentional focus. In other words, he had a mindset issue when it came to Majors.

Prior to the 2025 Masters Rory had still not broken through the mental barriers that were holding him back from not only winning the Masters, which would complete his career grand slam, but they were preventing him from winning *any* major championship for the past 10 years—a remarkable occurrence considering Rory's astonishing talent.

> "I am trying to improve mentally. I had freedom early in my career, but when expectations began, I started to play careful and second-guess myself—I want to play with freedom."
>
> —RORY MCILROY, MARCH 6, 2020, ON GOLF CHANNEL

During Rory's major championship drought (2014–2025), Rory had no problem winning big PGA Tour events. In Rory's press conference on the Tuesday of the 2025 Masters week, Rory was asked the question:

INTERVIEWER: You've been working with Bob Rotella for a bit. I'm curious in your words what he brings to the table for you, how valuable he's been to you, and are there any ways you guys have shifted your approach or altered your approach leading into this week?

RORY McILROY: Talking about not getting too much into results and outcomes, we talk about trying to chase a feeling on the golf course. Like if you're on the golf course, what way do you want to feel when you're playing golf. That's something that is a—ok it's not something I obviously just do here [playing the Masters], but I do every week that I compete. If I can chase that feeling and make that the important thing, then hopefully the golf will take care of itself.[16]

Chase a Feeling—Intrinsic Motivation & Results

Rory's first step is to break his emotional connections to expectations and result-oriented thinking—such as winning the Masters and what it would mean to him, extrinsic results and motivation. Rory stated in his post-round interview after the third round that he was the one who suggested "chasing feelings on the golf course," not Rotella. I thought that was interesting. This shift in thinking is the right move; it's an effort to detach his emotional connection to extrinsic results, motivation, and expectations, which interfere with his ability to perform—the thing that holds him back.

The Problem

Most golfers hold onto *extrinsic motivations* and *results* when they play, this is the source of the problem. This way of thinking will compound one's *expectations,* which can easily turn short putts into threating situations. Fear

16 Transcript by *ASAP Sports*, April 8, 2025 THE MASTERS, Rory McIlroy.

of this threat begins to occupy the player's mind, taking the player out of This Present Moment. Over time this threat—missing the putt—can easily turn into anxiety.

What I believe Bob Rotella and Rory were working on is precisely what MindTRAK Golf has already sorted out. MindTRAK has gone well beyond "chasing feelings on the golf course." It is a fully baked operating system designed to shift the player's motivation, attentional focus, and performance measurement from extrinsic results to intrinsic motivation and results. In my experience, being intrinsically motivated helped me get into and stay in This Present Moment.

When you make this shift to access This Present Moment, it removes anxiety and expectations of making the putt. It gives you freedom.

Rory Finally Pierced the Veil

On Saturday's third round of the 2025 Masters, Rory took off like a rocket, opening with six straight 3s on his scorecard. Rory shot 66 in the third round and took a two-shot lead heading into Sunday's final round. The proverbial question was, *Will working with Bob Rotella help Rory rid himself of his own thoughts and emotional incarceration?*

Prior to the start of the final round, I put out on X:

Richard Zokol
@RichardZokol

Today we will watch Rory play under more pressure than any other player has ever had to endure

He doesn't have to overcome his opponent, @brysondech

He has to overcome an old mindset, which can only be resolved in major championship play

@chambleebrandel & @mcginleygolf

1:01 PM · Apr 13, 2025 · **3,560** Views

Rory won the 2025 Masters in an emotional roller-coaster ride that finished in a sudden-death playoff win over his pal Justin Rose. The world of empathetic golfers went on this emotional ride with Rory that began on the first hole on Sunday when Rory made a double bogey. The golf world gasped—here we go again. This nightmare is going to continue. But what was so remarkable about Rory's final round was how well he reacted after each disaster, and there were many. Rory's internal struggle was on full display.

- Double bogey on his first hole—erasing his lead.
- Birdies on three and four to take the lead back.
- Birdies on nine and 10.
- He hit his 86-yard third shot into Rae's Creek on the 13th hole, making his second double bogey of the day and losing his three-shot lead once again.
- He made another bogey on his 14th hole.
- He made a remarkable 7-iron shot, hooking it around the group of trees on the left side of the 15th hole from 205 yards to 6 feet. Jim Nantz on CBS called this "the shot of a lifetime."[17]
- Then he made another remarkable 8-iron second on the 17th hole from 196 yards to 2 feet, making birdie to take a one-shot lead to the final hole.
- Executed a perfect tee shot on the 18th tee, leaving him only 125 yards to the pin on the 72nd hole, from the middle of the fairway—everyone thought it was all over. Rory was going to win.
- Then Rory blocked his simple 125-yard gap wedge into the bunker right of the 18th green and failed to get it up and down to win—letting Justin Rose into a sudden-death playoff.
- On the first sudden-death playoff on the 18th hole, Rory executed a perfect shot, once again from 125 yards, to 2 feet.

---

17 Jim Nantz on CBS telecast—Alex Myer, *Golf Digest*, April 17, 2025.

When Rory made that two-foot putt for birdie in the sudden death, he pierced the veil, and the whole golfing world felt his emotional relief as Rory fell to his knees, covered his head and broke down.

After his Masters win, Rory stated:

> "I really do think it's going to free me up in these things (major championships). It's been a long time coming. It's been over 10 years since I won a major championship. It will allow me to play with a lot more freedom."
>
> —RORY MCILROY, APRIL 14, 2025 ON TIKTOK

This Widespread Mental Problem Among Golfers

Most players have never been taught how to think properly. Perhaps more than in any other sport, golfers are perilously susceptible to mental mistakes due to their own corrupt thought habits. Most golfers have not been taught to think appropriately on the course. And only a few have learned through trial and error how to attain a healthy perspective while playing. Left to our own devices, even the most advanced players can slip down these mental rabbit holes and compound our thought-habit problems. Rory got stuck for 10 years in this trap. These thoughts, especially expectations, harmful self-talk, future projecting to what may or may not happen with the shot's outcome or results, or being concerned about what others may think, can lead to anxiety. These types of thoughts erode confidence by disrupting the player's ability to perform—affecting their ability to assess and execute shots on the golf course. That's Golf Insanity. I think all golfers can relate to this.

The Real Objective in Putting and All Shots

Most golfers, just like my friend and former PGA Tour colleague, Notah

Begay, fall down the same rabbit hole. Notah said, "The objective in putting is to get the ball in the hole,"[18] when he was explaining Scottie Scheffler's practice putting session on the Golf Channel on Tuesday of the 2025 Masters.

But in reality, getting the ball in the hole is an extrinsic result, which should not be the player's objective. The ball going in the hole should be a by-product of the player's Assessment and Execution of the putt. Our ego's objective is fixated on the result. Our ego projects forward and becomes emotionally attached to this extrinsic result—it takes the player out of This Present Moment, which disrupts the player's ability to execute the shot.

Constant projecting forward to what may or may not happen can lead to anxiety. It starts with result-oriented thinking, introducing a threat. When outcomes don't happen in the way our ego wants, frustrations build—the harder you try, the more difficult it becomes. We see this internal frustration cycle happen with many players. When golfers continually feed the Golf Insanity cycle (Tyrrell Hatton, Jordan Spieth, and Collin Morikawa come to mind), they get stuck in their frustration. Every serious golfer has experienced this.

The key is, what are you going to do about it?

Evidence suggests Rory McIlroy spent much of his time in this mindset when it came to major championships between 2014 and 2025—emotionally attached and pushing hard on extrinsic results—keeping him in this Golf Insanity cycle. McIlroy let the 2022 Open Championship at the Old Course in St Andrews, the 2023 US Open in Los Angeles, and the 2024 US Open in Pinehurst slip through his hands on the back nine on those Sundays because he didn't have the right mental discipline—yet.

Rory's putts for par on his last three holes now became a serious threat to him at Pinehurst. And Roy did make a great putt on 17. In this mindset, when you take hold of a putter, it can feel like you're holding on to a rattlesnake.

The two KPM measurements shift a player's focus and motivation. They detach from extrinsic results, then reattach to intrinsic results. Focusing on these two KPMs allowed me to access This Present Moment and gave me the freedom to pursue that I was looking for.

---

18 The Golf Channel's Masters *Golf Talk Live*, Tuesday April 8, 2025.

The Yips—They Happen in Other Sports Too

The yips, or as the medical community calls it, task-specific focal dystonia also happens to tennis players who find themselves in a state of anxiety prior to and during the execution of their serve. This involuntary flinch happens in the form of not being able to effectively toss the ball up into the air to initiate their serve. Even more significantly, the tennis yips affect the player's second serve. Anxiety accelerates when the player's attentional focus is on the threat, the fear of embarrassment of yet another double-fault result. Among the top tennis players who have suffered these thought afflictions are Alexander Zverev in 2019 and Aryna Sabalenka at the beginning of 2022. Sabalenka was able to overcome her psychological issues through biofeedback practices.

A number of Major League Baseball pitchers suffer from the same mental affliction. Just as with certain golf shots, or the toss up in the tennis player's serve, because the pitcher must consciously initiate motion to initiate play, the problem strikes those with the same thought disruptions that inevitably turn into an involuntary reaction during the pitcher's execution of his throw. The reaction is precipitated by fear, and it is compounded with continual poor thought habits.

Among notable MLB pitchers who have battled this affliction is Jon Lester. Lester got to the point where he couldn't throw the ball effectively to his first baseman if he stopped a grounder. He addressed his mental affliction a couple of times by throwing the ball to his first baseman *while the ball was still in his glove*. It was a certainly a creative remedy in the moment to get the runner out—but it's not a long-term solution. Lester had good company. Other notable players similarly stricken with this mental disability include players Daniel Bard, Matt Garza, Rick Ankiel, Mark Wohlers, Steve Blass, Jarrod Saltalamacchia, Chuck Knoblauch, and Steve Sax.

When a player is having the yips, I personally think the subconscious mind recognizes there is faulty technique in play, and is aware of what is about to happen with this shot—it is not going to have a happy ending. Understanding this, the subconscious mind hits the panic button during the shot in an effort to intervene. But it can't intervene effectively. This intervention at the last possible moment becomes the involuntary response or the flinch. Our subconscious also knows staying on this track will not work. It placed the player in an unhealthy mindset and perspective—Golf Insanity. Players in these situations need to correct the technical mistake first and then reprogram their new (corrected technique) and establish new neural pathways (neuroplasticity) that won't set off the subconscious alarm. The best example of this is when the player adopts a new method of gripping the putter. The claw-putting grip, or the pencil-grip removes the right-hand hinging motion, which can significantly and quickly remove the right-hand flinch. This grip causes the lead hand (the left hand for right-handed players) to structurally control the execution of the stroke.

The Fastest Way to Stop the Putting Yips—Separate Your Hands

The yips happen when our two hands stop working together. The problem occurs when there is an internal struggle to control the execution of the short putt. Tony Finau is an example of a Tour player who struggles from time to time with this. During the final round of the 2025 Memorial Tournament, on the 15th hole, Finau made an eight-foot nine-inch birdie putt—putting with just *one hand*. I am convinced this is evidence that Finau chose to putt with one hand in order to rid himself of this internal struggle and conflict of thoughts during the execution of his putts. Finau had more internal freedom to execute this shot with just his right hand than he did with both hands gripping his putter.

The player with the yips has established an unhealthy foundation—fear of missing this short putt and what that means: complete embarrassment. Over time, the dreadful thought loop plays out and compounds in the player's mind and performance declines. Fear builds into full-blown anxiety, and the player establishes anxiety during the execution of the putt, chip, or drive, which triggers an involuntary reaction—a flinch. With each short putt missed, this threat compounds into even more fear, which exacerbates the problem.

The origin of the yips begins with a combination of a flawed technique accompanied by how the player thinks—having expectations and constantly projecting forward and fearing the outcome. Let's say the player is faced with an important four-foot putt. Having an expectation—of making or missing this four-foot putt—is a mental mistake.

When expectations take a foothold in the player's mind, it can easily produce the threat of missing the putt. This threat triggers fear and turns into a conditioned response when the player's thoughts project to the possible outcome of missing this short putt and what it will mean. Secondly, the player with the yips has already built a foundation of emotional connectivity to result-oriented thinking—otherwise they wouldn't have the yips. The player's first reaction to this situation is pain avoidance, but not taking the shot is not a viable option. When you play golf, you must stand in there fully exposed.

The first step to build a healthy perspective is to stop all expectations and start construction on a high level of acceptance. If you want to be a top player at any level, you must accept the risk that comes with facing all golf shots, especially those short putts, with courage, focus, and a system designed to help—just because you have a short four-foot putt does not mean the putt is easy and you're going to make it. You must give your full Key Performance Marker attention on each shot. Every player needs to face and accept the risk that comes with these shots. If you don't bring a healthy or proper perspective and method to overcome this problem you will struggle.

Lucas Glover Solved his Yip with the Broomstick Putter

Yips almost brought Lucas Glover to his knees. Prior to going with the long putter Lucas was in a horrible place mentally. Most golfers can relate to this. He was desperate and was fortunate to find a solution. Glover said, "I've been struggling with putting a lot, especially short putts that you need to make . . . I made up my mind that something was going to change. And I was going to try the long one [broomstick putter], and if that didn't feel good, I was going to try left-handed. That's how far down the road [the Golf Insanity road] I was . . . my brain was fried."

When a player adopts a broomstick putter, they separate their hands in a new way. Their hands are no longer required to work directly together. Because the hands have different roles to play, this creates a neurological rewiring in the player's brain. Now that the hands are split they have different roles to play when executing the stroke than they did when they were connected to one another; when the hands split apart, there is no longer conflict in the messaging from the mind to the hands, so the internal struggle and involuntary flinch cease to exist. The player's mind calms and the player builds new neural pathways. With this rewiring Lucas transformed his ability to putt—he not only overcame his short putting yips, but he made putting a strength in his game. Unfortunately there is no broomstick method for chipping yips. Sometimes the best way to avoid chipping yips is to learn to chip with one hand only.

I in fact helped a good friend and member of Predator Ridge, Greg Bird, who relearned to chip effectively with using just his left hand. Greg was committed and put in the time to develop this skill requirement. Another option to deal with the chipping yips is chipping cross-handed, how Matt Fitzpatrick, Vijay Singh, Chris Couch, Chris DiMarco, and Matthieu Pavon have learned to chip.

What Is Confidence? (And What It Is Not!)

There is no doubt we all want to play golf with confidence. But to build stable confidence, an essential step is understanding what confidence is and more importantly what it is not.

Most golfers, coaches, and so-called experts think building confidence is a skill requirement. This notion adds another layer onto an already confused perspective for most golfers. This general misconception of how we perceive and use the word confidence is deeply embedded in golf culture.

> "The way people talk about confidence
> you'd think you could go down
> to the store and just buy some.
> It takes years to build up and after
> one or two bad shots it's gone."
>
> —JACK NICKLAUS

Adding to the muddle, too often we hear expert analysts make claims that this or that player "needs to find their confidence," but this is putting the cart before the horse.

Statements like these are evidence they don't have a proper understanding: it's all just a sound bite. Confidence cannot be conjured up because it is something you want. And confidence is certainly not something that all of a sudden will fall in your lap. Confidence is a feeling that we can cultivate, but how does it come about? And how can we get more of it?

Confidence can mean a few different things, but in the context used most often, from a micro-perspective, it's a feeling of capability based on recent performance in specific situations. Confidence is a pre-event feeling that can easily fluctuate—increase or decrease—based on recent performance, and thoughts and feelings relating to the ability of assessing and executing each shot in a given situation.

Here's an example. Golfer A has a high level of confidence and is comfortable facing a four-foot putt against his buddies on the 18th hole for a $5.00 wager. But if Golfer A faces a similar four-foot putt at Augusta National to win the Masters on the 72nd hole, Golfer A's mindset, emotions, comfort level, and confidence are drastically different. It's safe to say Golfer A would have a more difficult time with that four-foot putt.

The first thing we must do is stop getting ahead of ourselves in our thought sequence. Establishing the proper understanding of how we use the word confidence will go a long way in mitigating confusion. If you're looking to improve your mindset it's imperative you get on the proper thought track.

In his book *Golf Is a Game of Confidence*, Dr. Bob Rotella, the leading mental-game consultant for PGA Tour players dating back to the '80s, stated, "Confident athletes let their brain and nervous systems perform the skill they have rehearsed and mastered—without interference from the conscious mind." Dr. Bob is absolutely right and goes on, "Most golfers experience confidence only occasionally and only haphazardly. They normally play in a state of barely repressed tension."

In my way of thinking, *performance* always precedes and produces appropriate levels of confidence. Confidence is a by-product feeling generated by performance of a task.

Significant problems occur when our attentional focus shifts off performance. You cannot be confident in the task if you cannot perform the task. If your confidence level is low and you want to increase your confidence, your performance level must improve, otherwise your confidence will not increase.

In his books Rotella also states, "The golfers I work with refuse to wait until confidence descends upon them. Most of them are professionals whose dreams and livelihood depends on finding a way to play confidently. Some are amateurs, from scratch players to high handicappers, who simply want to play golf as well as they can. They understand that this requires confidence."

This is precisely where the understanding of confidence falls off the track and the misunderstanding occurs. Yes, confidence is a meaningful influencer in one's game, but I am sorry—there is a need to disrupt this notion from the title of Rotella's book, *Golf Is a Game of Confidence*. In my opinion golf is not a game of confidence—*Golf Is a Game of Performance*. Confidence is not the requirement, performance is the requirement, and confidence is simply the by-product of the performance. Confidence will increase or decrease based on one's performance in a particular situation.

Here is a metaphorical example of the sequence. You have an orange in hand and you want the juice inside the orange (let's call the juice *confidence*). In order to get the juice out of an orange you need to squeeze the orange (let's call the squeeze *performance*). You cannot get the juice without the squeeze. The juice is a by-product of the squeeze. The squeeze is not a difficult task like a golf shot, but it's the necessary task nonetheless. In the same way, you cannot get confidence or stable confidence without the act of performance.

Too many golfers, TV analysts, and performance coaches skip right over the squeeze but still expect the juice. Golf doesn't work that way. Every golfer's KPMs for each shot on the golf course is the squeeze. Every golfer's KPMs ultimately determine the by-product—the juice. Too many coaches and players focus on confidence when they should be focusing on performance.

So let's start focusing, measuring, and reporting on performance and let confidence be an effective by-product of performance and mitigate confusion.

When performance is measured,
performance improves. When performance
is measured and reported, the rate of
improvement accelerates.

The skill of the golfer's ability to assess then execute each golf shot, in any given situation, is what determines performance. As a golfer improves their two KPM capabilities, confidence will grow accordingly. Confidence cannot be developed any other way.

Everyone Is Talking About "The Process"

Most all players who play professional golf today openly talk about what they must do to play well—and they all say the same thing. They repeat the clichés, "I need to play one shot at a time, stay in the moment and follow my 'process.'" They are right. But . . . when you ask these players, "What is your process?" most are unable to explain it.

Too often these players explain their process as a result-based objectives, such as, "I need to get off to a fast start," or "I need to hit fairways and greens." Or they have a "target number in mind to shoot." These results-based objectives are expectations in disguise. Once again when your mind becomes fixated on results, which most golfers are, it's an invitation for problems as these thoughts take you out of This Present Moment. These are thoughts about *extrinsic results.*

The Process

The Process refers to the golfer's thought sequence, their attentional focus, the state of mind that involves how the player goes about executing each shot. The healthy process involves developing a high level of acceptance and establishing:

1. Pre-shot routine—the Assessment;
2. Shot routine—the Execution and;
3. Post-shot routine—Key Performance Marker (KPM) data capture.

The purpose of having these routines is to establish a method you can relay on, to assess and execute good golf shots, in difficult and stressful situations.

To develop the thought skills to perform under pressure, players should strive to develop a healthy perspective and invest in these three stages. When it comes to the second stage, the Execution of your shot routine, it should be short, tight, and have rhythmic cadence. When your pre-shot routine and shot routine is established it's important to condition them to become automatic. You want to rely on activating your pre-shot routine, then go into a tight and rhythmic shot routine, which will pull you into This Present Moment, The Zone, on a per-shot basis.

The shorter and tighter you make your shot routine, the less can go wrong to disrupt your concentration and rhythmic flow—your shot routine becomes your conditioned response to every shot. The rhythm is key; it acts like a mantra and gives you this rhythmic flow. When you become reliant on your shot routine, it will allow you to perform well in the most extreme and difficult situations that you will no doubt find yourself in on the golf course.

Ben Hogan famously said, "The most important shot in golf is the next one." Your last shot is in the past and your next shot is in the future. To be in This Present Moment, this statement should be restated, "The most important shot in golf is the shot you have right Now."

Step 1—Your Pre-Shot Routine

Your pre-shot routine is all about making the proper Assessment of the shot you face. Relating to the tee shot, this could mean deciding to hit or not hit driver based on the shot at hand and how you choose to play the hole. Your decisions also involve the weather, the distance, the lie, the situation, what the ball will do when it lands, the type of shot you decide to hit, the read of the putt, and how you feel. You need to go through this checklist to assess each shot in your pre-shot routine—they lead to the decisions you make.

Once you've made your decision(s) in the Assessment of the shot, the next step is to commit 100% to them. The shot Assessment in your pre-shot routine is the first of two Key Performance Markers (KPMs) for each shot. Part of this process is fully committing to your decisions and taking them into the next step—the Execution of the shot.

If you are not fully committed, or have any doubt, or hesitate in any part of your shot routine, it will compromise and collapse the rhythm/cadence of your shot routine during the Execution process. You will not be able to get the Drop required to get into the Still Point, which maintains flow to access The Zone in the shot.

The Assessment of the shot, the commitment to the shot, and the performance of the shot need to work together. And you also need to understand that you can be fully committed to the shot and still make a poor Execution. Too many people think your commitment to the shot and the performance of the shot are the same—they are not.

Step 2–Your Shot Routine

Your shot routine is an integral part of your shot Execution. Your objective is to work on developing a shot routine so it becomes habitual, even automatic. It should become your conditioned response to every shot. It is what you will rely on to perform well in difficult situations.

The shot routine is a key factor in your Execution. The Execution is the other Key Performance Marker (KPM). The Execution of your shot routine should be as tight and short as possible. The longer the player's shot routine, the greater the possibility that something will disrupt the rhythm of the shot's Execution.

You can change your shot routine from time to time, but you want to establish it or re-establish it so you can use it on every shot on the golf course.

As I mentioned in a previous chapter, the most nervous I have ever been was my tee shot in the final round of the 1992 US Open, and my shot routine allowed me to perform well in an extreme situation, where moments before I was hyperventilating.

My pulse was jacked and I was breathing deeply as I teed my ball, which was not an easy task considering how my hands were shaking. I went straight into my shot routine—standing behind my ball I connected my ball to my target and made my first step forward and stepped into my stance. I took a rhythmic practice swing with my club (a 2-iron), connecting to my target, then I took a breath in and then exhaled smoothly while saying to myself, "feeling the Drop." I took one last glance at my target, and with my target in mind I pulled the trigger on my takeaway and gave it everything I had.

I crushed that 2-iron down the middle of the first fairway. I had never struck a better 2-iron shot in my life, and I did it in the most nerve-racking situation I had ever been. As I picked up my tee, my heart was exploding out of my chest. I couldn't believe how fast my pulse was the moment after impact.

Walking down the first fairway in contention on Sunday of the 1992 US Open was as exhilarating as hell. I felt alive in that moment. Focusing on my breathing mantra, trying to settle into the round, I knew it would take a few holes. My primary objective was to establish my rhythmic shot routine and keep my shit wired tight—I kept saying to myself, *Breathe motherfucker, breathe.*

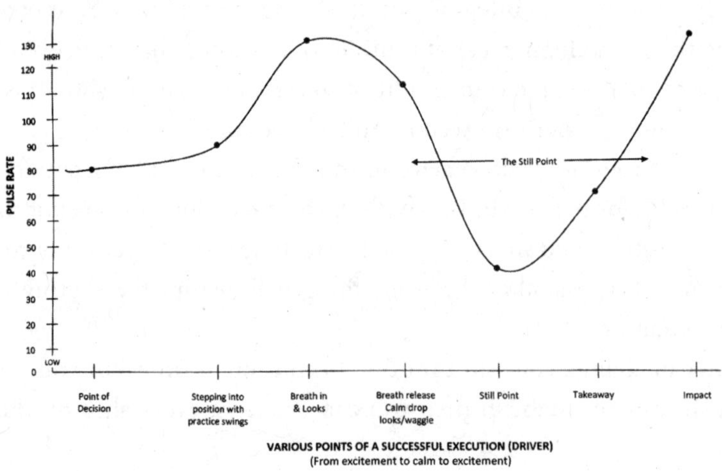

Step 3—Your Post-Shot Routine

The Post-Shot routine for many players is just an afterthought. But it's an important aspect of collecting Key Performance Marker (KPM) data. As golf is a subjective game, players should evaluate the data for each shot. The problem that often occurs, and it's a significant problem, is that many coaches and players evaluate the *result* of the shot rather than their KPMs.

KPM Data Capture and Vocabulary are Important

As mentioned, quite often you hear a caddie give their player a final directive to commit to the shot. As a player the commitment to the shot is not the same thing as the performance of the shot. I personally think the best directive a caddie can give their player after the commitment is the performance of the shot. Once the shot is gone, it is important you take stock of what happened and capture your KPM data. This process requires you to subjectively grade your performance of the two KPMs on the three-point Likert scale—Excellent—Satisfactory—Unsatisfactory—on each shot.

This specific aspect of the process will challenge some coaches and players to learn to distinguish the difference between the result of the shot and a player's KPM. The process-oriented player learns to focus on their KPM performance, regardless of the outcome. This system empowers the player to access This Present Moment on the golf course.

After Action Report (AAR)

The AAR objective is to review your KPMs of each shot after each round. You want to start to look and be accountable for all the Shot Lost Events and Shot Gained Events you had in the round. The purpose then is to attach every Shot Lost Event to the KPM that caused them. When I first started to account for all my Shot Lost Events, it blew my mind. I couldn't fathom how many shots I pissed away in every round. When I took responsibility for my KPMs, I started to shore up where I was making most of my mistakes. My wasted shot numbers improved, and I felt like I simplified my process—it pulled me into the present moment. Golf began to feel simple—I felt freedom.

This process begins to remove our mental barriers and starts to make playing this game much easier. It's the key to success in all performance anxiety situations—on and off the course.

arnold palmer

post
office
box
fifty-two
youngstown,
pennsylvania
15696

May 19, 2011

Dear Dick:

I was very pleased to learn of your impending induction into the Canadian Golf Hall of Fame.

You have been a fine competitor and a credit to the great game of golf during your career in Canada and on the PGA Tour.

Congratulations!

Enjoy the day at Marine Drive, your home club. It's nice that the ceremony is being held there.

Sincerely,

Arnold Palmer

Arnold Palmer

AP/dg

Richard Zokol

Jack Nicklaus

July 18, 2011

Dear Richard:

Please allow me to add my congratulations to the many others you will receive, as you celebrate your induction to the Canadian Golf Hall of Fame. I commend you on your dedication to the game and its traditions, and applaud your commitment and contributions over the years, not only to the sport, but to the countless others you have helped along the way to better understand and appreciate the values and fundamentals of the game.

Congratulations again Richard, and best wishes for a wonderful celebration.

Sincerely,

Mr. Richard Zokol

ACKNOWLEDGMENTS

First and foremost, I want to express my deepest love and gratitude to my family.

My parents, Joseph and Elsie Zokol, who are no longer with us, were truly exceptional people. They lived their lives guided by unwavering integrity, strength, and a deep, abiding love—for each other, for their family, and for the world around them. These were not just values they believed in—it was the essence of who they were.

Our parents passed these gifts on to their four children: my brother, Ron Zokol, my sisters, Janet Brooks and Deborah Zokol, and me, the youngest. We were raised in a home where love and family pride was a constant, where hard work was respected, and where family was everything.

Our parents taught us that with a strong dedication, and a belief in ourselves, anything was possible. They gave us not only a sense of pride and purpose, but also a legacy of love that continues to guide us every day. Their spirits live on in the way we care for one another, in the values we carry forward, and in the lives we strive to lead.

The best thing ever to happen to me was Joanie Zokol (née Kindrachuk). There are no words that can fully express how much she means to me. Marrying Joanie 40 years ago was, without question, the best decision I've ever made. She is not just my wife—she's my life partner, my steady hand, my greatest blessing.

Together, we built something special we are so proud of: our family filled with love, laughter, and support. Watching our children grow into incredible people, and now seeing our grandchildren light up the world—it fills our life with gratitude every single day.

To Garrett and Pauline, and their beautiful little Eloise.

To Conor and Bryana, and their two gorgeous little girls, Isla and Aria.

To Hayley and Colby, and our marvelous little angel, Liv, and our first grandson, West Richard Sutton.

Our children and grandchildren are the truest treasures in our lives—and they all carry a significant piece of Joanie's spirit with them.

Joanie is the soul of our family. She's our North Star. Her love and strength held us all together. Traveling across North America on the PGA Tour with three-month-old twins? That takes incredible courage and devotion. And Joanie never flinched. She faced every challenge with grace and grit, and she carried us through the toughest moments and the best ones.

She's been my anchor during the highs and lows of a professional golf career. But even more than that, she's been the force behind the values, the character, and the warmth our children grew up with. They are who they are because of her. She helped me in so many ways.

Joanie, thank you—for everything you've given us, everything you've carried, and everything you are. I'm grateful for you every single day—thank you and I love you.

I want to acknowledge Jim Nelford. I absolutely believe that had Jim Nelford not spoken to BYU's Men's Head Golf Coach Karl Tucker on my behalf in the summer of 1977, I would have likely not gone to BYU that gave me four years of incredible learning during such a critical time in my life. It was a wonderful feeling being part of such a successful NCAA team program, and it was so meaningful for my development—thank you, Jim.

I want to acknowledge Karl Tucker. BYU's Men's Head Golf Coach Karl Tucker gave me the opportunity to "walk on" the BYU Golf Team and placed me in the dorm room with Bobby Clampett our freshman year, and that meant so much to me at that time. Karl Tucker was brilliant in building a superb NCAA golf program. Coach Tucker was like a father to me and many of us on the team—thank you, Coach.

I want to acknowledge Clay Edwards. Moe Norman introduced me to Clay Edwards in 1984. I am not so sure I'd have been able to get the traction I needed to learn and to overcome the challenges and barriers of playing the PGA Tour without Clay. This is proof that "good fortune" does play a part in everything. Clay and I are like brothers. He was a difference-maker for me—thank you, Clay, for teaching me how to hit shots.

I want to acknowledge Mike Barnett. Mike Barnett is a unique sports agent. He had a corral of some of the best athletes in Canada and beyond. Our representation agreement was based on a handshake. His vision was always sharp, and his loyalty went above and beyond. In my story, Mike made a significant difference and became a source of inspiration when I needed help. He was so much more than a sport agent; he is family.

I want to acknowledge Russ Jordan. Russ was and always will be my best friend. We learned to play golf together. He was a better player than I was in our junior golf days at Marine Drive Golf Club. Playing with Russ taught me to how to compete in junior golf, and he taught me to love USGA events, particularly US Opens. Russ caddied for me in numerous US Opens. We particularly enjoyed the 2000 US Open at Pebble Beach—thank you, Russ.

I want to acknowledge my good friends Greg Olson and Mike Hood. Both Greg and Mike, a retired Lieutenant-General of the Royal Canadian Air Force, helped me with my writing structure. Greg and I battled it out in a couple Canadian Amateur Championships. Greg beat me out on the back nine to win in 1980 Canadian Amateur in Halifax, and then I got him back in 1981 in Calgary. Mike co-authored *Pathways to the Stars: 100 Years of the Royal Canadian Air Force*. Thank you Greg and Mike for your encouragement to write this book and for your assistance in doing so.

I want to acknowledge Chris Rivers. Chris has been my best friend since the fourth grade. We haven't spent a great deal of time together but we've had that special close friendship that made us best friends no matter what—thank you, Chris.

I want to acknowledge my dear friend Brad Pelletier. Brad Pelletier is one of those outliers in this world that combine a remarkable vision with follow-up action at IMG Canada and Predator Ridge. Brad accomplished making Predator Ridge Canada's leading relocation community. Under Brad's leadership, Predator Ridge announced the Ritz-Carlton Residences, Okanagan, Predator Ridge in 2024, the first global luxury brand in the Okanagan—a remarkable accomplishment.

I want to acknowledge Jeff Cox who told me, "You need to write a book."

Entertainment. Writing. Culture.

ECW is a proudly independent, Canadian-owned book publisher. We know great writing can improve people's lives, and we're passionate about sharing original, exciting, and insightful writing across genres.

Thanks for reading along!

We want our books not just to sustain our imaginations, but to help construct a healthier, more just world, and so we've become a certified B Corporation, meaning we meet a high standard of social and environmental responsibility — and we're going to keep aiming higher. We believe books can drive change, but the way we make them can too.

Being a B Corp means that the act of publishing this book should be a force for good — for the planet, for our communities, and for the people that worked to make this book. For example, everyone who worked on this book was paid at least a living wage. You can learn more at the Ontario Living Wage Network.

This book is also available as a Global Certified Accessible™ (GCA) ebook. ECW Press's ebooks are screen reader friendly and are built to meet the needs of those who are unable to read standard print due to blindness, low vision, dyslexia, or a physical disability.

This book is printed on FSC®-certified paper. It contains recycled materials, and other controlled sources, is processed chlorine free, and is manufactured using biogas energy.

ECW's office is situated on land that was the traditional territory of many nations, including the Wendat, the Anishinaabeg, Haudenosaunee, Chippewa, Métis, and current treaty holders the Mississaugas of the Credit. In the 1880s, the land was developed as part of a growing community around St. Matthew's Anglican and other churches. Starting in the 1950s, our neighbourhood was transformed by immigrants fleeing the Vietnam War and Chinese Canadians dispossessed by the building of Nathan Phillips Square and the subsequent rise in real estate value in other Chinatowns. We are grateful to those who cared for the land before us and are proud to be working amidst this mix of cultures.

ecwpress.com